The World Trading System

The World Trading System

Law and Policy of International Economic Relations

John H. Jackson

The MIT Press
Cambridge, Massachusetts
London, England

Second Printing, 1990

Editorial production: Editorial Services of New England, Inc.
Typeface: Palatino
Typesetter: Publication Services, Inc.
Printed and bound in the United States of America.

Library of Congress Cataloging-in-Publication Data

Jackson, John Howard, 1932-
    The world trading system : law and policy of international
economic relations / John H. Jackson.
        p.   cm.
    Bibliography: p.
    ISBN 0-262-10040-1
    1. General Agreement on Tariffs and Trade (Organization)
    2. General Agreement on Tariffs and Trade (1947)   3. Tariff — Law
and legislation.   4. Foreign trade regulation.   5. International
economic relations.   I. Title.
    K4602.2   1989   89-2400
    341.7'543 — dc19   CIP

Contents

Preface

Trade law and policy involves a remarkably intricate interplay of international law, national law, and nonlaw disciplines, including economics and political science. For some years it has been clear that for policymakers, practitioners, and scholars there has been a lack of an accessible entry into the subject. The purpose of this book is to fill that gap, and to provide an introductory text for sophisticated readers that can form the basis of their further work, study, and reflection on this perplexing subject. Unfortunately, the subject never stands still. During the course of preparing this book, several important national statutes have been adopted on the subject (particularly in the United States), and a new (eighth) trade round of negotiations in the context of GATT has been launched. Because the subject moves so rapidly, it has been my goal to focus on the core fundamentals, particularly the institutions and legal rules and constraints that shape those institutions, and the policies of international trade. There is no way, for example, that the latest details of the antidumping law can be presented effectively in a book of this type. Rather, this book attempts to help the reader relate some of the intricate subjects of international trade, such as antidumping rules, to the broader purposes of international trade policy, all set in the context of the world's institutions and laws (both national and international), which impose the "road map " on the subject.

There is no doubt in my mind that the reader will find certain aspects of this book frustrating. Some readers always need more detail on one or another subject, yet the author must limit the material. There is no way to escape this and keep a book within manageable production limits. For such interested readers, however, it is my hope that the notes will suggest sources of more detailed information about many specific subjects that may be of interest. Partly for this reason, a number of the notes refer to previously published works of mine.

Another purpose of this book, however, is to share with the reader certain of my reflections and perceptions developed over several decades of practice, teaching, and scholarship in the area of international trade law. Some of these perspectives and reflections are quite speculative — there is no way to "prove" or "disprove" them. Nevertheless, the reader may find such impressions at least provocative, if not indicative of further reflection and thinking to come in future years.

Acknowledgments

I would like to thank the Ford Foundation and the William W. Cook endowment of the University of Michigan Law School for support of many of the expenses of the research leading to this book.

I would also like to thank many other individuals who provided a remarkable amount of able assistance in the preparation of this book. A number of colleagues and other scholars, as well as practitioners, have kindly assisted me by reviewing various parts of draft manuscript material and engaging in extensive discussions of some of the points. Among these, I particularly thank Professor Alan Deardorff of the Economics Department at the University of Michigan, with whom I have jointly taught several seminars that have focused on some of the subjects of this book, including subsidies and safeguards. Needless to say, the discussions in those seminars, as well as in a number of other contexts, have been exceedingly valuable. In addition, I received very helpful comments on portions of the manuscript from Professor William Davey at the University of Illinois; Mr. Gary N. Horlick, a partner at O'Melveny & Myers, Washington D.C.; Mr. Ake Linden of the GATT Secretariat in Geneva; and Mr. Ernst-Ulrich Petersmann of the GATT Secretariat.

During the course of several years preparing this book, I have been fortunate to have the able secretarial assistance of Erika Hrabec and Barbara Shapiro, and the diligent and able research assistance of a number of very capable students. Most particularly I thank Ross Denton, my assistant during the final work on this book, and Edwin Vermulst, who assisted in an earlier phase of the work.

The World Trading System

1   The Policies and Realities of International Economic Regulation

1.1   Law, Politics, and the Dismal Science

Puzzles, or Why Do Officials Choose the Fourth Best Option?

Puzzle: Suppose you are the minister for trade of a small Asian country that is rapidly developing. Several of your small electronic components manufacturers export their products to various countries of the world, and you are informed that one of those importing countries has just decided to stop imports from your country. What steps can you take? As a small country, are you completely at the mercy of a larger economic power? In planning investment policies for your country designed partly to export and obtain foreign exchange to pay off a staggering external debt, what world market environment can you rely upon?

Puzzle: Suppose you are advising a large multinational corporation based in the United States, and this company is exploring the feasibility of a substantial investment in a plant in a small underdeveloped country in Africa. Inexpensive labor could give the products of this plant a substantial advantage on the world market, but in order to be economically viable this plant must ship over 80 percent of its output outside the small country which has only a tiny market for the product. A smaller plant would not be able to achieve the economies of scale necessary to make the enterprise flourish. Currently there are few government barriers to imports of the projected product into either the United States or Europe. Can you advise your client that he can depend on those circumstances continuing long enough into the future to ensure a satisfactory return on the proposed investment?

Puzzle: Economists, government policymakers, and many others tend to agree that barriers to international trade reduce world welfare and often the welfare of the countries that impose the barriers. If barriers must be imposed, such experts generally agree that a tariff (or price-effect measure) is superior to quantitative restrictions. Yet quantitative measures to reduce trade have proliferated around the world — particularly in recent years the so-called "voluntary export restraint" device, whereby the exporting country, at the request of the importing country, restrains the amount of export of a product that will be shipped to the importing country. This device seems favored even by the importing country, although it is often thought to have an even less favorable effect on the economy of the importing country than the alternative whereby the importing country itself imposes the quantitative measures. Why is it, then, that governments tend to opt for the fourth best measure?

These are only a few of a large number of puzzling questions embedded in the subject of international trade today. These puzzles cannot be solved by reference to only one academic discipline, be it economics, or law, or political science. Indeed, these questions may not be solvable at all. But the only potential for discovering reasonable explanations or solutions for these and many similar puzzles requires a pragmatic and empirical analysis of the motivating factors and circumstances of real transactions and government actions. Many different disciplines, certainly all of those just mentioned, are required to assist in that process.

The Meaning of Interdependence

In a world where trade across borders constitutes over 50 percent of the gross national product of some countries, and 14 percent even for as large an internal market as the United States,[1] it is no wonder that government leaders, businessmen, and almost anyone else feels some anxiety about those mysterious foreign influences that can affect daily lives so dramatically.[2]

Even these statistics don't tell the whole story. It is generally recognized that the influence of international trade on national economies has been growing for decades and can be much more profound than the stated percentages might indicate, both because the trade itself is often a much higher percentage of the goods-producing sectors of economies and because a multiplier or ripple effect amplifies the consequences of such sectors expanding or contracting.[3]

In sum, the world has become increasingly interdependent. With that interdependence has come great wealth: goods are produced where their costs are lowest; consumers have more choices; institutions of production are disciplined through competition; producers can realize the advantages of economies of scale. But with interdependence has come vulnerability. National economies do not stand alone: economic forces move rapidly across borders to influence other societies. Government deficits in the United States can have an impact on its interest rate, which can push heavily indebted developing countries to the verge of "bankruptcy." An embargo or price rise implemented by major oil-producing nations can cause deep and frustrating unemployment, farm bankruptcies, and dramatic rises in the cost of living in the United States. A recession in one part of the world is rapidly felt in other parts.[4]

These observations were underscored in an article by Martin Feldstein in the summer of 1985 in which the former chairman of the Council of Economic Advisors said: "The experience of the past few years has underlined the interdependence of the world economy. Sharp changes in international trade, in capital flows and in exchange rates have affected all major economies. The rise in real interest rates everywhere reflects the close links among capital markets."[5] Economic interdependence creates great difficulties for national governments. National political leaders find it harder to deliver programs to respond to needs of constituents. Businesses fail or flail in the face of greater uncertainties. Some laboring citizens cannot understand why it is harder to achieve the standard of living to which they aspire.

How did this interdependence, at least within the non-Communist world, come about? Perhaps the technological innovations of the post-World War II era alone would have created these conditions, at least in the absence of major military conflict. The time and cost of transport has fallen rapidly, so that this barrier to greater trade flows and service exchanges has also dropped. Communications have become spectacularly instantaneous: in our living rooms we watch foreign local wars broadcast on the T.V. news by satellite, and it is possible now to order goods or shift huge sums of money across oceans, literally in seconds. Information systems are changing the character of markets and also affecting business techniques, such as the control of inventories, the use of borrowed money, the response to changing interest rates, and the adoption of new developments of technology. But these scientific advances have little influence if they are resisted by governments, as we observe in the cases of those governments that do resist them.[6]

We must recognize that the international institutions erected or reinstated by governments after World War II have made their contribution. If some world organizations have failed to perform in the manner contemplated by their founders, they have nevertheless contributed symbiotically to the general trend of the world environment made possible by the scientific innovations. This is particularly the case with the economic institutions.

The 1944 Bretton Woods Conference launched the World Bank and the International Monetary Fund. A few years later came a failed attempt to add a complementary organization for trade, the ill-fated ITO of the Havana Charter, but into the vacuum grew the General Agreement on Tariffs and Trade (GATT). These institutions were later joined by others, including the OECD, UNCTAD, and some important regional systems. By the late 1960s, therefore, the liberalization of trade and financial flows promoted by this postwar system—sometimes broadly called the Bretton Woods System—had progressed far enough to foster an unprecedented surge of trade and to demonstrate the economic benefits that flow from such liberalization. But at the same time, new problems were emerging. The receding waters of tariff and other overt protection inevitably uncover the rocks and shoals of nontariff barriers and other problems. As the European Economic Community has in recent decades discovered, creating free trade requires attention to a group of interrelated activities such as the flow of capital, the flow of labor, and the flow of technology and services.[7] These in turn have revolutionized government methods traditionally used to control fiscal and monetary policy, taxation structure, environment regulation, product standards, and liability for product defects. The propensity for government summit meetings, both within Europe and on a worldwide basis, is obviously not unrelated to these world economic trends of interdependence. Likewise, the attempts of governments to combine their efforts through international organizations have a similar result. The question is not whether a government will play on the international scene; the question is, Where will it play and with whom (that is, what forum will it work in and which other governments is it willing to let into its "club")?

The problem of international economics today, then, is largely a problem of "managing" interdependence.[8] The success of the Bretton Woods System has created a host of new problems. When economic transactions so easily cross national borders, tensions occur merely because of the differences between economic institutions as well as cultures. In addition, the freedom of border "transit" sometimes allows unscrupulous entrepreneurs to evade national government regulation. Even morally sensitive entrepreneurs find their effective power enhanced when they can move activity quickly from one nation to another. Governments, by contrast, find themselves increasingly frustrated by effective evasion of their regulatory powers. Furthermore, governments find that actions of other governments can cause them great difficulties.

Governments respond to these problems in a variety of ways. Some join other governments in an attempt to create an international regulatory system to help ameliorate the "free-for-all" aspects of international trade (such as beggar-thy-neighbor policies), or to provide a unified posture to confront the less public-spirited entrepreneurs. Another common response is to develop internal policies designed to enable their nations to better cope with the challenges of the world economy. Thus, governments adopt "industrial policies," measures to enhance "competitiveness," measures (usually at the border) to offset foreign-governmental or private actions deemed potentially damaging, or reciprocal responses of various kinds.

In considering any of these responses, however, governments participating in the "Bretton Woods System" (as described in the next chapter) confront international as well as national sets of rules, procedures, and principles that may narrowly constrain their options. One of the purposes of this book is to describe one part of that system: the rules of international trade as developed principally in the context of GATT, but related closely to national laws which regulate trade.

Do The Rules Work?

Let us explore one example. In recent decades the so-called "injury test" has been one pillar of trade policy. When this test applies, an importing country will presumably only impose restraints on imports of a particular product if it can be established that such imports are "injuring" its domestic industry, which produces like or similar products. An "injurious" import is defined as one that competes with the domestic product and thus *causes* a decline in the domestic industry.

Under international treaties as well as the domestic law of major trading countries, the "injury" test is elaborately defined. In some cases an independent agency is charged with ascertaining whether the detailed legal criteria for "injury" have been met, and in other cases appeal to the courts may be permitted.

Thus it was surprising and revealing to me when some years ago I was having a detailed conversation about trade policy with a highly ranked trade official of a European country, and this official blandly stated, "Oh, we can always find 'injury' whenever we need to for political purposes."

This comment about the ease with which detailed legal criteria can be overcome for political purposes typifies a larger dilemma of implementing international trade policy in major market-oriented countries today: the tension that is created when legal rules, designed to bring the subject a measure of predictability and stability, are juxtaposed with the intense human needs of government to make "exceptions" to solve short-term or ad hoc problems. This tension poses difficult problems for the practitioner and the scholar. (Of course trade policy is surely not qualitatively different, in this respect, from tax policy, or unfair competition law, although it may be different in degree.)

Contours of This Study

This book is about trade policy. But it is about trade policy in the context of the legal, constitutional, and political realities that constrain it. These constraints mold policy so much that its resultant form scarcely if at all resembles the pure logic of the economic theorist. Yet the economic theory is clearly part of the "reality." Without the theory, the policy would often be directionless, lurching from one inconsistent approach to another.

Thus the purpose of this book is to examine the theory and real implementation of the policies of international trade in our contemporary world in a way that attempts to explain how the theories have been effectively constrained by the processes of real human institutions, especially legal institutions. The perspective of this book is that of a legal scholar, of course. (My "comparative advantage" would not realistically support any other perspective.) Yet my goal — not too ambitious, I hope — is to explore the multidisciplinary context of trade-policy rules. Charts, graphs, and formal mathematical proofs will be eschewed here, because fortunately I can rely on the extensive literature and expertise of generous economist friends for them. Nevertheless, I will state the basic economic propositions of international trade policy, and they will lie at the center of this exposition. However, I will also examine many other policies — sometimes called "noneconomic." Indeed, in many cases we will see a direct clash of inconsistent policies. In precisely those cases lurks the greatest challenge to government action and the law.

The basic purpose of this book is to provide policymakers, practitioners, students, and scholars of many different disciplines with an integrated knowledge of the way in which the international trade "system" operates in today's complex and interdependent world economic-legal-political environment.

Clearly the larger problem of international economics includes many subjects in addition to trade in goods. Monetary issues, investment flows, trade in services (such as transport, insurance, or banking) come easily to mind. But the observable fact is that the "legal system" for trade in goods, including both national and international rules, is the most intricate and elaborate system of rules that exists in the context of international economic relations.[9] This book is devoted to that system of rules regarding trade in goods, partly because to take on the broader field would make it impossible or at least much more difficult to formulate any meaningful generalizations or hypotheses.

Throughout this work there will be references to certain basic themes. One of these has already been stated in the previous subsection: the tension between the necessity for legal rules conducive to stability and predictability, and the human need for solutions to short-term and ad hoc problems. In another sense this dilemma is largely the well-recognized political-philosophy problem of the tug-of-war between rules and official discretion. Other themes will be stated elsewhere in this chapter, and in the final chapter.

This chapter continues in its next sections with some further introductory reflections. In section 1.2 I turn to the basic policy assumptions that underlie most of the law and policy described in this book, starting with the doctrine of "comparative advantage." Next I look at some of the policies, often termed "noneconomic," that compete with the doctrine of comparative advantage. Certain basic concepts of international law related to international economic affairs will be introduced in section 1.4. Finally I will reconsider some of the underlying themes of this book's exploration of trade policy.

Chapters 2, 3, and 4 outline the basic "constitutional structure" of the contemporary world trade system. Chapter 2 will examine its international structure, while chapter 3 will focus on domestic governmental structures, particularly those of the United States. Chapter 4 explores the much-discussed dispute-resolution and compliance problems.

Chapters 5 through 11 then take up specific "regulatory" subjects of international trade. These are the "substantive issues" of trade policy which are the core of the "system" today. Not all substantive trade policy issues can be taken up in this book, of course, but these seven chapters will cover the most significant and most frequently encountered.

Chapters 12 and 13 then introduce problems which relate to specific types of national economic structures. Chapter 12 examines trade policy and the operation of the current trading "system" with respect to developing countries. Here we explore briefly whether the system and its rules work for developing countries, or whether they introduce some biased constraints on those countries. Chapter 13 looks at a different set of national economic structures, namely those often termed "nonmarket." Of course, the sets of nations focused on in these two chapters overlap extensively. Nevertheless, the implications for policy modification can differ substantially in these two types of economies.

Finally, chapter 14 surveys the scene painted with such detail in the previous chapters, and asks some very large questions. Some hypotheses are offered as answers to some of these questions, but clearly some of the questions are (at least at present) unanswerable.

1.2 The Policy Assumptions of the International Economic System

"Liberal Trade"

The starting point for any discussion of policy for the international economic system of today is the notion of "liberal trade," meaning the goal to minimize the amount of interference of governments in trade flows that cross national borders. The economic arguments concerning this central policy concept will be discussed below, but regardless of their validity or intellectual persuasiveness, there is no question that they have been influential. The basic "liberal trade" philosophy is constantly reiterated by government and private persons, even in the context of a justification for departing from it!

The prominent economist Paul Samuelson says that "there is essentially only one argument for free trade or freer trade, but it is an exceedingly powerful one, namely: Free trade promotes a mutually profitable division of labor, greatly enhances the potential real national product of all nations, and makes possible higher standards of living all over the globe."[10]

The GATT itself begins with a preamble that includes phrases expressing goals of "raising standards of living" by, among other things, "expanding . . . exchange of goods." The recent Leutwiler Report prepared for the GATT expressed a similar view:

Ever since ancient times, people have found that they can increase their incomes by developing specialized skills and trading the fruits of their labor in the market-place. A farmer may know how to sew and a tailor may know how to raise chickens — but each can produce more by concentrating on doing what each can do most efficiently.

The same applies to countries. Trade allows countries to concentrate on what they can do best. No two countries are exactly alike in natural resources, climate or work force. Those differences give each country a "comparative advantage" over the others in some products. Trade translates the individual advantages of many countries into maximum productivity for all. This is the classic theory of international trade. It is still valid today. [11]

A 1970 Senate document notes "It had been the principal goal of American foreign policy since 1934 to strive for the removal of barriers to the free flow of international trade. The original trade agreements program has been extended several times, and since 1934 the Congress repeatedly, after careful scrutiny and examination, renewed the President's advance authority to negotiate reciprocal agreements to lower trade barriers."[12]

The July 1971 report of the President's Commission on International Trade and Investment Policy (the "Williams Commission"), in expressing the goals of U.S. policy, included this sentence: "The ultimate goal should be to achieve for all people the benefit of an open world in which goods and capital can move freely."[13]

Thus there can be little doubt of the general policy underpinnings of the post-World War II international economic system as it prevails at least among the so-called industrial-market economies. There is uncertainty, however, about what this basic policy implies in specific instances, and doubt that this basic policy is still viable in the face of changed circumstances. These are issues to which this book repeatedly returns.

Of course, this basic "economic goal" is not the only goal of international trade policy. A number of other goals can be articulated also. In some cases these other goals may be partly inconsistent with the central goal, requiring some "balancing" or "compromise." I won't at this point attempt to inventory all possible goals of international economic policy, but at least two more can be mentioned here. In the next section I describe some other policy goals, which could be classified as "noneconomic."

During the years near the end and just after World War II, as leaders of the victorious nations began formulating postwar plans for international economic institutions, one could detect in speeches and documents a strong political goal that accompanied the economic thinking of the day. The political goal stemmed from thinking that pointed to the interwar economic problems as partial causes for the disastrous Second World War.[14] The Great Depression, the mishandling of policy toward Germany after World War I, and similar circumstances weighed heavily on the minds of policy makers who wanted to design post-World War II institutions that would prevent a recurrence of these problems. For example, Harry Hawkins of the U.S. said in a 1944 speech, "Trade conflict breeds noncooperation, suspicion, bitterness. Nations which are economic enemies are not likely to remain political friends for long."[15] A 1945 presidential message stated: "The fundamental choice is whether countries will struggle against each other for wealth and power, or work together for security and mutual advantage. . . . The experience of cooperation in the task of earning a living promotes both the habit and the techniques of common effort and helps make permanent the mutual confidence on which the peace depends."[16]

Another policy underlying contemporary international economic rules and institutions became more prominent in more recent decades. This is the policy of promoting economic development in those countries which were not industrialized at the end of World War II. Many of the corollaries of this policy goal appear to challenge the appropriateness of rules and institutions assumed to be desirable for general "liberal trade" goals, and this development goal has led some leaders to question the fairness of the economic institutions established during the 1940s.[17]

Ricardo and the Theory of Comparative Advantage

Professor Peter Kenen writes: "The study of international trade and finance is among the oldest specialties within economics. It was conceived in the sixteenth century, a lusty child of Europe's passion for Spanish gold, and grew to maturity in the turbulent years that witnessed the emergence of the modern nation state. It attracted the leading economists of the eighteenth and nineteenth centuries, including David Hume, Adam Smith, David Ricardo, and John Stuart Mill. . . ."[18]

Early theorists developed a "mercantilist" viewpoint. Under this theory, the goal of nations in their economic relations was to amass gold or other treasure, so as to maximize national power (which was not well distinguished from the wealth and power of sovereigns).[19] The goal therefore was to "sell more to strangers yearly than we consume of theirs in value."[20] This theory was soon attacked as flawed by Hume and Smith, among others. For one thing, mere accumulation of money did not necessarily promise better living standards or even the instruments of power (warships etc.). For another thing, accumulating monetary assets could cause inflation, undermining a nation's world-competitive position. Eighteenth-century classicists focused on welfare of citizens rather than of sovereigns, and noted the advantages of international trade, Adam Smith saying: "What is prudence in the conduct of every private family, can scarce be folly in that of a great kingdom. If a foreign country can supply us with a commodity cheaper than we ourselves can make it, better buy it of them with some part of the produce of our own industry. . . ."[21]

It was Ricardo, in 1817, who went a step further and developed the theory of comparative advantage, which, despite refutations from skeptical politicians,[22] has provided a powerful intellectual underpinning, still respected by all major economists, for policies that generally stress the value of "liberal trade" — that is, of minimizing governmental interference with trade flows. We must, therefore, examine this theory in some detail.

The theory was originally based on a simple model of international trade involving two countries, two traded products, and one type of input for both products.[23] Often the model uses the United Kingdom and Portugal as the countries, cloth and wine as the products, and labor as the input. Assume that in the U.K. a yard of cloth takes 5 hours of labor to produce, and a gallon of wine 10 hours of labor to produce. Assume that in Portugal it takes 10 hours to produce the yard of cloth and 6 hours to produce the gallon of wine. It is obvious that the U.K. has an absolute advantage in cloth production and Portugal an absolute advantage in wine production. The total goods produced by an available 90 hours of labor in each country, absent trade, can be summarized as follows.

U.K. : 18 yards of cloth or 9 gallons of wine, or some combination of these, such as 10 yards of cloth and 4 gallons of wine.

Portugal: 9 yards of cloth or 15 gallons of wine, or some combination of these, such as 6 yards of cloth and 5 gallons of wine.

Since citizens in both countries want both products, then without trade both countries will produce some mix of the two products, such as the following:

	U.K.	Portugal	Total
Cloth	10 yd	3 yd	13 yd
Wine	4 gal	10 gal	14 gal

If trade between the two countries is opened and each specializes entirely, trading for the product of the other, then the products available or produced in each can be summarized as follows.

	U.K.	Portugal	Total
Cloth	18 yd	0 yd	18 yd
Wine	0 gal	15 gal	15 gal

The totals for both products are larger than in the autarky case, and thus more is available for consumption in both countries under trading conditions.

The model above shows a case in which each of two countries has an absolute advantage in one of the two products, and trade will help both. The question that immediately occurs, then, is, if one country has an absolute advantage in *both* goods, should these countries trade? Such a case would demonstrate the power of the theory of comparative advantage. The following table summarizes this situation, both before and after trade opens.

	U.K.	Portugal	Totals
Labor Available	90 hr	90 hr	
Labor Used			
Hours per yard	5 hr	10 hr	
Hours per gallon	10 hr	10 hr	
Autarky			
Cloth	10 yd	5 yd	15 yd
Wine	4 gal	4 gal	8 gal
Trade			
Cloth	18 yd	0 yd	18 yd
Wine	0 gal	9 gal	9 gal

Thus, it is not the difference of *absolute* advantage but of *comparative* advantage that gives rise to the gains from trade. Even when the U.K. can produce all goods in the model with no more labor than Portugal, there is an advantage for the two countries to trade if the *ratio of production* costs of the two products differs. In this second case, wine in the U.K. costs 2 yards of cloth, while in Portugal it costs only 1 yard of cloth; thus it is worthwhile for the U.K. to produce cloth and to trade its excess for wine.

In fact (going beyond Ricardo), with specialization may create economies of such scale that the gains from trade would be even more than those represented in this hypothetical case.

The discussion above presents the basic model of the theory of comparative advantage, but it is appropriate to ask whether the model has been confirmed by empirical evidence. The simple model above doesn't easily lend itself to empirical investigation, partly because it is so simple. However derivative and additive, theories complementing the model have been tested with some success.[24] The apparent importance of trade to national and world economic growth and well-being is sometimes seen in statistics showing that world trade over several decades has generally grown at a faster rate than the economy as a whole.[25] Strictly speaking, however, this fact does not necessarily confirm the theory of comparative advantage, since there are many other factors (including the significant decline of transportation costs and other "natural" barriers to trade) that could at least partly explain the fact.

Elaborations of the simple model, however, all seem to point in the same direction. A large number of studies exist, based on various plausible theories or analyses of the effects of restraints on trade, which show a loss in welfare for the world as a whole and often also for the countries imposing the restrictions. These restraints cause costs to be borne by the economies, usually costs which are imposed on the consumers of the imported product.[26]

The theory does have strong intuitive appeal. As consumers, individual citizens can easily see the advantage of international trade: it gives them greater choice of products at better prices. Travelers return to their homes raving about their purchases. Buyers in the marketplace observe better available values in some imported goods. Of course, the question remains whether Adam Smith was right when he claimed that what is good for families is also good for nations. Most assuredly one does not follow from the other. The advantages that buyers discover in individual cases may result in an overall disadvantage for a nation as a whole.

One thing does seem clear, however. Import trade provides an additional source of competition to domestic producers. Considered intuitively, and on the basis of a large number of studies, competition is almost always deemed beneficial to world or national-aggregate economic welfare. This can be seen intuitively from individual experiences in recent years with electronic consumer goods: calculators costing over $100 during the mid-1970s can now be purchased in better versions for under $8 (although surely some of this discrepancy is due to technological innovation).

Yet there are also groups in a national economy which experience loss from shifts to freer trade, such as the employees who lose their jobs in a domestic industry because of competition from imports. Of course, there are numerous other reasons, including other domestic competition, why firms or whole industry sectors decline, causing job loss as well as capital investment loss. Changes of taste, changes in government procurement programs, new technology and improved efficiency of production processes, can all be mentioned. The question is, Why should influences from beyond a nation's borders, ones requiring "structural adjustment changes," be treated differently than such influences from within a nation's borders?

An interesting article in the *Journal of Economic Literature* discusses some of these circumstances in the context of theories relating to "industrial policy."[27] Norton notes that the U.S. is a large integrated market with conditions similar to those of free trade among a group of smaller countries (such as in Europe). He advances the suggestion that "U.S. regional diversity has enforced a painful but therapeutic adjustment of a kind missing in Victorian Britain or contemporary Europe."[28] Unlike the relative stagnation in Europe during recent decades, he notes that ". . . regional diversity has enforced a rapid adjustment in the U.S. over the past 15 years. America's transition has been perhaps more painful but surely more effective than in Europe. The result has been rapid U.S. job growth over the period, during a time when new entrants flooded the American labor market."[29]

Challenging the Theory: Conditions and Assumptions of the Theory of Comparative Advantage

One of the ways to challenge the theory of comparative advantage is to demonstrate that some of the conditions required for it to operate do not exist in the real world, or similarly, that some assumptions on which the theory is based are not valid. A few of these conditions and assumptions will be discussed in this subsection.[30]

One of the more important arguments used to challenge the theory is that it depends on a relatively perfect competitive environment which only rarely exists. Thus, if markets are manipulated by monopolistic influences or any other situations of imperfect competition (including government regulation and other policies), the functioning of comparative advantage can be seriously impaired.[31]

The theory also is said to depend on a so-called static economic analysis. It has been alleged that it does not adequately take into account certain "dynamic" conditions of economic systems.[32] For example, when the importing nation's economy is in a period of declining demand, it is possible that import competition could exacerbate unemployment problems (at least during the time required for "adjustment" unemployment and factor shifts) which could cause an overall short-term decline in world welfare because of trade. In addition, another argument being forcibly put forward in recent years notes that government policies can themselves change the conditions of competition or "comparative advantage," particularly for products which require inputs that are not immutable. Immutable inputs might include sunshine, arable land, iron ore deposits, water etc. But for many recent products, particularly those of "high technology," important inputs include skilled labor and expertise, transportation, communication, and availability of risk capital. A nation's endowments of these inputs can be influenced by government policy (education, roads, communication infrastructure, capital-market structures, etc.).[33]

Finally, it is sometimes said that the model is too simple and thus not realistic. It deals in its original form only with two countries, two products, and one factor of production. Obviously the real world is vastly more complex, and different products have complex interactions of factor mobility and substitutability of demand. However, economists respond that this criticism of the model does not hold up. Modern elaborations of the model show that it supports the value of liberal trade in surprisingly general cases.[34]

Challenging the Theory: What Is Success?

Often statements about economic theory, including theory of international trade, seem to imply a goal of maximizing "real" wealth of more and better goods and services. Theorists note that there is room, in a market-oriented consumer choice system, for choices to be non-"real" or nonmaterial. Thus, some prefer leisure over television sets, or esoteric music over popular concerts, or religious values and meditation over other worldly goods. But it is worrisome that a purely market-driven system tends to reduce the opportunity for those choices, that somehow all the talk about "efficiency" or "competitiveness" or "gross national product" tends to overlook many of these nonmaterial choices.

This subject clearly cannot be extensively explored here. Yet it is raised in connection with international economic policies. There may indeed be a preference in some societies for preserving agricultural or nonindustrial social patterns. Likewise, some societies may be prepared to pay a large price (forgoing such basics as telephones or heath services) in order to preserve historic or aesthetic sites. These societies may be willing to do this even though it requires forcing individual citizens to relinquish choices in the market they would prefer. The international policy issue of this is whether the longer-term direction of international economic policy tends unnecessarily to make national choices about social patterns or "nonmaterial" preferences more difficult. It also raises the question of whether in some circumstances such national choices are made because the cost of those choices is somehow being thrust onto other nations which do not necessarily benefit from them.

Wealth maximizing, in the material sense, may not be as high a priority in the view of some as other goals, such as equitable distribution of income. Even though a nation as a whole may prosper with trade, particular groups within it may be seriously harmed.[35] Again this circumstance raises questions, some of which are termed "adjustment," to which I will return in later chapters. (See especially chapter 7, concerning safeguards.)

One example of a powerful goal which often cuts against traditional theories of international trade has been brilliantly recognized by the economist Max Corden. In his book *Trade Policy and Economic Welfare*[36] he speaks of a preference in many societies which he terms the "conservative social welfare function": "Let us now introduce the conservative social welfare function, a concept which seems particularly helpful for understanding actual trade policies of many countries. Put in its simplest form it includes the following income distribution target: any significant absolute reductions in real incomes of any significant section of the community should be avoided. . . . In terms of welfare weights, increases in income are given relatively low weights and decreases very high weights."[37]

This, Corden says perceptively, helps to explain the income maintenance motivation of so many tariffs in the past.[38] Corden argues that the income maintenance motivation has a number of elements. First, it is "unfair" to allow anyone's real income to be significantly reduced — especially as the result of deliberate policy decisions — unless there are very good reasons for this and it is more or less unavoidable. Second, insofar as people are risk averters, everyone's real income is increased when it is known that a government will generally intervene to prevent sudden or large and unexpected income losses. The conservative social welfare function is a part of a social insurance system. Third, social peace requires that no significant group's income shall fall if that of other groups is rising. Social peace might be regarded as a social good in itself or as a basis for political stability and hence for economic development. And even if social peace does not depend on the maintenance of the incomes of the major classes in the community, the survival of a government may. Finally, if a policy is aimed at a certain target, such as protection of an industry or improving the balance of payments, most governments want to minimize the adverse side effects on sectional incomes so as not to become involved in political battles incidental to their main purpose.

The Level Playing Field as a Policy Goal

In connection with international trade policy, one often hears expressed the importance of the "level playing field."[39]

The meaning and implications of this goal are anything but clear. To a certain degree it may imply preserving a competitive market atmosphere for world trade, just as some large societies (notably the U.S.) have such a goal for their internal markets. Thus, when foreign governments intervene in the world market to favor their own national objectives, or foreign manufacturers engage in various noncompetitive practices, these activities are thought to be unfair to competing producers in other countries.

But often something more is meant by the "level playing field" idea. Even "economically competitive" actions by foreign firms are considered in some cases to be "unfair," and thus to disturb the "level playing field." Certain categories of actions have for many decades been considered to be "unfair" by nations and the international rules of international trade. Among these are "dumping" and "subsidy" activities, as well as other actions, including patent, trademark, or copyright infringements. It is not always clear whether all the practices subsumed by trade policy experts under these categories really have a damaging impact on a world trading system, or whether they provide for uneven conditions of competition for producing firms in other nations. Yet the goal of promoting a "level playing field," through national and international policies designed to inhibit dumping or subsidies, seems to have a powerful political appeal (which I shall discuss in later chapters).[40]

1.3 Competing Policy Goals and Noneconomic Objectives

Even Adam Smith recognized two exceptions to his views about the value of liberal trade among nations. I have already discussed some circumstances under which nations might pursue goals that would not maximize material wealth. Goals of distributive justice and Max Corden's "conservative social welfare function" were mentioned in section 1.2. In this section we will look at a few of the national objectives which in a sense "compete" with the traditional goals of liberal trade theories.

The objective of "national security" is frequently recognized as justifying a departure from liberal trade policies.[41] Adam Smith recognized national security as a valid reason for such departure: "Defence," he wrote, "is more than opulence."[42] Thus a nation may feel that its national security requires an airplane (or shipbuilding) industry regardless of whether such industry has a "comparative advantage" or is even viable on world markets. Tariffs or other protection may be used by such a nation to preserve and enhance this industry. There are two problems which must always be considered in this context, however.

First, preserving or building a productive capacity for the contingency of war or for preventing a challenge to national economic survival may indeed be a valid goal, but there may be more economically efficient ways to achieve that goal. Economists argue, for example, that in certain circumstances direct subsidies may be preferable to restraints on imports.[43] Of course, the structure of domestic political and legal institutions will vitally affect the choice of means to support a domestic industry. The structure of governmental and political institutions may make it impossible or very difficult to use a direct subsidy: it is too obvious, it adds to the government budget deficit, it requires a long debate and a vote of a parliament, etc. In such cases national leaders may succumb to the temptation to fall back on the economically less desirable but politically more feasible techniques of import restraints to achieve goals they believe are important in the national interest.

A problem inherent in the national-security argument is that of determining its limits. Which industries (if any) are needed for security in a world of potentially instantaneous wars? It is all too easy for any economic group to argue its importance to national security as an excuse for import protection. One variation on this argument proposes that a nation must always have certain industries as part of its industrial "infrastructure." Thus, it says, a certain minimum steel-making capacity must be maintained regardless of its efficiency or competitiveness in the world economy. This argument invokes some concepts of "industrial policy": the national government makes choices and influences the structure of its economy. These arguments are much debated.[44]

A second, but related argument, is that a nation needs to avoid being too dependent on other nations (or even on the world economy). Such dependence, it says, reduces real sovereignty and makes a nation vulnerable to economic and political forces beyond its control and to decisions made by either political or business leaders outside its borders. Thus, those nations traditionally relying on one or a few types of exports (oil, copper, sugar, etc.) may legitimately feel that the ups and downs of the world markets pose too much strain and adjustment costs to their economies. In such cases a nation will often be willing to forgo some current or short-term economic welfare in order to achieve somewhat greater security and economic stability. The argument for maintaining certain basic "core" industries may be motivated by this goal. Thus a steel industry (and sometimes an airline) becomes an attribute of sovereignty. It is debatable whether the independence argument is valid even for very small economies. It is also debatable whether in today's interdependent world such argument is realistic. Like much else, there is probably some degree to which it has validity.

More subtle is the possibility that a national consensus could explicitly opt for a choice of policies that would not maximize wealth (in the traditionally measurable sense, at least), but would give preference to other noneconomic goals. For example, the choice might be to preserve an agricultural way of life for groups of citizens used to it. Philosophy or aesthetics might lead a public consensus to such a preference even though it means a lower standard of living for the whole population. Likewise one can imagine (and observe) choice of religious goals (and lifestyle demands of such religion), or aesthetic choices, such as a preference for classical music and opera (and extensive subsidization of music education and musicians). There is little in international trade theory which can refute the validity of such choices on the part of nations, with perhaps one exception. It can be argued that when a nation makes an "uneconomic" choice, it should be prepared to pay the whole cost, and not pursue policies which have the effect of unloading some of the burdens of that choice onto other nations. In an interdependent world, paying the whole cost is not often easy to accomplish.

Noneconomic social policy choices might also lead a nation to try to preserve or encourage certain types of economic activity for its citizens. For example, perhaps a national preference for "white collar" work (in clean, pleasant surroundings) can be observed. A nation, for this reason, might want to take steps to favor businesses of this type. Could it be that this will become more of a problem if the major nations begin to develop rules for trade in "services" such as banking or insurance?[45]

A commonly stated "exception" to liberal trade theory is the "infant industry" argument. This argument proposes the use of import barriers to enable a new or young industry to become established and viable. The barriers to imports give some shelter against foreign competition, until the industry is strong enough to meet that competition. There are also several problems with this argument. Economists can argue that there are better ways to achieve the goal of promoting the new industry, such as the explicit use of subsidies.[46] (The same constraints discussed in the case of national security may apply here as well, however.) And, as with the national-security arguments, there may be the problem of identifying which industries should receive the benefit of "infant" treatment. For small economies, the infant-industry argument for import protection may be relatively weak: such an industry may need to depend on exports to establish the economies of scale necessary for true viability.

This can lead to arguments about tariff and trade preferences which later chapters discuss.[47] One problem has been to determine when an "infant" industry has reached maturity, so as no longer to merit the exceptional treatment of import protection. There is often a tendency for industries to argue for perpetual infancy status.[48]

One noneconomic goal greatly affecting national trade policies is the goal to preserve political or economic power. At least in a democratic nation, national leaders will be observably influenced in their trade policy decisions by the desire to get elected or re-elected. But not only political leaders manifest the desire for power. Business leaders and labor leaders can also be seen to have similar tendencies. It has been queried whether liberal trade policies render labor unions more vulnerable and reduce their power. Although it may not yet be possible to answer this query definitively, it does seem that there is some evidence supporting an affirmative answer. (This relates to goals of distributive justice also.) But the reduction of power may occur not only to labor unions. Some industrial leaders and owners of capital may also find their power reduced. No one involved in trade policy questions can afford to ignore the often intense feelings that are engendered by these effects of international trade (or of other international transactions). No one can effectively explain the specially favored place which agricultural producers have preserved in trade policy measures without reference to some of these ideas.[49] An interesting study beyond the scope of this book would analyze the gains and losses of power among national groups, resulting from international economic interdependence and international trade. Do the nimble, well-managed multinational corporations find their effective power enhanced by these international economic trends?

1.4   International Law and International Economic Relations: An Introduction

International Economic Law

Increasingly in recent years one has heard references to "international economic law."[50] Unfortunately, this phrase is not well defined. Various scholars and practitioners have differing ideas about the meaning of this term. Some would have it cast a very wide net, and embrace almost any aspect of international law that relates to any sort of economic matter. Considered this broadly, almost all international law could be called international economic law, because almost every aspect of international relations touches in one way or another on economics. Indeed, it can be argued from the latter observation that there cannot be any separate subject denominated as "international economic law."

A more restrained definition of "international economic law" would, however, embrace trade, investment, services when they are involved in transactions that cross national borders, and those subjects that involve the establishment on national territory of economic activity of persons or firms originating from outside that territory.[51]

In any event, the subject of international trade, whether in goods or in services (or both), is clearly at the core of international economic law. This book focuses on the rules of international trade in products, but the implications of those rules for other subjects of international economic relations should be obvious. The rules of product trade, centrally served by the GATT, are the most complex and extensive international rules regarding any subject of international economic relations which exist. As such it is natural that they would have some influence on the potential development of rules for other international economic subjects. Already scholars and statesmen have mentioned a "GATT for Investment"[52] and a "GATT for Services."[53] For this reason there is considerable justification for focusing on the rules of product trade as they are reflected in the GATT system. This focus can be thought of as sort of a "case study" of the advantages and disadvantages, the positives and negatives, of an elaborate rule system at the international level.

There are two unfortunate bifurcations of the subject of international economic law, however. One is the distinction between monetary and trade affairs. Since both are, in a sense, "two sides of the same coin," there is a degree of artificiality in separating them as topics. Yet international organizations, national governments, and even university departments tend to indulge in the same separation, and since the whole world cannot be studied at once, there is great practical value in taking up the trade questions separately.

An even less fortunate distinction of subject matter is often made between international and domestic rules. This book will not indulge in that separation. In fact, domestic and international rules and legal institutions of economic affairs are inextricably intertwined. It is not possible to understand the real operation of either of these sets of rules in isolation from the other. The national rules (especially constitutional rules) have had enormous influence on the international institutions and rules. Likewise the reverse influence can often be observed. Consequently in this work I shall try to treat them both, and introduce them in the next two chapters.

International Law and Economic Relations

By way of introduction to the international law bearing on economic affairs, and as part of an historical introduction to it, several observations may be useful to the reader.

Sources of international law can generally be divided into "customary" or "conventional." The latter term refers to treaties, which are often termed "conventions." Customary international law is defined as rules of national behavior which can be ascertained from the practice of nations when such practice reveals that nations are acting under a sense of legal obligation (*opinio juris*).[54] Unfortunately, customary international law norms are very often ambiguous and controverted. On many propositions of customary international law, scholars and practitioners disagree not only about their meaning but even about their existence. The traditional doctrines of establishing a norm of customary international law leave a great deal of room for such controversy.[55]

In economic affairs, however, there are very few recognized norms of customary international law.[56] There is a heavily disputed jurisprudence relating to national-government taking of alien property.[57] In addition, there are some fairly well-recognized norms of the law of the sea which relate to economic matters regarding the sea.[58] Beyond these, there is very little in the way of *substantive* international law customary norms (that is, norms other than ones dealing with procedures for government-to-government relations, or of relations among firms or individuals in the few cases when international law is deemed to apply to firms or individuals).

One view argues that there is a customary norm of economic relations which prohibits "discriminatory" action between nations. This "most-favored-nation" ideal is embodied in many treaties, including the GATT,[59] but most scholars and practitioners do not seem to accept the argument that there is any customary international norm of MFN.[60]

Thus, when dealing with international economic law, one is dealing primarily with *treaties*.

Functional Approach to International Law

A critical question, almost always asked by anyone confronted with an international law norm, is "Why does it matter?" Put another way, there exists much cynicism about the importance or effectiveness of international law rules. Frequently the public can read news of violations of such rules by both major and minor nations. In some cases such violations, even when they are admitted to be such (often there is bitter and inconclusive argument on this question), are rationalized or declared just by national leaders.[61] Thus the cynicism about international rules cannot be surprising.

A more careful examination of the role and effectiveness of international rules is necessary, however. First, it should be observed that not all domestic rules are always obeyed either. Observe traffic at any stop sign, or recall teacher strikes in many U.S. states where they are illegal. Then observe the cases of enterprises violating economic regulations, evading taxes, or indulging in corruption of government officials. It is apparent that international law has no monopoly on breaches and violations. It is a matter of degree. At least of stable societies it can be said that domestic laws are more often obeyed and effective than are international laws, and few scholars or practitioners of international law would try to refute that statement.

Yet there are many international rules which are remarkably well observed. Why this is so has been the subject of much speculation which will not be repeated here.[62] Notions of reciprocity and a desire to depend on other nations' observance of rules lead many nations to observe rules even when they don't want to. The critical task for this book is realistically to evaluate the role of the international as well as the national rules in influencing real behavior of nations or persons or enterprises. I will have more to say on this in later chapters.[63]

At least in the context of economic behavior, however, and particularly when that behavior is set in circumstances of decentralized decision-making, as in a market economy, rules can have important operational functions. They may provide nearly the only predictability or stability to a potential investment or trade-development situation. Without such predictability or stability, trade or investment flows might be even more risky and therefore more inhibited than otherwise. If such "liberal trade" goals (for reasons discussed in section 1.2) contribute to world welfare, then it follows that rules which assist such goals should also contribute to world welfare.

1.5   The Tangled Web: Is There a Warp and a Woof?

Legal scholars sometimes refer to the "seamless web" of the law.[64] The phrase connotes the notion that each legal concept is in some way related to virtually every other legal concept. It also connotes a certain skepticism of theory and of simplifying concepts — a skepticism which in many ways is characteristic of the legal profession, which often views itself as uniquely, among the learned professions, coming face to face with the complexity and coarseness of reality with the aim of solving real problems. It is sometimes said that the economist tells us what should be done, while the lawyer is left to figure out how to do it. This brings to mind the anecdote of the person on a desert island who finds a can of vegetables and asks the theorist how to open it. "Use a can opener," the theorist replies. "But where do I find one?" asks the other castaway. "Don't bother me with details!" responds the theorist.

The converse problem can also be dangerous: there is always the risk of losing sight of the forest because one's gaze focuses on particular trees. Watch a lawyer and a social scientist argue. The lawyer often cites specific cases — the "anecdotal evidence" — to make his point. The social scientist, on the other hand, will often use statistics to make his point. There are dangers with each approach. In order to formulate statistics it is often necessary to develop categories for counting which are oversimplified. The specific case history can be a useful way to avoid this kind of oversimplification. On the other hand, the use of anecdotes can often seriously mislead policy makers. "Once does not make always"; the anecdotes may be atypical.

Thus we see the dilemma of a book like this. How can some meaningful generalizations be stated in the short space allotted for exposition of an extraordinarily complex subject? There is always the danger of an apparently "unifying hypothesis" seriously oversimplifying the subject and thereby misleading the policy-maker and problem-solver. Yet without some generalization it is difficult, if not impossible, to understand the subject. Perhaps one way out of this difficulty is to state issues or questions raised by the material, without in all cases trying to formulate answers. In this book I try to do a little of both.

Some important themes or problems of the "world trade policy system" have already been introduced. The dilemma of rule versus discretion is one such theme, to which I return particularly in chapter 4.[65] Closely associated with that theme is the question of "effectiveness" of the trade rules: How effective are they? How effective should they be? How can they be made more effective (if that is desirable)?

The puzzle of an apparent tendency to choose second-, third-, or even fourth-best policy options has also been previously noted.[66] In these cases there are often noneconomic policy goals operating, sometimes without it being obvious. Some of the conflicting policy goals have to do with the legal and constitutional structure of the "system." A certain constitutional political structure can impose severe constraints on decision-makers, as we shall see particularly in the next two chapters. For example, a constitutional requirement of parliamentary approval can often lead officials to seek nonlegislative ways to resolve problems, even if such ways appear to be less desirable (in economic theory) than the option selected. Yet there are important policy reasons for the existence of constitutional structure, e.g., preventing a monopoly of power or preserving a representative form of government. Sometimes the "obstructiveness" of lawyers ("You can't do that, it's unconstitutional!") is merely the exercise of a constitutional cautionary function ("Think about the really long-term consequences of what you want to do").

One persistent theme that becomes apparent in the study of trade policy and law is the close interaction of national and international institutions. Each has a strong influence on the other, and it is impossible to understand this subject fully (and many others in today's interdependent world!) without noticing and analyzing how these influences operate. The U.S. constitution had a direct influence on the shaping of the GATT (as the next chapter will show). Vice versa, much of current U.S. trade legislation can only be understood in the context of the GATT rules.[67] The tendency for academic subject matters to separate international from national or domestic issues becomes an important source of misunderstanding.

A frequently discussed and debated topic of current trade policy is the question of what is "unfair" government or private activity. Politicians and others commonly declare, "Of course I am for liberal trade, but it must be *fair* trade. We must take action against all those unfair trade activities of *other* nations, even if that means restraining imports from them." But how do we tell what is "fair"? In chapters 10 and 11 we struggle with this theme. Closely related to it is another theme, which I have called the "interface" problem. This refers to the difficulty, in the current interdependent world, of trade among different types of economies. Some of the "unfairness" problems are in reality "difference" problems. We come across this type of issue in a number of later chapters, but again, especially in chapters 10 and 11.

Thus I have expressed a sort of "consumer warning." Don't expect too much of this book. Problems which appeared intractable before you read it will in many cases still appear intractable afterward. But I hope that this monograph will contribute at least modestly to an understanding of *why* those problems appear to be intractable, albeit primarily from the perspective of a legal scholar, but also whenever possible from the direct vantage point of a participant.

2   The International Institutions of Trade: The GATT

2.1   The Bretton Woods System and Its Context

Introduction

Although the GATT is featured in headlines of major daily newspapers as the most important treaty governing international trade relations, the fact is that the GATT treaty *as such* has never come into force. How could this be? What were the institutional and historical events which occurred during the formation years of the GATT which led to this state of affairs? How has this history affected the operation and the vigor of the GATT? These are some of the issues with which we struggle in this chapter.[1] I must hasten to clarify, however, that the obligations of GATT are clearly binding under international law, because of the history that this chapter describes.

The Context of Treaty Obligations for International Economic Affairs

Before embarking on a history of the GATT, however, it may be useful to review the context of international norms relating to economic affairs. International economic relations under international law are (as I noted in the previous chapter) primarily governed by treaties, rather than by customary law. In many cases, the treaties establish organizations. In such cases, a number of interesting legal questions may arise concerning the constitution and operation of the institution, as well as its authority to establish "secondary" law in the form of decisions, regulations, or possibly subsidiary treaty-type instruments.[2]

The principal governmental organizations concerning economic relations include the International Monetary Fund,[3] the International Bank for Reconstruction and Development,[4] and the GATT. These institutions comprise the "Bretton Woods System." Although the GATT was not formed at the 1944 Bretton Woods Conference, nevertheless the Bretton Woods Conference contemplated the necessity of an International Trade Organization, or ITO.

There is no dearth of organizations relating to international economic relations. Of the 3,100 governmental international organizations listed in the *Yearbook of International Organizations*, at least 300 can be said to relate to economic matters.[5]

What does this "landscape" of international economic institutions look like? These institutions can be grouped into several categories. The first of these categories would include the general economic institutions, which are designed to address problems in a variety of economic sectors, and which affect many nations (but not necessarily all). The Bretton Woods System, consisting of the IMF, the World Bank, and the two World Bank affiliates,[6] as well as GATT, is the core of this category. Furthermore, two important international organizations can be included, namely the Organization for Economic Cooperation and Development (OECD),[7] although its membership is limited primarily to the industrial Western countries; and the United Nations Conference on Trade and Development (UNCTAD),[8] which is a United Nations subsidiary and therefore has as "members" all United Nations members. The UNCTAD has been identified most prominently with developing countries' issues, but is not technically limited to those. In addition, the UN's Economic and Social Council (ECOSOC) can be grouped with these.[9]

The second category of organizations includes the other United Nations specialized agencies, which tend to focus on particular problems or sectors of endeavor. For example, the Food and Agriculture Organization (FAO) focuses on agricultural problems; the International Civil Aviation Organization (ICAO) focuses on airline transportation; the International Labor Organization (ILO) focuses on improvement of working and living standards, and the International Maritime Organization focuses on shipping.[10]

A third category includes the "regional" organizations. In many cases these organizations are in the form of "customs unions," "free trade areas," or interim agreements leading to one or the other. The most prominent of these organizations, of course, is the European Community (EC) (technically, three different customs unions or communities) which currently has twelve member states in Europe, and is perhaps the most cohesive existing customs union.[11] In addition to the EC, however, there are a number of other regional economic organizations, with varying degrees of cohesiveness and stability. For example, in the past the

European Free Trade Area (EFTA) has been prominent,[12] although its role has decreased after the departure of several of its members to join the EC.[13]

A fourth category of institutions or international agreements relating to economic matters consists of the various commodity agreements which exist in the world.[14] As of mid-1985, there were basically eighteen agreements, each devoted to a specific commodity, such as sugar, tin, etc. Some of these agreements themselves have had checkered histories.[15]

A fifth category of agreements and institutions relating to economic affairs includes a very large number of even more specialized agreements. One example is the Customs Cooperation Council (CCC), headquartered in Brussels, which deals with problems of customs classification and works closely with the GATT.[16] This organization sponsored the negotiations which led to the "International Convention on the Harmonized Commodity Description and Coding System."[17] Another is the World Intellectual Property Organization (WIPO), headquartered in Geneva and dealing with such things as patent and copyright law.[18] Even more specialized agreements govern the relations of a very small group of states to a common watershed or river (such as the U.S.-Canada Boundary Waters Agreement of 1907,[19] or the Rhine River agreement[20]).

A final category includes the myriad bilateral agreements which exist to govern economic relations. In past decades or centuries, the Friendship, Commerce, and Navigation Treaty (FCN) was of central importance to bilateral relations;[21] but in recent decades, with the advent of multilateral treaties such as the GATT, the FCN treaties have become less important, and fewer new ones seem to be negotiated. On the other hand, in recent decades there has developed — at least for several industrialized countries, such as Western Germany and France — a major program to build a web of bilateral investment treaties. These treaties are more narrowly focused than FCN treaties, but cover many similar subjects, often providing for certain standards of compensation in the event of expropriation, as well as for certain other matters relating to the investment of capital from a capital-exporting country in a capital-importing country. The United States has recently embarked on such a program, although as of mid-1988 it has not completed and brought into effect any treaty under that program.[22] During the 1930s, there was a fairly elaborate network of reciprocal bilateral trade treaties, most of which have been superseded by the GATT.[23]

A key question is whether all these international organizations and treaties are adequate — either in number and subject matter coverage, or in their structure and institutional makeup — to cope with the new and complex problems that have been developing in the context of greater world international economic interdependence. Furthermore, the institutional arrangements embodied in these many treaties vary enormously. For instance, with respect to voting, some of the institutions have a weighted voting system;[24] but much more common is a one-nation/one-vote system,[25] sometimes tempered by an ancillary or elite body of selected member states who have some additional powers (such as a "council"). In addition, the degree to which there are measures for "effectiveness" of the norms of these treaties (for example, sanctions) varies enormously from treaty to treaty, as does the effectiveness of the treaties themselves.[26]

This, then, is a partial road map of the landscape on which we must place the international trade system. It is complex, constantly changing, and furnishes both pitfalls and opportunities for constructive diplomacy.

2.2 The Flawed Constitutional Beginnings of GATT[27]

Early Development of International Trade Rules

The history of international cooperation to discipline national actions affecting international trade can be traced back to the beginnings of recorded history.[28] During the middle ages the development of the city-states and the Hanseatic League were manifestations of this long history, and the "law merchant," later to be incorporated into the Common Law of England by Lord Mansfield in the late 1700s, was another example of the search for predictability and stability in international trading relations.[29] The Treaty of Utrecht of 1713 has been described as a forerunner of GATT![30]

The development of the bilateral Friendship-Commerce-Navigation (FCN) treaties during the seventeenth and eighteenth centuries was an important step in regulating economic relations among the developing nation-states.[31] These treaties also covered matters other than trade in goods, but involved clauses such as "most-favored-nation" (MFN) and "national treatment" which later became pillars of the GATT structure.[32]

Modern multilateral developments to regulate trade began mainly during the late nineteenth century. In 1890 a treaty was signed "Concerning the Creation of an International Union for the Publication of

Customs Tariffs."[33] International meetings or congresses to address problems of customs cooperation were held in 1900, 1908, and 1913. Conferences on this matter were also held in 1920, 1922, 1923, 1927, 1930, and 1933.[34] The 1923 International Conference on Customs Formalities, sponsored by the League of Nations, completed an International Convention Relating to the Simplification of Customs Formalities which covered many of the matters now treated in GATT. The League of Nations produced a series of studies on trade problems from 1926 to 1936 which had influence on later international initiatives concerning trade.[35]

World War II and Bretton Woods

The major initiatives leading toward the GATT were taken by the United States, during World War II, in cooperation with its allies, particularly Great Britain. There were two distinct strands of thought which influenced those countries during the war period. One of these strands stemmed from the program of trade agreements begun by the United States after the enactment of the 1934 Reciprocal Trade Agreements Act. This history will be further discussed in the next chapter, but it should be noted that between 1934 and 1945 the U.S. had entered into 32 bilateral reciprocal trade agreements covering trade,[36] many of which had clauses that foreshadowed those that are currently in GATT.

The second strand of thinking during the war period stemmed from the view that the mistakes concerning economic policy during the interwar period (1920 to 1940) were a major cause of the disasters that led to World War II. The Great Depression has been partly blamed for this war, as has the harsh reparations policy toward Germany.[37] During this interwar period, nations, particularly after the damaging 1930 U.S. Tariff Act, took many protectionist measures, including quota-type restrictions, which choked off international trade. Political leaders of the U.S. and elsewhere made statements about the importance of establishing postwar economic institutions that would prevent these mistakes from happening again.

Thus it was that the Bretton Woods conference was held in 1944.[38] This conference was devoted to monetary and banking issues, and it established the charters of the IMF (International Monetary Fund) and the World Bank (International Bank for Reconstruction and Development), but it did not take up the problems of trade as such. This was undoubtedly because the conference was sponsored by and under the jurisdiction of ministries of finance, while trade was under the jurisdiction of different ministries. (It is interesting to speculate, in light of the history of the trade conferences, how history might have been different if the Bretton Woods conference had indeed taken up the entire subject matter of economic relations, including trade.) Nevertheless, the 1944 Conference is on record as recognizing the need for a comparable institution for trade, to complement the IMF monetary institutions.[39]

The United Nations and Preparations for An ITO: 1945–1948

The two strands of thinking about an organization for international trade began to merge in 1945. In the United States, the Congress enacted the 1945 renewal of the reciprocal trade agreements legislation for a three-year period.[40] In December of that year, the United States government invited a number of other nations to enter into negotiations to conclude a multilateral agreement for the mutual reduction of tariffs. In the same year, the United Nations was formed, and in February 1946 its subordinate body, ECOSOC, at its first meeting adopted a resolution calling for a conference to draft a charter for an International Trade Organization.[41] The United States at this time published a draft of a suggested ITO charter, and a preparatory committee was formed and met in October 1946 in London.

Altogether, including the London 1946 preparatory committee meeting, four preparatory meetings were held to complete a draft charter for an ITO. The various official records of these meetings total more than 27,000 pages in over 100 volumes.[42] The second meeting was a brief limited meeting of a drafting committee at Lake Success, New York in early 1947. But the principal meeting was held in Geneva from April to November 1947, and was followed by the fourth meeting to complete the ITO charter, in Havana in 1948.

The history of the preparation of GATT is intertwined with that of the preparation of the ITO charter. The 1947 Geneva meeting was actually an elaborate conference in three major parts (sometimes referred to as a "three-ring circus"). One part was devoted to continuing the preparation of a charter for a major international trade institution, the ITO. A second part was devoted to the negotiation of a multilateral agreement to reciprocally reduce tariffs. A third part concentrated on drafting the "general clauses" of obligations relating to the tariff obligations. The second and third parts, together, constitute the GATT—the General Agreement on Tariffs and Trade.

The "general clauses" of the draft GATT imposed obligations on nations to refrain from a variety of trade-impeding measures. These clauses had evolved in the United States' bilateral trade agreements, and were seen as necessary to protect the value of any tariff-reducing obligations.[43] The GATT, however, was not intended to be an organization. Indeed, U.S. negotiators were called to task by committees of the U.S. Congress during 1947 for appearing to tentatively agree to draft GATT clauses which seemed to imply an organization. The U.S. president and his negotiators recognized that an ITO charter would have to be submitted to Congress for approval. But from the U.S. point of view, the GATT was being negotiated under authority of the 1945 extension of the trade agreements authority. The congressional committees pointed out that this 1945 act did not authorize the president to enter into an agreement for an organization: it only authorized agreements to reduce tariffs and other restrictions on trade. The general clauses of GATT were recognized as a necessary complement to any tariff-reduction agreement, but organizational clauses were a different matter. So the U.S. negotiators returned to Geneva and redrafted the general GATT clauses to eliminate the suggestion of an organization. Thus multilateral decisions under GATT are to be taken by the "CONTRACTING PARTIES acting jointly" and not by any "organization" body.[44]

The Geneva negotiators thus conceived of their task as preparing a draft ITO charter (to be completed at Havana in 1948), and also as negotiating the GATT which would consist of elaborate schedules of tariff reductions appended to the "general clauses" of GATT. These schedules consisted of thousands of individual tariff commitments which resulted from numerous bilateral meetings of negotiators.[45] These commitments ultimately resulting in generalized tariff reduction commitments applied to all GATT members through the MFN obligation.

The GATT was to be merely a multilateral treaty, not an organization; and it was to be similar to the bilateral treaties which preceded it, but designed to operate under the umbrella of the ITO when the ITO came into being. The general clauses of GATT were largely drawn from that chapter of the draft ITO charter which was devoted to trading rules, which in turn had been heavily influenced by clauses in bilateral trade treaties. The GATT contained a clause recognizing that after the ITO charter was completed, parallel GATT clauses would be revised to bring them into conformity with those of the ITO charter.[46] One important implication of this preparatory history, linking the GATT to the ITO draft charter, is that the ITO preparatory history, including in some instances the history of the Havana Conference (which occurred after some of the GATT obligations came into force), is relevant to the interpretation of GATT clauses.[47]

The Havana Conference of 1948 completed the draft ITO charter, but the ITO never came into being. The principal reason for this was the failure of the United States Congress to approve it. The U.S. president submitted it to Congress, but by 1948 wartime urgency for new institutions had given way to desires for return to "normalcy." In addition, the 1948 U.S. election returned a Congress that was Republican-dominated, while the presidency remained in Democratic hands. Various other factors undoubtedly contributed to this history,[48] but by the end of 1950 the U.S. Executive announced that it would no longer seek congressional approval of the ITO, and that ended any chance of an ITO coming into being. Although other countries could have gone ahead, at this time the U.S. was the preeminent economic power in the world, having emerged from the war largely unscathed, and no other country desired to enter an ITO which did not include the United States. The irony was that it was the U.S. that had taken the principal initiative to develop the ITO charter in the first place.

The GATT and the Protocol of Provisional Application (PPA)

At the beginning of this chapter I asked: How is it that the GATT as such has never come into force, and yet that it is known as the principal institution of international trade today? The answer technically lies in the Protocol of Provisional Application, through which the GATT is applied as a treaty obligation under international law. This situation was a direct result of the history I have outlined, but it takes a bit of explaining.

The GATT, including the various tariff obligations, was completed by October 1947 as the Geneva conference drew to a close. Even though the GATT was to be subordinated to the ITO, the ITO charter was to be finished only later, in 1948. Yet many negotiators felt that the GATT should be brought into force much sooner. There were several reasons for this feeling. First, the GATT consisted partly of thousands of individual tariff concessions. The U.S., for example, had committed to reduce the tariff on wood chairs from 40 to 20 percent, and on leather shoes from 30 to 20 percent. The U.K. likewise agreed to reduce tariffs on soya beans, coniferous wood and timber, and many other products.[49] Although these concessions were still secret, the negotiators knew that it was inevitable that the content of the concessions would begin to creep into public knowledge, and as they did so traders would be influenced by them. Sellers might anticipate a forthcoming tariff reduction by holding their product back until the new tariff came into force. World trade patterns could thus be seriously disrupted if a prolonged delay occurred before the tariff concessions came into force.[50]

Another reason for early implementation of the GATT particularly influenced U.S. negotiators. They were negotiating under the authority of the U.S. trade legislation which had been renewed in 1945. Under this authority they would not need to submit the GATT to Congress (in the next chapter we will see how some members of Congress disagreed with this). But the 1945 act expired in mid-1948.[51] Thus there was a strong motivation on the part of the U.S. (shared by knowledgeable allies) to bring the GATT into force before this act expired. It was unlikely that this could be done if the participants in these events waited until after the 1948 Havana Conference and the completion of the ITO charter.

On the other hand, there were several difficult problems in bringing the GATT into force. Of course, some of the language of the general clauses of GATT would have to be made identical to the final ITO language, but this could be handled by amending the GATT at a later date to bring it into conformity with the results of the Havana Conference.

More troublesome was the fact that some nations had constitutional procedures under which they could not agree to parts of the GATT (particularly some of the general clauses) without submitting this agreement to their parliaments. Since they anticipated the necessity to submit the final draft of the ITO charter to their parliaments in late 1948 or the following year, they did not want to give their legislatures "two bites of the apple." They feared that to spend the political capital and effort required to get the GATT through the legislature might jeopardize the later effort to get the ITO passed. They preferred to take both agreements to their legislatures as a package.[52]

The solution agreed upon was the adoption of the Protocol of Provisional Application (PPA).[53] By this protocol eight nations agreed to apply the GATT "provisionally on and after 1 January 1948," while the remaining members of the twenty-three original GATT countries would do so soon after. The Protocol contained two other important clauses which resulted in changing the impact of the GATT itself. The Protocol required only a sixty-day notice period for withdrawal from the GATT, compared to the six months required by the GATT agreement itself. This, however, is essentially meaningless, since withdrawal from GATT is not a very viable option in practical terms, at least for any major participant. (Some would argue that it is unnecessary anyway, since it is so easy to "get away with" nonobservance of most of the rules.)

The second and much more important impact of the PPA, however, is its statement of the manner of implementing GATT. Parts I and III of GATT are fully implemented without a PPA exception, but the PPA called for implementation of Part II "to the fullest extent not inconsistent with existing legislation." Part I of GATT contains the MFN and the tariff concession obligations, while Part III is mainly procedural. Part II (Articles III to XXIII) contains most of the principal substantive obligations including those relating to customs procedures, quotas, subsidies, antidumping duties, and national treatment. As to these important obligations, each GATT Contracting Party was entitled to "grandfather rights" for any provision of its legislation which existed when it became a party, and which was inconsistent with a GATT Part II obligation.

These "grandfather rights," or the "existing legislation" exception of the PPA, solved for most countries the problem of executive authority to agree to GATT. This exception allowed most governments, which would otherwise need to submit the GATT for legislative approval, to approve the PPA by executive or administrative authority without going to the legislature. Obviously it was determined that after the ITO charter was ready to submit to legislatures, the GATT would also be submitted for "definitive" application (pursuant to GATT Article XXVI). In the meantime, GATT Contracting Parties could deviate from those GATT Part II obligations to which they could not adhere without legislative authority. They were to accept fully the MFN obligation of Article I of GATT and the tariff cuts of Article II incorporating the tariff schedules, but in most cases the executives had authority to do this. (The United States had such authority, of course, from its 1945 trade act extension. Whether the United States had authority to fully accept and implement the GATT in 1947–8 on a definitive basis without submitting it to Congress can be argued. We return to this question in the next chapter.[54]) Governments that later joined the GATT did so on treaty terms that incorporated the same "existing legislation" exception.

Although there have been attempts during subsequent GATT history to obtain definitive application of the GATT, none has succeeded.[55] Thus, even today one witnesses the invocation of grandfather rights to justify certain national actions regarding international trade.[56] This legal context was an important part of the U.S. bargaining position in the Tokyo Round negotiation of a countervailing duty code[57] and was also a central issue of a GATT panel proceeding that concerned the so-called manufacturing clause, which limited copyright protection in the U.S. on certain imported English-language books.[58] Many of the grandfather rights have, however, become extinct. Any new legislation does not qualify for this PPA exception, and gradually some of the old provisions have passed out of existence, or for other reasons have become either nonoperative or superceded.[59]

The GATT Begins to Fill the Vacuum

Since the ITO did not come into being, a major hole was left in the fabric intended for post-World War II international economic institutions: the "Bretton Woods System." It was only natural that that institution which did exist — the GATT — would find its role changing dramatically as nations turned to it as a forum to handle an increasing number of problems of their trading relationships. More countries became contracting parties, sometimes in groups (nine in 1949, four in 1951), sometimes individually.[60] The Contracting Parties (CPs) met almost every six months, usually for several weeks, and discussed a wide range of problems including disputes about the implementation of GATT rules. Because of the fiction that GATT was not an "organization," there was considerable reluctance at first to delegate any activity even to a "committee." Gradually that reluctance faded, and soon there was even an "Intercessional Committee" which met between sessions of the Contracting Parties.[61]

No secretariat existed for the GATT. After Havana, however, an Interim Commission for the ITO (ICITO) was set up, in the typical pattern of preparing the way for a new international organization. A small staff was assembled to prepare the ground for the ITO, and this staff serviced the needs of the GATT.[62] As years passed and it became clear that the ITO was never to come into being, this staff found that all of its time was devoted to the GATT, and it became *de facto* the GATT secretariat (technically as a kind of "leased" group, whereby the GATT "reimbursed" the ICITO for the costs of the secretariat).

During the early 1950s the GATT CPs decided that it would be necessary to review the GATT, and to amend it so as to better prepare it for its developing role as central international institution for trade. The CP's ninth regular session, scheduled for 1954-55, was designated a "review session"; and at this exceptionally long session extensive protocols were prepared to amend the GATT — one for those parts of GATT requiring unanimity to amend, another for the other parts requiring only two-thirds acceptance. (Ultimately the latter protocol came into effect, amending portions of Part II of GATT, but the protocol requiring unanimity never came into force and was withdrawn in 1967.[63])

The 1955 Review Session also drafted a new organizational protocol. Under this protocol an Organization for Trade Cooperation (OTC) was to be established to provide the institutional framework for the developing organizational role of GATT. This short treaty agreement was much less elaborate than the ITO, but even it failed to get the approval of the U.S. Congress, so the OTC also died stillborn.[64] Thus, the GATT has limped along for nearly forty years with almost no basic "constitution" designed to regulate its organizational activities and procedures. Even so, today the GATT by any fair definition must be deemed an "international organization," and as we shall see in other parts of this book, it has in some cases evolved through trial and error some fairly elaborate procedures for conducting its business. That it could do so, despite the flawed basic documents on which it had to build, is a tribute to the pragmatism and ingenuity of many of its leaders over the years.

One person in particular must be singled out for his influence on the evolution of GATT. This is Sir Eric Wyndham White, a British citizen (knighted in 1968) who was the chief administrative officer of the United Nations group which provided service for the drafting conferences of the ITO and GATT. He became the first GATT executive secretary, a post he held (later embellished by the title of director general) until he retired in 1968.[65] Although he was careful to give the appearance of playing the role of the typical international civil servant, to be neutral among all parties, and to avoid the appearance of taking initiatives which should be left to the nation-state participants, nevertheless Sir Eric had a profound sense of the "possible" while continuously working toward the basic goals of the GATT agreement. Some attribute important evolutionary steps of the GATT dispute settlement procedure to Sir Eric's actions behind the scenes. In the Kennedy Round of world trade negotiations from 1963 to 1967, Sir Eric's role was reportedly crucial, particularly during the last few weeks of the negotiation, in helping nations to break a stalemate and achieve a final agreement.[66]

During the Kennedy Round period, the GATT Contracting Parties adopted an amendment to the GATT general clauses which is the last such amendment to date. A protocol to add Part IV to GATT, dealing with problems of developing countries, was approved in 1965, and finally came into force in 1966.[67] The three articles (XXXVI, XXXVII,

XXXVIII) of this part are primarily expressions of goals, and impose few if any concrete obligations. Nevertheless, their language has been relied upon in legal and policy argumentation in GATT, and has had considerable influence.

A later section will describe the seven major trade- and tariff-negotiating rounds held through 1984 under the aegis of GATT. The last of these, the Tokyo Round (1973–1979), resulted in a major expansion of the activity and competence of GATT, not through amendments to the treaty text, but through the negotiation of a series of separate instruments, sometimes called "codes," each of which is technically a stand-alone treaty. These "codes" address a number of nontariff measures which distort international trade flows, such as government procurement regulations or the use of product standards to restrain imports. In various other chapters of this book, some of these codes will be considered in some detail, since they have important effects on the GATT rules regarding their subject.[68]

2.3 The Obligations of GATT and Their Legal and Institutional Setting

What Are the Rules?

This section serves a dual purpose. First, it introduces the GATT and its obligations and institutions. This constitutes an overview, since many of the particular obligations and institutional questions will be taken up much more extensively in other parts of this book. It will be noted that the obligations, in the light of the history previously explained, are binding under international law as applied by the Protocol of Provisional Application.

Second, this section discusses several important legal and policy issues that tend to "cut across" many GATT articles and principles. For example, it examines some problems of ascertaining which GATT obligations apply to which nations. It also explores the question, To whom, within a nation, do obligations apply, particularly in the context of subordinate units of government in a federal system?

One important subject which affects many other GATT issues is that of procedures and techniques for interpreting the GATT. This subject, touched on in this section, will be taken up more extensively in chapter 4 when I discuss dispute resolution and rule application problems of GATT. Certain key legal issues are more closely related to problems of contracting-party domestic law, such as the issue of "self-executing" or "direct" effects of GATT law. These I will examine in chapter 3, which explores national law issues.

The GATT Obligations and Code of Conduct

The central obligations of GATT are the tariff "concessions," by which contracting parties commit themselves (in Article II and the schedules) to limit the level of tariffs they will impose on imports from other GATT contracting parties. These obligations were the original reason for negotiating the GATT agreement. It is probably fair to say also that these obligations have been the most effective obligations of the GATT. Through a series of tariff reduction negotiations in GATT, the general average of tariffs of industrial countries on industrial goods has declined significantly during the history of GATT, to about 4.7 percent or less today.[69] Many observers feel that such a low tariff level is not a significant barrier to imports: it acts more as a low sales tax, one that most efficient producers abroad can effectively "hurdle" by increasing their productivity and decreasing their costs.[70]

A second and equally central obligation is that of most-favored nation (MFN). Both of these obligations are extensively considered in other chapters (chapters 5 and 6 respectively), so I will not elaborate further here. It will be remembered that these obligations form Part I of GATT, amendments which require unanimity[71] and which are not subject to the "existing legislation" clause of the Protocol of Provision Application.[72]

In Part II of GATT, Articles III through XVII comprise most of the other substantive obligations of GATT, and can be thought of as the "Code of Conduct" for government behavior in regulating international trade. It will be noted that these obligations (as well as MFN) apply to all products regardless of whether such products appear in a tariff concession schedule. This code applies to all goods, both imported and exported, although most of the rules are relevant only to imports. Most of these obligations are also treated more extensively in later chapters. They include the following:

National treatment (Article III, treated in chapter 8)

Antidumping and countervailing duties (Article VI, treated in chapters 10 and 11)

Valuation of goods for customs purposes (Article VII, treated in chapter 5)

Procedures of customs administration (Articles VIII and X, treated in chapter 5)

Marks of origin (Article IX, treated in chapter 5)

Quantitative restrictions (Article XI, treated in chapter 5)

Subsidies (Article XVI, treated in chapter 11)

State trading monopolies (Article XVII, treated in chapter 13)

One policy question which may be asked is whether it is beneficial to have a general code of conduct on trade. An alternative would be to apply rules only to agreed lists of goods (like the tariff schedules). A variation on this idea would incorporate notions of "reciprocity" so that a rule would apply to a product from another contracting party only if that party also applied the rule to its imports of the same product. These variations would obviously add greatly to the complexity, and therefore probably to the confusion and difficulty, of predicting compliance.[73]

In fact, because of the legal and sometimes not-so-legal measures taken to affect various products, there is substantial variation in the application of the GATT rules. Under the amending rule of GATT, a contracting party is not obligated to an amendment which it does not accept (even if more than two-thirds of the CPs have accepted the amendment).[74] Due to a peculiar history relating to the Article XVI subsidy obligations, only a few of the GATT contracting parties are bound by a portion of that article.[75] The grandfather "existing legislation" exception has already been noted, and various other exceptions in the GATT itself, including a waiver authority, may exempt particular products or countries from certain GATT obligations.[76] Finally, with the trend in GATT since 1965 to develop separate "codes" of conduct not integrated into the GATT text, only those countries which accept these codes are bound by them, so even more differentiation in legal GATT treatment can occur.[77]

De facto nonlegal differentiation also occurs when compliance with GATT legal norms varies. This subject will be addressed in chapter 4 (dispute settlement) and other chapters, but it is well known in GATT that many countries have used "Balance of Payments tariff surcharges" which technically are inconsistent with GATT rules.[78] Likewise, the proliferation of various types of "voluntary export restraints" during the last two decades often involves breaches of GATT obligations as well as contraventions of the basic policies of GATT. These restraints raise interesting jurisprudential questions about international law.[79]

To Whom Do GATT Obligations Apply? Private Enterprises and Subordinate Government Units

The wording of GATT makes it reasonably clear that this agreement applies only to treatment of *products* (and not to services, for example).[80] It is also reasonably clear that the agreement applies only to *government* action, and not to actions of private firms or individuals. Newer trends of international law entertain the possibility that treaties or customary international law may apply to individuals as well as to nations and international organizations. There is no longer much jurisprudential problem with these developments.[81] Nevertheless, the GATT wording is almost all phrased in such a way as to apply only to governments.[82] One important result of this circumstance is that the GATT (in contrast to the ITO Charter) has virtually nothing to say about monopolistic practices of private firms, even though such practices can substantially undermine the basic policies on which GATT is based.[83]

Whether or not it is worded to apply to governments, treaty language may additionally have, in some legal systems, so-called direct effect.[84] In the U.S. this would be called the "self-executing" effect, and would allow private parties to rely on the treaty language in private litigation in the domestic courts.[85]

Another question is, To what extent do the GATT norms apply to units of government subordinate to the nation which is the contracting party? Such units might include states in a federal system (e.g., California), or municipal or county units of various kinds. The GATT is not entirely clear on this question, but language in Article XXIV, paragraph 12 requires the contracting party to take "such reasonable measures . . . available to it to ensure observance." For the United States this probably means that the proclamation of GATT has already made it applicable to subordinate government units directly, and courts have so held.[86]

GATT Legal Exceptions to the Obligations

The GATT agreement itself provides a large number and variety of potential exceptions to its other norms. A simple enumeration will introduce them (many are taken up elsewhere in this book):

Grandfather rights of the PPA (see preceding section)

Waivers voted under Article XXV (see following section)

Balance of payments exceptions allowing use of quotas (Articles XII–XV)

Exceptions for developing countries in Article XVIII and also in Part IV (Articles XXXVI–XXXVIII)

The important exception for customs unions and free trade areas (Article XXIV; see chapter 6)

The escape clause of Article XIX (see chapter 7)

The general exceptions of Article XX, which cut across all GATT obligations, but are themselves subject to "soft" MFN and national treatment requirements (see chapter 9)

National security exceptions of Article XXI (see chapter 9)

The renegotiation procedures for tariff concessions of Article XXVIII (see chapter 5)

The "opt-out" provisions of Article XXXV (see following section)

Two of these exceptions are sufficiently general as not to be treated elsewhere in this book, yet are important enough to merit additional discussion here. These are the waiver provision (Article XXV) and the "opt-out" provision (Article XXXV). The latter will be taken up in the next section.

The waiver authority of Article XXV authorizes the CONTRACTING PARTIES acting jointly to grant a waiver to any party "in exceptional circumstances not elsewhere provided." The vote must be by two-thirds of those nations voting, to include a majority of all contracting parties. In practice the "exceptional circumstance" language has not been a constraint. It was once argued that it would be inappropriate to grant a waiver of obligations in Part I of GATT (MFN and tariff concessions) because amendment of that part required unanimous action while the waiver required a lesser vote.[87] Sufficient practice to amount to an "interpretation" of GATT has occurred to the contrary, however. In effect, some waivers have been almost the equivalent to "amendments," since they have no time limits. In some cases waivers have fundamentally altered the rights and obligations of contracting parties,[88] and in some cases the right to deviate from a GATT norm has been granted on conditions which almost amount to impositions of new obligations on contracting parties.

Omissions and Sectorial Exceptions

Certain subjects have been purposely omitted from GATT cognizance. We have already noted that GATT language applies to products, so services are not covered (although services are included in a new round of GATT negotiations, presumably with a view to drafting a separate agreement or agreements on the subject).[89]

In addition, although the ITO draft charter contained a whole chapter on anticompetitive practices, the GATT includes none of that language, and subsequent GATT interpretations have established the view of the CPs that it would be inappropriate to try to use GATT too fully to control such practices.[90]

There are also a number of "loopholes" in GATT — particular practices unanticipated when GATT was drafted — that have been utilized by various governments to evade GATT obligations or to subvert the general policy thrust of GATT in order to promote liberal trade. It has been argued that the variable levy used by the European Community is one such practice — one which is probably technically legal under GATT as a tariff on products that are not "bound"; yet one which amounts to an evasion of the idea to limit the protective effect of border measures to stable and predictable levels of tariffs.[91]

Although the GATT on its face applies to all product sectors of economic activity (with some differentiation between industrial and primary goods),[92] nevertheless noncompliance with GATT rules has resulted in some sectors being effectively beyond the discipline of the GATT rules. The most striking example of this is agriculture. So ineffective have GATT rules been, with respect to trade in agricultural goods, that some writers or practitioners have made the error of stating that the GATT does not legally apply to agriculture goods. One of the reasons for this state of affairs was the Congress of the United States, which early in GATT history adopted legislation mandating certain import restrictions on some agriculture goods — such that the U.S. would be in violation of GATT obligations.[93] In 1955 the U.S. government sought and obtained a GATT waiver for the requirements of this legislation.[94] This waiver is much criticized, and even though other governments may not have the legal cover of a waiver, they engage in practices similar to those covered by the waiver, arguing that what is fair for the U.S. must also be fair for others. The question of bringing GATT discipline to agriculture goods trade has been much discussed in GATT, and has been one of the most difficult negotiating problems of recent and currently proposed negotiations in GATT.[95]

Another sector which has been troublesome for GATT is textiles and clothing. Since 1961, world trade in textiles has basically evaded the discipline of GATT because of a series of negotiated "side-agreements" which establish a special regime of quotas for trade in these products.[96]

2.4   The GATT as an Organization: Membership and Institutional Measures

GATT as an Organization

Despite the original theory of the draftsmen of the GATT that GATT was not to be an international organization, the history previously outlined in this chapter forced GATT to assume a role for which it was never intended, and effectively that role became one of an organization for consultation, negotiation, and application of rules regarding international trade.

Who Belongs to GATT

Since in theory GATT is not an "organization," it does not have "members." The terminology used to emphasize this theory in the agreement itself is "contracting party." Yet we can fairly speak of "membership," in the light of the evolution of the GATT into what it is today.

Apart from the twenty-three nations which were original GATT CPs, nations become GATT contracting parties by one of two methods. The normal method is governed by Article XXXIII of GATT and requires a two-thirds vote of approval by the existing contracting parties for a nation to be accepted into GATT. The key part of obtaining sufficient votes for this purpose is the candidate nation's willingness to negotiate tariff concessions which existing GATT CPs deem to be adequate to fulfill their views of "reciprocity" to the various existing GATT concessions now binding the existing GATT members. It would be unfair to let a nation enter GATT and receive the advantage of over forty years of various trade concessions and obligations, which the existing membership had accepted, without requiring the new nation also to commit itself to equivalent obligations. This is sometimes referred to as "negotiating the ticket of admission."

A second path to membership also exists, however. Article XXVI (5c) provides that if a parent country has accepted the GATT in respect of a dependent customs territory (such as a colony), and if that customs territory later becomes independent, such territory can become a GATT contracting party merely through sponsorship by the parent country.

Since the origin of GATT, over thirty newly independent nations have entered GATT membership by this route. The advantage to those nations is that they need not negotiate a ticket of admission. The GATT is deemed to apply to these newly independent sponsored nations to the same extent that it applied to their territories before independence. If a subportion of the parent country's tariff schedule applies to a territory, then that becomes the GATT schedule for the new contracting party. Often this has only a few tariff obligations. If the parent country has no such tariff schedule portion, however, then the new GATT party has the great privilege and advantage of belonging to GATT without having the obligation of any tariff concessions.[97]

Some contracting parties have subsequently added to their schedules by negotiation, but the provisions of Article XXXVI (8) of GATT which say that developing countries should not have an obligation to furnish reciprocal concessions in tariff or trade negotiations have influenced industrial countries to tolerate very short schedules of concessions from developing countries, even though these countries all benefit from the industrial country concessions by virtue of MFN.[98]

Article XXXV of GATT has an important measure which affects to whom a contracting party's GATT obligations apply. This article, introduced in the original 1947 GATT draft when the voting requirement for new members was reduced from unanimity to two-thirds, allows either a prior member or a new member to "opt out" of a GATT relationship with the other at one time only—the time when the new member enters GATT.[99] This "opt out" was used extensively against Japan when it became a member, and it has been used by other countries for a variety of reasons. Often the reason to object to a GATT relationship is political in nature, as in the case of India's original 1948 invocation of Article XXXV against South Africa.[100] This "opt-out" clause has been carried into several of the 1979 Tokyo Round "codes," and has been used in some cases in connection with those codes also.[101]

Membership in GATT is not limited to "sovereign nations." The actual GATT language allows a "separate customs territory possessing full autonomy in the conduct of its external commercial relations and of other matters provided for in this Agreement" to become contracting parties. Among the original GATT "members" were Rhodesia and Nyasaland, Burma, and Ceylon (now Sri Lanka), although at the time they were not independent nations. Perhaps the most interesting recent example of this rule is the case of Hong Kong, as we see below.

Several interesting "membership" questions exist in connection with current GATT practice. One is the status of the European Community (EC) in GATT. It is possible to argue that the EC is a "separate customs territory possessing full autonomy" over GATT matters so that it could itself become a contracting party. Yet it has not taken steps to do so. The EC represents its member states (all of whom are GATT CPs) in the GATT. However, the Treaty of Rome allocates competence over member states' external trade relations with the EC institutions. The EC Commission provides a mission at GATT and asserts the sole right to speak on trade matters for the member states at GATT. There have been occasional instances, however, when because of this some tension has developed between the EC Commission representatives and the member states. In addition, in several instances it was decided that the Commission did not have competence to discuss a matter at GATT, and in such cases the member states spoke and acted for themselves. When actual voting occurs in GATT (somewhat rarely) each member state casts its vote as a contracting party (supposedly coordinated by the EC), and thus the EC effectively has twelve votes.[102]

China was one of the original contracting parties of GATT, but arguably withdrew from GATT in 1950 (the matter is disputed).[103] In the Uruguay Round the People's Republic of China is negotiating for "resumption" of its seat, a matter explored in chapter 14. China joined the GATT Multi-fibre Agreement in 1984, and became an observer to GATT in that same year.[104]

The case of Hong Kong is also very interesting in connection with GATT "membership." For many years Hong Kong has participated in GATT as a colonial entity of the United Kingdom, which is a GATT contracting party.[105] In April of 1986, after declaration of the U.K. under Article XXVI, Hong Kong was accepted by the GATT contracting parties as a full contracting party. To become such a "member," however, a determination was necessary that Hong Kong was an independent-customs territory with full autonomy over its external trade relations. The U.K. possession of Hong Kong and adjacent territories ends in 1997 and an agreement has already been reached between the U.K. and the People's Republic of China about the reversion of Hong Kong to China and the status which Hong Kong will have after that time. Before Hong Kong was accepted as a contracting party to GATT, assurances were received from the People's Republic of China that Hong Kong's status would remain sufficiently independent to fulfill the GATT Article XXVI requirement.[106]

The Contracting Parties Acting Jointly and Their Power

For a treaty that was not supposed to form an "organization,"[107] the GATT contains some clauses which appear to authorize a very broad exercise of authority. The principal body of GATT is the CONTRACTING PARTIES (specified in capital letters in the agreement when they are to "act jointly"). A number of GATT clauses call for joint action, but Article XXV of the Agreement gives general authority to the CPs to meet "from time to time for the purpose of giving effect to those provisions of this Agreement which involve joint action and, generally, with a view to facilitating the operation and furthering the objectives of this Agreement."[108] Each CP gets one vote, and unless otherwise specified, a majority of cast votes controls an issue.

From the language of Article XXV it can be seen that there is the potential of very broad CP authority. In practice this has not been exercised. Many governments (including the U.S.) could have some serious constitutional problems if the CPs purported to exercise this language of Article XXV to its limit. Nevertheless, the use of waivers has been extensive and in some cases nearly like an "amendment."[109] (The degree to which the CONTRACTING PARTIES have the authority to definitively interpret the GATT in a manner binding on all contracting parties will be taken up in chapter 4.)

The CONTRACTING PARTIES carry out their business today with an elaborate group of committees, working parties, panels, and other bodies.[110] The most significant sub-body of the CPs is the "Council," which was set up by resolution of the CONTRACTING PARTIES in 1960. This group consists of representatives of all GATT contracting parties who wish to assume the responsibility of such membership, and meets almost monthly. Partly because of the formation of this group, but also partly because diplomacy has increasingly become a process of referring to national capitals for instructions and even of voting by telex, the sessions of the CONTRACTING PARTIES as such have been reduced to annual meetings which last only a few days. The ordinary "grist" of GATT business is carried on by the Council, supervising the many other bodies of GATT.

Now that GATT has ninety-six or more nations as contracting parties, it is no longer the "cozy group" that formed it in 1947. Its size has made effective operation more difficult. There is some trend for major GATT trading countries to take their business elsewhere — to annual "summit" meetings, for example, or to other private meetings of trade ministers of the major participants.[111] Even though GATT may try to work by "consensus,"[112] voting will often play against the interests of the most powerful CPs. For these various reasons, it has sometimes been suggested that GATT needs some sort of high-level super committee which can act more like an executive, and which would reflect more accurately the real-power relations in the organization. The weighted voting technique of the IMF and World Bank are not deemed realistic options, but a small group of nations which included the most powerful trading entities as well as representatives of major categories of other CPs has been suggested. In 1975, during the Tokyo Round negotiations, a "Consultative Group of 18" was set up, partly with the considerations just mentioned in mind. It has not played a powerful role, however.[113]

For each major negotiating round in GATT, there has been formed a Trade Negotiating Committee (TNC) to act as a steering committee. Since usually nations which are not GATT CPs are invited to participate in the negotiation (sometimes with the hope that they will negotiate to accede to GATT), the TNC is not always precisely considered a sub-body of GATT, but is more like an ad hoc body set up by a group of nations deciding to negotiate.[114] For the Uruguay Round, the supervising structure became more complex because of some nations' objections to GATT negotiations on services trade. Their compromise has a typical group (called the Group on Negotiations of Goods [GNG]) for trade negotiations on goods, but a separate supervising group for services (called the Group of Negotiations on Services [GNS]). Some argue that the services group is not a GATT entity. Over both, however, is a broader supervising mechanism, traditionally called the TNC.[115]

Voting

The CONTRACTING PARTIES acting jointly would be governed by majority vote on many matters; however, in much of GATT business there is a decided preference for "consensus" approaches. There is in fact some fear of voting, possibly for good reason. The voting structure, like that of so many international organizations today, bears little resemblance to real power relations of the participants. The practice in GATT generally is to avoid formal voting, although this practice is conditioned by the amending, membership, and waiver language of the agreement, so that for waivers, or for membership or treaty amendments, at least, formal votes (or treaty acceptances) are considered necessary.

Unfortunately, the legal structure of potential voting still has a great influence on any organization, no matter how hard the organization tries to avoid voting. Consensus approaches often involve negotiating to resolve differences, but such negotiation is in the context of the participants' knowledge of the likely outcome if the negotiation breaks down. This can be complex and subtle. The outcome may be a vote, in which case the voting structure will in fact influence the negotiations toward a consensus. On the other hand, voting an unrealistic proposition will likely lead one or more powerful participants to ignore the vote result. This too becomes one of the constraints in a negotiation, at least when the negotiators are responsible and reasonably realistic.

A consensus approach has other problems. Strictly applied, it gives every country a veto, and thus reduces any potential initiative to the least common denominator. If not strictly applied, there will often be deference to the real "power structure" of the participants, and this may in fact give the most powerful of the group an even larger share of the power than policy or equity might dictate. During the Tokyo Round, the actual negotiation often began with major decisions being made by only the United States, the European Communities, and Japan. Canada or a few others might elbow their way into these discussions, but even then the vast majority of the Contracting Parties and other negotiating nations would be excluded from real influence on the drafting of a proposed agreement until near the end of the process, at which time it was difficult to get changes made.[116]

Likewise, the voting-consensus question has posed great problems for the GATT dispute-settlement procedure, rendering it difficult if not impossible to obtain Council approval of a panel report in a dispute, when the nation dissatisfied with the outcome expressed in such a report refuses to go along with a "consensus" for Council approval.[117]

A similar problem exists for many of the "code" agreements which resulted from the Tokyo Round. The institutional clauses are even more ambiguous than GATT, often not specifying voting arrangements at all.[118] In such cases "consensus" is supposed to be the approach used, but if this breaks down (which becomes more likely as more nations join the various codes), then general international customary practice will almost inevitably lead to the interpretation that the one-nation, one-vote with majority rule will prevail. Since these agreements usually provide for a "committee of signatories," consisting of a representative of each signatory, and since the EC is listed on each as a potential signatory, it was possible for the EC when it had 10 member states to exercise 11 votes (the number would be 13 now). This will not likely occur, however, since for many agreements only the EC has signed (a matter which involved considerable internal constitutional debate in the EC).[119]

The following breakdown of characteristics of GATT membership, illustrates various voting or other influence possibilities (as of March 1989):

Total number of CPs of which:	= 96
Industrial	= 25
(EC member states	= 12)
Advanced developing	= 9
Developing	= 56
Nonmarket economies	= 6

EC member states, plus the EFTA countries as well as the GATT members associated with the EC in the Lome convention total at least 54, which could be a formidable block; although no particular evidence of EC large-bloc voting (beyond the member states) can be detected.

Obviously, the advanced developing and the developing countries comprise more than a two-thirds vote of the GATT, opening the possibility that there could be some waivers that might displease the industrial countries.

The overall experience and current practice of these voting institutions in GATT and the various GATT-associated codes, however, suggests more potential for paralysis than for voting abuses.

Amending the GATT

In the light of what I have just described, the problems of amending the GATT become clearer. Governed by Article XXX of GATT, amendments to Articles I, II, and XXIX of GATT require unanimous acceptance, a circumstance that has never occurred. Amending the remainder of GATT requires two-thirds acceptance on the part of all contracting parties, but such an amendment obligates only those CPs which accept it (a potentially messy arrangement).[120]

In recent years it has generally been considered impractical to attempt to amend the GATT general clauses. (Technically, of course, the tariff commitments resulting from each trade negotiation round become part of the "text" of the agreement through Article II, but the methods of changing the schedules differ from those for amending the general language of GATT.[121]) Thus it was considered impossible to embody the nontariff measure results of the Tokyo Round negotiation into amendments to the GATT. Getting more than ninety (or even more than sixty) parliaments to accept the results would likely have been too time-consuming; and besides, such an approach would effectively have given much more negotiating power to the large developing country majority.

On the other hand, the development of "side codes," or stand-alone ancillary treaties, to enlarge and elaborate the GATT rules poses some technical legal and administrative difficulties. I have written about some of these difficulties in the following terms:[122]

The interrelationships between the various Codes and the GATT will become increasingly complex. Such complexity, in turn, will make it harder for the general public to understand the GATT-MTN system, perhaps resulting in less public support for that system over time. The complexity will hurt those countries that cannot devote additional governmental expertise to GATT representation problems. In addition, such complexity inevitably will give rise to a variety of legal disputes among GATT parties. Finally, it will contribute to the belief that the richer nations can control and can manipulate the GATT system for their own advantage.[123]

The most striking characteristic [of the Tokyo Round results] is the Balkanization or fragmentation of dispute settlement under the various Agreements. . . .[124]

One of the questions raised by side codes, which purport to obligate only those nations which separately accept them, is the relationship of those codes to the obligations of GATT itself. We come back to this question in the next section.

2.5   GATT and the Trade Negotiation Rounds

Trade Negotiation Rounds and the Evolution of GATT

An important but intermittent feature of GATT has been the series of trade negotiating rounds which it has sponsored. Through 1985, seven of these rounds (counting the 1947 original negotiating and drafting of GATT as the first) had occurred, and in September 1986 a decision was made to launch the eighth.[125] The first five of these rounds were devoted almost exclusively to tariff negotiations, although during the time of the fourth round, at the "review session" of 1954–55, the GATT contracting parties separately drafted the protocols revising non-tariff measure clauses of the agreement. The sixth round, named the "Kennedy

Round," had as one of its goals the negotiation of non-tariff measure obligations, but it succeeded only in a limited way to achieve this goal. The seventh round, the 1973–1979 Tokyo Round, was more devoted to non-tariff measures than to tariffs.

Over the forty years of GATT history, its most resounding success has undoubtedly been the reduction of tariff levels among the contracting parties.[126] As a result of these seven rounds, and of other activity between them, many tariffs on nonprimary goods imported into the industrialized contracting parties have been so reduced that many economists and businessmen feel that they are no longer a meaningful barrier to imports. Indeed, this very success (as I mentioned in section 1.1), has been one of the causes of today's "interdependence" problems. As previously mentioned, the story regarding primary goods, particularly agricultural products, is not nearly so encouraging. Likewise many developing countries have extensive tariff or other barriers to imports, as we shall explore in chapter 12.

The tariff schedules are incorporated into GATT by language in Article II, and thus changes might technically be considered amendments to that article. However, in GATT practice they generally are not considered to require unanimity. Instead, the acceptance of each contracting party whose schedule is affected is considered a prerequisite for the coming into force of those schedules.[127]

The following table gives some indication of the scope and success of the tariff-reducing activity of GATT. (The tariff averages refer to tariffs on nonprimary products of industrial countries. Figures for many rounds were unavailable.[128])

Round	Dates	Number of countries	Value of trade covered	Average tariff cut	Average tariffs afterward
Geneva	1947	23	$10 billion	35%	n/a
Annecy	1949	33	Unavailable		n/a
Torquay	1950	34	Unavailable		n/a
Geneva	1956	22	$2.5 billion		n/a
Dillon	1960–61	45	$4.9 billion		n/a
Kennedy	1962–1967	48	$40 billion	35%	8.7%
Tokyo	1973–1979	99	$155 billion	34%	4.7%

The Kennedy Round and Non-Tariff Measures

Although the contracting parties intended the Kennedy Round to deal with the increasingly troublesome problems of non-tariff measures, the results of that round for NTM were very modest. Only one basic side-agreement "code" resulted, namely the 1967 Antidumping (AD) Code.[129] This code had a troubled history because of United States constitutional and legal problems,[130] and was replaced in 1979 by a second AD Code resulting from the Tokyo Round.[131]

Another result of the Kennedy Round was a separate protocol agreement complementing the tariff protocol and embodying some NTM matters. The United States had a system of valuation of imports for Customs that, for certain products, used the American Selling Price (ASP) technique. Under this method, imported goods were valued by reference to the price of competing domestically produced goods in the U.S. This procedure was a clear violation of GATT, but the U.S. claimed grandfather rights for it. It applied to a few selected categories of goods, primarily shoe products and petrochemicals.[132] Other contracting parties, eager to obtain a commitment from the U.S. to change this system, were willing to negotiate reciprocal concessions on a variety of tariffs and a few other matters. Since under U.S. law, changes in ASP could not be agreed or implemented without reference to Congress, this matter and the reciprocal commitments to it were embodied in a separate protocol at the end of the Kennedy Round (1967), so as not to hold up implementation of the main tariff protocol. This ASP side agreement was then submitted to the U.S. Congress for approval, but the Congress never concurred and the protocol died. In fact, the side agreement never reached the floor of either the House or the Senate, due to various procedural devices engineered by domestic interests desiring to protect the products involved from foreign competition. This sad experience, reminiscent of congressional treatment of the ITO and the OTC,[133] was one factor leading to some foreign nation reluctance to enter into a new (Tokyo) round of negotiations during the 1970s. In the next chapter I will discuss some of the legislative devices designed to avoid repetition of this experience.

The Tokyo Round: "Side Agreements" and the GATT (Legal Status of Agreements Resulting from the Tokyo Round)

The last completed round of negotiation occurred from 1973 to 1979, and was called the "Tokyo Round," or sometimes the MTN (for multilateral trade negotiations). In this round non-tariff in addition to tariff measures were addressed extensively for the first time. Except for the original drafting of the GATT itself, the MTN results may well be the most far-reaching and substantively important product of the seven major trade rounds. The MTN results included, in addition to tariff-reduction protocols, nine special agreements, and four "understandings," dealing with subjects as follows:[134]

Agreements on

1. Technical barriers to trade

2. Government procurement

3. Interpretation and application of Articles VI, XVI, and XXIII (subsidies)

4. Arrangement regarding bovine meat

5. International dairy arrangement

6. Implementation of Article VII (custom valuation)

7. Import licensing procedures

8. Trade in civil aircraft

9. Implementation of Article VI (antidumping duties)

Understandings on

1. Differential and more favorable treatment, reciprocity and fuller participation of developing countries

2. Declaration on trade measures taken for balance-of-payments purposes

3. Safeguard action for development purposes

4. Understanding regarding notification, consultation, dispute settlement, and surveillance

The overall impact of these results was to substantially broaden the scope of coverage of the GATT system.[135]

The legal status of these various agreements and understandings, however, is not always clear. The nine agreements are drafted as "stand-alone" treaties, each with signatory clauses, in most cases with institutional measures which include a committee of signatories with certain powers, and with a dispute settlement mechanism (part of the "Balkanization" mentioned previously). Of these agreements, seven have sufficiently precise obligations to be called "codes." The others tend to confine their terms to the development of consultation mechanisms, statements of objectives, and only a few weak provisions which actually provide binding obligations. In one case, an agreement has apparently been sufficiently troubled that the United States and some other signatories have formally withdrawn from it.[136]

The "understandings" have a much more ambiguous status. Not signed as independent agreements, these instruments mostly express goals or very general obligations, or (in the case of dispute settlement) describe procedures which arguably were already followed. The CONTRACTING PARTIES adopted these understandings in November 1979.[137] The implication of some of the provisions in these understandings is such as to suggest a "waiver" from other GATT obligations,[138] while other provisions elaborate procedures in the manner in which a "decision" under GATT Article XXV might do.

As "stand-alone" treaties, the "codes" obligate only those nations which sign and ratify them. A number of questions can then be raised about the legal relationship of these codes to the GATT itself. First, in theory, GATT parties which do not sign the agreements are not bound by them, and no provision of a "code" can alter their GATT rights. Since the GATT obligations include the most-favored-nation clause, however, if a code provides treatment for the trade of any other code signatory which is more favorable than that provided in GATT, such treatment is arguably required for the GATT member who has not signed the code. The GATT CONTRACTING PARTIES in November 1979 adopted a decision which takes this position.[139] However, some codes may not fall within the terms of the GATT MFN clause, so we return to this question in a later chapter.[140]

Some of the "codes" have titles that relate them to the GATT, such as the "Agreement on Implementation of Article VI," and another on "Interpretation and Application" of several GATT Articles. Again, nonsignatories may argue that they are in no way bound by such codes. However, if these codes can be deemed to be "practice" of the GATT contracting parties, they may themselves be evidence of evolving interpretation of the GATT language itself. This could be especially true if further practice in GATT develops, without protest from nonsignatories of the codes, which follows a code interpretation. In these ways GATT parties who have not signed a code may find that they effectively become obligated to code terms which "interpret" the GATT.

One question already posed concerns the issue of "membership" in some of the codes, when a customs territory becomes a contracting party through "mother country" sponsorship.[141] In such a case, does the new contracting party also automatically become a "member" of such "codes" as the sponsoring parent country has signed?[142] The fact that the GATT secretariat is servicing the codes and their committees also raises questions about the relationship. Are all GATT members at least entitled to be observers in a code committee of signatories, even if they do not themselves sign the code? So far the code committees have all taken the position that they are entitled to decide which governments may be observers and attend meetings of their code. Most have, however, always accepted requests from other GATT members to be observers. On the other hand, the code committees have reserved the right to meet occasionally without observers, and to limit the participation of nonsignatories. It should be noticed, incidentally, that certain nations who are not GATT members are allowed to become signatories for some codes.[143]

Finally, it should be recalled that many of the codes have independent dispute-settlement mechanisms. This raises questions about whether a particular dispute should be brought into the general GATT procedure, or into the separate code procedure. This also may give rise to questions about what happens when an interpretation of a code by a code-dispute panel differs from an interpretation on a similar GATT issue by a GATT panel.

3   National Institutions

3.1   Introduction

Interrelationship of National and International Institutions

The erosion of the concept of "sovereignty" in international affairs has been much commented on.[1] Perhaps in no context more than international economic affairs has this erosion actually occurred. One occasionally still hears national officials (including those from the United States) argue against either international rules or foreign government demands for consultation or representation, on the basis that it "interferes with our sovereignty," or that it encroaches on the "internal affairs" of a given government. But this is usually a misplaced argument in today's world. The effects of national government actions on other societies, and on general world economic conditions, are so often significant that it would seem that the time has come for all governments to be prepared at least to listen to the arguments and representations of other governments, or of citizens of other societies, before taking action that has such effects. The old tired argument that "it is premature" for a foreign party to weigh in with its ideas, or for it to ask for consultation, before a government acts, is often only an excuse to enable the acting government to create a *fait accompli* situation before foreign objections can have any meaningful influence.

Apart from these considerations, it is also clear today that any coordinated activity of governments, especially in connection with economic affairs, requires a complex set of individual governmental actions by both international and national institutions. This is particularly important, of course, for the large and powerful economies which participate in world economic affairs. For example, to achieve any meaningful initiative by the GATT requires not only action by some body of that organization, but also action by at least the United States and the European Community — and probably also by Japan, Canada, and certain other key countries. In every such case, each government responds to a complex set of internal institutional constraints. As we see in this chapter, the United States Constitution mandates certain procedures (often requiring action by both the executive and the Congress), and this immediately imposes a set of legal/constitutional/political constraints on any proposed course of international action.

United States Law and the International System — Synergy or Conflict?

It is not difficult to find cases in which national and international legal systems have interacted to influence each other. A prime example is the effect of the U.S. Constitution and laws on the GATT-ITO history.[2] The 1967 GATT Antidumping Code was also heavily influenced by U.S. legal constraints imposed on U.S. negotiators; and the difficulty of implementing that code in U.S. law because of congressional criticism illustrates the interaction point.[3]

Other countries, especially the more powerful ones, have similar problems. The EC is a particularly interesting example, since it is so influential in GATT. Under the Treaty of Rome the troubled and evolving nature of the EC institutions has a constant influence on many GATT matters.[4] Controversy about appropriate competence or authority — between the EC institutions and the member states, or between the EC Commission and the EC Council — can slow up GATT action, or impose constraints on that action, just as it does to United States law. The Treaty of Rome cedes competence in "commercial policy" to the Community, and such policy arguably includes almost all matters presently within the scope of GATT. "Commercial policy" is not defined within the Rome Treaty, nor is the competence said to be exclusive. Member states often argue, therefore, that certain matters are not within the exclusive competence of the Community. Good examples of areas of controversy are monetary matters and trade in services. In such circumstances, the Community may allow member states to participate in the process alongside the Community.

At the end of the Tokyo Round, a number of these issues suddenly came to prominence. In the U.S., the Congress began considering legislation to approve and implement the Tokyo Round agreements. The EC, rightfully concerned that this national procedure would influence potential future interpretations of these agreements, retained legal and economic consultants located in Washington, D.C., to monitor and report to Brussels about these Congressional proceedings—once again illustrating the departure from theories of strict sovereignty and traditional diplomacy. On at least one important issue, EC officials felt it was necessary to communicate with the U.S. government to influence the direction of Congressional measures to be included in the Trade Agreements Act of 1979.[5] The EC itself had some difficulties in designing the procedure for its approval of the Tokyo Round agreements.[6]

3.2 The United States Constitution and Its Effects on Trade Relations

The Constitution and Its Constraints: Congressional Power to Regulate Commerce

The founding fathers who wrote the U.S. Constitution in the 1780s distrusted government and concentrations of power. Consequently, they built into the Constitution the concept of distributing power among three principal branches of the federal government (the presidency or executive branch, the Congress, and the courts), and between the federal and state governments. Among the results of this structure is a constant tension between the Congress and the executive branch. This tension sometimes results in actions of one branch or another which seem mysterious unless they are viewed in the context of this constitutional structure. However, this power struggle between the branches of the U.S. government is precisely what the founding fathers contemplated. They viewed it as a system of "checks and balances," which would prevent any one branch from becoming too powerful.

During recent decades, beginning with the crises of the 1930s, the U.S. presidency has grown considerably stronger. A Supreme Court case in 1936, The United States v. Curtiss Wright Export Co., even propounded the theory that the United States president has certain inherent powers over foreign affairs that do not depend on the Constitution![7] Although many scholars reject this theory,[8] for practical reasons the presidency has developed a preeminent role in the conduct of U.S. foreign affairs, stemming partly from various clauses in the U.S. Constitution.

With regard to international economic affairs, the Congress can point to several clauses which appear to indicate that power has been delegated to the Congress. These include Article I, section 8, of the U.S. Constitution which grants to the Congress the power to "regulate commerce with foreign Nations," and to "lay and collect Taxes, Duties, Imposts and excises."[9] Consequently, the Congress thinks that it has a special power over matters of international trade, and it likes to remind the executive branch of this special power.[10]

Although the power of the presidency was enhanced by the necessities of World War II, during the postwar period this power continued to be great, particularly in foreign affairs. However, in 1952 the U.S. Supreme Court, in the case of Youngstown Sheet & Tube Co. v. Sawyer, held that President Truman had exceeded his power by seizing the steel mills in order to keep them operating in the face of a strike.[11] Constitutional language in that case was relied upon as support for arguments limiting presidential power in matters relating to both domestic and foreign affairs. Although there have been few cases subsequently in which the Supreme Court has limited presidential powers in foreign affairs, some lower court cases have suggested the possibility of further limitations.[12]

The Vietnam War and the Watergate crisis caused the Congress to reassert its powers, especially in international affairs. Consequently, during the last decade, the Congress has taken a number of actions which have imposed restraints upon the president's authority.[13]

Treaties and Executive Agreements

As we have seen in previous chapters,[14] treaties are the main international law methods of implementing norms concerning economic relations. The way by which a particular nation enters into and treats treaties from a domestic-law point of view thus becomes extremely significant.

The U.S. Constitution requires that "treaties" be submitted to the U.S. Senate for "advice and consent" (requiring a two-thirds affirmative vote) before the president can enter into them on behalf of the United States. Nevertheless, during two centuries of constitutional history, there have developed alternative forms of approval of international agreements. United States practice divides international treaty agreements into "treaties" (in the U.S. constitutional sense, agreements which must be submitted to the Senate) and "executive agreements." All of these instruments, from an international law viewpoint, are "treaties," but from the U.S. constitutional perspective on domestic law, this different terminology is significant.[15]

There are several ways in which "executive agreements" may be approved under U.S. constitutional practice: (1) they may be submitted to the Congress, for approval by the passage of a statute which grants the authority to the president to accept the international agreement (many trade agreements get approved in this manner, a primary example being approval of most of the Tokyo Round GATT agreements by the 1979 Trade Agreements Act); (2) the Congress may pass a statute which in advance authorizes the president to negotiate, enter into, and accept for the United States an international agreement (this is the approach to tariff agreements of the Reciprocal Trade Agreements Acts); (3) a *treaty* may give the president advance delegated authority within limits to enter an executive agreement designed to implement the treaty; and finally, (4) there are some executive agreements which under the Constitution the president may enter into on his own "inherent" authority, without any participation either before or after the negotiation by the Congress or the Senate. These would be agreements which are authorized by explicit constitutional grants of authority to the president (such as his authority as commander-in-chief of the armed forces), or which are implied by the Constitution as falling under presidential authority ("executive power").[16]

Some countries, including the United States, make a distinction between international law and domestic law. This distinction concerns whether an international treaty will be treated by courts and government agencies as part of the domestic law, similar to statute law, of a country. Some countries, notably the United Kingdom, are considered "dualist," and their treaties do not become part of domestic law. In order for domestic-law implementation of a treaty to occur, the Parliament must enact a statute, or some other legal instrument (such as executive decree or regulation) must be promulgated. Other countries have legal systems which tend to incorporate international agreements into domestic law without the intervention of further governmental acts.[17] These are often called "monist" systems. The United States falls in between. International agreements (including the five types just described) can sometimes be deemed to apply automatically as statute-like law in domestic U.S. courts. In U.S. jurisprudence such agreements are (unfortunately) called "self-executing."[18] Some agreements, however, cannot be deemed to be domestic law, and may require further governmental acts to be implemented.

It must be recognized that a treaty norm may well be valid and binding under international law, but not under domestic law. This gives rise to the possibility that the domestic law which prevails in specific cases is inconsistent with the international law treaty norm. In such a case the country concerned may be in violation of its international law obligations, although its domestic law will be "valid" in its own government institutions, including its courts. These issues can be very significant in connection with, for example, the GATT and the various "side codes." Furthermore, the legal treatment of trade agreements may differ from country to country, giving rise to perceptions of unfairness or lack of reciprocity.[19]

There is a great deal of confusion about U.S. law relating to domestic application of international agreements, and this confusion is reflected in court opinions and secondary literature.[20] In U.S. law, if an international agreement has direct statute-like ("self-executing") legal effect, then in relation to statutes or other such agreements, the latest in time will prevail.

Presidential Powers

Even though the Congress has been reasserting its powers in connection with foreign affairs, the presidential powers are formidable, and still dominant. The president has authority to negotiate international agreements and to carry on international diplomacy. Consequently, as I have indicated, he may enter into executive agreements on his own constitutional authority, although the number that fall into this category is rather small. More significantly, however, over the years the Congress has delegated to the president a wide variety of powers relating to international affairs. Since the president is the chief "actor" in international affairs, he may sometimes interpret these delegations expansively, and effectively exercise great power indeed.

The extent of presidential power in international economic matters is not clear.[21] Several significant court cases have addressed the issue of the president's power to enter into international agreements, formal or informal. In the 1953 case of United States v. Guy Capps, Inc., the Fourth Circuit U.S. Court of Appeals held that the president's officials exceeded presidential authority by entering an agreement with Canada concerning the importation of potatoes to the United States[22] There was no explicit statutory authority for such an agreement, and indeed a relevant statute was deemed to require different procedures for the circumstances involved. The U.S. Supreme Court affirmed the case, but did so on other grounds, and historical evidence exists that the Court intended to avoid taking a position on the presidential power issue.[23]

During the late 1960s and early 1970s U.S. government officials "promoted" an informal understanding by which steel producers in Japan and in Europe sent "unilateral" letters to the United States government, containing assurances that steel shipments to the U.S. market would not exceed certain quantities. In Consumers Union v. Kissinger, this voluntary restraint arrangement was challenged as a violation of U.S. antitrust laws, and as exceeding the president's power.[24] The antitrust portion of the lawsuit was dismissed because of lack of investigative resources by the complainant. On the *ultra vires* issue, however, the Court of Appeals for the District of Columbia circuit ruled two-to-one, in favor of the president, largely on the ground that the arrangement did not involve any *formal* agreement on behalf of the United States. The dissenter vehemently argued that the informality of the arrangement should not prevent the court intervention, since the *effects* on trade were just as real as if the agreement had been formal. The Supreme Court refused to take the case; and the Congress, in the 1974 Trade Act, enacted a provision immunizing the participants in these *past* steel arrangements from antitrust liability, partly on the ground that key congressional leaders had been consulted before the arrangement had been encouraged and had condoned it.[25] We shall return to some of these issues in chapter 7, where I discuss voluntary restraint arrangements in general.

The Congress and International Economic Relations

It is sometimes interesting to speculate whether the Congress or the president has been more "protectionist" or "trade restrictive." This question is not easily answered, although many would quickly answer that the Congress is the more protectionist. It is true that congressmen, senators, and a plethora of committees often seem bent on adopting a certain proposal to please specific constituent groups by restricting imports. Yet, since 1945, the Congress has never adopted a *general* trade statute designed as primarily protectionist trade legislation. It is true that the Congress has sometimes adopted "riders" or other "tack-on" measures in bills principally designed for other purposes, which have restricted imports of specific product groups (such as English-language books, or steel for mass transit systems). But despite threats and occasional near-misses, the Congress since 1945 has always pulled back from the "brink" of any overtly protectionist statute.[26] The lessons of the 1930 Smoot-Hawley tariff seem still to have some force.[27] The 1988 Trade Act is considered by some to be rather protectionist, but close examination leads others to ambivalence on that issue.[28]

The president, on the other hand, has implemented several programs with broad and extensive import-restricting results, including programs on textiles,[29] steel,[30] and autos.[31] In terms of trade coverage or impact, the president wins this contest hands-down. However, the president's action is often motivated by the threat of imminent congressional action — which would be worse — if he does not act first.

The fact is that the role of the Congress in trade policy is extremely important, and to some, very troublesome. The authority of the U.S. executive branch in this subject derives principally from enactments of the Congress. A number of these are enactments which the executive has sought from the Congress. When the Congress grants authority in this area, however, it usually extracts some "price," requiring certain procedural or judicial restraints on executive action, or mandating certain trade-policy activity which may have import-restricting consequences. (We will explore these enactments in the next section.)

There are, however, several general topics relating to the exercise of congressional authority which need examination. One of these is the question of constitutional constraints on congressional delegation of authority to the president. In past decades this has been a seriously debated question, but no jurists or scholars seem to deny that there is *some* constitutional limitation on the extent to which the Congress may delegate authority to the president. The Congress, for example, could not delegate "all legislative authority" to the president, since the Constitution sets forth a division of powers inconsistent with such sweeping delegation. However, no Supreme Court case since 1935 has held a congressional delegation to be unconstitutional,[32] and the rule articulated by the Supreme Court is that, so long as a delegation contains an "intelligible principle" on which the executive branch or other official shall act, the delegation will be upheld.[33] Even a 1971 delegation to the president authorizing him "to issue such orders and regulations as he may deem appropriate to stabilize prices, rents, wages, and salaries at levels not less than those prevailing on May 25, 1970" was upheld,[34] and trade statutes commonly contain some very broadly stated principles.[35]

The Congress, however, often does not wish to delegate much authority to the president, and this is particularly noticeable in connection with authority regarding international economic matters. Although the Congress has delegated the president authority to act in certain emergencies, in matters relating to trade (particularly export controls and the negotiation of agreements on tariffs), the Congress has kept the executive on a relatively "short leash," with statutory delegations which expire and require renewal every few years. Even then, executive authority is usually hedged with many conditions and requirements, as we shall see.[36]

The Courts and International Economic Relations

Federal Courts in the United States, in exercising their constitutional role of mediating the division of powers within the U.S. government, have played a relatively cautious role. With respect to foreign affairs, they seem to have given a great deal of deference to the president.[37] This deference has carried over into international economic affairs, with the Supreme Court making statements like the following in 1948:[38]

The President, both as Commander-in-Chief and as the Nation's organ for foreign affairs, has available intelligence services whose reports neither are nor ought to be published.... The very nature of executive decisions as to foreign policy is political, not judicial. They are delicate, complex and involve large elements of prophecy.... They are decisions of a kind for which the Judiciary has neither aptitude, facilities nor responsibility and have long been held to belong in the domain of political power not subject to judicial intrusion or inquiry....[39]

The Court has also noted that the Congress, "in giving the Executive authority over matters of foreign affairs — must of necessity paint with a brush broader than it customarily wields in domestic areas."[40]

Whether it is wise for the courts to be so deferential might well be questioned in a world of growing international interdependence.[41] Such interdependence causes greater portions of government activity to be "international," and thus potentially removed from close court scrutiny. In any event, in some international economic matters, courts are not so deferential. The Congress, perhaps partly because it feels incapable of restraining the executive itself, has in a few areas delegated considerable powers of judicial review over executive branch administrative decisions. This has been particularly the case with respect to antidumping[42] and countervailing duty[43] cases, where the Court of International Trade has intruded deeply into the decisions of the U.S. Department of Commerce and the International Trade Commission.

Federal-State Relations in the United States

The United States is a federal system, and the Constitution grants certain powers to the states. However, with regard to international economic matters, there appears to be no significant constitutional limitation on the powers of the federal government because of state powers. Thus, any valid international agreement which has direct application, or any valid federal statute or regulation regarding foreign economic affairs will likely prevail over inconsistent state law. One well-known Supreme Court case held that a valid international agreement may even extend federal powers of regulation beyond what would be permissible in the absence of such an agreement.[44] Several cases[45] have addressed the matter of conflict between state law and GATT, and all such cases have recognized that the federal law — or directly applicable international agreements — regulating international commerce will prevail over state law.

Perhaps the most interesting recent issue in this context concerns the international Government Procurement Code[46] negotiated in the context of GATT. This code imposes international obligations on procedures by which signatory governments handle certain parts of their government purchases, requiring them to treat imports equally to domestic goods. During the negotiation the question arose whether such obligations should be applied to government subdivisions, including states in a federal system. U.S. negotiators apparently took the position that the U.S. could validly enter into a commitment on the subject which would obligate state government purchases to follow the code. Negotiators from other nations, however, found more difficulty in such a provision and, in the end, the code excluded political subdivisions from its ambit.[47]

Such authority in the central government of a federal state is not common to certain other countries, however. In Canada the provinces have considerably more power over international trade,[48] and in the European Economic Community the relationship between the EC's powers and those of the member states is an evolving and controversial subject.[49]

3.3 United States Law and International Trade

Introduction

Even though the president has broad and ill-defined powers in foreign affairs, in economic affairs (for reasons I have already described[50]) his inherent or direct constitutional powers are considerably constrained. The Congress normally must delegate authority to the president, for him to be able to act. In fact, the Congress has delegated many powers to him, and "creative interpretation" on the parts of the president and his lawyers has undoubtedly extended the limits of those delegations beyond what the Congress intended.

The frustration of the Congress in this matter is expressed in a statement made in 1985:

Before I get into the national security section of the new [export control] law, I want to talk about the foreign policy section for just a moment. I have with me a copy of the committee report for the supplemental appropriations bill that we took up recently. The first page of the report says that the American agricultural community is near bankruptcy because of past foreign policy controls. It went through and listed at least four different executive branch actions that called for either trade embargoes or termination of contracts on agricultural exports. It then listed recent statements by the Administration that it will never again consider embargoes on agricultural products, in full recognition that they do not work and that they harm American farmers. At the same time that this page in the committee report was being printed, the President was imposing a new trade embargo on Nicaragua. Where was the authority? The EAA [the old export control law] has expired.

The President found the authority in the International Emergency Economic Powers Act (IEEPA). So when the State Department appeared before the committee I asked, "If the EAA had been alive and well, and if we had no contract sanctity provision, which would you have chosen, IEEPA or the EAA to impose that embargo?" The official response was IEEPA. All of the work that we have put into contract sanctity to protect American businessmen with long-term commitments in the work community goes out the window because the President at any time, through a mere whim, can invoke IEEPA.[51]

The U.S. statute books are full of a variety of delegations of authority to the president to deal with various aspects of international economic relations.[52] Furthermore, the approval of treaties has extended additional powers to the executive. Our focus here will be on the trade-agreements acts which concern the GATT and on related matters of international trade regulation.

Smoot-Hawley and Progeny

The infamous Tariff Act of 1930 led the Roosevelt administration, elected in 1932, to consider ways to reduce the damage done to the world economy by high tariffs. Under the leadership of the then secretary of state, Cordell

Hull, the executive proposed and the Congress adopted a statute, the Reciprocal Trade Agreements Act of 1934, which was designed to allow the president's officials to negotiate with foreign nations for the mutual reduction of tariffs. During the debate in Congress on this act, one senator noted: "[O]ur experience in writing tariff legislation . . . has been discouraging. Trading between groups and sections is inevitable. Log-rolling is inevitable, and in its most pernicious form. We do not write a national tariff law. We jam together, through various unholy alliances and combinations, a potpourri or hodgepodge of section and local tariff rates, which often add to our troubles and increase world misery."[53]

The 1934 act was limited in duration, but until the mid-1960s, renewals came regularly—in 1937, 1940, 1943, 1945, 1948, 1951, 1953, 1954, 1955, 1958, and 1962.[54] During recent years these acts have concerned much besides tariff matters, and large portions of them have been permanently added to the statute books. The "tariff-negotiating authority," however, has always been limited in duration. The authority granted for the Tokyo Round expired in January 1980 (although section 1102 of the 1988 Omnibus Trade and Competitiveness Act renewed that authority, for a new round, until June 1, 1993).[55]

The basic negotiating authority of the series of trade acts has provided a two-part power to the president. First, it authorizes him to negotiate and accept an international agreement on the reduction of tariffs, specifying certain goals and certain defined limits on his authority to enter into agreement. The agreement itself is the "executive agreement pursuant to congressional authority granted in advance" which I described in the preceding section. Second, these statutes authorize the president to "proclaim" such agreements on tariffs, so that they become part of the domestic law which customs officials and others apply to actual transactions and other events. A Senate report stated in 1943: "Under the Trade Agreements Act changes in our tariff rates are made, so far as our domestic law is concerned, by the President's proclamation under the authority of the Trade Agreement Act. Changes in the Tariff rates are not made by the agreements, per se. . . ."[56]

The 1962 renewal of trade agreements authority saw a shift in emphasis from fairly simple renewal or date-extension legislation to more elaborate legislation intended to deal with a number of different issues of international economics. The 1962 Trade Expansion Act set up the framework for U.S. participation in the sixth GATT trade-negotiating round, the Kennedy Round, and explicitly mentioned the goal of reducing non-tariff measures on the flow of trade.

From 1967 to 1975 there was a hiatus (the longest since 1934) in the trade agreements authority. This was finally corrected in the 1974 Trade Act (effective in 1975), which provided the framework for U.S. participation in the seventh trade round, the Tokyo Round. The 1974 act renewed the "advance authority" for the president to enter into tariff agreements until January 5, 1980. It also made some permanent changes to the escape clause and certain other legislative provisions. Most significantly, however, it added to the books some major titles of law concerning non-tariff measures, provision for industry group "liaison" to the negotiators, treatment of communist or "nonmarket" economies, and provisions for preferential treatment of developing countries.[57]

The next major U.S. trade act was the Trade Agreements Act of 1979, which approved the agreements which resulted from the Tokyo Round agreement under the so-called "fast-track procedure." In 1984 the Congress passed the Trade and Tariffs Act,[58] which made some significant changes in U.S. trade law, but did not purport either to generally overhaul that law or to establish new negotiating authority. In fact, since World War II, this statute was the first major trade act concerning imports which was not the result of a comprehensive proposal from the executive branch. Although the executive branch in 1984 wanted basically two things— renewal of the preference title concerning developing countries, and authority to negotiate a bilateral free trade area with Israel—the Congress had a number of other matters on its mind, and various pieces of draft legislation from various congressional committees were rather suddenly pasted together near the end of the 1984 congressional session, to form the 1984 act.

Since 1984 there have been hundreds of proposals in Congress for further trade legislation, and several comprehensive or broad-scope bills. Since a new, eighth round of negotiations was launched in September 1986, it was acknowledged that some U.S. legislation would be needed within the next several years to assist U.S. participation in that round. The Congress, however, threatened to require an expensive *quid pro quo* for such legislation, making various proposals concerning a variety of trade-policy issues, many of which would have had a trade-limiting effect.

Finally, in mid-1988, the Omnibus Trade and Competitiveness Act[59] became law (after much maneuvering between the president and the Congress, an earlier version of the act being vetoed). This act, similar to that of 1984, was primarily due to a congressional initiative, again reflecting a considerable shift from the traditional pattern of major trade acts since 1934.

Congressional Attempts to Keep the Executive in Check: Legislative Veto Procedures and the "Fast Track"

Imagine you are a congressman, and the president comes to you and says he needs authority to negotiate with foreign nations for the reduction of non-tariff measures (NTMs) which are restricting trade. The tariff problem, although not extinguished, has been largely resolved by multiple rounds of GATT negotiation, but now NTMs are proving damaging to the principles of comparative advantage and to world welfare. The president would like advance authority for NTM negotiations along the pattern of the traditional tariff authority. The problem is that non-tariff measures reach deeply into the interstices of domestic policy and regulation. The Congress has fought lengthy battles on many such issues, including environmental standards, product liability, and purity requirements for medicines. The Congress does not relish the prospect of a president changing all its work through the implementation of international agreements. So you advise the president to negotiate all he wants, but to bring back for congressional approval any agreements he completes.

The president's answer is that such a procedure is not acceptable to foreign governments, who see it as a way for U.S. negotiators to get "two bites of the apple." The negotiators and their political superiors spend "political chips" in the form of compromises necessary to obtain an international agreement. These will cost foreign governments some loss of votes in the next elections, but will be worth it if negotiators can demonstrate that some advantage will ensue from the agreement. But when the delicately balanced draft agreement is submitted to Congress (or to other Parliaments) then it can all come unraveled, as those bodies find clauses objectionable or feel their negotiators should have obtained more. Major portions of the results of the Kennedy Round were never approved by the U.S. Congress, and foreign officials remember this. They also remember the history of congressional refusal to approve the ITO and the OTC.[60]

What should one do? Some sort of middle way must be sought. This was the thinking of the draftsmen in the early 1970s as they prepared the bill that finally became the 1974 Trade Act. One idea was to turn to a procedure that had a long but controversial history in the United States—the legislative veto. This procedure basically called for the president to establish an order, regulation, or international draft agreement; submit that to the Congress; and if the Congress did not—within a specified time by a specified majority—*dis*approve the measure, it came into effect and became valid law. But, although many foreign governments, and a number of state governments in the United States, have used the legislative veto, the constitutional doctrine of "separation of powers" has been used to argue against it.

Early drafts of the 1974 legislation provided a fairly elaborate legislative veto provision as a way to resolve the apparent dilemma of the need for U.S. NTM negotiating credibility,—i.e., a procedure that improved the chance that U.S. officials could "deliver" upon a commitment to accept an international agreement, but did not give the president a "blank check." Under this draft procedure, the president, before final completion of a draft international agreement,[61] would consult with the Congress and be partly guided by their views of the draft agreement in progress. Then, when the draft agreement was completed, he would prepare proposed legislation to approve and implement it which, if the legislation was not disapproved by the Congress, would become law.

The House of Representatives accepted this procedure, but when it went to the Senate, the political atmosphere was different. The Watergate scandal had recently broken, and the Senate Finance Committee was reluctant to approve delegations of authority to a president under such a cloud. (In fact, the bill did not make much progress until after President Nixon resigned and President Ford took office.) Even though in the same bill there were other legislative veto procedures which were not challenged, the one relating to non-tariff measures was too significant. Consequently the Senate Committee drafted an alternative which became law, and this has been called the "fast-track" procedure.

The fast-track procedure for approval of the results of international negotiations on non-tariff measures was an attempt to retain the essential features of the legislative veto. In addition to the consultation requirement, the fast-track provided three essential rules: 1) a bill, when introduced, would not be amendable; 2) committees to which the bill was referred would be required to report out the bill within a short period of time;[62] and 3) debate over the bill in both houses would be limited. These rules were not statutory, however. They were included in the rules of each house of Congress, and were subject to change through parliamentary procedure which excluded the president. Thus the procedures were not quite so stable as a statutory legislative veto would have been.

It should be noted that this procedure is constitutionally the same as that of adopting a statute. Further, if a statute is also adopted, the statute itself cures most conceivable departures from the fast-track procedure. For example, if the proposed bill were to go beyond the scope of subject matter contemplated in the fast-track procedure, but the Congress were to adopt it anyway (and the president were to sign it), then the statute would be valid since the Constitution would be fulfilled, and the deviance would be "cured."

The fast-track procedure worked very well during the 1979 enactment of approval and implementation of the Tokyo Round results. Surprisingly, the relevant congressional committees developed a procedure for the consultation period, under which those on the committee played a role very similar to their role in normal legislation, with "nonmark-up" and a "nonconference" to reconcile differences between the House and the Senate. These committees and the lawyers for the Congress actually developed the draft legislation, which they wished the president to introduce for the fast-track procedure. The president's bill was almost identical to the bill developed by the Congress,[63] and partly for this reason the bill was adopted by an astounding 395 to 7 in the House, and 90 to 4 in the Senate. During the consultation period several concerns of congressional interests had resulted in negotiated changes in the draft agreements, proving the efficacy of the procedure.[64]

Subsequently, in 1983 the U.S. Supreme Court, in the case INS v. Chadha,[65] held that a legislative veto procedure was not permissible under the U.S. Constitution.[66] Fortunately, the trade act NTM procedure was not threatened. Certain other trade-act "vetoes," however, were subsequently changed because of this case.[67] The fast-track procedure has in fact been suggested as a plausible alternative to legislative vetoes in other types of statutes.

The Trade Act fast-track procedure, like the tariff authority, however, has a duration limit. Satisfaction with the procedure led the Congress in the 1979 act to extend the original time of expiry from January 5, 1980 to January 5, 1988. This procedure is now considered so important that in 1986, at the beginning of negotiations between Canada and the U.S. for a free-trade area, Canada insisted on the fast-track application for the negotiation results.[68] The deadline of the current law on this procedure was extended by the 1988 act so that it will be available for the new round of trade negotiations begun in 1986 in GATT.[69]

GATT and Its Codes in Domestic United States Law

A critical and intriguing question concerning the GATT and, more recently, some of the "codes" related to GATT, is whether these agreements have a "direct application" in the domestic law of signatory countries. As I previously noted, the answer to this question varies from country to country. The issue, for example, has been addressed in Luxembourg by the Court of Justice of the EC.[70] Here I will examine the issue only insofar as it pertains to the United States.

First, about GATT. The GATT language itself was intended by negotiators[71] to be precise enough for direct application by courts, and its phraseology is such that a U.S. court would likely find most of the GATT clauses to be self-executing. However, it must be remembered that the GATT as such is not in effect under international law. It is the Protocol of Provisional Application which brings GATT into effect, and this protocol has language suggesting a requirement of an added governmental action to implement the GATT. Thus, this language would likely be treated by a U.S. court as *not* self-executing. But (another "but"!) the president negotiated the GATT under the authority of the trade agreements act renewal of 1945, which contained the typical two-part authority: — to accept an agreement, and to proclaim it. In fact, the president has proclaimed all of the general language of GATT except Part IV (added in the 1960s to address problems of developing countries).[72] Thus the key parts of GATT are all domestic U.S. law because they have been proclaimed, and not because they are self-executing. U.S. courts which have had to decide the issue of GATT direct applicability have all held that GATT was part of U.S. domestic law, but usually without realizing or discussing the intermediate steps in the logic required for such finding.

For the Tokyo Round codes, the Congress and the executive anticipated this question of direct application, and provided explicitly in the approval of the Trade Agreements Act of 1979 that the agreements approved would *not* be self-executing. This provision is not crystal clear in the language of the statute,[73] but the legislative history shows the clear intent of both the executive (which proposed the bill), and the Congress (which adopted it) that the agreements the statute approves are not to be self-executing. It is virtually certain that U.S. courts will therefore follow this intent.[74] Thus the source of domestic U.S. law is the implementing statute (Trade Agreement Act of 1979) and not the agreements themselves. However, the agreements are most certainly part of the legislative history of the statute, since the congressional committee reports state, "This bill is drafted with the intent to permit U.S. practice to be consistent with the obligations of the agreements, as the United States understands those obligations."[75] In addition, the well-accepted rule in U.S. jurisprudence that courts, when confronted with several possible choices for interpreting a statute, should prefer that choice which is consistent with U.S. international obligations, must be remembered.[76]

While addressing these questions of statutory interpretation, another wrinkle caused by the fast-track procedure should be noted. The legislative history of the 1979 implementing statute is different from that of most bills, since a bill is theoretically drafted by the president and amendments to it in Congress are prohibited. Thus it can be argued that the statement of the executive branch[77] is of primary importance. However, the actual history of the process, which I have described, suggests a somewhat different argument. Although the Congressional Committee reports were issued at a time in the procedure when no amendments or changes were possible, the reports explain:

> The Committee emphasized that virtually all of the provisions of H.R. 4357 [which became the TAA of 1979] reflect the decisions of the House and Senate committees, as coordinated in the joint meetings.... The implementing bill was drafted in the offices of the House and Senate Legislative Counsel with the participation of staff members of the committees of jurisdiction in both Houses and representatives from the Administration. The bill reflects the understandings achieved on all issues, as explained in this report.[77A]

Structure of the United States Government for Trade Policy

Dozens of U.S. government agencies have at least some jurisdiction over various aspects of trade policy. For example, the Agriculture Department has considerable authority on matters relating to agricultural commodity trade. The Defense Department has great power in the procedures relating to export controls. The Labor Department is concerned with workers who have become unemployed because of imports. The Commerce Department has the line authority on antidumping and countervailing duty measures, while the Departments of State and the Treasury also have important roles not only in international economic affairs generally, but in trade particularly.[78]

A key agency is a small one attached to the executive office of the president, namely the office of the U.S. Trade Representative. The position of trade representative (originally created by the 1962 Trade Expansion Act, partly as a compromise between competing jurisdictional claims of the U.S. Departments of State and Commerce) was first called "Special Trade Representative," or "STR." During several decades the office serving this official has become increasingly important to U.S. trade policy; and in the 1974 act the Congress upgraded the USTR position to cabinet status, one of few such positions not heading a department. The position also carries the rank of ambassador. The office of the USTR chairs many of the interagency committees which formulate trade policy and negotiating positions for the U.S. government, including the Trade Staff Committee (TSC) and the cabinet-level Trade Policy Committee (TPC).[79]

In addition to the many executive branch agencies which participate in trade policy and trade regulation, and to the interagency trade-policy committees, there is an important quasi-independent agency: the International Trade Commission (ITC). This agency of six commissioners — appointed for 9 year terms, with a staff of approximately 400 — is not strictly under the wing of the executive branch, and is often considered closely allied to Congress. It has the task of making various factual determinations, usually on the question of whether imports are "injuring" domestic U.S. industry (as in cases of the escape clause, antidumping duties, and countervailing duties). It plays a central role in Section 337, unfair trade complaints against imports.[80]

3.4 The Variety of National Constitutions and Their Impact on the International Trading System

National Constitutions and International Economic Relations

We have already remarked how the international trading system is a complex interaction of international and national legal norms, political institutions, and economic systems. The legal and constitutional requirements for treaty-making of national governments can profoundly influence the international negotiating processes, and can sometimes impose crippling constraints on the nature of possible agreements. When international agreements are completed by the negotiators, the difficult processes of completing the ratification by national governments begins. These processes vary enormously from nation to nation. When they are completed, different legal and constitutional systems may cause the implementation of the agreements to not be uniform.[81] In some systems the executive branch may be operating under laws which are "mandatory" and allow it little discretion. In others, open-ended legal authority may allow government officials considerable leeway, which can sometimes be valuable in fashioning an international settlement on some controverted point. In certain systems, private firms and citizens may have the power to invoke procedures which raise international trade issues requiring the attention of foreign nations against their will.[82] On top of all this, of course, lurk the major problems which occur when the economic systems of the various nations also differ.[83]

I have here examined the U.S. legal system at some length. A scientific approach to understanding the trading system would require a similar examination for many other countries. GATT now has over ninety-six member countries, however, so there is no practical way to analyze the national constitutional, legal, and governmental structures of even a significant fraction of that number of countries in relation to international trade. Fortunately, regarding some of the key countries, other works on this subject exist.[84] However, some brief descriptions of two other major players, the EC and Japan, are useful, partly because these along with the U.S. so dominate world trade. The U.S., EC, and Japanese trade now exceeds $1,224 billion for exports and $1,295 billion for imports. The total value of world trade in exports is $2,119 billion and in imports $2,200 billion; U.S., EC and Japanese trade therefore amounts to 57% of world exports and 59% of world imports. GATT countries all together comprise over 85% of world trade.[84A]

The European Community

In recent years, the largest number of disputes under GATT rules, and generally the most acrimonious, have been those between the United States and the European Community (EC) and its member states. The EC is a very complex institution, viewed by some as a budding "federal state," but by others as still an international organization. This institution, it is safe to say, is in a process of a difficult constitutional evolution which clearly has had an impact on what its representatives at GATT and other international fora have been able or willing to say or do. The internal difficulties of the communities have probably led to the cautious approach of the EC diplomats when dealing with other countries or international organizations and norms. There undoubtedly has been an internal political need to keep the pressures of the outside world from constraining the potential options for compromise needed internally in order to keep the whole institution from falling apart. Thus the EC has in the past stiffly resisted an international negotiating agenda which would include attention to agriculture policies, since the EC has viewed the Common Agricultural Policy (CAP) as so centrally important to the continued viability of the EC itself.[85]

Here I can only sketch the outlines of the EC constitution as it relates to the world trading system. The starting point is to realize that there are essentially five entities or groups of entities which play the key constitutional roles in the EC: the "Commission," the "Council," the "Court," the "European Parliament," and, finally, the "member states." Each of these entities plays a distinct role, which is constantly evolving in a sort of dance of power contests and struggles, not unlike that which the United States experiences with its separation-of-powers problems between the executive and Congress.

One of the very interesting features of the EC, at least to members of the legal profession, is the degree to which the EC as a whole is heavily influenced by legal structures and concepts. Even though many of the largest member states of the EC have constitutional structures that do not permit judicial review of parliamentary action, the EC effectively has a judicial review system in which its Court plays a central role. Likewise, although an unwritten constitution is a feature of one of the largest member states, the EC to which it belongs has an elaborate written constitution (the 1957 Treaty of Rome and related treaties[86]) which is subject to definitive interpretation by the Court. It appears that on a number of issues, the types and styles of government which member states have become used to are not deemed appropriate in the larger continental arena. Nations which have what have been called "one-city governments," in which one city has a virtual monopoly on governmental and business decision-making as well as on intellectual and cultural activity, find that the methods of operating (involving quiet genteel meetings at pubs and cocktail parties) no longer are feasible when the affairs of a whole continent, involving many different languages and cultures, are at stake.

The institutional structure of the European Community was recently subject to alteration as a result of amendments to the treaties known as the Single European Act.[87] This act aimed to enhance the effectiveness of the community decision-making process (in particular the completion of the internal market by 1992[88]), encouraging use of simple or qualified majority voting in the Council and a diminishing use of the "Luxembourg Compromise" (see below). It also enhanced the role of the European Parliament in the decision-making process,[89] formalized the European Council, and introduced an embryonic Community foreign policy.[90]

The Commission is the EC's counterpart to the executives of member states. In the current EC, the Commission consists of seventeen commissioners, each given a certain "portfolio" of activities and generally heading a "directorate general." The commissioners are appointed for terms of four years by the joint action of the member states. The directorate generals each have a director-general who is likely to be a career civil servant of the EC. This person presides over the staff. The Commission totals about 12,000 employees, and has the task and competence to implement the laws and policies of the EC, and to propose law changes.[91]

The Council, formally the Council of Ministers, is composed of representatives of each of the member states, who sit as representatives, and not as civil servants or executives. The Council reviews and controls the actions of the Commission, except to the extent that the foundation treaties delegate direct responsibility to the Commission, or to the extent that the Council itself has so delegated. The "legislative" process most often consists of an interaction between the Commission and the Council, whereby the Commission proposes, and the Council must approve of, a proposal before it becomes law. The foundation treaties allow the approval in some cases to be by a "qualified majority" which is less than unanimous; but several decades ago, in 1965, the EC constitutional evolution nearly foundered on shoals of national sovereignty, and the result was the so-called "Luxembourg Compromise." Under this, it was tacitly agreed that, despite rules to the contrary in the foundation treaties on matters which any member state designates as "very important" the Council will act only by consensus—*i.e.*, by unanimity. This compromise is slowly evolving, having been influenced by the override of the U.K. veto in 1982,[92] the addition of more member states, and the Single European Act. Through this process, *inter alia*, regulations and directives are adopted. The former are directly applicable to the domestic law of the members, while the latter tend to be addressed to member states, requiring some further government action at the national level in order for them to be directly utilized in cases before national courts, etc.[93]

The member states have supported (sometimes reluctantly) the enhancement of the role of the European Parliament, which has been rather weak. With direct elections, and some other modest tinkering with its authority, the Parliament has begun to play a somewhat more substantial role in EC government decision-making. The Single European Act gave the Parliament an enhanced role with respect to EC decisions, including a modest new role in approving certain types of external relations treaties (but not those likely to emerge from GATT negotiations).

The European Court of Justice (ECJ) is a central and significant part of the EC institutional structure, and has evolved into a rather strong constitutional court for the EC. Its influence is felt daily in the other EC institutions, and officials often find their discourse directed toward questions about how the Court might react to this or that proposal. The ECJ has thirteen judges, and following a continental European pattern, six advocates general who prepare cases for the Court and give their opinion as to how the Court should decide each case.[94]

Finally, of course, there are the member state governments, jealously trying to preserve their national sovereign power, and with some success. For some years European summits of national heads of states have been held, although there is no provision for them in the original EC foundation treaties.

A key question for the international trading system is the treaty-making authority of the EC, and the method by which the EC can participate in such organizations as GATT. The Treaty of Rome provides that in matters relating to the conduct of "commercial policy," the community is to have exclusive competence.[95] The negotiation of commercial agreements with third countries was to be undertaken by the Commission alone, and was to be concluded by the Council on behalf of the community by a qualified majority. This exclusive power of negotiation has been carefully guarded by the Commission and has often been challenged by the Council acting on behalf of the member states' interests.[96] Relationships with international organizations such as GATT are dealt with in specific articles.[97] Another significant question is the domestic-law effect of international agreements accepted by the EC institutions. Can these agreements become direct parts of the jurisprudence of the EC, both at the EC level (e.g., before the Court in an EC matter), and at the member-state level (e.g., as directly applicable before member-state domestic courts)? The answer appears to depend on a combination of factors, but it is anything but clear to what extent EC international agreements will be given domestic-law effect.[98]

Japan

The government of Japan differs considerably from those of the U.S. or the EC. Japan is essentially a parliamentary form of government, and thus its executive is headed by a number of ministers, including the prime minister, which are almost always members of Parliament belonging to the party which has the parliamentary majority. However, most legislation in the Japanese system is drafted by the relevant ministry, and this is particularly so with respect to international trade matters dominated by MITI.[99] Thus, as compared to the other governments I have discussed, there would seem to be less tension between the executive and the Parliament in this system, and it would appear that the government would more likely be able to implement international agreements, as well as other initiatives, since it would have considerable control over the parliamentary majority. Even in such a country, however, there are institutional power rivalries and tensions. The ruling party has a certain apparatus for its own decision-making, and thus must be persuaded of the desirability of measures which require parliamentary approval. A Supreme Court in Japan presides over the legal conflicts, including constitutional rules. Although Japanese society has been described as less litigious than U.S. society, and operates in a social climate that tends to discourage resort to formal court processes to resolve differences, a few cases relating to international economic measures have gone to the courts in Japan, and there has been speculation that the number of such cases may increase.[100]

4

Rule Implementation and Dispute Resolution

4.1 The Effectiveness of International Law

Introduction

In chapter 1 I described briefly some of the general concepts of international law.[1] I noted there the tendency of many observers, particularly those not well acquainted with international relations or transactions, to dismiss international law rules as ineffective. I mentioned, however, that many domestic law rules are equally ineffective. Although it may be the case that international law rules are somewhat less effective than domestic law rules for those nations with stable legal systems and a generally effective central government, it is not always the case that domestic laws are implemented efficiently.[2] It is important for the policy advisor, the statesman, or the practitioner to accurately evaluate the real impact of the international rules recognizing that some of those rules (often the ones that do not reach the headlines) do have considerable effect and influence on real government and business decisions.[3] For example, despite cynical statements by members of the U.S. Congress that GATT rules are "irrelevant," there are a number of proven instances when congressional committees and their staff members have taken considerable trouble to tailor legislative proposals so as to minimize the risk of a complaint to GATT. Not all of these efforts have been successful, but in other cases Congress has been persuaded to drop a proposal because of its inconsistency with GATT provisions.[4] The U.S. executive branch also is influenced in its actions by GATT legality arguments, although it too does not always defer to these.

In later chapters of this book, I will attempt to evaluate various rules regarding trade and their effectiveness, and in the final chapter I will come back to this issue to see if any generalizations about the various rules are warranted. For example, the ability of nations to unilaterally apply antidumping or countervailing duties often has a powerful influence on potential transactions or even on government policy. The constraints on the nation applying those duties stem from the GATT and MTN code rules on those subjects, and thus those rules have considerable utility for determining what would be the likely response of an importing country to certain dumping or subsidy-like practices in an exporting country.[5]

In addition to the difficulty of evaluating the effectiveness of existing international rules, there are several important policy issues about rule implementation which often do not get explicitly addressed. First, should the legal system be improved to make rules more effective? Second, should new rules be added and made effective? It might seem at first that these questions are trivial and that most persons would answer them in the affirmative. Indeed, most governmental and private practitioners would probably privately answer this way. But in actual practice, they would act differently. To put this another way: realistic observations of the operation of the legal system, even as it pertains to international economic affairs, will lead one to perceive that many government and private practitioners are not all in favor of an effective international rules system![6]

Why is there real (albeit concealed or implicit) opposition to the effectiveness of international rules? Some of the reason for this can be traced to the older concepts of national sovereignty. As one astute European observer put it, one reason for the difficulty of welding a more effective European union is that national leaders would then lose a number of "photo opportunities" — i.e., news coverage of summit meetings, decisions and conflict on various issues among national leaders, playing to their constituencies with a "tough stance" against other foreign leaders. In short, power is fun, and international rules reduce the power of national leaders and government officials. The chance to go "tooting off in private jets to negotiate with other national leaders at comfortable locations or three-star restaurants" is a key plum of otherwise dull government jobs, a high government or official once indicated.

It would be unfair to implicate this type of motivation as being too much the cause of antagonism to international rules. However, the international rules do cause real difficulties for national leaders. In chapter 1 we noted the problems posed for national leaders by growing international economic interdependence. It is harder to deliver on promises to constituents. Several situations lead even the wise national leader to cause his government to breach or consider breaching international rules. One such situation is when the international "rule" is patently unfair or bad policy. This may be because the rule is outdated and not in tune with current actual practice and conditions. (I noted in chapter 2 the difficulty of amending GATT rules, one example of an activity which creates this "out-of-date" problem for some rules.[7]) It may also be because the current international rule-making process is faulty—as when voting procedures allow rules to be created which are unrealistic and which do not recognize real power relationships.[8]

Another situation in which it can be argued that rules *should* be breached, is when reform of the rule is badly needed, but the international and national institutional system for some reason makes the reform impossible. It could be argued that the U.S. departure from the currency par value system of the IMF in 1971 was such a case, leading quickly to a major revision in the IMF Charter to allow "floating exchange rates," which had been advocated for decades by many eminent economists.[9]

Nevertheless, every departure from the rules carries some risks. It causes respect for the rule system itself to be weakened. It makes it easier in the next hard case to depart from the rules. If rules are viewed as one tool for ordering or improving human affairs, then weakening a rule system tends to reduce the utility of that tool in all its contexts.

Power-Oriented Diplomacy Contrasted with Rule-Oriented Diplomacy

One way to explore the questions raised above is to compare two techniques of modern diplomacy: a "rule-oriented" technique and a "power-oriented" technique. This perhaps puts the issue in too simple a dichotomy (because in practice the observable international institutions and legal systems involve some mixture of both), but it is nevertheless an useful way to examine the policy issues involved. This dichotomy may be explained as follows:

In broad perspective one can roughly divide the various techniques for the peaceful settlement of international disputes into two types: settlement by negotiation and agreement with reference (explicitly or implicitly) to relative power status of the parties; or settlement by negotiation or decision with reference to norms or rules to which both parties have previously agreed.

For example, countries A and B have a trade dispute regarding B's treatment of imports from A to B of widgets. The first technique mentioned would involve a negotiation between A and B by which the most powerful of the two would have the advantage. Foreign aid, military maneuvers, or import restrictions on other key goods by way of retaliation would figure in the negotiation. A small country would hesitate to challenge a large one on whom its trade depends. Implicit or explicit threats (e.g., to impose quantitative restrictions on some other product) would be a major part of the technique employed. Domestic political influences would probably play a greater part in the approach of the respective negotiators in this system, particularly on the negotiator for the more powerful party.

On the other hand, the second suggested technique—reference to agreed rules—would see the negotiators arguing about the application of the rule (e.g., was B obligated under a treaty to allow free entry of A's goods in question?). During the process of negotiating a settlement it would be necessary for the parties to understand that an unsettled dispute would ultimately be resolved by impartial third-party judgments based on the rules so that the negotiators would be negotiating with reference to their respective predictions as to the outcome of those judgments and not with reference to potential retaliation or actions exercising power of one or more of the parties to the dispute.

In both techniques negotiation and private settlement of disputes is the dominant mechanism for resolving differences; but the key is the perception of the participants as to what are the "bargaining chips." Insofar as agreed rules for governing the economic relations between the parties exist, a system which predicates negotiation on the implementation of those rules would seem for a number of reasons to be preferred. The mere existence of the rules, however, is not enough. When the issue is the application or interpretation of those rules (rather than the formulation of new rules), it is necessary for the parties to believe that if their negotiations reach an impasse the settlement mechanisms which take over for the parties will be designed to apply fairly or to interpret the rules. If no such system exists, then the parties are left basically to rely upon their respective "power positions," tempered (it is hoped) by the good will and good faith of the more powerful party (cognizant of his long-range interests). . . .

All diplomacy, and indeed all government, involves a mixture of these techniques. To a large degree, the history of civilization may be described as a gradual evolution from a power-oriented approach, in the state of nature, toward a rule-oriented approach. However, never is the extreme in either case reached. In modern Western democracies, as we know them, power continues to play a major role, particularly political power of voter acceptance, but also to a lesser degree economic power such as that of labor unions or large corporations. However, these governments have passed far along the scale toward a rule-oriented approach, and generally have an elaborate legal system involving court procedures and a monopoly of force, through a police and a military, to insure that the rules will be followed. The U.S. government has indeed proceeded far in this direction, as the resignation of a recent president demonstrates. When one looks at the history of England over the last thousand years, I think that the evolutionary hypothesis from power to rule can be supported. And more recently, when one looks at the evolution of the EC, one is struck by the evolution toward a system that is remarkably elaborate in its rule structure, effectuated through a court of justice, albeit without a monopoly of force.

In international affairs, a strong argument can be made that to a certain extent this same evolution must occur, even though currently it has not progressed very far. The initiatives of the World War II and immediate postwar periods toward developing international institutions is part of this evolution, but as is true in most evolutions there have been setbacks, and mistakes have been made. Likewise, when one focuses on international economic policy, we find that the dichotomy between power-oriented diplomacy and rule-oriented diplomacy can be seen. We have tried to develop rules, in the context of the International Monetary Fund and the GATT. The success has been varied.

Nevertheless, a particularly strong argument exists for pursuing gradually and consistently the progress of international economic affairs toward a rule-oriented approach. Apart from the advantages which accrue generally to international affairs through a rule-oriented approach — less reliance on raw power, and the temptation to exercise it or flex one's muscles, which can get out of hand; a fairer break for the smaller countries, or at least a perception of greater fairness; the development of agreed procedures to achieve the necessary compromises — in economic affairs there are additional reasons.

Economic affairs tend (at least in peace time) to affect more citizens directly than may political and military affairs. Particularly as the world becomes more economically interdependent, more and more private citizens find their jobs, their businesses, and their quality of life affected if not controlled by forces from outside their country's boundaries. Thus they are more affected by the economic policy pursued by their own country on their behalf. In addition, the relationships become increasingly complex — to the point of being incomprehensible to even the brilliant human mind. As a result, citizens assert themselves, at least within a democracy, and require their representatives and government officials to respond to their needs and their perceived complaints. The result of this is increasing citizen participation, and more parliamentary or congressional participation in the processes of international economic policy, thus restricting the degree of power and discretion which the executive possesses.

This makes international negotiations and bargaining increasingly difficult. However, if citizens are going to make their demands heard and influential, a "power-oriented" negotiating process (often requiring secrecy, and executive discretion so as to be able to formulate and implement the necessary compromises) becomes more difficult, if not impossible. Consequently, the only appropriate way to turn seems to be toward a rule-oriented system, whereby the various citizens, parliaments, executives and international organizations will all have their inputs, arriving tortuously to a rule — which, however, when established will enable business and other decentralized decisionmakers to rely upon the stability and predictability of governmental activity in relation to the rule.[10]

Exploring These Concepts

In this chapter, we will examine the rule effectiveness and implementation of the international trade system, centering on GATT. Any effective system probably needs at least two workable procedures: a procedure of "norm formulation" or new rulemaking, and a procedure for applying and implementing those rules. An implementing/applying procedure requires a "dispute settlement" mechanism as part of its tools. Somehow the existing rule must be applied to specific facts in particular cases. Inevitably there will be disagreement about such application, that is: disagreement on the interpretation of the rule, its scope, appropriate exceptions, etc. The dispute settlement mechanism could be based on brute force, of course, but as I have noted, there are significant reasons to avoid recourse to that type of behavior. The GATT (and the associated MTN codes) have a variety of more or less formal dispute settlement mechanisms, and we will examine these in this chapter.

The norm application system is not entirely an international procedure. National governments play extremely important roles in the process. In this chapter we will examine some very interesting procedures which have been devised in the U.S. and the EC to complement the international procedures of GATT and the codes.

4.2 Legal Power to Interpret GATT Agreements

Legal interpretation of the GATT and associated MTN agreements must be considered in the context of the general principles of international law regarding interpretation of treaties. These general principles are probably best summarized today by Article XXXI of the Vienna Convention on the Law of Treaties, although that convention does not technically apply to the GATT (which preceded it), and would not technically apply in a controversy involving a nation — such as the United States — which has not yet ratified the Vienna Convention. Nevertheless, this portion of the Vienna Convention is considered by many nations, including the United States, to codify generally accepted rules of customary international law, and thus is a definitive text describing those rules.[11]

The principles of treaty interpretation include "ordinary meaning" of the words, other agreements or instruments influencing the treaty which were accepted by the parties to the treaty at the time it was concluded, subsequent agreement between the parties to the treaty, "subsequent practice in the application of the treaty which establishes the agreement of the parties regarding its interpretation," and other relevant rules of international law. In some circumstances the preparatory work may also be relevant.[12]

Each of these principles of interpretation plays a role for the GATT and associated agreements. The original GATT contains an annex with a series of originally agreed interpretations which are considered definitive.[13] Subsequently there have been formal agreements which purport to interpret the GATT. Among these are the Tokyo Round subsidies and antidumping codes, although these clearly go beyond mere "interpretation." Whether these codes can influence the GATT interpretation for GATT contracting parties (CPs) which do not accept the codes is not yet clear.[14]

The preparatory work of the GATT itself, as well as the drafting of the amendments which came into force, have often been relied upon in GATT proceedings. Indeed, a document prepared by the secretariat, entitled the "Analytical Index," lists many aspects of the preparatory work as interpretative material.[15] A major question is whether the text and preparatory work for the Havana Charter (ITO) could also be considered interpretative material for the GATT.[16] I have taken the position that it can, because it is contemporaneous with the preparation of the GATT (the Geneva conference preparations were simultaneous with the GATT drafting, with the same national negotiators involved). Even the 1948 Havana Conference is, in my view, relevant to GATT, since the GATT draftsmen clearly anticipated later changing the GATT to accord with the changes made at Havana to the corresponding provisions of the ITO Charter, and since some of those changes were later incorporated into the GATT while others were not (on the grounds that the GATT language was already sufficiently similar to that of the Havana revisions).[17]

The actual practice in GATT has also played a major role in the interpretation of that agreement. Technically, to be "binding," practice must be sufficient to "establish the agreement of the parties." Exactly how far the evidence must go in this regard is not clear. Additionally, it should be noted that under accepted doctrines of international law, *stare decisis*, or the common-law concept of "precedent," does not apply.[18] Thus a

World Court decision in a dispute between countries A and B provides no binding precedent as such in a dispute between C and D, nor for A and C, nor even for another dispute at another time between A and B.[19] Yet, in practice, the diplomats and officials who participate in the GATT system are very influenced by "precedent," and often mention precedents in some detail in GATT deliberations, as well as in the formal dispute-settlement panel "findings." A common-law lawyer would find himself very much at home in GATT legal discussions!

From time to time GATT interpretations have been made by a short statement by the chairman of the contracting parties.[20] Sometimes these are offered in the context of a "consensus view" of the CPs, without any objection from any CP. At other times, interpretations are made as statements of the chair without any explicit connection to an agreement or a vote (without objection) of the CPs. In all such cases, however, it is safe to assume that the text has been carefully negotiated in advance and deemed acceptable to the interested CPs. Similarly, often dispute-settlement panel findings will contain rulings interpreting the GATT application in the particular dispute, and the CPs adopt most of these findings. These findings may be binding on the disputing parties,[21] but it can still be asked, What is the status of such "interpretative statements" as to future disputes? Although their status is quite indefinite, the procedure suggests, in Vienna Convention phraseology, that it is one of "practice . . . establishing agreement."[22]

Another interesting question is whether the CONTRACTING PARTIES of GATT, under their Article XXV powers, have the authority to make a legal and binding interpretation of GATT. Some international organizations are explicitly given such power in their charters, so that an interpretation adopted by the procedure specified would carry with it a binding treaty obligation to accept the interpretation even for nations disagreeing with the interpretation and even in the absence of sufficient practice to establish "agreement of the parties."[23] The language of GATT itself does not explicitly grant this power, although it gives authority for "joint action" with a view to "facilitating the operation and furthering the objectives of this Agreement. . . ." This language seems broad enough to include the power to interpret, but caution is necessary for several reasons. First, since binding interpretative power for other organizations has been explicit in their charters, the absence of explicit power in the GATT could argue against the existence of that power. Second, the ill-fated ITO Charter contained explicit provisions for interpretation, whereas these provisions were not included in the

GATT (because the GATT was not considered to be an "organization").[24] In the light of the Vienna Convention codification of customary international law, as well as the general language of GATT Article XXV, it seems likely that at least where there is no formal dissent by any GATT CP, various "practice" actions of the GATT would be deemed very definitive interpretations. In the case of only the majority of CPs agreeing, however, there is still some ambiguity. It is quite possible that the practice of GATT during its four decades of existence has itself established an interpretation of the Article XXV powers to include the power to interpret.

No dispute involving GATT or its associated agreements has ever been taken to the World Court (formally the International Court of Justice or ICJ).[25] One may ask whether that court would have jurisdiction over such a dispute, or whether the internal GATT interpretative processes would be held to be exclusive. The ITO charter would have provided both a requirement to exclusively use dispute procedures of the ITO charter, but also a reference to the ICJ in certain circumstances.[26] No such provisions are included in the GATT, but in any event, so far, no GATT contracting party has been motivated to bring a GATT case to the ICJ.[27]

Similar questions may be asked regarding the agreements resulting from the Tokyo Round negotiations, and the answers are even more difficult. Although these agreements were undertaken after the Vienna Convention,[28] many of the parties which accepted them have not accepted the Vienna Convention. The agreements themselves do not explicitly grant the power of formal binding interpretation, although many of them have dispute-settlement procedures. The agreements do not contain the phrase found in GATT Article XXV, so no claim on that basis can be made.[29] The phraseology of the procedures contained in the GATT side agreements varies greatly, sometimes calling for exclusive procedures,[30] at other times "permitting" use of specified procedures.[31]

4.3 GATT and Its Dispute-Settlement Procedures

The Fundamental Goal of GATT Dispute-Settlement Procedures: Negotiation or Rule Application?

One of the interesting and certainly more controversial aspects of the GATT as an institution is its dispute-settlement mechanism. It is probably fair to say that this mechanism is unique. It is also flawed, due in part to the troubled beginnings of GATT.[32] Yet these procedures have worked better than might be expected, and some may argue that in fact they have worked better than those of the World Court.[33] A number of interesting policy questions are raised by the experience of the procedure, not the least of which is the question of what should be the fundamental objective of the system—to solve the instant dispute (by conciliation, obfuscation, power-threats, or other means), or to promote certain longer-term goals. In this section we will look at some of the fundamental policy controversies about the dispute settlement procedures of GATT, and then examine those procedures and those of GATT-associated agreements. In the next section we will explore how the system has worked by looking at overall statistics of cases as well as some detailed examinations of a few specific troubling cases.

The difference of opinion about the basic purpose or goals of the dispute settlement process in the GATT system has not often been explicit, and the same individuals sometimes express a preference for opposite poles of this difference without realizing it. Of course, the matter is more one of appropriate balance along a spectrum than it is of choosing one extreme or the other; but nevertheless it is important to understand the difference, and to describe the dichotomy helps to do so. Perhaps the following two statements help to illustrate the differences I have mentioned:

As a part of the increasingly pragmatic policies of the secretariat and the recognition by all contracting parties that legalism does not contribute to trade liberalization, emphasis has shifted from the formal role of the GATT as third-party arbiter to its informal role as catalyst for the resolution of disputes by the disputing parties themselves.[34]

International economic policy commitments, in the form of agreed rules, have far-reaching domestic effects. . . . They are the element which secures the ultimate co-ordination and mutual compatibility of the purely domestic economic policies. They form the basis from which the government can arbitrate and secure an equitable and efficient balance between the diverse domestic interest: producers v. consumers, export industries v. import-competing industries. . . . Only a firm commitment to international rules makes possible the all-important reconciliation, which I have already alluded to, of the necessary balance on the production side and on the financial side of the national economy. . . .[35]

There are at least two important questions here: one historical, one of future policy. The historical question is whether the GATT preparatory work and practice through its decades establishes a goal of dispute-settlement more oriented toward "conciliation and negotiation" or toward "rule integrity." The future policy question is, Which of these *ought* to be the goal? These questions relate to the "power- or rule-oriented diplomacy" discussion in section 1 of this chapter.

With regard to the first question, the record is somewhat mixed. Despite the many statements of some writers[36] and diplomats that the GATT is merely a "negotiating forum" primarily designed to "preserve a balance of concessions and obligations,"[37] there is considerable historical evidence to the contrary. At least one draftsman of GATT said at the preparatory meetings that the agreement "... should deal with these subjects in precise detail so that the obligations of member governments would be clear and unambiguous. Most of these subjects readily lend themselves to such treatment. Provisions on such subjects, once agreed upon, would be self-executing and could be applied by the governments concerned without further elaboration or international action."[38]

The original intention was for GATT to be placed in the institutional setting of the ITO, and the draft ITO charter called for a rigorous dispute-settlement procedure which contemplated effective use of arbitration (not always mandatory, however), and even appeal to the World Court in some circumstances.[39] Clair Wilcox, vice-chairman of the U.S. Delegation to the Havana Conference, notes that the possibility of suspending trade concessions under this procedure was "... regarded as a method of restoring a balance of benefits and obligations that, for any reason, may have been disturbed. It is nowhere described as a penalty to be imposed on members who may violate their obligations or as a sanction to insure that these obligations will be observed. But even though it is not so regarded, it will operate in fact as a sanction and a penalty. ...."[40] He further notes the procedure for obtaining a World Court opinion on the law involved in a dispute, and says, "A basis is thus provided for the development of a body of international law to govern trade relationships."[41]

The shift in GATT from a committee or "working party" procedure to a "panel" procedure (see below), with its connotation of impartial third-party findings, can also be used as evidence that the practice evolved in a direction of "rule integrity"[42]; and a number of panel reports during the first several decades of GATT contained reasoning which closely resembled that of an opinion of a court of law, with reference to precedent, etc. Then, during the 1960s, the GATT dispute-settlement procedure fell into disuse. Some CPs feared that invocation of the procedure would be deemed an "unfriendly act," or for other prudent policy reasons abstained from formal procedures to resolve disputes. Countries with less bargaining power, however, seemed to feel differently. Indeed, the developing countries pushed through a proposal in GATT designed to strengthen the dispute-settlement procedures as they applied in disputes with developing countries.[43] In a celebrated exercise, Uruguay brought a series of complaints against industrial countries' treatment of Uruguayan exports (with mixed results).[44] It was during this case that the doctrine of "*prima facie* nullification or impairment," which has had a continuing effect in GATT, developed.

The Procedures of Dispute Settlement in GATT

The ITO Charter would have established a rather elaborate dispute-settlement procedure,[45] but the GATT, not intended to be an "organization," has only a few paragraphs devoted to this subject.[46] Although one can argue that there are a number of "dispute settlement" procedures distributed throughout the GATT (raising the issue of what we mean by that phrase),[47] the central and formal procedures are found in Articles XXII and XXIII. The first of these simply establishes the right to consult with any other contracting party on matters related to the GATT—a right which does not impose a major obligation, but which is nevertheless useful.[48] Indeed, I would argue that Article XXII should be interpreted to rule out the all-too-frequently heard argument against allowing a request to consult on some potential legislative or executive action, namely that the matter was "premature."

Article XXIII is the centerpiece for dispute settlement. It also provides for consultation as a prerequisite to invoke the multilateral GATT processes. Three features of these processes should be stressed: 1) they are usually invocable on grounds of "nullification or impairment" of benefits expected under the Agreement, and do *not* depend on actual breach of legal obligation; 2) they establish the power for the CONTRACTING PARTIES to not only investigate and recommend action, but to "give a ruling on the matter"; and 3) they give the CONTRACTING PARTIES the power in appropriately serious cases to authorize "a contracting party or parties" to suspend GATT obligations to other contracting parties. Each of these features has important interpretations and implications, and although Article XXIII does not say much about them, the procedures followed to implement these principles have evolved through the four decades of practice into a rather elaborate process.

The key to invoking the GATT dispute-settlement mechanism is almost always "nullification or impairment,"[49] an unfortunately ambiguous phrase. It is neither sufficient nor necessary to find a "breach of obligation" under this language, although later practice has made doing so important. An early case in GATT[50] defined the nullification or impairment (N or I) phrase as including actions by a contracting party which harmed the trade of another, and which "could not reasonably have been anticipated . . ." by the other at the time it negotiated for a concession. Thus the concept of "reasonable expectations" was introduced, and it is almost a "contract"-type concept.[51] But even this elaboration becomes very ambiguous. Consequently, a later practice in GATT developed to enumerate three situations in which the CPs and their panels might find "*prima facie* nullification or impairment." One of these situations was the breach of an obligation. The other two were the use of domestic subsidies to inhibit imports in certain cases[52] and the use of quantitative restrictions (even when they would have been otherwise legal in GATT).[53] In such cases, the burden of proof that no N or I occurred as the result of the breach, subsidy, or quantitative restriction shifted to the country which breached or used those actions. Lacking a clear showing that no N or I occurred, the GATT practice assumes that the panel is obligated to make a *prima facie* N or I ruling, usually calling for the offending nation to make its actions conform to the GATT obligation.

At the beginning of GATT's history, disputes were generally taken up by the plenary semi-annual meeting of the Contracting Parties. Later they were brought to an "intersessional committee" of the CPs, and even later were delegated to a working party set up to examine either all disputes, or only particular disputes brought to GATT.[54] Around 1955 a major shift in the procedure occurred, largely because of the influence of the then director general, Eric Wyndham-White.[55] It was decided that rather than use a "working party" composed of nations (so that each nation could designate the person who would represent it, subject to that government's instructions), a dispute would be referred to a panel of experts. The three or five experts would be specifically named and were to act in their own capacities and not as representatives of any government. This development, it can be argued, represented a shift from primarily a "negotiating" atmosphere of multilateral diplomacy, to a more "arbitrational" or "judicial" procedure designed to arrive impartially at the truth of the facts and the best interpretation of the law. All subsequent dispute procedures in GATT have contemplated the use of a panel in this fashion.[56]

Although the CONTRACTING PARTIES are authorized (by majority vote) to suspend concessions (by way of retorsion, retaliation, or "rebalancing" of benefits—a term which is not and never has been clear), they have actually done so in only one case (up to mid-1988). That instance was the result of a complaint brought by the Netherlands against the United States for the latter's use, contrary to GATT, of import restraints on imported dairy products from the Netherlands.[57] For seven years in a row, the Netherlands was authorized to utilize restraints against importation of U.S. grain,[58] although it never acted on that authorization. This had no effect on U.S. action, however. Recently there have been some moves to seek authorization to suspend obligations.[59] Also, the U.S. has taken measures without authorization.[60]

During the Tokyo Round negotiation, there was some initiative taken to improve the dispute settlement processes of the GATT. The so-called "Group Framework Committee" of the negotiation was given this task, among others. However, partly because of the strong objection of the EC to any changes in the existing procedures, this effort did not get very far. The result was a document entitled "Understanding Regarding Notification, Consultation, Dispute Settlement and Surveillance," which was adopted by the CONTRACTING PARTIES at their thirty-fifth Session in Geneva, November 1979.[61] Like the other "understandings" resulting from the Tokyo Round, the precise legal status of this understanding is not clear. Unlike the Tokyo Round codes and other agreements, it is not a stand-alone treaty. It is also not a waiver under Article XXV of GATT, but is presumably adopted under the general powers of Article XXV to "facilitate the operation and further the objectives" of GATT. This document is, nevertheless, very interesting and also very influential, since it, along with its annex, consists of a detailed description of the dispute-settlement processes of GATT. It thus forms a sort of "constitutional framework" for these processes.

The most salient features of this "restatement" of procedures is the explicit provision for a conciliatory role for the GATT director general, the provision for panels (with some ambiguity about whether a complainant has a right to a panel), reinforcement of the prima facie nullification or impairment concepts, the outline of the work of a panel including oral and written advocacy, language that permits the use of nongovernment persons for panels while stating a preference for government persons, recognition of the practice of a panel report with statement of facts and rationale, and understanding that the report is then submitted to the CONTRACTING PARTIES for final approval.[62]

Subsequent to the 1979 understanding, there has been much dissatisfaction in GATT about the dispute-settlement procedures. At the 1982 ministerial meeting, a new attempt to improve them was made, again with modest success. The resulting resolution suggests the possibility of departing from the tradition of requiring a consensus to approve a panel report, so that the "losing" party could not block or delay that approval,[63] but subsequent practice has not seemed much improved. As of this writing, many GATT members continue to talk of the need for improving the procedures, and this subject is included in the Punta del Este declaration, establishing the framework for the eighth round of trade negotiations.[64]

Many of the treaty agreements resulting from the Tokyo Round negotiations included special procedures devoted to the settlement of disputes relating to a particular agreement. Some of these follow very closely the traditional GATT procedure, and unfortunately they utilize the language "nullification or impairment." In a few cases, special "expert" groups have been called into the process to handle highly technical problems involving such things as scientific judgments.[65]

Dispute settlement provisions in the Tokyo Round agreements[66]

Agreement	Article	Measure
Protocols on tariffs	None	Depend on GATT
Technical barriers to trade	XIV	Consultations, committee investigation (w/technical experts if needed), panel report, committee ruling, suspension of obligations
Government procurement	VII	Consultations, committee investigation, panel report, committee recommendation, suspension of obligations
Interpretation, etc., Articles VI, XVI and XXIII (CV)	XVIII, XVII, XIII	Consultations, committee review, panel report, committee recommendation, suspension of obligations
Regarding bovine meat	None	
Dairy arrangement	None	
Implementation of Article VII (Valuation)	XIX, XX	Consultations, committee investigation, panel report, committee ruling, suspension of obligations

Agreement	Article	Measure
Import-licensing procedures	IV	Subject to GATT Articles XXII and XXIII
Trade in civil aircraft	VIII	Consultations, committee recommendation, resort to GATT Articles XXII and XXIII
Implementation of Article VI (AD)	XV	Consultations, committee panel governed by GATT Articles XXII and XXIII

4.4 GATT Dispute Procedures in Practice

The Dimensions and Targets of GATT Cases: Who Are the Disputants?

The history of dispute settlement and procedures in GATT was outlined in the previous section. This activity in GATT has had its ups and downs, beginning as a relatively informal process, moving to more formal and objective third-party panels, and gradually developing not only procedural but substantive legal concepts.

During the 1960s, the use of GATT dispute-settlement procedures fell off, but during the 1970s the United States began bringing a number of cases in GATT (partly reflecting its internal law, which called for utilizing this process),[67] and during and after the Tokyo Round many more cases have been brought, so that at times more than a dozen cases have been underway in GATT at once. As I previously mentioned, both the 1982 ministerial meeting and subsequent proposals for the Uruguay Round of trade negotiations have given considerable stress to strengthening the procedures for dispute settlement, generally in the direction of "rule integrity" rather than "negotiation/conciliation."[68] Indeed, some diplomats have suggested privately that most developing countries, as well as many industrial countries (including the U.S. and most smaller independent countries), appear to favor strengthening the dispute procedures, leaving the EC almost alone in open opposition to them.

From a study designed to inventory all disputes formally brought to GATT under Article XXIII or under another GATT agreement,[69] it appears (as of September 1988) that the number of cases initiated was approximately 233, of which 9 were brought under the MTN Code provisions (not the GATT itself). Of the cases for which further data exists, approximately 42 (18 percent) were settled or withdrawn before a panel or working party was constituted, and another group were settled or withdrawn before a panel (or working party) reported its findings. In all, panel or working party reports were completed in about 73 cases.

Of the panel reports forwarded to the CONTRACTING PARTIES, most were "adopted." Some others were merely "noted," or otherwise were not explicitly approved (although none were explicitly rejected), and several are still pending. The procedure of "adoption" by the CPs is one of the most troublesome parts of the current procedure, since the losing contracting party can generally block acceptance by refusing to join in a "consensus" decision to accept.[70] Of the findings approved, all but a few have gained compliance, although in some cases compliance took many years to achieve. Nevertheless, some of the cases of noncompliance are very significant and troublesome, as we shall see.

Who brings the cases? Against whom? About what? The inventory study, summarized in the following table, shows some revealing information.

GATT Disputes 1947–1986[71]

	Total	Percent
Total Cases	233	100.0
DC as complainant	179	76.8
DC as respondent	205	88.0
Cases w/DC	229	98.3
ADC as complainant	15	6.4
ADC as respondent	14	6.0
Cases w/ADC	29	12.5
LDC as complainant	35	15.0
LDC as respondent	13	5.6
Cases w/LDC	46	19.7
NME as complainant	4	1.7
NME as respondent	1	0.4
Cases w/NME	5	2.1
All other	0	0.0
U.S. as complainant	77	33.0
U.S. as respondent	48	20.6
Cases w/U.S.	125	53.7
EEC as complainant	26	11.2
EEC as respondent	42	18.0
Cases w/EEC	68	29.2
Cases between U.S. & EEC	35	15.0

DC   = developed country   LDC = less developed country
ADC = advanced developing country   NME = nonmarket economy

Thus, over 76 percent of complaints are by industrial countries, and nearly 88 percent of the complaints are against industrial countries. Of the 50 complaints brought by ADCs and LDCs, 47 or 94 percent are against industrial countries. Of the 179 complaints brought by industrial countries, 24 or 13 percent are against developing countries. The procedure is thus primarily used by and against industrial countries. What are the issues and products involved?

Product Type[72]

	Industrial	Agricultural	Primary	Other	Total
Total	51	100	16	61	228
percentage of all cases	21.9	42.9	6.9	26.2	
U.S. as complainant	11	37	4	25	77
U.S. as respondent	15	17	2	14	48
EEC as complainant	9	5	3	9	26
EEC as respondent	4	28	0	10	42
GATT Article I	3	4	2	6	15
GATT Article II	8	4	0	8	20
GATT Article III	9	7	1	14	31
GATT Article VI	3	0	0	2	5
GATT Article XI	3	44	6	9	62
GATT Article XVI	0	14	0	4	18
Subsidies code	2	5	0	1	8
Technical (Standards) code	0	1	0	0	1

The importance of agricultural products is apparent in the dispute-settlement cases, especially with regard to cases brought against the EC. Likewise, the article of GATT most frequently invoked is Article XI, which concerns the obligation not to use quotas. GATT Articles III (national treatment) and XVI (subsidies) also figure prominently in the disputes. Separate proceedings under MTN code procedures had not had much time (as of late 1988) to develop, but there have already been a number of cases under the subsidies code.

Several Cases Examined

Although the compliance record of GATT panel recommendations is very respectable, (perhaps higher in percentage terms than that of the World Court),[73] there has been much concern during recent years about noncompliance. It is very difficult to assemble data on this question, but our explorations suggest that of approximately 117 cases for which we have information, only about 8 to 10 have resulted in panel reports which have not been followed.[74] In some cases, the concerns about the GATT processes are partly to blame: a disputing nation can block "adoption" of a report and then argue that there is no binding requirement for it to follow the report. Furthermore, merely counting cases does not adequately reveal the relative importance of some cases compared to others. If compliance occurs only in the relatively unimportant cases, the percentage record may look good but not be too meaningful.

Two cases in GATT pose some substantial problems in this regard, and in addition point to some of the considerations which lead nation-states to be cautious about international dispute-resolution procedures. Both of these cases involved processes brought under the so-called "Subsidies Code"[75] of the GATT, and in both the United States brought a complaint against the EC. The cases are the "Wheat Flour" case, in which a panel found itself unable to rule on the critical legal issue; and the "Pasta" case, in which a different panel ruled in favor of the U.S. position. Neither report (at this writing) has been adopted by the committee of signatories of the code, although the U.S. and the EC have settled the Pasta dispute.[76] A brief look at these two cases may be revealing for our purposes.

The Wheat Flour case[77] involved a complaint by the U.S. that EC subsidies (as much as 75 percent) to aid exports of wheat flour to third markets (including Egypt) were a violation of the code and of the GATT rules regarding export subsidies. Export subsidy rules for agricultural products differ from those for manufactured or "nonprimary" products. There seemed to be little doubt that the EC subsidies would have been violating the rules if manufactured products had been involved. But the rules are less absolute regarding agricultural products, requiring only that a subsidy not result in a nation "having more than an equitable share" of world export trade. The U.S. argued that the EC share of the world export market had increased from 29 percent to 75 percent over a relevant period and that the EC market share in a number of important and growing markets had increased, while U.S. export share of those markets had decreased. Yet the panel, partly influenced by special characteristics of the marketing of U.S. wheat flour, including aid under the U.S. PL 480 food aid program to assist developing countries, did not find that the EC had achieved "more than an equitable share." The panel refused to be guided in this case by an earlier export subsidy case in GATT history, also dealing with wheat flour, which might have been seen as a sort of "precedent" for some meaningful definition of "equitable share."

The Pasta case[78] also involved a U.S. complaint against EC subsidies for exports (pasta), which in this case went to the U.S. market (particularly harming a U.S. regional pasta industry). The EC claimed that its subsidies to EC pastamakers for exporting were only such as were necessary to equalize the effective cost of the more expensive European durum wheat (which EC pastamakers presumably used) with the world-market price for wheat. The EC price was higher because of its Common Agricultural Policy program of maintaining grain prices. For the pastamakers to be able to export, they needed to have inputs at prices equivalent to those of foreign competitors, so the EC provided a "cereals refund" to make up the difference. The EC claimed, therefore, that the subsidy was really one for wheat (and thus was governed by the rules for agriculture products). The panel, however, found both that the payments were made to the pastamakers for pasta exports and, more significantly, that pasta was not a primary or agricultural product, but was a processed good and therefore came under the rules for nonprimary products. In this case, the subsidies were forbidden by the code.

Both of these cases sorely tested the GATT-type processes. The Wheat Flour case is viewed by some observers as one in which the panel members, for diplomatic reasons, essentially "ducked" their responsibility. Yet it has to be recognized that the treaty language is exceedingly vague. A restrained view of "judicial behavior" might legitimately lead to a refusal to rule on such an issue. If no prior precedent existed, such a refusal seems fair.

The Pasta case was approached differently by its panel. Clearly the EC was surprised to find that processed agricultural goods fell afoul of the subsidy rules for non-primary goods, and arguably would not have agreed to some of the language of the agreement if it had realized what would be the eventual result. The panel nevertheless was willing to come to that conclusion, in what was perhaps the opinion of the GATT dispute system in which a dissenting opinion was offered. Again, a more restrained view of judicial behavior in these circumstances might lead to the conclusion that the issue is one which the interested nations should negotiate toward a solution, by refining the rule. Persons with this view would argue that the nation-states did not intend to delegate so important a question (which, the EC argues, goes to central issues of its all-important Common Agricultural Policy) to a trio of disinterested panel members.

Each side has its point. There is considerable ambiguity about the appropriate role of third-party decision making in these cases. But there is also a need for an institutional process that will effectively resolve disputes (which otherwise can fester for lengthy periods of time), and will do so in a way that reinforces rule integrity. The jurisprudence and philosophy of these processes need considerable attention.

4.5 National Procedures for Citizen Initiation of International Economic Disputes

The United States and Its Section 301 Procedures

Under traditional international law doctrines, nations were almost the only "subjects" of international law, and international procedures were open only to nation-states, or in some cases also to international organizations. This is generally still true today, although there is a developing body of practice and thought that permit individuals as well as business firms to be "subjects." Nevertheless, the primary international law procedures for dispute settlement, such as the World Court, are available only to nation-states or international organizations. When individuals have a complaint against some foreign nation, the traditional approach requires those individuals to get their own governments to bring up the matter in international diplomatic processes or tribunals. This is called "diplomatic protection."[79]

Under traditional practice of diplomatic protection, the nation whose citizen has urged it to take up his or her cause is the "owner" or controller of the case. If that nation refuses to proceed, the individual usually has no recourse under international law.[80] That nation's domestic law may give the individual some recourse, such as under laws regarding taking of property, but under international law the national government officials have the final say as to whether to bring a citizen's complaint to the attention of an offending nation or to an international proceeding. The theory supposedly is that national policy may in some cases make it more important for a nation to refrain from pursuing its citizens' problems. A desire to preserve its good relations with a more powerful state may lead a small nation to refrain from aggravating the powerful state by supporting the complaints of a few of its citizens.

In the United States, the traditional approach for an American citizen who has a complaint against actions taken by a foreign nation is to bring that complaint to the attention of the U.S. government (usually the Department of State), and try to get the U.S. government to intervene on behalf of the citizen with the foreign authorities. This was true in foreign economic matters, as when a foreign nation expropriated property of an American citizen. It is true when a foreign nation violates an international treaty obligation which would otherwise protect the economic or trade interests of an American citizen or firm. Thus, if a foreign country imposes a tariff which exceeds the limit set in its GATT obligations on imports from an American firm, the American firm will probably not find help in the courts of that foreign nation, and certainly cannot itself go directly to the GATT about the matter. It has to prod the U.S. government to take the matter up at GATT.

Dissatisfaction with the U.S. government's handling of such complaints led the Congress to insert into the 1962 Trade Expansion Act a provision[81] which explicitly granted to the U.S. president some authority to take retaliatory actions when foreign governments harmed the trade interests of American firms.[82]

In the 1974 Trade Act, the Congress overhauled this authority and set up a more regular procedure for handling such cases. The procedure gave American firms and citizens the right to formally petition an agency of the U.S. government alleging that American commercial interests had been harmed by illegal or unfair actions of foreign governments. This agency was charged with the responsibility of investigating the allegations, trying to get redress for the U.S. citizen, and ultimately recommending various retaliatory actions to the president which were authorized by the statute. The 1979 Trade Agreements Act amended this law, as did the 1984 Tariff and Trade Act. The recent 1988 Omnibus Trade and Competitiveness Act also contains amendments to section 301 These have several objectives. First, they move the responsibility for the disposition of the action from the president to the USTR. However, the USTR is subject to the direction of the president. Second, under certain circumstances, the use of section 301 is to be nearly "mandatory," with presidential discretion reduced in certain cases of "unjustifiable" actions (for example, breach of legal obligations) by foreign governments. Certain exceptions are specified which restore some of the president's discretion, but on the whole Congress "tightened" the

301 process and made it at least politically more difficult for the president *not* to retaliate. This seems to be part of the source of rather bitter criticism from foreign government officials of the 1988 act.[83]

Thus, today, the United States has a procedure which until 1984 was virtually unique in the world, under which U.S. firms and citizens could petition the U.S. government, in any case involving trade or commerce, for U.S. government aid to redress any foreign-nation action which is deemed to be a violation of "rights of the United States under any trade agreement . . . ," or which denies "benefits to the United States under any trade agreement . . ." or which is "unjustifiable, unreasonable, or discriminatory and burdens or restricts United States commerce."

Section 301 Procedure

The U.S. section 301 procedures allow the government to "self-initiate" a case, or a citizen to file a petition. A citizen petition must be addressed to the United States Trade Representative, who must then determine within forty-five days whether to initiate an investigation. If an investigation is opened, the Trade Representative must publish a summary of the petition, provide opportunity for a public hearing, and request consultation with the foreign country or instrumentality concerned. If the case involves a trade agreement and no mutually acceptable resolution is obtained, the U.S. must involve the dispute-settlement procedures of the agreement. Finally, the Trade Representative must (with certain time limits) make a published determination of what action the U.S. should take. The statute delegates broad powers of response to the Trade Representative, including suspending or withdrawing trade agreement concessions, imposing duties, fees, or other restrictions on the offending country's trade. It makes clear that the procedure applies to trade in services as well as products, and allows responses through either MFN measures or discriminatory measures targeting the offending country.[84]

As I have noted, the 1988 Omnibus Trade and Competitiveness Act strengthened the political pressure on the U.S. executive to take concrete action in the case of "unjustifiable" foreign actions.

Several other features of the U.S. procedure should be noted. Although it is required in some cases to follow an international procedure, the U.S. government is not required to abide by the outcome of that procedure, and in some cases does not even need to refrain from action until the international procedures are formally completed. This feature reflects considerable congressional dissatisfaction with the GATT dispute procedures.[85]

Furthermore, a 301 case need not depend on foreign actions which violate international rules (actions which the statute usually terms "unjustifiable"): it may also be based on the statutory criteria of "unreasonableness," which gives the U.S. much latitude in which to unilaterally define practices it deems to be unfair and deserving of countermeasures.[86]

Finally, section 301 does not have an "injury requirement" specifically; but, for practices not in violation of a trade agreement, it does require something which "burdens or restricts United States commerce," which might be interpreted as a kind of injury requirement.[87]

On the whole, it is apparent that the language of section 301 is extraordinarily vague and imprecise, and partly for this reason it offers considerable discretionary power to the president to impose retaliatory measures against foreign trade. In several cases this broad power has been relied upon in connection with self-initiation to justify presidential measures restricting trade in cases which do not quite fit the traditional trade actions on congressional delegations. For example, section 301 was used as part of a package to settle a countervailing duty case concerning Canadian lumber[88] and to impose the so-called "computer chips agreements" on Japan.[89]

The Practice and Cases under Section 301

From the 1974 enactment of section 301 until April 1989 there have been at least seventy petitions accepted by the office of the USTR. Of these, nineteen concerned practices of the EC, while four more concerned actions of the EC member states. Ten cases involved trade in services rather than goods, and three concerned the protection of intellectual property. As of April 1989, twenty-one of the cases are still pending. Of the remaining cases, thirty were settled by bilateral agreement or some change in the practice of the foreign state. Only ten have resulted in U.S. government retaliatory sanctions of some type.[90]

The utility of the procedure does not result from the counteraction itself, but from the negotiation process assisted by the potential of counteraction, as the draftsmen anticipated.[91] One of the lawyers who has most often used section 301 explains:

In practice, a petition filed under Section 301 by a private party carries an effective threat of potential retaliation, combined with the threat of adverse publicity and a general souring of trade relations. These potential ramifications alone may bring the offending government to the bargaining table. Indeed, astutely using the threat of filing a Section 301 complaint as leverage to achieve a desired end may lead to better results than casually filing a complaint and pursuing the case through administrative channels. Conversely, a sound legal case coupled with inept commercial diplomacy by either the petitioners or the U.S. government may lead to wasted effort and negligible results. More than any other U.S. trade law, Section 301 works through feints and threats, rather than through formal legal processes.[92]

Although most of the section 301 cases regarding products were concerned with damage to U.S. exports from some foreign government action, some of these cases involved imports to the U.S. When section 301 is used in connection with foreign practices regarding exports to the U.S., the question of overlap or conflict between section 301 and various other U.S. laws regarding unfair trade practices is raised. For example, the complaint about pasta imports from the EC argued that the EC export subsidies were unfair. Presumably the countervailing duty laws were designed for such a case. However, section 301 does not contain all the same criteria for U.S. government response which one finds in the countervailing duty law. Section 301 does not explicitly require an injury test, although it appears to be normally interpreted to require some "injury" because of the statutory language of "burdening commerce."[93] The definition of "industry" for purposes of an injury test could also vary. Section 301 criteria may also differ in other ways from those of an unfair trade statute. Nevertheless, there is no *a priori* exclusion of a complaint from a section 301 procedure merely because the facts are similar to or sufficient for a different proceeding. Since section 301 gives the government considerably more discretion than the principal unfair trade laws (countervailing duties and antidumping duties), it is usually not preferred by complainants. Furthermore, in one set of section 301 cases regarding steel products, the government decision was to invoke the escape-clause procedures for the complainants, in essence transferring each case to a different statutory provision and a different U.S. government agency.[94]

The New Commercial Policy Instrument" of the EEC

In 1984 the EEC adopted a regulation on "the strengthening of the common commercial policy with regard in particular to protection against illicit commercial practices."[95] This regulation is designed to give individuals or firms in the EC the right to petition the EC commission to begin an investigation of foreign government practices which are harming EC trade, and possibly to take action to counter those practices. The regulation seems to have been partly inspired by the U.S. section 301 procedure, but as adopted it has some significant differences. In addition, it would be a mistake to assume that the same motivations were behind the EEC regulation as were behind the U.S. law. The EEC regulation is set in a very different governmental context and arguably has an important effect of altering the balance or allocation of power among EC institutions. For example, for the EC to react to foreign unfair practices before the new regulation, practice and the "Luxembourg Compromise" effectively required that a proposal of the Commission be accepted by the Council without objection.[96] This meant that a member-state government with a liberal trade position could "veto" such reaction (under principles that allowed any member state to object). Under the new regulation, once certain procedures are followed, a Commission proposal to take counter-action cannot be so easily overturned in the Council by a member state. In the debate leading to its adoption, it was argued that this aspect of the regulation would allow some governments (such as France) which traditionally were able to influence the Commission to have a greater opportunity to influence the adoption of trade-restricting measures.

In addition, the balance of power within the EC was altered by this regulation in several other ways. For example, the Commission is now authorized to launch a GATT dispute-settlement procedure (subject to a "guillotine" vote of the Council), whereas previously this required an affirmative decision by the Council.

Several interesting differences between the EEC regulation and the U.S. section 301 law exist. First, under the regulation, an international proceeding, if applicable, must always be invoked and followed through to its conclusion before the contemplated counteractions may be utilized.

Second, the regulation provides that it "shall not apply in cases covered by other existing rules in the commercial policy field."[97] This seems to suggest, for example, that anti-dumping and subsidization cases are more appropriately brought under other regulations relating to those actions.

Finally, ". . . the shift in emphasis from inward-looking protective measures to export promotion which has come to be identified with Section 301 is not reflected in the EEC instrument. Reg. No. 2641/84 primarily seeks to protect the Common Market against foreign unfair trade practices. Securing access to export markets for Community industries clearly has been a secondary objective in drafting the regulation."[98]

However, in fact the several cases brought under the regulation have been directed at practices which effect EC exports.[99]

Obviously, the U.S. and the EC developments raise the question of whether they represent a trend toward more formalistic procedures available to private individuals or firms in connection with the application and enforcement of international trade rules, at least under GATT and associated agreements. I will have more comment on this in the next section.

4.6 Looking at the Future of Dispute Settlement and Rule Application in GATT

There has been considerable comment about the weaknesses of the GATT dispute-settlement processes, and much mention of the necessity of trying to improve these as one of the tasks of a new round of negotiations.[100] Clearly there are many obstacles to any serious reform, not the least of which is the fundamental disagreement on the policy and goals of the procedure, outlined in the first section of this chapter. Nevertheless, since so much attention is being directed to the question, it does not seem out of place to speculate a bit on what types of reforms might be desirable.

First, it might be useful to list briefly some of the goals for such a system.[101] A valid and improved system should encourage settlement by the disputants, giving them assistance in the process of settlement, but it should encourage that settlement primarily with reference to the existing agreed rules rather than simply with reference to the relative economic or other power which the disputants possess. The mechanism should be designed so that as time goes on, greater and greater confidence will be placed in the system, so that it will more often be utilized, and so that gradually greater responsibilities may be given to it.

In order to establish that the dispute-settlement mechanism relies primarily on reference to rules and their application, the fulcrum of a mechanism should be the opportunity to obtain an impartial and trusted decision as to the interpretation or application of a previously agreed upon rule. To avoid tainting the process of that judgment — that is, to avoid reducing the trust placed in that decision because the process of obtaining it might be mixed with other goals — the impartial third-party decision of rule interpretations or application should be (as it most often is in the various legal systems of the world) relatively isolated from other processes, such as the process of assisting in negotiation for settlement, or the process of rule formulation (left to legislatures in typical legal systems).

One possible framework for an improved dispute-settlement procedure is a five-part approach, which can be outlined as follows:[102]

1. Bilateral consultations between the disputing parties, without outside presence (as now provided)

2. Conciliation process, with the assistance of trained persons probably from the secretariat, to assist the parties in resolving their dispute

3. Panel and rulings similar to those of the current procedure, with more emphasis on the impartiality of the panel members, utilization of a broader cadre for panels, and a separation of the conciliation process from the panel process. A goal is to increase the integrity and credibility of the "findings," so these can have greater moral force (even without the use of sanctions). The panel report should therefore *always* be published quickly.

4. Policy body approval similar to that of the present procedure. A panel ruling will be submitted to the highest policy body, such as the GATT CONTRACTING PARTIES, for approval. This will allow some "play in the joints" for special circumstances or the recognition of the need for a new rule. The procedure should not allow either disputant to block approval of the panel report, and it should be recognized that the policy body considerations go beyond the strict rules or the law—invoking, for example, "equitable" principles.[103] Over time, the persuasiveness of the panel report and the credibility of the panel process would obviously have a great impact on the policy body consideration of the panel reports.

5. Sanction, such as suspending GATT concessions as now provided. History suggests that there is limited utility for sanctions, and not much willingness by the international community to accept or strengthen sanctions. Thus, at present, the system may well be designed to operate mostly without sanctions.

Making progress in a body of more than ninety-six nations is always difficult,[104] and recognizing the divergence of opinion regarding dispute-settlement procedures even between the EC and the U.S., it may be necessary to turn to methods of evolving a better procedure other than full GATT participation. In short, a "minilateral" approach[105] may be useful, allowing a small group of nations to develop an improved procedure to use in disputes among themselves, keeping the door open for other nations to join these procedures as time goes on.

Bilateral approaches are also an important option, although they worry some who think they may undermine the multilateral system. The 1988 Free Trade Agreement between Canada and the United States has several far-reaching bilateral dispute settlement provisions which cover many GATT subjects also covered in the bilateral agreement.[106]

One of these provisions created an international panel procedure which not only substitutes for appeal to domestic courts in antidumping and countervailing duty cases in the two countries, but is empowered to issue a decision which becomes directly applicable in the domestic law of the country concerned so as to bind the administration officials there.[107]

At some point in the future (certainly not soon), the participants in the international multilateral trade system might consider an approach to disputes and rule application that allows some modified means of direct access to procedures by individuals and private firms, perhaps after an appropriate international "filter" to prevent spurious complaints. I explained, with several co-authors, in our 1984 book:

There are some interesting potentials in these precedents for the GATT and the international economic system, although they will probably not be readily accepted by the governments that participate in the GATT. But governments and business firms do desire greater predictability of national government economic actions in an increasingly interdependent world, and do desire greater balance and equality in actual implementation of negotiated international rules on economic matters. Those factors could lead governments to be willing to accept some sort of a mechanism by which individual citizens or firms could appeal directly to an international body like the GATT to determine whether a government obligated under the GATT or one of its codes has taken an action that is inconsistent with its international obligations. . . .

Clearly, the typical governmental reluctance to relinquish any power or to constrain its field of discretion would discourage a move in the direction of the procedures described. On the other hand, it should be recognized that there are some advantages for governments in such a procedure. For one thing, if it were carefully designed and became reliable, governments might well find that the procedure would tend to deemphasize and depoliticize many relatively minor trade or economic complaints that now exist between nations. For example, let us assume that Mr. A, a citizen in country A, finds that his exports to country B are being restrained improperly by country B, inconsistent with country B's international obligations. Under the current procedure, Mr. A must go to his own national government and get it to take up his matter with the foreign government. Thus, his case has immediately been raised to a diplomatic level. That quite often means, by the nature of things, that it has been raised to a fairly high level of official attention and consequently of public perception. On the other hand, if an appropriate international procedure existed, when Mr. A came to his government to complain about country B, country A officials could refer Mr. A to that procedure and encourage him to use it, without taking any stand on the matter. It is quite possible that the issue could then be handled more expeditiously and routinely. The case would continue to be Mr. A's case, and [would] not become country A's case. The issue would be Mr. A versus country B, instead of Mr. A and country A versus country B.

It is the view of at least one of the authors of this book that in all probability, early versions of such a procedure would have to allow the individual governments to exercise some kind of right of veto over their own citizens' attempts to invoke the process. However, this right could be accorded to national governments as a way to make them more comfortable with experimenting with the procedure, and could be designed to gradually die out (at least for all but the most exceptional cases).[108]

Once again, we need to return to the dichotomy of policy pointed out in the first section of this chapter. A European author, in a book quoted approvingly by a major European diplomat, suggests that international resolution of disputes, at least regarding economic matters, has as its prime objective neither ascertainment of right or wrong, nor establishment of responsibility of a particular nation, but instead the most rapid cessation of the violations.[109] That author, and others,[110] stress the importance of diplomatic means and negotiating approaches to resolving disputes.

Unfortunately, in my estimation, these viewpoints miss important policy considerations and are often misleading. In the first place, there is considerable utility in publicly designating (or threatening to do so) the "wrongdoer" in an international dispute, especially if there is widespread acceptance of the validity of the process which determines the wrongdoing. But, more significantly, it must be recognized that in most cases it is *not* the resolution of the specific dispute under consideration which is most important. Rather, it is the efficient and just future functioning of the overall system which is the primary goal of a dispute-settlement procedure. Thus, it may be more important to clarify and provide predictive guidance about the application of a rule, than it is to determine that a "judgment" is acceptable to either or both parties of the immediate dispute. Indeed, in some GATT proceedings, contracting parties other than the disputants have expressed a strong interest in a dispute process because the resultant "precedent" effect of a panel ruling could affect them.[111] If the policies of a "rule-oriented diplomacy," as mentioned in section 1, make sense, they also tend to suggest a broader goal than just the settlement of a particular dispute to the satisfaction of the disputants.

These questions are not absolute "either/or" ones, however. There is a spectrum of utilities involved in the considerations discussed here. If a rule is too rigidly applied, so that the application is consistently ignored, that too will damage the broader international trading system. On the other hand, too much concern for the "feelings" of the parties, with too much concern for "diplomatic approaches" designed to sweep differences under the rug, or the use of studied ambiguity to "paper over" differences, will have costs also.

Finally, there are other mechanisms and techniques for improving the "rule integrity" of the GATT trade system. One approach is called "surveillance." One technique is to have committees or working groups systematically examine the trade measures of particular countries (perhaps on a rotating basis) and comment on the GATT consistency or policy appropriateness of such measures."[112] Another is for a GATT body to report semiannually (as is now done) on the "status" of the trading system, to flag discrepancies between measures actually taken (such as "gray area" or export-restraint arrangements)[113] and GATT rules, or to raise questions about the policy appropriateness of such measures.

5   Tariff and Non-Tariff Barriers

5.1   Import Restrictions and GATT Obligations

The first four chapters of this book have dealt with the institutional and legal structure of the world trade system related to GATT. Now we turn to the substantive regulatory policies of that system. In the next seven chapters I describe in turn the most important of those policies and their legal implementation both nationally and internationally. These chapters deal both with the affirmative obligations (such as tariff bindings, MFN, and national treatment) and with a series of exceptions to those obligations. In some cases, when the exceptions are most closely identified with a particular affirmative policy, they are discussed in the chapter relating to that policy.

The diplomats who wrote the GATT and the ITO Charter had broadly in mind a regulatory system that would essentially inhibit the use of restrictions on imports other than tariffs, and then provide for negotiation of reduced tariff levels.[1] It was recognized that the mere agreement to reduce tariff levels could be easily evaded unless other obligations were established to prevent that evasion. A simple example would be a negotiated limit of a 10 percent tariff on bicycles but evaded by a national government which imposes a quota on bicycle imports, thus frustrating the purpose of the tariff limit to liberalize trade.

It has been said that the drafters of GATT addressed primarily five types of border barriers to imports: tariffs, quotas, subsidies, state trading, and customs procedures.[2] For tariffs, the approach was to allow them to continue, but to provide for reduction negotiations. For quotas, the approach (with the experience of the 1930s well in mind) was to establish a prohibition on their use. For customs procedures, the GATT (in Articles VII – X) established norms of reasonableness, with limits on delaying or costly measures. With respect to subsidies and state trading, however, the draftsmen were not so rigorous.

State trading agencies, such as a government agency given exclusive rights to import, could be used to restrict trade in a number of ways. The agency could simply refuse to buy more than a certain quantity of the goods each year. Alternatively, it could buy goods but set a resale price for domestic buyers at a level high enough to inhibit sales and, therefore, imports. The agency could argue that in each case it did this as a matter of internal proprietary decision, and not by government regulation, so that most GATT rules didn't apply. Yet the government in most cases, certainly when it owned the agency or company, could have great "influence" on these "proprietary" decisions. The GATT rules on state trading (Article XVII) do not establish very much discipline.[3]

Likewise, domestic subsidies can be used to allow domestic producers to undersell and inhibit imports. Once again, the GATT rules on such subsidies are not very strong.[4]

This pattern of regulation—negotiate tariffs, eliminate quotas, and not enforce too much discipline on subsidies and state trading—has been the basis of one early argument used by developing countries to suggest that the GATT was biased in favor of industrial-country trading patterns.[5]

There are some important economic and other policy reasons to favor tariffs over quotas, however. The price effect and competitive distortion caused by quotas tend to be much less transparent than those of tariffs. Quotas as well as tariffs yield "monopoly rents"—that is, the domestic producers will be able to price their goods higher, and thus will receive more profits. While under a tariff the government captures some of these monopoly rents (from tariff payments), that often is not the case with quotas (unless the government charges for the quota licenses). Depending on how it is constructed, the quota may also allow foreign producers to pocket these added rents. In addition, the administration of a quota often is by "license," and licensing procedures lend themselves to corruption of government officials.[6] Some of these policies can also apply to use of other non-tariff measures. For these reasons, the policy preference given to tariffs has considerable rationale behind it.

The history of the tariff in the United States has been ably chronicled by well-known economists.[7] A broad characterization of that history is that U.S. tariffs were high during the early 1800s (averaging up to 60 percent), then dropped to a low of about 20 percent during the 1850s, only to climb back to high levels during the 1860–1914 period. Tariffs were cut sharply in the Wilson administration (1914–1920) but then climbed again, to peak with the 1930 Smoot-Hawley Tariff.[8]

One of the true success stories of the GATT is the effect it has had on tariffs during its nearly forty years of existence. The seven GATT trade negotiating rounds[9] (the latest was the Tokyo Round, completed in 1979) have resulted in an overall reduction in the weighted-average tariff on industrial products to a level of about 4.7 percent. In chapter 2 I presented a table which overviews the results of these prior negotiations.

The first five of these rounds negotiated tariffs on an item-by-item basis, under a procedure explained in section 5.2, below. The last two rounds turned to a "linear cut" approach (as I explain in that section), and also tried to emphasize negotiations on non-tariff measures. As I noted earlier,[10] the Kennedy Round was not very successful in this regard, but the Tokyo Round resulted in more than a dozen treaty agreements and "understandings" regarding non-tariff measures. I will describe most of these agreements in this and later chapters of this book.[11]

Tariffs of under 5 percent *ad valorem*, arguably constitute more of a "sales tax," or a nuisance, than an import barrier. Producers who can become sufficiently more efficient can "hurdle the tariff" by selling at a lower cost to offset the tariff. There may, however, be special circumstances in which even a low tariff could be important. For example, Canadians sometimes note that even a low tariff can have a substantial impact on an investment decision about where to locate a plant. If a substantial portion of the output from a Canadian plant must be sold in the U.S. market, a 5 percent U.S. tariff could be instrumental in leading investors to locate in the U.S. so as to enhance the long-term rate of return on the capital allocated to build the plant.[12]

In addition, the low tariff is an average which may conceal a few relatively high tariffs. Some U.S. tariffs (even MFN rates), for example, are above 20 percent *ad valorem* (even as high as 40 percent). Such very high tariffs may reduce the volume of trade such that trade-weighted tariff averages do not give adequate significance to their effect. Furthermore, the depressing experience of the GATT period is that as tariffs have declined, there is reason to think that various (often ingenious) non-tariff measures have been introduced or enhanced to limit imports and for reasons discussed above, these may be less desirable from a policy standpoint than tariffs.

One interesting study, by R. Stern and A. Deardorff, attempts to use a large computer model at the University of Michigan to measure the effects of the Tokyo Round tariff-cutting and NTB agreements. Their results show four broad effects. First, employment dislocations in most countries will aggregate only a fraction of one percent. Second, exchange rates will change to a small extent. Third, import and therefore consumer prices will fall to a limited extent. Finally, economic welfare will be increased in most countries, including the major economies of the U.S., the EC, and Japan. In general, however, the effects of tariff and certain NTB changes seem quite minor.[13]

Treaties relating to trade restrictions have for almost a century been concerned with the use of customs procedures as disguised import barriers in themselves. Like almost every other governmental activity, delay, excessive documentation, or arbitrary application of seemingly neutral rules can operate to prevent or inhibit business activity, and customs enforcement is no exception. The GATT treats these activities in its Articles VII through X, which call for opportunity to appeal arbitrary decisions, notice of regulations, minimization of fees and formalities, and reduction of the impact of requirements for marks of origin.[14] Perhaps the most flagrant recent abuse of the customs procedure for protectionist reasons occurred in 1982 in France, when that government required all Japanese imports of VCRs (video cassette recorders) to be entered for customs at the inland city of Poitiers, France. It happened (not coincidentally) that few customs inspectors were available at Poitiers, so in addition to the transportation and inconvenience, customs procedures were notably slow.[15] Unfortunately, GATT procedures appeared not to be too helpful.[16]

5.2   GATT Bindings and Tariff Negotiations

The Bindings and Their Meaning[17]

Since the GATT derived partly from the line of history begun with the 1934 Reciprocal Trade Agreements Act,[18] it is not surprising that commitments to limit the level of tariffs are the central feature of this agreement. The tariff commitments are called "bindings" or "concessions." They are contained for each country in that country's "schedule of tariff concessions," which in turn is incorporated into GATT by language in Article II of GATT. These schedules are voluminous; they consist of lists of product descriptions, followed by a tariff level — either specific or *ad valorem*[19] — which is the treaty obligation for *that product* or *that country*. A typical item might look as follows:

Tariff item number	Description of products	Rate of duty
734.45	Archery equipment, and parts thereof	3.8% ad val.
737.21 737.22	Dolls and parts of dolls, including doll clothing Doll clothing imported separately Other	8% ad val. 12% ad val.

Since there are many products, and since for the major trading countries almost all products are "bound" in GATT, a schedule for such a country will take up many pages—750 for the United States, for example. Also, since there have been a series of trade negotiations resulting in new schedules, and since the older schedules are still technically in force (and can sometimes have some effect),[20] the complete text of the schedules for GATT comprises many volumes.

A binding is a maximum tariff: contracting parties are treaty obligated not to allow their tariff level on a particular product to exceed the GATT binding. They may, however (and sometimes do), set a tariff lower than the binding.[21] When no binding exists, a country may charge any tariff amount it pleases, even a prohibitive tariff of 1000 percent or more.[22] Some GATT contracting parties (especially developing countries) have very short schedules, so that they have wide discretion to change very high tariffs on most imports.

There are a number of possible exceptions to the tariff concession obligation. The escape clause is one (see chapter 7) which allows temporary departure from tariff bindings. Waivers by the contracting parties can be another. In addition, there is a provision in the GATT agreement that essentially allows a contracting party to withdraw a concession at any time. However, on doing this, the CP becomes obligated to grant "compensation" or "renegotiation rights" to other CPs which are affected. These renegotiation rights require that the CP withdrawing a concession either grant a different equivalent concession, or be prepared to endure equivalent withdrawals of concessions from other CPs regarding the exports of the original withdrawing CP. This "rebalancing" feature of the agreement has been one of the more significant factors for maintaining the discipline of the tariff-schedule obligations.[23]

Negotiating Tariff Concessions: Item by Item Procedures[24]

Before the Kennedy Round (1962–1967), in the first five GATT tariff negotiating rounds the procedure for negotiation was followed on an item-by-item basis. Each country tabled, with each other country that had a potential to import from it, a "request list" of products and tariff concessions desired. Then each country prepared an "offer list" of concessions it was prepared to make in return. The national negotiators would then meet in two-country meetings to negotiate reciprocal concessions. The whole process was supervised by the GATT Negotiating Committee and the secretariat, with copies of all lists and notifications being kept by the secretariat and normally available for inspection by any negotiating party. Since each concession was applied on an "MFN" basis, when a pair of nations had arrived at preliminary agreement on their mutual concessions, each would then try to obtain other concessions, by way of reciprocity, from other contracting parties who would benefit from the concessions.

For example: If country A agreed to limit its tariffs on bicycle imports to 8 percent in exchange for B's agreement to limit its tariffs on cheese imports to 12 percent, and if country C also exported bicycles to A, then, as reciprocity for the benefit C would get from the A-B agreement, A would ask C for a concession on radio imports from A. If C refused, then A and B might have to rethink their tentative agreement. None of these preliminary agreements would be final until the end of the negotiation, when all parties were notified and all agreements were assembled into one treaty document by the GATT secretariat. At that time each contracting party would have to decide whether on balance it was willing to sign the "tariff protocol." Its decision would be partly based on the total balance of what it would give up, compared to what it expected to receive.

Needless to say, this process was very complex, and in later years it became increasingly cumbersome. When the EC was formed by the 1957 Treaty of Rome, it began negotiating as an entity for its six member states. But each bargaining position had to be internally worked out within the EC, and this added great difficulty to the GATT negotiating process. Consequently a search for a different procedure was undertaken.

Negotiating Tariff Concessions: The Linear Procedure[25]

Beginning with the sixth round, the Kennedy Round, the GATT CON-TRACTING PARTIES decided to conduct the main portions of the tariff negotiations on a "linear" basis. With this procedure, most industrial countries (the developing countries and a few primary product nations were allowed to opt out of the linear offer) were required to make their initial "offer," an across-the-board cut in tariffs of 50 percent for nonprimary products (agriculture products were not included in this offer). The 1962 U.S. statute set a limit to the U.S. president's authority to agree to a tariff cut at 50 percent, and this figure strongly influenced the GATT decision on the linear cut offer. Under such a maximum cut, a 14 percent *ad valorem* tariff would become 7 percent.

Each nation was then allowed to table "exceptions lists," which had to be defended in the Negotiating Committee and thus became the focus of the negotiation. The advantage of this procedure was that the negotiations focused primarily on the "exceptions," and not on every item in the tariff schedule. Agricultural goods, however, and all goods for those countries which stayed out of the linear procedure, were negotiated on an item-by-item basis.

The result of this new procedure at the end of the Kennedy Round (1967) was an average tariff reduction of about 35 percent, not as good as the original goal of 50 percent, but very significant nevertheless.[26]

Negotiating Tariff Concessions: The Tokyo Round

When the Tokyo Round was launched in 1973, it was assumed that a linear cut approach would be used again. The authorizing U.S. statute this time allowed the president to agree to up to a 60 percent cut, but the negotiations at Geneva took a somewhat different approach. It was argued by some countries, especially those of the EC, that higher tariffs should be cut deeper than lower tariffs.[27]

The argument was that tariffs which were fairly low already did not have the actual protectionist effect at the border that their level might imply. On the other hand, a high tariff, say 20 percent, might have a very powerful effect in keeping out imports. At some point a tariff becomes virtually prohibitive and keeps out almost all imports. If that point were, for example, 30 percent, with a current tariff of 60 percent, a 50 percent reduction of that high tariff would result in almost no additional imports. The EC approach was influenced also by the fact that the EC

Common External Tariff (CET) was a relatively level one, because it had been set primarily by averaging the various tariffs of the member states of the EC. On the other hand, the EC argued, the U.S. tariff had more "peaks and valleys," and therefore for proper reciprocity to occur in a tariff reduction negotiation, the peaks should be lowered further than the average or the valley tariffs.

Although the objective for the Tokyo Round negotiation was to place priority on non-tariff measures, the search for an appropriate linear "tariff-cutting formula" was a protracted and extensive part of the negotiation. Whether it was worth it, in tariff-cutting terms, is uncertain.[28] But some observers noted that during many months, and even years, when very little progress was made in the Tokyo Round negotiation, the tariff-cutting discussions were the only parts of the effort that seemed to engage the attention of the participants. For that reason, the tariff negotiations have sometimes been called the "glue" which held the negotiation together. Much staff effort and many computer runs were regained by the process of evaluating a variety of proposals for tariff cuts.

In the end, the negotiators agreed on an interesting formula for tariff cutting (subject to "exceptions-list" item negotiations, like those in the Kennedy Round). The formula is expressed as follows:

$$Z = \frac{AX}{A + X}$$

where X was the starting tariff (before the Tokyo Round), Z was the tariff which would result, and A was some constant coefficient. This coefficient could differ for different contracting parties, and so some of the negotiation was about the amount of this coefficient. For the U.S. it was set at 14; for the EC it was set at 16.[29]

Taking these two coefficients and the formula above, the following example enables us to see the effect of the agreement:

A =	Start tariff X =	End tariff Z =	Calculation
EEC = 16	10 %	6.15	(16 × 10)/(16 + 10) = 160/26
	20 %	8.89	(16 × 20)/(16 + 20) = 320/36
US = 14	10 %	5.83	(14 × 10)/(14 + 10) = 140/24
	20 %	8.24	(14 × 20)/(14 + 20) = 280/34

As noted, the tariff-cutting results of the Tokyo Round, for dutiable industrial products imported to industrial countries, has been estimated to be about 35 percent, reducing average tariffs from about 7.0 percent to about 4.7 percent.[30]

The Question of Reciprocity

The GATT does not require "reciprocity " (and indeed by amendments made during the mid-1960s urges industrial countries to refrain from seeking it from developing countries[31]). Usually, U.S. statutes authorizing U.S. participation in GATT negotiations also did not explicitly require "reciprocity." Nevertheless, the practice in GATT among the major negotiating parties was always to seek reciprocity, whatever that means. The 1934 U.S. statute, it will be recalled, was entitled the "Reciprocal Trade Agreements Act"[32]; and it was implied, and the Congress assumed, that tariff and other barrier reductions would be agreed on a mutual and equivalent basis.

In fact, it may be argued as a matter of economic policy that reciprocity does not make much sense. The theories of comparative advantage can demonstrate that a particular country can often gain a welfare advantage even by unilaterally reducing its tariff.[33] Of course, if more than one nation reduces its tariffs, this creates even greater welfare; so there is some advantage in using various "bargaining chips," including reduction of your own tariff, to persuade others to reduce tariffs also. However, regardless of the economics of these moves, one thing is very clear: the principle of reciprocity has had a very powerful political effect. It has been a significant motivator of public and government opinion in favor of inducing tariff reductions, even if the principle is fallacious, or partly so.

Assuming a goal of reciprocity, however, the question arises: How do nations measure it? One way, often used but rather simplistic, is to measure the value of a particular tariff concession by multiplying the total value of imports of the product, in the most recent year for which statistics are available, by the number of percentage points of the tariff reduction. Thus, if bicycle imports to A totaled 100 million dollars last year, and the tariff concession being considered would reduce the tariff from 14 percent to 7 percent, the value of the concession would be .07 × 100 million, or 7 million dollars. If one-half of these imports came from B, then the value of the concession to B would be 3.5 million dollars, and A would ask B to give A in return a concession worth that amount.

This "trade coverage" approach, however, does not get at what is really desired by reciprocity, which is to influence roughly the same amount of *future* trade. Under an approach to estimate the "future value" of trade, one would try to estimate the amount of additional trade which would occur if the tariff were lowered a certain amount. This would require using "price elasticities of demand," which are figures not always easy to obtain and sometimes suspect. Nevertheless, using the hypothetical case of the previous paragraph, one would take such elasticity and compute how much additional bicycle imports would occur if the tariff were lowered from 14 percent to 7 percent. This should have an effect on the importing country price of imported bicycles of slightly less than 7 percent (even less of the retail price, since imports are normally valued at wholesale). If one ascertained that the effect would be to sell 25 percent more imported bicycles, the value would arguably be 25 million dollars, and A would seek that amount in equivalent concessions from all the bicycle-exporting countries in the negotiation.

Although some countries in the negotiation tried to utilize these calculations in their appraisal of offers and reciprocal offers,[34] obviously this process is rather imprecise as well as difficult. In the end, the negotiators generally admit that "reciprocity" is mostly a "political judgement." Thus, at the end of a negotiation, nations which have been negotiating with each other may both claim to have "won" the negotiation! Different techniques of calculating the "reciprocity" effects of the agreement could enable them both to make such a claim. Furthermore, it has been suggested to me that at the end of the Kennedy Round, for example, when the political judgment "at the highest level" was made to approve the results for a major country, the political leader nevertheless required his officials to return to their offices and recalculate the "advantage" for his country, so that when made public the advantage would look more favorable!

Another problem of tariff negotiation is the difference of classification and valuation techniques in the different countries. For example, most GATT countries use a CIF valuation for imported products, while the U.S. uses FOB valuation (generally lower because it excludes insurance and freight costs). When calculating the reciprocity value of a tariff reduction, some allowance must be made for the different effects of a tariff due to the different techniques of valuing goods. A change from a 15 percent tariff to 10 percent tariff on imports to the EC, which uses CIF valuation, might be worth somewhat less reciprocally than a like change by the U.S. which uses an FOB method.[35]

Are there other principles which could be politically useful to encourage trade liberalization? One idea which became reasonably prominent in the legislative consideration of the Trade Act of 1974, was that of "sector harmonization."[36] Under this principle, an attempt would be made to reach an international agreement among key nations to achieve in each of them, for a particular product sector (for example, "aircraft" or "steel"), roughly the same level of import restraint. Whereas under traditional "reciprocity" concepts, concessions could be swapped across sectors (A reduces bicycle tariffs in exchange for B reducing radio tariffs), in a sector approach the goal would be to achieve, at the *end* of the negotiation, approximately the same level of restraint for a product sector in all agreeing nations. An important enhancement of this principle is to include non-tariff measures also, and to add up the values of the effects of those measures, probably as some sort of "tariff equivalents."[37]

Economically this approach has much merit. It means that firms are competing on a "level playing field" against other firms in the same business, regardless of nationality. However, it is very difficult to negotiate this approach. Indeed, although this approach was stated in U.S. legislation to be an important goal for the Tokyo Round, in the end only one trade liberalizing sectorial agreement—that on aircraft—was completed in that round. The difficulty is clear when one considers that two nations might begin the negotiation with vastly different levels of protection in a particular sector. Suppose country A has 15 percent tariffs on imports of steel and various non-tariff restraints on imports that are the equivalent of another 10 percent tariff. This total of 25 percent protection could be compared to that of B for steel, and if the latter totals only 5 percent, how can B induce A to reduce its protection to the 5 percent level? Maybe B can offer A some comparable inducement in another sector where the ratios are inverse, but often there is little incentive for the higher-restraint country to move its protection toward a harmonized level.

During the early 1980s, Congress began discussing yet another concept of reciprocity.[38] Legislation was proposed which would have the U.S. government impose new import restraints on products of those foreign countries (often meaning Japan) which did not reciprocally allow imports of U.S. products.[39] This "negative reciprocity" approach had much political appeal, but it obviously poses many questions. If used as a sector-by-sector approach, it defeats some of the results of traditional reciprocity whereby cross-sector swaps have induced reduction of tariffs and other restraints. It also is likely to cause violation of current GATT and other international obligations, not the least of which is MFN.[40] For some of these reasons, the executive branch of the U.S. government has generally opposed these negative-reciprocity proposals, and the Congress (at present) has not adopted them.

A very difficult question is how to utilize reciprocity concepts in negotiating *non*-tariff measures. Theoretically, one might try to compute tariff-equivalent values of various non-tariff measures. Some scholars have tried this, but obviously it is difficult, and it does not answer some important questions anyway. For example, when nations draft and sign an agreement on the treatment of subsidies in international trade, how can "reciprocity" play a role? First, how can one calculate the trade effect of such an agreement (especially when there exist certain ambiguities or imponderables about future implementation)? Second, all nations may receive a value from the establishment of certain common and predictable rules of behavior regarding international trade, even if the value each receives is not always equal.[41]

5.3   Classification for Tariff Purposes

Virtually every tariff system depends on descriptions of products contained in a classification system. If a tariff were the same on all imported goods (similar to many sales taxes), then presumably no such classification system would be needed (except for statistical and reporting purposes). However, since tariffs vary greatly — from zero to levels as high as 30 percent or 40 percent or more — it is necessary to classify imported products in order to ascertain what tariff level will apply. The difference between a "work of art" and a "toy" may not always be obvious to a customs official, but may make the difference between tariff-free treatment and a duty of 25 percent. Thus, officials at the border must constantly make classification judgments; and in most major trading countries, like the U.S., there is a system to appeal these judgments to the courts.[42] An elaborate jurisprudence with various principles of classification, such as *ejusdem generis* and *noscitur a sociis*, has grown up to aid courts, administrators, and importers in predicting the classification of goods. The GATT obligates contracting parties to publish regulations and provide for fair and judicial-type procedures (Article X). It also contemplates the importance of classification rulings and the danger that these could undermine the value of a concession. In such a case it provides for negotiation and "compensatory adjustment" (Article II: 5).[43]

Many countries, including the EC and Japan, have used the "Brussels Tariff Nomenclature" (BTN) of product classification for tariff purposes, which was developed by the Customs Co-operation Council in Brussels.[44] The United States, on the other hand, has adhered rather resolutely to its own classification system, now known as the Tariff Schedules of the United States (TSUS).[45]

Negotiating tariff reductions and evaluating reciprocity is further complicated by differences in nomenclature. Translation tables are necessary. Since these problems occur even between negotiating rounds, for purposes of "compensatory concessions" in an escape clause or binding withdrawal case, the nomenclature problem is a constant one. For this reason, and from a desire to improve statistical reporting, a number of nations (including the BTN members and the United States) negotiated to formulate a unified and revised product classification system which they all can accept. This "Harmonized Commodity Description and Coding System" was opened for signature in 1984 and has been adopted by many nations.[46] However, the implementation of the Harmonized Code by the United States was complicated by the political battles over the 1988 Trade Act[47] which delayed its enactment until the statute became law in September 1988.

The most-favored-nation (MFN) obligation often has the effect of increasing the complexity of classifications. If nation A is willing to grant a concession to nation B, but discovers that if it does so in an MFN manner it will benefit C while C won't reciprocate, then A has an incentive to subdivide the classification of the product so that even on an MFN basis it will tend to allow B's goods into A, without extending such benefit to C. This will work if there are identifiable differences between B's and C's exports. The classic and well-known example of this occurred in the 1904 Swiss-German Treaty reducing German tariffs on the imports of " ... large dapple mountain cattle or brown cattle reared at a spot at least 300 meters above sea level and having at least one month's grazing each year at a spot at least 800 meters above sea level. . . ."[48]

A 1982 GATT panel decision, however, upheld a Brazilian challenge to the subdivided classification of coffee imports by Spain, saying that the "tilt" against types of coffee produced in Brazil was inconsistent with the phrase "like product" in the GATT MFN obligation.[49]

5.4 Valuation for Customs Purposes

Classification and valuation comprise the two important "pillars" of administering a customs tariff. Of course a tariff may be "specific" (for example, 50 cents per pound) and not need valuation. But most tariffs are *ad valorem* (for example, 12 percent). Gradually many nations have shifted specific tariffs to *ad valorem*, since the latter tend to keep pace with inflation.[50] After the customs official values the products and classifies them, he can calculate the actual tariff amount that must be collected: i.e., he "liquidates" the import entry.

As with classification, there are many problems with valuation. It has already been noted that differences in valuation methods make tariff reduction negotiations more complex. Whereas most countries use a CIF basis for customs valuation, the U.S. has always used an FOB method of valuation.[51] It has even been argued that the U.S. Constitution requires this.[52] Prior to the Tokyo Round, the U.S. law was particularly troublesome. For various historical reasons, this law contained nine different methods of valuing goods for customs purposes, depending sometimes on classification, sometimes on other facts.[53] One objective of many countries in the Tokyo Round was to reduce the costs and delays associated with troublesome valuation systems. The result was a code (side agreement) entitled "Agreement on Implementation of Article VII," GATT Article VII being the article which governs customs valuation procedures.[54]

The Valuation Code establishes a series of definitions of value for customs purposes, with a ranking of how they are to be used. First, a contracting party should use "transaction value" (i.e., the value set by the price of the goods in the particular transaction leading to the importation, provided it is genuine). Second, if the first approach will not work for stated reasons, the contracting party should use the "transaction value" of *identical* goods exported at about the same time and place. Third, if the first two approaches for some reason do not work, the transaction value of *similar* goods shall be used. If these three approaches cannot be used, two more approaches are mentioned, along with some choice as to which to use: Fourth, the price at which similar or identical goods are sold, adjusted by subtracting commissions, transport, and insurance incurred within the country of import, should be used. Fifth, the contracting party shall use a "constructed" value method by adding amounts for profit, administrative expenses, and other adjustments to the original cost of materials and fabrication, to make this method comparable to the transaction costs of the first few methods.

The Valuation Code also has provisions for dispute settlement, and a "committee of signatories." A separate "protocol" for this agreement was added at the end of the Tokyo Round to modify the original code, because of some objections to the original from developing countries.

This code has been one of the more successful of the Tokyo Round results. As of January 1989, twenty-seven countries (including the EC as one "country") had accepted the code, including five developing countries. In the United States, the rules of this code have replaced the prior archaic and complex valuation system, and the result has been a dramatic decrease in appeals to the courts from administrative determinations of valuation—another good sign of success for the code.[55]

5.5 Quantitative Restrictions and Other Non-Tariff Measures

Quantitative Restrictions

GATT Article XI prohibits the use of quotas or measures other than duties to restrict either imports or exports. Other articles in GATT provide exceptions for balance of payments reasons[56] and for developing countries.[57] In section 5.1, I outlined the reasons why government officials and economists generally think that quotas are a less desirable import restraint than tariffs. The experience of widespread and escalating use of quotas during the 1930s also influenced the ITO-GATT draftsmen to try to abolish this technique of trade restraint.[58]

Despite this GATT obligation, the attempt to eliminate the use of quotas has not been nearly so successful as the tariff-reduction obligations of GATT. During the early years of GATT, many nations other than the U.S. could claim some legal cover for quotas under the balance-of-payments exceptions (BOP) of GATT. When in 1958 the major Western European trading nations established external currency convertibility, the BOP excuse began to fade, and the GATT undertook a program to try to get quotas eliminated. This program had some success, but it was least successful with respect to agricultural products, partly because the United States was using quotas on such products under the 1951 statute for which the U.S. had obtained a waiver. Other countries in GATT felt that, waiver or no waiver, if the U.S. could use quotas, they would also. With respect to nonagricultural products, many countries continued to maintain at least some quotas. These gradually obtained the name "residuals," and many of them still exist.[59]

The government procedures for administrating quotas can be abused, leading to corruption or to delay and expense from the procedures themselves. For these reasons, the Tokyo Round negotiations completed an "Agreement on Import Licensing Procedures"[60] designed to impose fair and efficient procedures in those cases when quotas are used. This agreement obligates nations accepting it[61] to avoid using licensing procedures in a manner which would have trade-restrictive effects, calling for published information about quotas, equality of opportunity to apply for quotas, reasonable duration of quota periods, etc. Only twenty-seven countries (all but ten being industrial countries) have accepted the agreement, and there is some indication that this agreement has not yet been very effective in achieving its objectives.[62]

Non-Tariff Measures (NTMs)

The ingenuity of man to devise various subtle as well as explicit ways to inhibit the importation of competing goods is so great that any inventory of such measures quickly becomes very large. In addition, it is clear that this ingenuity will never cease: like ways to avoid income tax, human invention of non-tariff barriers will undoubtedly go on forever. The international and national institutions designed to cope with this problem must recognize this as part of the circumstances which they must contend with.

During the 1960s the GATT undertook an exercise to catalog non-tariff barriers of all participating countries. One purpose of such an inventory was to prepare factual background that could be used in the next trade-negotiating round. By 1973 the catalog contained well over 800 NTBs, listed by country.[63] The UNCTAD has also conducted a research project to inventory trade barriers, and by 1986 had many more items on its country-by-country lists.[64] Some restrictions are the results of valid domestic policies, such as those to do with product standards or pollution control. The key question, as I will explain in later chapters, is whether such valid domestic policies have been implemented in such a way as to unnecessarily or arbitrarily restrict international trade.

Scholars have tried to estimate the "tariff-equivalent" effect of the various non-tariff measures, but have found this to be no easy task. A monograph by P. Morici and L. Megna of the National Planning Association contains one such effort, suggesting the aggregate tariff-equivalent value of most U.S. non-tariff measures is approximately 9 percent.[65] Professors R. Stern and A. Deardorff of the University of Michigan have written about the conceptual difficulties of such measurements, and have made tentative estimates of their own.[66]

Examples of measures which appear to be designed to restrict the amount of imports are sometimes amusing. For example, in one case a country required canned foods to have labels in the language of that country *and no other* (so that economies of scale are lost by the requirement of different labels for different markets). Another example: an importing nation requires VCRs to be imported only through one customs office, which is located in an interior city and has a limited amount of staff to process the goods. Sometimes inspection requirements handily exclude imports, as in the case of the importing nation who requires inspection of the production process itself, but will not send an inspector abroad![67]

One particularly important measure has been the "variable levy," utilized by the EEC in its Common Agriculture Policy (CAP). Under the various CAP systems of levy, a tariff is charged on imports, but the tariff varies frequently, even day to day. The tariff is usually set at a level calculated to offset any price advantage which foreign agriculture goods might have over goods produced within the EC. Since the levy is a tariff, and if the EC either does not have bindings on some of the imported products or withdrew bindings on other imported products (and paid the "renegotiation compensation"), the EC can argue that the variable levy is consistent with GATT, in that it functions as a tariff on unbound items. However, the variable aspect of the levy certainly defeats one of the basic policies behind the GATT preference of tariffs as trade restriction. If the tariff is fixed, then efficient foreign producers may be able to "hurdle" it, by becoming more efficient and lowering their prices. A maximum amount of protection against foreign competition is set, and when domestic producers become unable to compete even with the advantage created by such a tariff, pressure to become more efficient will be put on them by imports. When the tariff varies, however, in a manner explicitly designed to prevent foreign competition at virtually any price, then the "hurdle possibility" of other tariffs is defeated.[68]

6

The Most-Favored-Nation Policy

6.1 Most-Favored-Nation Obligation and Its Politics

There are two important principles of "nondiscrimination" in GATT and most international trade policies. The first is that of the "most-favored-nation" (MFN) principle, expressed in Article I of GATT and in a number of bilateral and other treaties. Despite some confusion derived from the phrase "most-favored," which seems to imply a specially *favorable* treatment, the concept is one of equal treatment, but to that *other* party which is most favored. In the GATT the MFN obligation calls for each contracting party to grant to every other contracting party the most favorable treatment which it grants to any country with respect to imports and exports of products.

The second obligation of nondiscrimination — that of "national treatment" — is the obligation to treat foreign goods equally to domestic goods, once the foreign goods have cleared customs and become part of the internal commerce. In this chapter we deal with MFN, and defer until a later chapter the national-treatment subject.[1]

The MFN obligation has a long history which is easily traced back to the twelfth century,[2] although the phrase seems to have first appeared in the seventeenth century. Growth of commerce during the fifteenth and sixteenth centuries seemed to be a major cause of MFN-type treaty clauses, as European nations competed with each other to develop networks of trading relationships. The United States included an MFN clause (albeit "conditional") in its first treaty, a 1778 treaty with France.[3] It has sometimes been speculated that early MFN clauses were "shorthand" means of including series of trade obligations in new treaties, without laboriously writing out those obligations.[4] In later centuries, the MFN clause, either conditional or unconditional, was frequently included in a variety of treaties, and particularly in the various Friendship, Commerce, and Navigation (FCN) treaties.[5]

One question which has sometimes been debated is whether there is any sort of MFN or economic nondiscrimination obligation independent of a treaty clause, under customary international law. While the issue is disputed, the prevailing view of scholars is that such an obligation exists only when a treaty clause creates it. Lacking a treaty, nations presumably have the sovereign right to discriminate against foreign nations in economic affairs as much as they wish. It may be that the "national treatment" obligation differs in this respect, however.[6]

What are the policy arguments which underpin the MFN principle? We now turn to an examination of some of those arguments, as well as to some arguments against the MFN idea.

Sometimes MFN is equated with the concept of "multilateralism," but it must be recognized that the two concepts can be distinguished. Multilateralism is an approach to international trade and other relations which recognizes and values the interaction of a number, often a large number, of nation states. It recognizes the dangers of organizing relations with foreign nations on bilateral grounds, dealing with them one-by-one. MFN, on the other hand, is a standard of equal treatment of foreign nations.

Many of the policies favoring MFN also favor multilateralism. It is, of course, possible to have multilateral approaches that do not depend on MFN; but the reverse seems relatively unlikely, although not impossible (for example, MFN clauses can be contained in bilateral agreements).

There are at least two groups of arguments that buttress the policy of MFN. First, there are some arguments that we may loosely call "economic." Second, there are a group of political or "not-so-economic" arguments.

With respect to the first category, several economic policy arguments in favor of MFN can be stated. To begin with, nondiscrimination can have the salutary effect of minimizing distortions of the "market" principles that motivate many arguments in favor of liberal trade. When governments apply trade restrictions uniformly without regard for the origin of goods, the market system of goods allocation and production will have maximum effect. Lamb meat will not be shipped halfway around the world when nearby markets could just as easily absorb it.

A second economic argument is that MFN often causes a generalization of liberalizing trade policies, so that overall more trade liberalization occurs (the multiplier effect of the MFN clause).

Third, MFN concepts stress general rules applicable to all participating nations, which can minimize the costs of rule formation (such as the difficulty of negotiating a multitude of bilateral agreements). Some theoretical arguments incidental to the "prisoner's dilemma" suggest that an optimum approach to avoid mutually destructive actions is to enter into an agreement that effectively restrains attempts by any party to engage in "exploitative" behavior. When many parties are involved (such as ninety-six or more member nations of GATT), a generalized rule seems the best approach. In addition, of course, attention must be given to making the rule effective.

Finally, MFN helps minimize transaction costs, since customs officials at the border may not need to ascertain the "origin of goods" to carry out their tasks with respect to goods controlled by MFN.

Turning to the second group of arguments, the "political" side of MFN policies, we first can note that, without MFN, governments may be tempted to form particular discriminatory international groupings. These special groupings can cause rancor, misunderstanding and disputes, because those countries which are "left out" resent their exclusion. Thus MFN can serve the functions of lessening tensions among nations and of inhibiting temptations for short-term *ad hoc* government policies which could be tension-creating in a world already too tense.

It must be recognized, however, that there are certain counterarguments, and that certain categories of nations take a position on some of the MFN policies that acts contrary to a full implementation of MFN obligations. During recent decades this has been particularly true of the developing countries,[7] who have argued that the GATT world trade system operates in such a manner as to inhibit the economic development of many societies who have a weaker economic status in the world. In the view of these countries, "preferences" should be arranged to compensate for the operation of this system, and generally for charitable reasons to assist the poorer nations to develop faster. Obviously, these arguments have merit. However, the risk is always that these arguments will be used to rationalize preferential systems that do not have the intended function of promoting economic development, but rather are used to assist national governments in certain short-term nationalistic political objectives not materially related to overall economic development. In addition, the experience of the Generalized System of Preferences in the GATT System, during the last fifteen years or so, is that for a number of different reasons each of the preference-granting national entities (the industrialized countries) succumbs often to the temptation to use the preference systems as part of the "bargaining chips" of diplomacy.

A second set of counterarguments stresses the risk of a unilateral unconditional MFN approach. These are the "foot-dragger" and "free-rider" arguments. To negotiate a general rule applicable to all nations in a system that stresses unanimity and consensus often means that a hold-out nation can prevent agreement or cause its provisions to be reduced to the least common denominator. This can greatly inhibit needed improvement in substantive or procedural rules.[8]

On the other hand, for like-minded nations to go ahead with reforms and agreements without the "foot dragger," but to grant (as unconditional MFN requires) all the benefits of the new approach to the non-agreeing parties, gives the latter unreciprocated benefits without any of the obligations. This furnishes an incentive to nations to stay out of the agreement. It was this which led the United States to require nations to accept the Subsidies Code obligations as a condition to receiving beneficial United States treatment in countervailing duty cases (as specified in the Code).[9]

6.2   The Meaning of MFN

Introduction

What does MFN treatment mean? Essentially, it is an obligation to treat activities of a particular foreign country or its citizens at least as favorably as it treats the activities of any other country. For example, if nation A has granted MFN treatment to B, and then grants a low tariff to C on imports from C to A, nation A is obligated to accord the same low-tariff treatment also to B and its citizens. The result of a nation being a beneficiary of an MFN clause is that that nation can comb all the treaties and all of the actual treatment of the granting nation, to see if some obligation or real treatment is more favorable than that granted to it, in which case the beneficiary can argue that such better treatment is owed to it.[10]

The subjects to which MFN applies depend on the treaty clause. The GATT clause (Article I), for example, applies to trade in goods—both imports and exports. However, it does not apply to the "right of establishment" (often found in FCN treaties, which often apply MFN to it), nor to "services" trade (e.g., banking, insurance, etc.).[11] Nevertheless, the GATT language is quite broad, and covers a lot of territory.

MFN clauses can be "conditional" or "unconditional," and in recent decades yet another MFN concept has arisen, which I will call "code-conditional."

Conditional and Unconditional MFN; Code Conditionality

Under conditional MFN, when country A grants a privilege to country C while owing MFN to country B, then country A must grant the equivalent privilege to B—but only after B has given A some reciprocal privilege to "pay for it."

Under unconditional MFN, in the case above A must grant the equivalent privilege to country B, without receiving anything in return from B. The United States pursued a "conditional MFN" policy prior to World War I, although many other major nations had by that time moved to an unconditional approach. The United States changed to an unconditional policy in 1923.[12]

Several arguments are often voiced in preference of the unconditional approach over the conditional. In the first place, it is very difficult to negotiate for reciprocal concessions from a third-party beneficiary of benefits. When A grants to C a privilege, and B knows that MFN obligations require that privilege to go to B also, albeit after "payment," there is not a very strong incentive for B to be forthcoming in a bargaining process with A. Such negotiations can generate more rancor and trouble than they are worth. Second, unconditional MFN can help spread trade liberalization faster, since any concession by a particular country is generalized to apply very broadly.[13] The GATT MFN clause is clearly unconditional.

A different type of MFN concept has arisen in connection with various "codes," or side agreements on trade matters, negotiated in the Tokyo Round. In some of these codes, certain code members have taken the position that the benefits of code treatment will only be granted to other nations who have become members of the code (or at least reciprocate with code treatment). Thus, if A, B, and C belong to a code which calls for an "injury" test requirement before countervailing duties may be applied to imports, A could argue that it need not give such a test to the imports from X, who is not a code member.[14] Sometimes this has been called "conditional MFN," but in fact it is not the same as the traditional "conditional MFN" concept, since it does not require a particular negotiation of reciprocal benefits. Instead, the code itself defines the nature of the "reciprocity" which is owed in order to receive the advantage of this type of MFN. The advantage of "code conditionality" is that it creates an incentive for other nations to join a code and submit to its discipline. If a general (e.g., GATT) MFN obligation required all code nations to grant the favorable code treatment to nations who did not become code members, there would be substantially less incentive for such nations to join. They could take a "free-rider" approach, and claim the benefits without having to incur the discipline of code membership.

Applying the Clause

It is not always easy to determine the way the MFN obligation applies. First, in the GATT and many other agreements, the language of the obligation speaks of MFN treatment for "like products." So the question often arises as to what "like products" are.[15] This question relates frequently to the question of classifications for tariff purposes which I described in chapter 5. When country A wishes to differentiate its treatment of countries B and C, regarding tariffs on radios, for example, one way to do this is to analyze the imports from B and from C to see if there are distinguishing characteristics. If it is discovered that B ships FM radios, while C ships AM radios, then A will be tempted to charge a higher tariff on FM radios, if it intends to favor C or disfavor B. As I noted in section 5.3, this is one of the reasons for narrower classifications within tariff schedules.

A 1952 GATT dispute case reveals an important consideration in the process of applying MFN clauses.[16] Norway and Denmark complained that a Belgian law levied charges on imported goods which differed according to the nature of family allowances in the exporting country. Although the language of the report in this case was not very clear, the report did conclude that Article I of GATT had not been fulfilled. The case can be interpreted to support the proposition that while treatment can differ if the *characteristics of goods* themselves are different, differences in treatment of imports cannot be based on differences in characteristics of the *exporting country* which do not result in differences in the goods themselves. On the other hand, as chapter 5 noted, a 1982 GATT panel found in favor of Brazil that Spain had not lived up to GATT MFN obligations when it subdivided its customs classification of coffee into sub-parts and applied a much higher duty on those types of coffee imported from Brazil. The panel stated that the coffees were so nearly the same that they were "like products," and that this must be treated nondiscriminatorily even though there were no tariffs binding by Spain on the product.[17]

6.3 Exceptions to MFN and Potential for Bilateralism

The Variety of Exceptions

Despite the policies and legal obligations which support MFN, it is widely recognized that there are substantial departures from MFN in international trade practice. Indeed, it has been estimated that more than 25 percent of all world trade moves under some form of discriminatory regime which is a departure from MFN principles.[18]

Some of these departures were anticipated by the original draftsmen of the MFN clauses, such as the MFN clause in GATT. For example, it has been recognized for centuries that although a tariff may be established on an MFN basis, classifications of tariff items can to some extent operate effectively to discriminate between the goods of various countries (as I noted in the previous section).[19]

In addition, when the GATT was drafted there were a number of preferential systems in existence, most prominently the Commonwealth Preference System. The GATT recognized that some of those preferential systems could continue as something like "grandfather exceptions" to the GATT, with the assumption that in due time the effect of those preferences would decline. Thus, annexes to GATT explicitly provide for such exceptional treatment from MFN.[20]

Other exceptions include some which are discussed elsewhere in this book, such as the problem of Article XIX (escape clause),[21] questions which have arisen in the context of the Tokyo Round codes,[22] and the opportunity for nations to "opt out" of a GATT relationship pursuant to Article XXXV of GATT.[23] It should be noted that if the GATT authorizes a responding action under the disputes provision, Article XXIII, such action need not be taken on an MFN basis.[24]

Furthermore, waivers sometimes authorize departures from MFN. Two important examples of this are the United States–Canada Automotive Products Agreement, (allowing a free trade area for automotive products),[25] and the United States preferences granted to the Caribbean Basin.[26] The Generalized System of Preferences (GSP) program to favor trade of less developed countries operated under the benefit of a waiver from GATT MFN from 1971 to 1981.[27] Presently it is presumed to be authorized by the Tokyo Round Understanding, called the "enabling clause" but officially entitled the understanding on "Differential and More Favorable Treatment, Reciprocity, and Fuller Participation of Developing Countries."[28]

The GATT Article XX "general exceptions"[29] can allow departures from MFN, but there is in that article another "soft" MFN obligation.[30]

Quantitative restrictions often pose an important conceptual challenge to the MFN principle. If a licensing system is used which is based on a "global quota," open to all equally on a first-come, first-served basis, or on a system of auctioning licenses to the highest bidder, then MFN seems realized. But, as is often the case, when quotas or licenses are allocated on a geographical or enterprise basis, even if they are related to historical trading patterns, then to some extent MFN is not completely fulfilled, since different countries or enterprises will have different types of fixed rights. GATT Article XIII establishes a "quasi" MFN principle for many such cases, which primarily relies on historical patterns.

In a similar context, the explosion of use of export-restraint arrangements in world trade provides one of the most significant recent challenges to the MFN principle of GATT. In the widespread use of so-called "voluntary restraint agreements," or "orderly market arrangements," the typical application is on a bilateral basis, and often provides *de facto* discrimination. Thus, countries that have proved most successful in rapidly expanding their exports of particular products become the targets of importing country governments' pressures to adopt export restraints of one form or another. In this context Japanese automobile restraints on the United States market immediately come to mind.[31]

Finally, this brief inventory of some of the discriminatory or non-MFN activities within the current world trading system is not complete without noting the real difficulty of this problem for nonmarket economies. When the enterprises doing the trading—either in imports or exports—are doing so not according to market principles but according to government commands, it is very hard to police any notion of MFN nondiscrimination. A government can always argue that it is not discriminating, and can often conceal the noneconomic motivations which have led it to command differential orders for imports or treatment for exports. In this connection, the problem of reconciling the forms of economic organization of nonmarket economies with the particular obligations of GATT which were designed for market economies is not unique.[32] This problem comes up in a number of different types of obligations of the GATT.[33] A similar group of problems arises in the context of so-called "countertrade."

Customs Unions and Free Trade Areas

One of the most prominent and difficult problems engendering exceptions to MFN and GATT is that of Article XXIV, which provides an exception for customs unions (CU), free trade areas (FTA), and interim agreements leading to either. This article has furnished a very large loophole for a wide variety of preferential agreements.[34]

GATT Article XXIV is based partly on the historical precedent of special regimes of frontier traffic between adjacent countries, but also on the policy that total world welfare can be enhanced by regimes of trade which totally eliminate restrictions on trade among several countries. This is sort of an "all-or-nothing" idea, which is prepared to tolerate some of the disadvantages of preferential treatment of trade in exchange for substantial liberalization of trade among several nations. It recognizes the "free-rider" or "foot-dragger" disadvantages of MFN, allowing particular departures from MFN to facilitate trade liberalization if such liberalization goes far enough to provide substantial advantages to the world. This article is also designed to allow such departures from the MFN principle for the purpose of trade *creation*, while discouraging regimes leading to trade *diversion*.

For these reasons, the GATT exceptions for customs unions and free trade areas provide several significant limitations on the exception.[35] First, the MFN departures are in theory allowed only for CUs or FTAs which are defined to require liberalization on "substantially all" the trade involved. Second, regarding CUs, the GATT article requires that the common tariff arrangements of the preferential group, toward third-country "external" trade, be not "on the whole" more restrictive than the "general incidence of" duties and regulations before the CU was formed. These are, however, difficult legal concepts to apply, and have caused much controversy in the GATT. In addition, the GATT exception allows an "interim agreement" — one which leads to a CU or FTA within a reasonable time — to depart from MFN. This has opened a loophole of considerable size, since almost any type of preferential agreement can be claimed to fall within the exception for "interim agreement," and "reasonable time" is exceedingly imprecise.[36]

Indeed, despite notification of five dozen or more Article XXIV-type arrangements, some of which provide very loose preferences as "interim agreements" and no set date for completion of the FTA, there is no formal record of GATT "disapproval" of such arrangements.[37]

6.4   Rules of Product Origin

The customs laws of many nations require identification of the country of origin for imported goods. If true MFN were followed for all goods and all origins, then presumably there would be no need for such rules.[38] In fact, however, there is considerable differentiation of treatment of imports, depending on their origin. For example, if six countries who are GATT members form a customs union so as to free all trade among them from tariffs, then at least three levels of tariffs may apply to goods imported into one of the six: the GATT bound-tariff level for GATT members who are not in the customs union; tariff-free treatment for customs union goods; and tariffs on goods from other countries who are not GATT members. Thus, when widgets are imported, it may be necessary to determine from which of the three groups of countries the goods originated. In some cases there may be more than three categories, when other special preferential areas exist.[39]

In addition to the problem just mentioned, there is also the "transshipment" question. Let us say the countries A, B, and C belong to GATT, but country X does not. Suppose X ships tires to B, which then ships them to C, where C plans to charge a tariff of 12 percent. If C's tariff binding on tires is 10 percent, and C actually charges 8 percent on tires from A, can B claim benefits from either the GATT binding (10 percent maximum) or GATT's MFN clause for its tire shipment to C? The answer is no, because the products are not products of B. They are products of X, and the GATT obligations apply only to the *products* of GATT members.

Now imagine that X produces plastic pellets which are shipped to B. In B these are melted and extruded into combs. Can B ship the combs to C and claim GATT benefits? The key question is whether the products are those of B. Merely transshipping, or even merely repackaging X products, would probably not obtain for B the GATT treatment for the combs. But when substantial processing occurs, then B can claim the goods are now B's product. But how much processing is necessary?

GATT does not offer a single definitive answer to this question. Instead, each country, within the bounds of reasonableness, has the sovereign right to define its "rules of origin," which will govern the determinations of its customs officials about the "origin" of goods presented for import. Indeed, the same country may have several different "rules of origin" depending on the purpose of the regulation which governs the particular imports. However, there is a multilateral convention covering rules of origin. The Kyoto Convention[40] (concluded under the auspices of the Customs Cooperation Council in 1974) contains, in Annex D:2, certain rules for the determination of origin. The EC adopted the convention's rules in 1977. However, the U.S. only partially ratified the convention in 1983,[41] and did not accept the provisions on rules of origin.

The U.S.–Canadian FTA contains a measure regarding rules of origin, and this has already proven somewhat controversial.[42]

Two fundamental approaches to this problem have been widely used. One approach is a "substantial transformation" principle, by which a product becomes attributed to the most recent exporting country only if within that country there has been a "substantial transformation" of the input goods obtained from another country. One test, sometimes mentioned, is whether the goods have been changed sufficiently to cause them to be listed under a different heading in the tariff classification. The problem with this approach is that different parts of the tariff classification have different levels of detail, and somewhat arbitrary results can occur.[43]

A second approach is a "value-added," or percentage-value, approach. Under this principle, goods are attributed to the last country of export if that country has added a certain percentage of value to those goods. For example, the U.S. rule-of-origin law governing goods imported to the U.S. under the Generalized System of Preferences (GSP) rules is that the goods must in general contain 35 percent of their value in materials or processes originating in beneficiary developing countries.[44]

Occasionally, rules of origin generate complaints from exporting countries when such rules are deemed to unfairly restrict imports from the complainant. For example, the United States became quite upset about standards for rules of origin in some free-trade agreements between the EC and other European countries (former EFTA partners). Allegedly, the rule required 95 percent of the value of goods to be attributed to the free trade partner,[45] thus reducing the opportunity for the U.S. to sell parts or partly completed products to EC countries in competition with favored third-country goods.

6.5 The Tokyo Round Agreements and MFN

For reasons noted in earlier parts of this chapter,[46] there is a rational policy reason to require "code conditionality" for the application of benefits of a "side agreement" regarding particular trade principles such as antidumping, countervailing duties, or government procurement. None of the Tokyo Round codes actually requires "code conditionality"; that is, none of the codes prevents signatories from extending the benefits of trade treatment required under the code to GATT member nations who have not signed the code. Nevertheless, discussions during the Tokyo Round negotiations (1973-1979) noted the advantages of providing an incentive for nations to enter the disciplines of the codes, and limiting the benefits of the codes to signatories was observed to be a major incentive.

Still, GATT has a broad MFN obligation, and this can be deemed to require at least some of the code benefits to apply to all GATT members. For example, if fourteen GATT members sign a side agreement (or "code") which limits certain trade-restrictive practices in antidumping duty procedures, GATT members who did not sign the side agreement can claim that such beneficial treatment should be accorded their exports to the code signatories, because of the GATT MFN clause. Indeed, a GATT ruling in 1968 stated with regard to the 1967 Antidumping Code that GATT nations were entitled to beneficial treatment under the Code even if they had not signed the Code.[47]

The same issue has come up with regard to the Tokyo Round agreements. Anticipating this problem somewhat, the GATT Contracting Parties at the end of the Tokyo Round in 1979 adopted a decision which noted "that existing rights and benefits under the GATT of contracting parties not being parties to these Agreements, including those derived from Article I, are not affected by these Agreements."[48] This language, of course, leaves somewhat open the question as to when the MFN obligation specifically applies to the benefits under a Tokyo Round agreement.

The United States, when it implemented the Tokyo Round codes through its Trade Agreements Act of 1979,[49] did not extend the code treatment of three agreements to all other GATT parties. These three exceptions to MFN application by the U.S. of the codes were:

1. The Subsidies-Countervailing Duty Code
2. The Government Procurement Code
3. The Technical "Standards" Code

In each of these three cases, the U.S. statute required nations to themselves apply the code provisions before being entitled to code treatment by the United States. Thus, the question arises whether this approach violates U.S. obligations under Article I of GATT.

With respect to the second and third agreements listed above, there are significant arguments why MFN is not required. Government procurement is excepted from GATT Article III (national treatment) by explicit clauses in paragraph 8 of Article III. Article III treatment is incorporated by reference into GATT Article I, and so it has been argued and apparently accepted by tacit consent and practice that the GATT MFN obligation does not apply to government procurement.[50]

The Standards Code is essentially a set of procedures. Its substantive rule merely restates the principle of national treatment found in GATT Article III. Thus it can be argued that MFN does not apply to the mere offer of certain consultation procedures to foreign nations.[51]

The tough question has to do with the Countervailing Duty Code, and particularly with the code requirement that importing nations extend an "injury test"[52] so that imports found to be subsidized will not be subject to countervailing duties unless they are found also to be "injuring" the competing industry of the importing country. Although there are some arguments to the contrary, this particular code benefit appears to be the type of treatment of imports contemplated by the MFN language of GATT. Thus, when the United States denies the injury test to subsidized imports from countries who do not apply the code discipline, it arguably violates GATT Article I.

A definitive solution to this problem has not yet been formulated. In a complaint brought in GATT in 1981, India raised this issue after the United States refused an injury test for certain industrial fasteners imported from India. A GATT panel was appointed,[53] but before the panel got into the substance of the case, the United States and India came to a settlement agreement, which seemed to satisfy India.

6.6 MFN, Bilateralism, and Possible Trends: Some Conclusions

During the last decade, United States policymakers have been seriously tempted to use bilateral approaches to trade relations.

One of the earliest post-1945 departures from MFN by the United States was its exclusion of communist countries from such treatment in 1951.[54] During the 1960s, however, the United States began a series of moves that related to its more traditional trading partners, with the development and 1965 implementation of the U.S.–Canada Automotive Products Agreement.[55] The United States obtained a GATT waiver from its MFN obligations for this agreement, and there was at least some comment at the time that the agreement and waiver efforts helped undermine United States advocacy of MFN and multilateralism in connection with other GATT exercises such as GSP.[56]

Despite the various U.S. reservations and hesitations about GATT and some of its rules (chronicled in other chapters),[57] in general the United States has been a strong supporter both of the principles of multilateralism and of nondiscrimination as embodied in the unconditional MFN clause of GATT. These were pillars of United States policy during the drafting and formative years of the GATT. Through the 1960s, for example, the United States continued to express skepticism and hostility toward the proposal of developing countries to carve out an exception to MFN so as to allow a "generalized system of preferences" to provide particularly favorable conditions of trade for developing country exports. The United States was the last major industrialized country to implement the GSP policy, which had been called for by the international and multilateral institutions, including the GATT.[58]

Likewise, although the United States had tolerated and perhaps even favored the formation of the European Economic Community, partly for broad strategic reasons the United States found itself well into the 1970s increasingly skeptical about the benefits and directions of that and other regional trade groups in international trade. The United States particularly viewed the series of agreements between the European Community and about four dozen developing countries in the world, the so-called "Lomé Conventions" and their predecessors, as departing from MFN principles of GATT. The Congress specified certain conditions regarding this convention in its 1974 legislation, refusing to extend GSP benefits to developing countries who afforded preferential treatment to developed countries (so-called "reverse preferences").[59]

In the Tokyo Round (1973–1979), the United States also took some steps that departed from unconditional MFN. The Congress mandated in the 1974 Trade Act that the United States try to offset the "free-rider" problem, at least of industrial countries, by withholding MFN treatment from certain countries if they did not provide reciprocal advantages in the results of a negotiation. In addition, as we have seen, the United States has refused to give unconditional MFN status to all GATT members in connection with the obligations of three of the Tokyo Round codes.[60] Clearly, however, the United States was again concerned about the "free-rider" problem, and the need to provide an incentive for countries to enter into the discipline of the codes.

More recently, one of the most visible and acrimonious trade relationships has become that of the United States and Japan. The United States has essentially dealt with this on a bilateral level, rarely going to a multilateral forum, possibly partly because it has distrusted the effectiveness of that forum. At the end of the Tokyo Round, the United States entered into bilateral negotiations with Japan for additional and special concessions under the Government Procurement Code, for purchases by the Japanese telephone company, NTT.[61] Subsequently, United States and Japan bilateral meetings have occurred frequently, and certain institutional mechanisms have been set up to try to ameliorate their problems.[62] Europe also has had similar difficulties with Japan. Yet there does not seem to be an inclination on the part of either the United States or Europe, or for that matter Japan, to focus these troubled bilateral relationships in the multilateral forum of GATT, although some specific cases and representations have been made in GATT about the "Japan problem."[63]

From the beginning of the Reagan administration in 1981, statements by the United States Trade Representative and his deputies hinted at a willingness of the administration to consider the potential of bilateral actions, at least where multilateral activities seemed ineffective. For example, in November 1985, Ambassador Yeutter said:

We simply cannot afford to have a handful of nations with less than 5 percent of world trade dictating the international trading destiny of nations which conduct 95 percent or more of international commerce in this world. . . .

We would still like to go the GATT route with a new round. . . . That is the preferred course of action; but if those discussions bog down in Geneva two weeks from now to where it becomes evident that a new GATT round is not likely to occur, or simply could not occur with those issues included, then we would prefer to pass on a GATT round. In our judgment, this is not a negotiable issue. Services, in particular, must be in the Round or we are just not going to have a new GATT round from the U.S. standpoint; and we will have to confront those issues in a different way—plurilaterally or multilaterally.[64]

President Reagan reiterated this tough stance of the U.S. Administration:

To reduce the impediments to free markets, we will accelerate our efforts to launch a new GATT negotiating round with our trading partners, and we hope that the GATT members will see fit to reduce barriers for trade in agricultural products, services, technologies, investments and in mature industries. We will seek effective dispute-settlement techniques in these areas. But if these negotiations are not initiated or if insignificant progress is made, I am instructing our trade negotiators to explore regional and bilateral agreements with other nations.[65]

More recently, additional statements by high administration officials have hinted at a growing impatience on the part of the United States with multilateral approaches.[66] Congressional efforts to promote reciprocity also seemed to tilt away from multilateralism towards bilateralism in many respects.[67]

Even when ostensibly carrying out an MFN policy, sometimes an examination "beneath the skin" detects a strong bilateral effect. For example, in the escape clause case on motorcycles, the quotas that were actually implemented seem to affect Japan, but very few other countries.[68] Likewise, during the massive group of antidumping and countervailing-duty cases on steel brought in 1982, the United States found it convenient to negotiate extensively with the EC. In many ways, the EC and the United States bypassed the GATT in working out their conflicts in the context of that series of cases.[69]

In 1983, the United States proposed and subsequently implemented a preference for Caribbean basin nations.[70] Some suggested that this may have represented a major watershed in United States policy, although it was not particularly noticed to be such at the time. Later, a bilateral free trade area was negotiated and implemented with Israel.[71] Subsequently, a free trade agreement between the United States and Canada was completed.[72] Other such possibilities have been mentioned, such as Mexico (or more broadly, a North American FTA), Japan or ASEAN countries, although there seems to be considerable resistance to those possibilities.[73]

In sum, the inconsistent history of U.S. policy makes it difficult to forecast its future, but there are ample situations which have occurred, particularly during the last decade, that suggest the possibility that the United States has gradually moved away from its earlier adamant support of MFN and multilateralism, toward a more "pragmatic" (some might say "ad hoc") approach, of dealing with trading partners on a bilateral basis, and of "rewarding friends."

7   Safeguards and Adjustment Policies

7.1 The Policies and History of the Escape Clause and the International Structure for Safeguards

Introduction to the Policies of Safeguards

The term "safeguards" is generally used to denote government actions responding to imports which are deemed to "harm" the importing country's economy or domestic competing industries. These mechanisms often take an "import-restraining" form, whether they be increased tariffs, quantitative restrictions, "voluntary" restraints by the exporting countries, or other measures. As such, the term "safeguards" embraces a number of legal and political concepts, including that of the "escape clause" which for many decades has been built into national and international rules regarding international trade.[1]

If there were no "liberal trade" policy or practice, we would not need to consider safeguards as such. It is only because international economic policies have emphasized reduction of border barriers to trade that the subject of safeguards, as an exception to the general rule of liberal-trade opportunities, comes into play. Thus the question arises, Why should there be this type of exception to normal liberal-trade policies? In other words, what are the policies that justify the use of import restraints for escape-clause or safeguard reasons?

In general there seem to be two arguments for safeguard/escape-clause actions. There are other arguments for the use of import restraints, such as those related to national security needs.[2] But for safeguard actions — often described as actions of a temporary nature taken to impede imports which are causing "injury" to competing domestic industries — the policies seem to focus on an "economic adjustment" goal, plus a more general "pragmatic" recognition of practical politics.[3]

The economic-adjustment argument for safeguards can be stated briefly as follows: Imports, particularly recently increasing imports, often cause harm to selected groups within an importing society, even though they may in the long term and in the broader aggregate increase the welfare of that society. Competing domestic firms will be forced to "adjust" to the imports, either by improving their competitiveness (productivity, price, quality, etc.) or by moving resources out of production of the competing products into production of other products. This adjustment process has often been viewed as "temporary," even though it may be costly. Consequently, it is argued that a temporary period of time of some relief from imports will allow the domestic competing industry the opportunity to take the necessary adjustment measures.[4]

The problem, of course, is not this simple. There are many other causes of adjustment in an economy: consumer tastes change; government programs (pollution controls, defense spending, fiscal and monetary measures, energy conservation) change; and these also can create great adjustment costs and pressures.[5] Why, then, should adjustment caused by imports be a justification for government intervention and aid, when adjustment caused by other forces is not? Answers vary. First, the fact is that adjustments caused by forces other than imports do sometimes cause government responses to soften their impact; special additional unemployment compensation, investment aids, community actions, etc. are all occasionally employed to assist those affected by onerous adjustment demands.[6]

Second, it is often observed that producers are better organized to bring pressure on government than are consumers.[7] In addition, if adjustment is analyzed as an action required by the relative few so as to bring about broadly spread benefits to the many (like the government taking of property for public purposes such as a highway) there may be an equity argument for shifting the burdens of adjustment, from concentration on those few to the many who benefit, by distributing the burdens through taxes or higher prices.[8]

This leads easily into the second category of argument for safeguard policies, the pragmatic or political argument. This argument also recognizes that producers often are better organized to influence governments. It also recognizes that with respect to imports, an important interested party is the foreign producer-seller. However, this party does not vote in the importing country, so its influence in the decision-making process of that country is likely to be very small. In short, the political forces for border protection against imports are often formidable. Those who accept the policy arguments favoring liberal trade (i.e., disfavoring import barriers) feel that to insist too rigidly on the fullest application of their principles could lead to a general dismantling of the policies of the last several decades which have reduced import barriers. Consequently, they argue, it is better pragmatically to give in to the idea of temporary and limited import barriers for specific (and hopefully not too significant) cases as a way not only to alleviate some of the burdens of adjustment but also to diminish the pressures for a more drastic departure from the general approach to imports. Some would describe this approach as "buying votes."

Of course, burdens of adjustment can be alleviated by means other than import barriers (and some would challenge whether border barriers really do alleviate adjustment burdens). Direct government assistance (or tax relief) is another way to provide relief. Programs of this type also have been utilized in varying degrees. In the United States, for example, since the 1962 Trade Expansion Act there have been various programs of "trade-adjustment assistance," as we will see later in this chapter.[9]

The concept of safeguards, when safeguards are justified on "adjustment" grounds, bears a strong relation to concepts of so-called "industrial policy." If adjustment truly is the rationale for temporary safeguard actions to limit imports, then it follows that it might be appropriate for the government to demand an effective adjustment program from the industry concerned, and/or to tailor government policies (including direct or tax aids) to encourage and assist such adjustment. It is commonly thought that the government of Japan does a fairly effective job of this type (although some would challenge that proposition), and it is clear that Europe has tried this approach, albeit with varied success.[10]

What has been said in this section does not depend on the import trade being in any way "unfair." Traditionally, in trade policy circles "fair" trade has been sharply distinguished from "unfair" trade.[11] "Unfair" trade is normally deemed to include trade which has been influenced or promoted by such activity as "dumping," or government subsidies, or attempts by foreign sellers to evade legitimate regulations regarding the environment, fair competition, intellectual property protection, etc. To counter these activities, it is often said that an importing nation is justified in taking import-restraining actions of various types. Safeguards policies, on the other hand, are justified for those imports which are perfectly "fair" — i.e., untainted by any activity just described. Even if they are "fair," imports can cause burdens of adjustment for which there are arguments for granting government relief.

It often becomes extremely difficult, however, to keep the concepts of fair trade separate from those of unfair trade. First, what is fair in an increasingly interdependent world with a variety of economic systems is very hard to define.[12] Second, unfair trade also causes burdens of adjustment and so arguably qualifies for safeguards policies. The traditional GATT (and many national) systems often try to distinguish between unfair trade policies and safeguards policies by requiring a higher standard of harm to domestic competing industries, and a more stringent test of "cause by imports," for the safeguard policies to come into play. In practical institutional terms, due partly to the vagueness of the concepts involved (How does "serious injury" differ from "material injury"? How does "substantial cause" differ from "ordinary cause"?), nations have found it very difficult to keep these categories separate. Domestic complainants who are facing major burdens of adjustment comb the statutes and laws for ways to prevent imports, whether those laws be designed for unfair imports or based on safeguard policies. Escape-clause cases are sometimes brought when industries feel that imports are "unfair" but have difficulty in establishing the proof of unfairness required by the national administrative processes.[13]

In a world of increasing economic interdependence, there may be additional arguments which support safeguard programs. For example, let us suppose that there is trade between two countries with different economic systems. If one country is primarily "market economy oriented," while the other is "nonmarket" oriented, entrepreneurs in one may feel that economic practices in the other pose an unfair competitive threat.[14] American firms sometimes argue that they can compete as long as they do not have to compete against the treasury of the foreign country.

There is some validity to this argument. But to try to design national or international rules to respond to the situation is difficult. Many foreign practices are not unfair in the eyes of the foreign firms. The problem is rather that the differences between the two economies create stresses upon one of the economies when the two trade extensively. There may be nothing unfair about the practices of either, but the differences cause perceptions of unfairness, and in fact those differences may create political and adjustment pressures in one of the societies to change their system. Foreign government subsidies of exports cause importing-country government officials and businessmen to consider offsetting subsidies or other practices so as to preserve the values of their own economic system. By so preserving them, however, the system may in fact be altered. Arguably the international trading rules should be designed to allow at least some measure of independent choice of economic systems for societies. (We will explore these issues further in later chapters.[15])

One possible solution could be part of a safeguards policy. In this sense, safeguards become a sort of "border buffer" to prevent too much pressure for change of the domestic economic structure resulting from increased international trade originating in economies which are structured differently. But this "solution," as is true of so much of safeguards policy, runs the considerable risk of being overused as an argument for a variety of protectionist measures which could erode the basic principles of liberal trade.

History of Safeguards Measures

The modern era of safeguards measures stems from the beginning of the U.S. Reciprocal Trade Agreements program of its 1934 Act. It was this statute that launched the program of trade liberalization which is still the fundamental part of U.S. trade policy today, over fifty years later. Even in that original program, however, there were the germs of a safeguards policy.[16]

The "escape clause," as we currently think of it (a provision to allow temporary border barriers to imports when imports are increasing and can be shown to "injure" domestic competing industry), was first introduced into a U.S. Reciprocal Trade Agreement in the U.S.–Mexico Agreement of 1943.[17] In 1947, as the United States and twenty-one other countries began negotiating the texts of GATT and an ITO,[18] President Truman issued an executive order requiring that an escape clause be included in every trade agreement entered into under the authority of the U.S. Reciprocal Trade Agreements program. This order was amended slightly by subsequent executive orders, until 1951, when the escape clause was included by Congress in the Trade Agreements Extension Act.[19] It has remained a part of U.S. statutory law ever since, revised from time to time in the various extensions or amendments to the U.S. trade law.

The evolution of the language of the U.S. escape clause provides an interesting barometer of liberal or protectionist sentiment in Congress, but that also is not a story for this book.[20] It can thus be seen that the GATT escape clause (Article XIX) was a direct descendant of the U.S.–Mexican Trade Agreement clause of the same nature.

Types of Safeguard Actions

Although Article XIX is the central and most prominent safeguards provision of GATT, there are a number of measures that are taken under GATT (or in evading GATT) which also can be termed "safeguards."[21] Various GATT clauses afford an opportunity to nations to impose border-import restraints, some of which may be "safeguards" in the sense discussed above. For example, Article XXVIII of GATT provides a means by which a Contracting Party can permanently withdraw a tariff "binding" (obligation as to a maximum tariff). In doing so, a country becomes obligated to negotiate with other GATT parties interested in exporting the product concerned, with a view to establishing "compensation" by equivalent other concessions, or counterwithdrawals of concessions by the exporting countries.

Article XII of GATT provides some exceptions for Balance of Payments (BOP) situations, while Article XVIII also provides some exceptions for BOP problems of developing countries. These measures, as well as other measures of Article XVIII designed for developing countries, can often provide a GATT-legal cover for various border-import restraints that are motivated by safeguards policies. Waivers can be voted under GATT Article XXV, and one could analyze various other GATT explicit exceptions and see the possibility of using them for safeguards reasons. Finally, of course, there are a variety of techniques other than those permitted by GATT to effectively burden imports for safeguards reasons. The most prominent of these in recent years has been the "voluntary export restraint" (discussed later in this chapter).

During its history, the GATT has been more or less permanently concerned with the safeguards issue. From time to time discussions have been held in GATT on various aspects of the problem. Some of the later discussions, those in the Tokyo Round and after, relating to a proposed safeguards code and concerning "adjustment," will be discussed in section 7.8. Other exercises on the subject in GATT include the elaborate textiles program (with a series of textile agreements or "arrangements" being negotiated, even though they probably violate GATT obligations). During the early 1960s, partly in connection with textiles problems, the GATT Contracting Parties discussed generally the concept of "market disruption" and in November 1960 adopted a decision describing it and expressing the desirability of establishing consultative procedures for dealing with it.[22]

7.2   The Escape Clause in GATT and the United States

The most significant safeguard mechanism of the international trading system has been the escape clause. This mechanism exists in GATT as Article XIX. The escape clause also exists in the law of the United States and of other GATT contracting parties.[23] It will be recalled from section 7.1 that the GATT article was essentially drawn from earlier versions of United States law, but United States law has evolved through a number of texts over the more than thirty years of GATT history, whereas the GATT article has remained virtually the same as it was in the original GATT text.[24]

To grasp an overall picture of the mechanics of the escape clause, it is necessary to analyze it in five parts, as follows:

1. Prerequisite of increasing imports

2. Prerequisite of injury caused by increasing imports

3. Permitted responses or remedies

4. Responses of exporting countries, or "compensation"

5. Procedures

In this section, we will introduce both the GATT and the U.S. escape clauses, make a few comments about the strengths or weaknesses of some of the details of those clauses, and try to compare them. The next section will deal with the two prerequisites for some import-restraining action which would be permitted under Article XIX. The following section will deal with what actions are permitted, the response that is entitled to other interested parties, and a brief note about procedures generally.

To further map the law of the GATT escape clause, the analysis proceeds as follows:[25]

1. It must be shown that imports of a product are increasing either absolutely or relatively, *and* such increase must be a *causal* result of (a) unforeseen developments *and* (b) GATT obligations.

2. It must also be shown that domestic producers of competitive products are seriously injured *or* threatened with serious injury, *and* that this injury or threat is *caused* by the increased imports.

3. If 1 and 2 are shown, then an importing nation is entitled to suspend "such" GATT obligations in respect of such product for such time as necessary to prevent or remedy the injury.

4. The importing nation must consult with contracting parties (CPs) having a substantial interest as exporters. If agreement is not reached, exporting CPs have the right to suspend "substantially equivalent concessions."

5. Various procedures are defined under GATT or national laws.

As we shall see in the next section, for each of the two prerequisites for action under Article XIX, namely that 1) imports be increasing and 2) those increasing imports be causing injury to domestic industry (or a threat thereof), there exist several variable concepts that can give considerable difficulty to persons attempting to interpret the language of Article XIX (or comparable escape clauses in domestic law such as that of the U.S.). These variable concepts include the concept of "like or competitive product" and the concept of "domestic producers of competitive products" (i.e., the "industry"). For many cases these two concepts can become extremely significant. This is also true, incidentally, for injury tests applied under other trade policies, such as subsidy/countervailing-duty policy, and anti-dumping policy.[26]

In general, the GATT language of Article XIX with regard to these variable concepts, as well as to the various criteria, is quite ambiguous. This becomes particularly obvious when one compares that language to United States domestic law, which has evolved under the pressure of conflicting special and policy interests over thirty years of congressional activity. The language in the U.S. law has become increasingly detailed and elaborate, with particular definitions offered for much of it. GATT language is so general and ambiguous (and for the most part has not been articulated by interpretive decisions during its history) that nations can often claim to fulfill the GATT language prerequisites in many plausible but marginal circumstances.[27]

One interesting feature of the United States' relationship to GATT is that the increasingly detailed articulation of the United States escape-clause law has led to a situation where in some (but not all) respects the United States escape clause is a much more rigorous and disciplined body of law than the GATT. This means that industry groups within the United States who seek escape-clause relief find that in many circumstances they are not eligible under United States law for that relief, although they might well be eligible for such relief if the GATT language were the applicable legal standard.[28] This does not mean that the United States should abandon its own law and re-embrace the ambiguous GATT standards. There may be sound policy reasons, and certainly the congressional draftsmen thought there were sound policy reasons, to define U.S. law as has been done. Even so defined, many observers have felt that the International Trade Commission of the United States government has been given extraordinarily broad discretion and leeway within the U.S. statute to act either affirmatively or negatively in response to a petition for import relief.[29] On the other hand, it is probably true that the United States' law and procedures have led the United States to decline to utilize the explicit measures of escape-clause relief in cases (such as the automobile case[30]) where clearly other governments would not be so inhibited. One of the questions to be asked is whether such restraint leads to pressures on the United States government to evade its own law in applying safeguard measures that are not explicitly provided for in the statutes.

In summarizing some of these escape clause requirements in following sections of this chapter, I will mention some of these troubles, but space limitations will not enable me to go into all of them in detail.

The United States also has a specified procedure for escape-clause cases spelled out in its law. This procedure beautifully illustrates the uneasy tension among various branches of the United States government, particularly between the Congress and the executive.[31] An escape-clause procedure is initiated by petition to the International Trade Commission (ITC) of the U.S., where the six commissioners, sitting as an impartial body, must make the various determinations I have listed. Only if this body rules affirmatively on the existence of the necessary prerequisites (by a majority or tie vote) can a case be eligible for the remedies specified in the statute. If the determination is negative, the president has no authority to invoke the escape-clause remedies. He may try various other measures, such as "voluntary restraints," but often there are constitutional or other constraints on him which prevent him from doing so. If the ITC finds affirmatively, the case is forwarded to the president with a recommendation of remedial action. The president may, however, decide differently from the ITC whether any remedy is warranted, or what remedy to grant. Prior to the 1983 Supreme Court case which held legislative vetoes to be unconstitutional, the Congress was authorized in the statute to override a presidential determination which differed from that of the ITC.[32] Since then, however, although the Congress could enact a law changing a presidential escape clause determination, it would need a two-thirds vote of both houses to override a president's veto of such a law.

Since January 5, 1975 the U.S. ITC has received sixty-one[33] petitions for escape clause. It has turned down twenty-seven of these. Of the thirty-two cases received by President Reagan (two were pending at the

ITC as of September 1988), the president imposed some sort of import restraining measure on at least eleven occasions. However, in some cases, while the president technically turned down the ITC case, he through other means under other laws proceeded with action that has had an import restraining effect. The most notable case of this type was that of steel, in the early fall of 1984. A petition on carbon and certain alloy steel products[34] had been purposely timed so that the ITC ruling would land on the president's desk only several months prior to a presidential election, with the obvious attempt to put the president under political pressure to give some relief. In this case, while technically turning down the escape-clause cases, the president ordered his officials to embark on a world-wide extensive program of negotiating "voluntary restraint arrangements," to effectively lower the amount of steel being imported into the U.S. market.[35]

A 1985 GATT document[36] lists 123 explicit invocations or notifications of the GATT escape clause, but also notes that the list is likely to be incomplete. In many cases of explicit reliance on GATT Article XIX, no notification is sent to the GATT secretariat. Even more questionable, however, is the use of a large variety of import-restraining techniques, including voluntary restraints and "customs officials bottlenecks" (for example, those operating in France on video cassette recorders[37]), essentially for safeguards reasons without any explicit reference to safeguards rules. In most of these "implicit safeguard" cases, some of which in recent years have been called "gray area measures,"[38] there is little or no GATT discipline which effectively applies.

7.3 The Escape Clause: Legal Prerequisites and Practice

Introduction and the Problem of the "Variable" Legal Concepts

In the previous section I presented an overview analysis of escape clause law, as we know it from both GATT and U.S. statutes. Of the five parts of that analysis, in this section we take up the two which concern the "legal prerequisites" of the privilege to utilize escape clause remedies, namely:

1. It must be shown that imports of a product are increasing either absolutely or relatively, *and* such increase must be a *causal* result of (a) unforeseen developments, *and* (b) GATT obligations.

2. It must also be shown that domestic producers of competitive products are seriously injured, *or* are threatened with serious injury, *and* that this injury or threat is *caused* by the increased imports.

As I have indicated, there are several problematic "variable" concepts which cut across these prerequisites, and which merit some attention.

First, regarding the "product" definition: Is the product to be defined broadly, like "motor vehicles," or more narrowly, like "passenger vehicles with a value less than six thousand dollars"? The definition of the product can often be the determining factor of whether there have been increased imports, or whether those increased imports are causing injury to domestic producers of "like or directly competitive products."[39]

Likewise, the concept of "industry" is a variable one that causes great difficulty. In GATT the phrase is "domestic producers"; the phrase "domestic producers" is used in U.S. law, but more often the phrase "domestic industry" is determinative. Once again, whether this phrase is interpreted broadly or narrowly can be very significant. If the industry is deemed to consist of all "specialty steel" producers, significant declining employment and other harm to only the producers of tools may not provide the basis for an affirmative determination for relief.

A third variable concept is implicit in GATT Article XIX and comparable domestic laws, but is not expressed precisely. This is the contemplated time frame, particularly in the cause test. When trying to ascertain whether imports have increased, should one use a one- or a two-year period, or is it appropriate to use a much longer period? Obviously, the longer the period, the more likely it is that one can find at least some increase in imports, in a world where trade generally is increasing. Likewise, in considering a causal relationship, suppose that a GATT obligation was incurred in 1960, but that only in 1980 imports began to increase. Does the twenty-year gap insulate the relationship of the two events as being linked by cause?

Now we turn to some (but not all) of the specific legal elements of the escape-clause prerequisites, partly to illustrate some of the points I have made previously—namely, that the ambiguity of some of these elements reduces the effective discipline which the GATT escape clause was at least partly designed to impose on the use of "exceptional" import-restraining measures.

Increased Imports and Cause Thereof

What might seem to the layman to be a simple concept turns out on close examination to be very complex. Under GATT Article XIX, several questions are involved in examining the first prerequisite of safeguard relief, that of "increased imports." The language of GATT Article XIX states: "If, as a result of unforeseen developments and of the effect of the obligations incurred by a Contracting Party under this agreement, including tariff concessions, any product is being imported into the territory of that Contracting Party in such increased quantities. . . ."[40] Questions include:

1. What are "unforeseen developments"?

2. What are the obligations mentioned? Which type of obligations are meant?

3. What is the time frame for increased imports?

4. How is "product" to be defined—broadly or narrowly?

5. Must the increase be "absolute," or will "relative" increase suffice?

We will examine three of these five questions, namely questions 1, 2, and 5 (questions 3 and 4 involve the variable concepts already mentioned, and space does not permit going further here. The jurisprudence of the USITC is quite extensive in its coverage of these concepts).[41]

With respect to one of the tests for the "first cause requirement," that the increased imports be a result of "unforeseen developments," a major case was brought to the GATT early in its history concerning a United States escape clause action regarding imports of hatters' fur. In October 1951 a GATT working party reported on this case, and a portion of that report focused on the question of whether "unforeseen developments" had existed. It appeared that the basic development that had occurred since the negotiation of the concession was a change in the style of women's hat bodies. The United States argued that this change was an unforeseen development, whereas the chief exporting country, Czechoslovakia, argued the contrary. The working party basically fudged the issue. It said that it was "satisfied that the United States authorities had investigated the matter thoroughly on the basis of the data available to them at the time of their inquiry and had reached in good faith the conclusion that the proposed action fell within the terms of Article XIX. . . ."

The working party noted that "any view on such matter must be to a certain extent a matter of economic judgment and that it is natural that government should on occasion be greatly influenced by social factors, such as local employment problems."

Thus the working party concluded that there was "no conclusive evidence that the action taken by the United States under Article XIX constituted a breach of that government's obligations under the General Agreement."[42]

One is tempted to conclude that if change of style of women's hats is deemed to be an "unforeseen development," then there is nothing that could not be such a development! (The same could be said for the width of men's neckties!) In short, it is argued that the prerequisite cause of "unforeseen developments" has been essentially "read out" of the GATT agreement. Almost any increase in imports could arguably be an "unforeseen circumstance" itself. The need for follow-up to review this language of GATT was noted in a 1963 GATT report, but follow-up has not occurred.[43]

The causal prerequisite that increased imports be a result of "obligations" on the part of GATT requires a more extensive examination. The language seems clearly to include GATT obligations other than tariff concessions. Since certain parts of the GATT obligations (such as Article XI, prohibiting the use of quantitative restrictions) apply to all goods, it can be concluded that an escape clause case is possible for any imported good whatsoever, not just for those that are listed on the Schedule of Concessions of a GATT member. Of course, if the Schedule of Concessions of a GATT member does not include the product concerned, then the country has the freedom under GATT to raise the tariff on the product at its own discretion. It is only bound to maximum tariff on those items which it has agreed to place on its schedule.[44]

Until 1974, the United States law provided a causal link requirement between GATT obligations and increased imports. The expression of this causal link differed in various statutes. For example, in the 1951 statute the language read "increased quantities . . . as a result, in whole or in part, of the duty or other customs treatment reflecting such concession . . ." Thus, earlier U.S. law seemed to be focused on a tariff concession of a previous trade agreement. In reviewing United States trade policy in the early 1970s, the Williams Commission noted that this causal "link" requirement of the United States law had been responsible in a large number of escape-clause cases for a negative determination. The Williams Commission concluded that the credibility of the U.S.

escape-clause procedures was lessened by the rarity of affirmative determinations, which placed pressure on government alternative and on less explicit procedural devices. For these reasons the Williams Commission recommended that the United States change its law, and the Congress subsequently complied in the 1974 Trade Act. The "causal link" between obligations of GATT and the increased imports was deleted from United States law.[45]

It therefore can be argued that United States law, at least in this respect, no longer complies with its obligations under GATT. A counterargument, however, is that since in every escape-clause case there is a GATT obligation (such as Article XI) which applies, and since if there were no GATT obligation the United States would have the freedom to prevent such imports, any increased imports automatically have been at least partly caused by GATT obligations. Furthermore, the argument continues, the U.S. practice can in fact never be in violation of GATT obligation in this regard, even though the U.S. law makes no explicit mention of the particular GATT prerequisite.

Turning to a third issue—whether or not the increased imports can be relative, compared to "absolute"—the GATT has generally been interpreted to include the concept "relative increase." Thus, the absolute level of imports may remain constant or even decline, but if there is an increase relative to total domestic consumption in the percentage that those imports represent, there has been a "relative increase" of imports which satisfies the first prerequisite of GATT Article XIX. This interpretation stems from action in drafting the ITO charter at the 1948 Havana Conference, where the word "relatively" was inserted in the comparable text. Although this word was not added to the GATT text, a working party report adopted by the GATT CONTRACTING PARTIES in September 1948 stated that it was the understanding that the existing language of Article XIX was intended to cover such cases.[46]

It may be asked whether "a relative increase" should ever be the basis of a safeguards measure, since it would be hard to argue that imports are a cause of injury in such a circumstance. (The cause would, arguably, be found in the reasons for overall decline in consumption, such as change of taste, general economic decline, increase in consumer interest rates, or the like.) On the other hand, it might be argued that a "relative increase" concept addresses some of the "buffering" and "share the burden" policies necessary in an increasingly interdependent world.

The 1988 Trade Act retained the essential criteria for the U.S. escape clause, but the language of the new law places much more stress on the issue of "adjustment," giving the ITC an opportunity to recommend actions to facilitate adjustment and the president more opportunity to use remedies toward that end. Whether the actual results of cases will differ from those under the prior law is hard to predict.[47]

The "Serious Injury" Test and Cause Thereof

The GATT language states that the increased imports must be such as "to cause or threaten serious injury to domestic producers in that territory of like or directly competitive products . . ." This language also poses a series of interpretive problems, including: (1) the degree of causal link required between increased imports and the serious injury; (2) the definition of "threat" of injury; (3) the definition of "like or competitive product"; (4) the definition of "domestic producers," i.e., the scope of the "industry"; and (5) how to define "serious injury."

The problem of defining "industry" or "domestic producers" in this context is similar to the problem of identifying what are to be considered "like or directly competitive products." It should be noted that the word "competitive" is included—which is not the same as the phrase "like product," found in a number of other GATT clauses (such as Article I, relating to "Most Favored Nation"). This inclusion is clearly appropriate, since the objective in the escape clause is to ascertain when the imports are harming domestic industry, and obviously competitive products can so harm. The question remains, however, which products will be construed as being in a "competitive" relationship with others? Are apples competitive with oranges? Are black-and-white television sets competitive with color sets? Presumably, economists could develop some sort of "cross-elasticity" test, and thereby provide some interpretive assistance here. Nevertheless, the GATT jurisprudence being so sparse, there appears to be considerable leeway for interpreting this phrase. The approach taken by a particular government on this issue can strongly influence the outcome of whether an industry or group of firms is eligible for escape-clause relief.

For reasons mentioned before, we will put aside the time-frame matter again (which lurks in a number of these issues), leaving three additional issues for discussion here: the cause, the "threat," and the question of how to define "serious injury."

With respect to cause, one should note how broad and simple the GATT language is. The question of cause in the United States law, however, has been an extremely important one, being the determinative factor in the largest escape-clause case ever brought (the 1980 automobile case). Over the years contending factions in Congress have struggled with the definition of cause. The Williams Commission in 1972 recommended some relaxation of the causal test, suggesting the words "primary cause" in lieu of the statutory language which then required that imports be "the major factor in causing, or threatening to cause, such injury."[48] This language had been interpreted to denote a cause that was more significant than all other causes put together. The Congress went even a little further than the Williams Commission recommendation, in the Trade Act of 1974, lowering the cause requirement with the phrase "substantial cause." Standing alone, the phrase "substantial cause" could be very relaxed or ambiguous (implying anything that is not "insubstantial"?), but in close negotiations, the contending parties in Congress developed a definition which states: "the term 'substantial cause' means a cause which is important and not less than any other cause."[49]

One critical question is, How does one disaggregate causes? If, for example, a general depression or general condition of slack demand is considered one single cause, it would be very difficult for imports to override or equal that cause in importance. On the other hand, if one disaggregated the "depression" cause into components such as higher interest rates, increased oil prices, and declining government programs, then it would be easier to find that imports were not only important, but also not less so than any other cause.[50]

The GATT has no jurisprudence which helps on this question. Thus, governments in GATT can often justify their safeguard actions under the loose language of Article XIX, although the United States would not be able to act under its own escape clause, which has a more rigorous standard. Again, this does not necessarily mean that the United States should change its law; there are important policy reasons which led to the careful formulations of that law. Nevertheless, it is clear that if the policy reasons were to change, the United States would have scope to relax the criteria of its escape clause while still complying with its GATT obligations.[51]

"Serious injury" is also a phrase that is considerably ambiguous. It should be noted that GATT clauses concerning antidumping and countervailing-duty measures require "material injury," a concept which should be contrasted with the "serious injury" concept of Article XIX. U.S. law likewise tracks this difference (and also specifies several other degrees of injury).[52]

It is generally thought that the escape-clause standard for injury should be the highest or most difficult to establish, since the escape clause is designed to respond to situations which do not necessarily involve any unfair action by foreign exporters. Antidumping and countervailing-duty law, by contrast, are designed to respond to actions deemed improper, and therefore a less rigorous standard of injury is thought appropriate.

Nevertheless, it is often difficult to determine what precisely should be the criteria for determining serious injury. The United States statute has a detailed list of factors,[53] but the GATT jurisprudence is once again very sparse. The question of "threat of serious injury" is even more ambiguous. Since the concept of threat suggests trying to predict the future, even greater discretion is granted by this concept to national government authorities who desire to justify their safeguard actions under Article XIX of GATT.

It can be seen from the discussion in this section that the GATT escape clause can be quite easily abused or ignored. In any sort of strict jurisprudential sense, it is probably virtually impossible to determine with any degree of precision or clarity that a nation has not fulfilled its obligations under Article XIX. There will, of course, be cases in which reliance on Article XIX would clearly be considered subterfuge. Nevertheless, there is considerable room for clarification and negotiation leading to greater discipline in connection with safeguard measures as compared to Article XIX of GATT.

7.4 The Escape Clause: Remedies and Procedures

In this section, we turn from the prerequisites for invoking the escape clause to the nature of the remedies under that clause and the procedures involved in obtaining them.[54] I will describe these under three subtopics. First we will look directly at the remedy afforded by Article XIX. The second subtopic in this section will be that of "compensation" negotiations, which are the compliance or enforcement technique of GATT Article XIX and, more basically, of the bindings and concessions in the schedules. Third, we will turn briefly to a few other procedural questions.

Escape-Clause Remedies

The GATT language states that if the prerequisites of Article XIX are found, "the Contracting Party shall be free, in respect of such product, and to the extent and for such time as may be necessary to prevent or remedy such injury, to suspend the obligation in whole or in part or to withdraw or modify the concession."[55] Apparently what is contemplated is a temporary measure. This can be contrasted with Article XXVIII, where the privilege of a permanent withdrawal of a concession or tariff binding is given, subject to conditions and compensatory negotiations.[56]

Three questions come immediately to mind: What type of government action is contemplated by the remedies mentioned in Article XIX? How long may such remedies remain in force? And, of course, the all-important MFN question (discussed in section 7.5).[57]

It will be noticed that a contracting party is given the freedom to "suspend the obligation in whole or in part or to withdraw or modify the concession" of "such product." It seems clear that this concept embraces more than simply withdrawing or modifying the tariff concessions; it appears to apply to any of the obligations of GATT, including the obligation of Article XI which prohibits the use of quantitative restrictions. Certainly the practice in GATT, and in United States law under GATT, has been to utilize non-tariff barriers on a number of occasions.[58] U.S. law explicitly authorizes not only an increase in tariff, but the use of quantitative restrictions, tariff quotas, combinations of those, and orderly marketing agreements.[59] The 1988 Trade Act puts more stress than does previous law on the use of the measures "to facilitate adjustment"—which, however, include the above remedies as well as adjustment assistance.[60] Other countries have likewise used all these measures, but have not always notified GATT that they are acting under Article XIX. In any event, the practice seems well enough established in GATT that almost any import barrier can find legal cover in the language of Article XIX when responding to the prerequisites of an escape-clause situation. In policy terms, of course, there are strong arguments that any import restraints should be "price" and not "quantity" oriented. Any use of quotas or restraints based on quantity will unfortunately reduce incentives of producers to be competitive in price or other product characteristics.[61] Yet it seems the GATT rules, at least in practice, do not reinforce these policy goals.

The time requirement is also ambiguous. The language says "for such time as may be necessary to prevent or remedy such injury," which seems to suggest a temporary measure, although the language at the end of the sentence, about "withdrawing or modifying" a concession could imply a more permanent measure. In any event, a country has

Article XXVIII if it wishes to do something permanent.[62] Article XIX seems designed for the application of temporary measures. The U.S. law, for example, had a five-year time limit for measures under its escape clause, which now has been extended to eight years under the 1988 Trade Act.[63] How long a measure may be invoked as "temporary," in the Article XIX sense, is again a subject which could use further clarification.

The remedy language of Article XIX also says "to the extent . . . as may be necessary to prevent or remedy such injury. . . ." How much in the way of import restraints is necessary, to "remedy" the serious injury caused by imports, is obviously a determination which is subject to great discretion of national governments.

Compensation and Compliance

In general, observers believe that the GATT tariff concessions and bindings, resulting from the seven rounds of trade negotiations and embodied in many thousands of pages of country tariff concessions, have been among the most stable and most followed of the GATT obligations. For some reason, although the temptation to evade the GATT obligations has been very great over the years (and some would say has grown stronger), the tariff concessions perhaps because of their explicitness and detail, have been widely complied with. One reason for this compliance may be the visibility or explicitness of a government's departure from a tariff binding. Some suggest that another of the reasons for this is the effective "sanction" built into the GATT structure for departure from tariff obligations.

The GATT does not use the term "sanction," nor the term "retaliation," but it has a structure for requiring a "payment" from a country which departs from its schedule obligations in the context of the escape clause of Article XIX or elsewhere. This structure has been embellished by considerable practice over four decades of GATT history, and is not immediately apparent in the GATT language. Article XIX requires that a Contracting Party using the escape clause shall give notice to the GATT. Article XIX also gives to exporting countries having a substantial interest in the product concerned an opportunity to consult (unless the "critical circumstance" exception is invoked). If consultations do not result in any "agreement," the importing country can nevertheless act under Article XIX, but in that case "the affected contracting parties shall be free . . . to suspend . . . such substantial equivalent concessions or other obligations under this Agreement . . . which the CONTRACTING

PARTIES do not disapprove." This is deemed to be the "compensation" requirement of Article XIX.

Because it is generally recognized that suspension of obligations has a negative impact on the general policies of liberalization under GATT, it has been the practice in GATT for negotiations to include the possibility that the importing country invoking the escape clause will grant to interested exporting countries alternative concessions on other products by way of compensation, so as to avoid the need of the exporting countries to counter the escape clause by suspending liberal trade concessions.[64]

In fact, in the political discourse of countries considering import barriers, one can note the importance of arguments that potential "retaliation" or "compensation" will be damaging and will therefore provide reasons to avoid using import restraints. One of the problems of recent years, as the general average of tariffs has declined to a very low point, is that it has become increasingly harder for countries invoking safeguard measures to effectively compensate affected countries by granting alternative concessions. Usually the "compensation bill" is sufficiently large that it becomes very difficult to find any products which have a sufficiently high tariff to make an alternative concession meaningful, except for products which are already very sensitive and subject to the pressures of domestic interests who claim they are already harmed by imports. This "compensation bill" then adds pressure upon government to find alternative or "nonescape clause" safeguarding techniques, such as voluntary restraints. One option that Contracting Parties might consider in negotiating a more disciplined safeguard system would be the relaxation of the compensation requirement in appropriate circumstances, such as cases where higher degrees of the otherwise ambiguous criteria have been fulfilled.[65]

The risk of any such reform, however, might be to lessen the effective enforcement or compliance with the GATT schedule obligations. Indeed, when escape-clause measures are contemplated it has sometimes been the case that the interested exporting nation has "leaked" lists of potential products that might be subject to "retaliation," as a way to focus the attention of the importing country on the possible consequences of its action.[66]

Under U.S. law, the executive sometimes did not have authority to give "compensation" to foreign governments by lowering alternative U.S. tariff rates. When the so-called general "negotiating authority"[67] was in effect, the president could use that authority to enter a "trade agreement" which supplied the compensation; but in periods such as 1967 to 1975 such general authority had lapsed, and so the president lacked authority to offer compensation when the U.S. exercised escape-clause remedies. Section 123 of the Trade Act of 1974 remedied that lacuna, and explicitly gives the president a certain amount of compensation authority.[68] This is an interesting example of the influence of GATT on U.S. law[69] and of a U.S. statutory provision that makes sense only in the context of U.S. participation in GATT.

Some Procedural Questions

GATT Article XIX requires notice, as I have mentioned, and also establishes some time limits for the completion of compensation negotiations. Almost invariably these time limits are missed, and the GATT, by concerted action, or by agreement of the parties (including the negotiating parties), extends the time limits.[70]

The procedural requirements of Article XIX do not speak to the nature or process by which a nation shall determine its own escape-clause procedures. This raises the question of whether a nation has complete freedom in that regard. For example, a nation which has a powerful executive endowed with the authority to limit imports whenever it desires, might invoke Article XIX by a simple statement of the executive, arguing that the prerequisites of Article XIX have been fulfilled. There is nothing explicit in GATT that prevents that possibility. On the other hand, it is possible that a parliamentary body, such as the United States Congress, could make the necessary "finding" that the prerequisites of Article XIX have been fulfilled, and could take action that it could defend as permissible under Article XIX.[71] Of course, in all such cases, the "compensation" requirement would be inhibitory. But it may be asked whether a revised international surveillance mediation for safeguards actions should establish some norms for national procedures — including, for example, adequate notice, the right to present counter evidence and arguments, "transparency" (published statement of facts and reasoning), and possibly some appeal process.

7.5 The Escape-Clause MFN Question

During the past decade, the most controversial issue of Article XIX of GATT has been the question of whether a remedy under it must be applied in a nondiscriminatory manner, i.e, on a "MFN" basis. What does this mean?[72]

If a country becomes authorized to utilize Article XIX, because the prerequisites have been fulfilled, then when it applies the remedy (which would generally be import restraints of one type or another), it might do so in two ways. First, if it were to apply that remedy in a MFN manner, and if it were to utilize tariffs, there would be one tariff for the products of all MFN (GATT) nations. If it were to utilize quantitative restrictions, the concept of MFN would become considerably more difficult. Quotas are almost "inherently discriminatory," unless a country uses so-called "global quotas," or auctions the quotas[73]. Generally speaking, however, since global quotas can cause a rush by importers to fill them early in a prescribed time period (and thus may result in no trade at the end of that time period), and since governments have not used an auction system very often, governments tend to prefer a more explicit allocative system of quotas. Usually quotas are granted on a country-by-country basis. In practice and under the language of GATT Article XIII that deals with quotas, as well as in the general practice under that article and in GATT history, it is generally considered that a nondiscriminatory quota system establishes the amount of quotas by referring to a recent historical period, "a previous representative period," and the amount or proportion of trade that each country had during that period. This, of course, often discriminates against any new entrants to the market.

This is a source of considerable bitterness for countries, such as developing countries, who are trying to develop new industries. It is probably not entirely a fair approach for that reason, and consequently countries may use some discretion to try to accommodate new market entrants. The result, of course, is that governments have considerable discretion in the setting of quotas; and thus, although they may claim to be applying import restraints on a MFN basis, upon close examination it might be determined by impartial observers that considerable discrimination has resulted from their actual application of quotas.[74]

Moreover, a government may expressly desire to depart from MFN application under Article XIX. Often the argument is made that it is wise to do so, because there are only a few countries which "cause" the increase of imports that has led to the invocation of Article XIX. These would be countries whose share of the importing country's market has grown fairly rapidly and recently. Obviously, these are likely to be the new market entrants. Some argue that in applying a safeguard measure, it is least disturbing to do so to only a few countries, rather than in a non-discriminatory across-the-board manner. It is sometimes asked: "Why should countries who are not responsible for the increase in imports have to bear the burden of an escape-clause action?"

The counter policy argument is that the escape clause is designed to provide temporary relief from fair imports, not to respond to unfair imports.[75] Those countries whose share of the importing country's market have been increasing most rapidly are doing exactly what they are supposed to do under world trade policies of the GATT. They have become more efficient; they are producing better and less expensive goods, and therefore the market is responding by favoring them. To penalize those economies is to target the very industries which have been achieving the results which international trade policy is designed to achieve. It is therefore argued that only MFN or nondiscriminatory application of the escape-clause import barriers will allow the more efficient to continue on their praiseworthy path of providing better goods for less cost.

Those are the basic policy arguments. Now let us turn to the "legal" arguments.[76] The language of Article XIX states that the invoking Contracting Party shall be free "to suspend the obligation" of GATT, which is deemed to be linked to the increased imports. It is not explicit as to which obligations are considered. It is therefore argued that the Article I MFN obligations of GATT are within the scope of those which can be "suspended" in Article XIX. For this reason, it is claimed that Article XIX legally and technically allows a discriminatory import restraint remedy.

A counterargument focusing on the language of Article I, is that it is unlikely that the MFN obligation is responsible for the increased imports. The increased imports are related causally to the domestic demand for imports of the goods generally, and the domestic consumer is usually indifferent to their origin.

An important interpretive practice in GATT is invoked by the latter argument. One result of the 1948 negotiations for an ITO charter held in Havana was an interpretive note inserted in the draft charter that stated: "It is understood that suspension, withdrawal or modification under . . . [the escape clause provision] must not discriminate against imports from any Member country, and that such action should avoid to the fullest extent possible, injury to other supplying Member countries."[77]

A GATT working party in 1953 indicated that the same approach was taken for the GATT escape clause.[78] Despite its ambiguity, this ITO language has been one basis of the legal argument that the GATT Article XIX requires MFN application.

Starting in the Tokyo Round safeguards negotiations, the contrary position has been taken by the European Economic Community. The community, as well as some Scandinavian countries, have offered arguments mentioned previously that they are authorized to take discriminatory measures under Article XIX. This position has aroused intense opposition from many developing countries who see themselves as the potential targets (as "new entrants" to the market) of safeguards measures. It has also resulted in some debate on this subject among scholars.[79]

One of the arguments used in favor of a discrimination approach is that in fact the practice in GATT for several decades has shown a tolerance for the use of discriminatory safeguards measures. For example, it is noted that there are many voluntary-restraint agreements, and that these agreements are inherently discriminatory in their approach.[80] It has also been pointed out that on several occasions the United States and others have either used quotas in a *de facto* discriminatory manner or have negotiated orderly marketing agreements under U.S. domestic escape-clause law which were effectively discriminatory.[81] In addition, in at least one case there has been a fairly explicit application of a discriminatory safeguards measure by another country.[82]

In a recent GATT panel determination, however, the panel seemed explicitly to endorse an MFN obligation for Article XIX remedies, saying: "The Panel was of the view that the type of action chosen by Norway, i.e. the quantitative restriction limiting the importation of the nine textile categories in question, as the form of emergency action under Article XIX was subject to the provisions of Article XIII which provides for non-discriminatory administration of quantitative restriction. . . ."[83]

The United States position in the GATT negotiations has varied a bit. It began in early parts of the Tokyo Round negotiations by strongly supporting the nondiscriminatory approach of Article XIX. At one point, however, it seemed to relax this stance. In recent years, however, the United States apparently has been taking a stronger pro-MFN approach to Article XIX.[84]

Where does this all leave us? As is true of so many legal issues in the GATT (or other international obligations), it is hard to say with complete assurance and precision what the interpretation of an international obligation should be. Pragmatically, one would try to predict (as U.S. lawyers often do with respect to the U.S. Constitution and the Supreme

Court) what would be the outcome of the controversy in the procedures of GATT, such as a panel determination if a dispute were taken under Article XXIII of GATT. More difficult, one would try to predict what practice would be considered and tolerated in GATT as consistent with the GATT obligations, over a longer period of time. It is very hard to make such predictions, given the fairly strong opposing stands of important trading partners. It does seem to me that if the MFN matter were to go to a panel in GATT, the panel would likely rule on the basis of the Havana Charter and the early GATT report that MFN is required by Article XIX remedies. The fact that there have been departures from a rule over a period of time, and that those departures have been "tolerated" (but not tolerated as fulfilling or changing the legal obligation) is not evidence of practice of an interpretation of an international agreement. Virtually all agreements are violated at some point or another, and some are violated more than others. A pattern of violations should never be the basis on which to argue that the underlying obligation itself has been changed. Something more would be needed, such as expressions consistent with the customary international law concepts of *opinio juris*.[85]

In addition, since there is at least some ambiguity in the MFN question, it seems important to examine the underlying policies of the GATT agreement as a whole, and particularly of Article XIX in the context of that GATT agreement. Those policies seem to reinforce the concept of MFN. As I have stated, it seems doubtful that one could argue that the MFN obligation is one of those which is "causally linked" to the increase of imports. In addition, the economic concepts of comparative advantage and the goal of liberal trade policies to allow more efficient producers to develop and enter the market reinforce an approach that would negate discriminatory application of Article XIX remedies.

It can be argued pragmatically, however, that there are so many substantial deviations from the nondiscriminatory approach in safeguards that world welfare would be better served by some (even grudging) recognition of those deviations if they could then be channeled and disciplined so that the worst abuses would be inhibited. This is a "second best" (or third best) argument for the real world.[86] The dilemma is that to "recognize" the deviations might be to entrench or encourage more of them. One diplomat has therefore argued (somewhat cynically, perhaps) that the "law" should not be changed, even though "Professional trade policy administrators know that measures can usually be devised which deal with the category of imports which give rise to the perceived problem."[87]

7.6 Law and Practice Regarding Adjustment

Adjustment and Adjustment Assistance

Early in this chapter[88] I noted that there is a significant argument which supports government intervention in the market to ease the pain of the costs of adjustment which are caused by imports. I suggested the eminent domain analogy. Import restraints, of course, do some of this, but they may be not only costly but self-defeating in the long run, when uncompetitive industry sectors are induced to continue production by the subsidization which import restraints confer. Many economists would argue that it is preferable to grant government financial assistance to the adjusting producers, especially if such assistance is designed so as to "nudge" the recipients toward effective adjustment policies. Such policies may involve moving completely out of production of particular uncompetitive products, or restructuring the producer plants and organization so as to become competitive.[89] Since the source of such aid is spread generally through the government fiscal policies, it is arguably fairer than import restraints, which impose costs only on certain segments of the population. For example, restraints on the imports of computer chips impose additional costs on domestic companies, which use such chips in their products. Whether those costs can be passed on to another limited segment of the population—those who buy computers—may depend in turn on whether restraints are imposed on the imports of computers.[90]

The problem is that many observers feel that the adjustment assistance programs that have been tried, in the U.S. and elsewhere, have failed to accomplish their purpose and have been very expensive. In times of budget constraints, as well as of skepticism about government "welfare" subsidies, it has become increasingly difficult to persuade political leaders to fund adjustment assistance.

International Norms

Very little exists in the way of legal norms or explicit institutional obligations, in the sense of positive obligations to promote or create advantageous conditions for economic adjustment in world trade. Most of the international legal and institutional activity concerning adjustment has been in the context of safeguards and escape-clause questions. From time to time, the issue has been raised as to whether there could be designed an international obligation upon nations to promote internal structural adjustment to facilitate the economic policies which lie behind the GATT/Bretton Woods System for international trade. It is possible that some sort of obligation could be implied from some of the looser or more general clauses of GATT. For example, in Article XXXVI of GATT there is a desire expressed that developed countries provide favorable and acceptable conditions of access to world markets for products on which developing countries depend. Likewise, in Article XXXVII of GATT, developed contracting parties are called upon to "give active consideration to the adoption of other measures designed to provide greater scope for the development of imports from less-developed contracting parties. . . ." Article XXXVIII of GATT also reinforces this viewpoint, with general admonitions for contracting parties to collaborate "in seeking feasible methods to expand trade for the purpose of economic development."

In addition, from time to time there have been committees or working parties in GATT that have studied the problem of structural adjustment. In November 1980, the GATT Council established a working group on structural adjustment which has examined several studies by the secretariat with respect to this problem.[91]

At the November 1982 ministerial meeting of the GATT Contracting Parties, the CONTRACTING PARTIES decided to continue the "work on structural adjustment and trade policy in order to focus on the interaction between structural adjustment and the fulfillment of the objectives of the General Agreement. . . ."[92] Subsequent GATT activities have not changed this picture of little progress.[93]

By way of comparison, it is interesting to note the impact of International Monetary Fund actions, including the IMF "Standby Agreements." With the pressure it can bring with the bait of financial resources and threat of withdrawal of those resources, it can be argued that the IMF has had some profound impact on economic policies of its members.[94] Whether it has been able to influence micro policy to achieve "structural adjustment" would be a subject for another study.

Although it has occasionally been suggested that an international norm should be adopted which would obligate structural adjustment measures in the context of GATT and safeguard actions, so far such a norm seems to be only a question for discussion in the future.

United States and Adjustment Assistance

An innovation of the 1962 Trade Expansion Act in the United States was the introduction of the concept of "adjustment assistance" payments to workers dislocated due to imports. The Act provided for special unemployment compensation benefits for workers and certain tax benefits and other assistance to import-affected firms. These benefits, however, were tied to the then criteria of the escape clause, and as noted in section 7.3(b), under those criteria few escape-clause cases succeeded. Likewise, few petitions for adjustment assistance succeeded. (Similar but slightly relaxed provision put into the legislation implementing the U.S.-Canada Automotive Products Agreement also provided little actual relief.)

One of the 1971 Williams Commission recommendations was to make the adjustment assistance prerequisites easier to fulfill than those for the escape clause, and thus to suggest a policy preference for such assistance. The 1974 Trade Act accomplished this, establishing easier criteria for units of workers to obtain "certification" so that workers could obtain special benefits due to imports. These criteria were that a "significant number or proportion" of workers in a unit be totally or partially separated from employment and that sales or production of the unit be declining, all because imports had "contributed importantly" to these conditions.

At the same time, the benefits for workers were considerably improved, including weekly unemployment compensation often much better than that provided by state unemployment benefit plans, plus special allowances for retraining, job search, and relocation. (In addition, while assistance to firms was cut back, some modest provision for assistance to "communities" affected by imports was provided.)

One result was a surge in cost of the program, which peaked in 1980 when 530,000 workers received a total of $1.6 billion. At that point the "budgeteers" interceded, and in subsequent years the program was cut back by various administrative and legislative changes. In 1985 the Reagan Administration urged repeal of the program, but the Congress extended it in 1986 for six years. The 1988 Trade Act added further refinements to the program, and in addition changed the language in the basic escape clause to stress the adjustment goal.[95]

Adjustment assistance, although seemingly based on sound economic principles, has in the eyes of many failed to achieve its goals of either assisting adjustment or winning additional support for a liberal-trade policy. Labor unions have called it "burial insurance" and have refused to be overly impressed by the program. Costs have been difficult to contain without imposing inequities on workers (why should *trade*-affected workers be treated more favorably than other unemployed workers?). Possibly part of the reason for this less-than-happy appraisal is that the program assumes workers are "mobile," when in many cases they are not. Workers have deep ties to their communities, own homes there, have spouses with jobs there, have children with school and activity ties there. Maybe they don't want to move. Why, then, should a government program be based on measures which seem to ignore such preferences? Alternatives to the program need study. Would it be better to use a "regional aids" approach (as in Europe) to assist communities to develop new businesses which would utilize the idled manpower resources already there? Or would this approach too closely resemble the notion of "industrial policy" despised by some?

7.7 Export Restraints, Agreements, and Arrangements

ERAs and Their Policies

One of the most troublesome and increasingly common types of safeguard action during recent decades has been the export restraint imposed by an exporting country on behalf of or at the request of an importing country.[96] A variety of terms have been used for these, including "Export Restraint Agreement" (ERA), "Orderly Marketing Agreement" (OMA), "Voluntary Export Restraint" (VER), "Voluntary Restraint Agreement (or Arrangement)" (VRA), etc. There is no definite or preferred term, although there are a number of different types of arrangements, and some of the terms fit the different types better than others. For example, one can identify three particular categories of arrangements:

1. Government-to-government arrangement
2. Private exporting industry to private domestic competing industry
3. Importing government contact with the private exporting industry

Other variations exist, of course, and another dimension is the degree of formality that is involved. The formality could be as high as an explicit international agreement between governments, or something considerably lower, such as mere "predictions" by an exportation industry association as to what would be their "likely" exports to a given country during the next brief time period. On many occasions, an exporting government will act "unilaterally," without any formal indication of international agreement or even any consensus arrangement; but of course it will have done so because it has received signals of one type or another from the importing government or competing industry, that there are risks in continuing to export at the existing or potential level.[97]

These arrangements have been very troublesome and have been the subject of considerable criticism from GATT bodies as well as from economists and government officials. One of the problems is their "lack of transparency": many of the arrangements are secret, or at least there is an attempt to keep them secret. Another problem is that almost invariably these arrangements have not been subjected to the scrutiny or checks of concrete domestic or international proceedings. Consequently, there is a considerable lack of discipline over the issues that have been analyzed in previous sections of this book. One suspects that the arrangements can often result from particular political favors being rendered by governments to certain domestic constituent groups to enhance the possibility of reelection or other favors from the constituent groups. Finally, in most cases the arrangements have dubious legal status.

Legal questions involve both international obligations and national laws. In many countries, there is no essential inhibition of these types of arrangements by national law, with the possible exception of restriction of executive authority to enter into such arrangements without some parliamentary action. When legal obstacles appear to be present, often a very informal type of arrangement is utilized, so that no sustainable constitutional argument of *ultra vires* is possible. In the United States, the *ultra vires* argument has considerable importance, given the constant tensions between the executive and the Congress and the limited nature of delegations of authority under the Constitution to either body.[98] But as to very informal arrangements, it is probably the case that the executive has very broad discretion to "encourage" or to "inform" foreign governments who are inclined to impose some sort of export restraints on a product which has been causing "difficulties" for a competing domestic market in the United States. In addition, in the light of the Tariff and Trade Act of 1984, the U.S. government has somewhat stronger arguments that even explicit export restraint agreements with foreign governments are authorized by Congress, at least for steel.[99]

U.S. Law

In the United States, there is an extremely important additional legal inhibition on certain types of arrangements for export restraints, namely the United States antitrust laws.[100] Under the "effects doctrine" of that law, private firms abroad who collude to limit exports to the U.S. market may find themselves liable either to criminal prosecution under U.S. law or to private civil treble damage actions by aggrieved plaintiffs in the United States. Since the arrangements are often at least tacitly encouraged by the United States government, the risk of criminal prosecution by bodies of the United States government is usually small. However, the government is not able, under existing United States law, to control the possibility of private treble damage actions, and it is the threat of the exposure to these actions that has been a major inhibiting factor for the United States to use voluntary or other kinds of export-control arrangements as a major part of its trade policy. Consequently, the United States generally wants the exporting country's restraints to be in the form of governmental measures which could sustain the "sovereign compulsion" defense in an antitrust lawsuit.[101]

Of course, under the U.S. escape clause, there is explicit authority for the president to negotiate "orderly marketing agreements" on a government-to-government basis, and this authority has been used on a number of occasions.[102] In addition, the president has certain other explicit statutory authorities to enter into arrangements with foreign governments whereby those governments will limit exports of certain commodities to the United States.[103] This is true in the categories of agricultural commodities and textiles. When the products do not fall within those categories, the legal situation becomes more complicated.

GATT and ERAs

Under the GATT obligations, many and probably most of the so-called "export restraint arrangements" are probably inconsistent with the obligations of GATT. GATT does not apply to the actions of private companies, so this amounts to a major loophole which allows those governments who are not inhibited by antitrust or other laws from encouraging private-firm restraints on exports from doing so. But with respect to government actions which restrain exports, GATT Article XI is clearly attracted. This article states: "No prohibitions or restrictions other than duties, taxes or other charges, whether made effective through quotas, import or export licenses or other measures, shall be instituted or maintained by any Contracting Party on the . . . exportation or sale for export of any product destined for the territory of any other Contracting Party." This sweeping language would seem to embrace virtually any export control maintained by governmental authority.[104]

The problem in GATT is a more pragmatic one: Who will make any sort of formal complaint? The country establishing the restraints is usually doing so at the behest or signal of an importing country. The country which establishes the export restraints would hardly complain against itself in GATT. The country who is most affected, namely the importing country that sent the signal, would hardly complain either, since the action is precisely what it had hoped for. Other countries in GATT would find it difficult or awkward to complain, because they normally would not be able to establish that they themselves have been harmed (under doctrines of nullification or impairment of Article XXIII, or with other less formal considerations). Thus, there have been a paucity of cases in GATT with respect to export restraints. One possible complainant country in the GATT context might be a country C, who felt that as a result of an export-restraint arrangement between A and B, exports of A were diverted from the B market, thus putting greater competitive pressure on the market in C. This was basically the complaint of the United States steel industry in a domestic United States proceeding under the U.S. Section 301, in 1976.[105] In that proceeding, however, the United States government declined to take the case because there had not been established adequate evidence of actual diversion or harm.[106]

More recently, in GATT the European Economic Community has successfully challenged a U.S.–Japan agreement concerning Japanese exports of computer chips. The panel found, *inter alia*, that Japanese monitoring (with "administrative guidance") of export prices was inconsistent with GATT Article XI commitments.

Economists generally view the export restraint agreement as one of the more damaging devices affecting principles of trade policy of the GATT. In addition, from the point of view of the importing country, it is probably economically the most costly procedure that could be followed. Unlike a tariff, the export restraint does not give the government any revenue to offset some of the general welfare economic costs of the import restraints.[107] Indeed, it generally appears that the exporting country, or at least the exporting industry, can reap substantial "monopoly rents" through the process. This probably explains why some countries seem to be so willing to enter into such arrangements. Indeed, these rents have in some cases been viewed as a substitute for the GATT compensation requirement.

Textiles and the Multifiber Arrangement (MFA)

One of the most pronounced anomalies of the GATT system and the liberal-trade policies of the post-World War II period is the elaborate system of "voluntary agreements," which perpetuates a quota system for international trade in textiles and clothing. Today this is called the "Multifiber Arrangement" (MFA).[108] An extensive study entitled "Textiles and Clothing in the World Economy" was completed by the GATT Secretariat in 1984,[109] and this report (noting origins dating back to 1936) describes the thirty-year history of this arrangement—starting with a Short-Term Arrangement (STA) on textiles in 1961 and 1962, followed by a succession of long-term agreements (LTAs) lasting from 1962 to 1973, when the LTA was replaced by the first MFA in 1974. Subsequently, MFA II entered into force in 1978, and MFA III in 1982 (extended in 1986 to last until 1991).[110]

All of these arrangements involved a substantial departure from the policy and rules of GATT. It is noted in the GATT study that "the most common feature of trade policy in the textiles (and later clothing) area over the past century is the above-average level of government intervention". The study observes that most developed countries, especially in Western Europe, began the postwar period with very restrictive trade regimes, and trade policies affecting textiles remained largely untouched by GATT trade liberalization. In some cases, countries invoked various GATT articles to justify their action. However, these GATT departures were developed in the textile and multifiber arrangements into a regularized and constant form of government intervention for textile and clothing trade. It is recognized that this intervention is inconsistent with GATT, but the countries who have accepted the textile or multifiber arrangements have arguably partially "waived" their GATT rights. Of course, the pressure to enter into these agreements for the textile-exporting countries was very great, and the fear was that the importing countries would make matters worse without the arrangements. At least the arrangements were a result of the tugging and pulling of international negotiations, and the argument was that these arrangements would allow the progressive and predictable liberalization of trade for the products concerned.

The basic approach of these arrangements is to set up a framework by which the importing countries (the developed or industrial countries) would negotiate bilaterally with the exporting countries for the establishment of a series of voluntary restraint arrangements, subsidiary to the overall textile or multifiber arrangements. Certain rules in the overall agreements constrain the nature of the bilateral agreements. For example, a target was introduced in some of the agreements for annual expansion or gradual liberalization of the imports into the importing countries. This figure has stood nominally at 6 percent since 1973, but it is clear that exceptions introduced in the agreement provide a number of circumstances in which nations may use a much lower rate of increase in imports. If agreement cannot be reached on the level of imports to be accepted, the arrangement provides that a limit within certain boundaries may be set by the importing country. Provision is also made for interim "emergency" restraining agreements on measures. In addition, a Textiles Surveillance Body (TSB) is set up to provide a forum for disputes and generally to supervise the arrangement.

Some of the factors that seem to have influenced these special arrangements in the textile and clothing sectors are well known. In particular, clothing industries are often a very large part of an economy, employing many people; and these are often distributed among a wide variety of locations, which adds to their political importance. The original Short-Term Arrangement is traced by many persons to commitments made by John F. Kennedy during the 1960 presidential election campaign in the United States.[111] The GATT report notes the arguments that were used by proponents of these arrangements, including the concern that developing countries often find it most convenient to begin their industrialization in the textile sector, since the machinery to do so is not too complex, and since clothing for the domestic market is an important marketing consideration. Thus, low-wage textile employees in developing countries became a threat to textile workers in developed countries.[112]

Currently, approximately forty countries are formal participants in the MFA, and of these about nine (including the EC as one) are developed importing countries.[113] The 1984 GATT report, as well as other studies, has pointed out the very high costs to consumers (world wide) caused by textile trade restraints. W. Cline notes in his book:

Yet the reality . . . has been one of successive tightening of practices under the MFA' and the creation of a protection regime of unrivaled longevity and scope. . . .

In sum, quota protection for textiles and apparel appears to have been rising over time through the successive tightening of the MFA and its implementing mechanisms. Today the tariff-equivalent of apparel quotas is probably in the range of 25% (beyond the tariff), and that on textiles some 15%....

Total consumer costs of protection amount to $17.6 billion annually in apparel and $2.8 billion in textiles.... The average American household thus pays $238 every year to retain some 235,000 jobs in the textile and apparel sectors rather than elsewhere in the economy. The consumer cost per job saved is approximately $82,000 in apparel and $135,000 in textiles.[114]

There have been demands to phase out the arrangements, possibly as part of the Uruguay Round Negotiation. The likelihood of this result does not seem high, however. Indeed, the risk seems to be that other economic sectors will find the textile example appealing. For example, some are already talking about the "textilization" of steel, in the light of the elaborate world-wide quantitative arrangements for steel trade (strongly enhanced by the U.S. program, begun in 1984, to set up a large number of VRAs for steel exports aimed at the U.S. market).[115]

7.8 Perspectives and Proposals: Attempts to Reform GATT Safeguards Rules

The Attempts to Negotiate an International Safeguards Code: The Tokyo Round and After

One of the major objectives of the Tokyo Round of negotiation, reflected in the September 1973 Tokyo Ministerial Declaration,[116] was to develop a new "Safeguards Code" which would enhance the international discipline of safeguards.

It is well known that this objective of the Tokyo Round negotiation ended largely in failure. The Contracting Parties could not come to a mutual agreement on the subject of safeguards during that negotiation, despite extensive sessions and hard work. The director general's report, at the end of the Tokyo Round in 1979, noticed the difficulties of this negotiation,[117] mentioning the controversy about discriminatory application of safeguards measures, as well as difficulties to do with surveillance and dispute settlement, the definition of "serious injury," and the broader issues of "structural adjustment." Additionally, the question of how to bring some discipline to the burgeoning and chaotic use of export restraints, was addressed, again with little agreement.

At the conclusion of the Tokyo Round, the Negotiating Parties did agree that a committee of the GATT Contracting Parties continue negotiations, and that committee still operates today. At the November 1982 Ministerial Meeting, the Ministerial Declaration noted the need for a comprehensive understanding, to include *inter alia* the following elements:

i. transparency;

ii. coverage;

iii. objective criteria for action including the concept of serious injury or threat thereof;

iv. temporary nature, degressivity and structural adjustment;

v. compensation and retaliation; and

vi. notification, consultation, multilateral surveillance and dispute settlement with particular reference to the role and functions of the Safeguards Committee.[118]

Apparently little progress has been made on this subject since then, but the matter is one of the subjects included in the Uruguay Round of negotiations.[119]

Perspectives About Safeguards

Two general propositions can be stated with considerable confidence. First, the international rules, centered in GATT, concerning so-called safeguards and the problems of economic "structural adjustment," are too weak and ambiguous to provide a very effective level of discipline on national practices in an increasingly economically interdependent world, although some measure of discipline through the GATT System and its "compensation rules" has been effective. Second, so far, attempts to reform the safeguards or adjustment process in the international trade institutions have resulted in no concrete advances, although considerable information has been developed.

The question remains, In what direction should the system evolve in the future? A number of troublesome issues need further elaboration: (1) Are the underlying policies for safeguards institutions still valid, or do they need to be rethought? (2) Do the conditions of greater economic interdependence, as well as the increasingly dynamic character of "comparative advantage" wherein nations can, through governmental policies, influence the structure of international trade, call for a rethinking of some of the fundamental safeguards and liberal trade policies? (3) Is it possible to effectively develop a safeguards policy and set of institutions which attempt to continue to differentiate safeguards from notions of responding to "unfair trade"?

If one concludes that greater international discipline on national safeguard measures is important and feasible, is it appropriate to ask what might be its characteristics? The following, while not constituting a draft or even a complete agenda for this troublesome area of endeavor, offers some suggestions, gleaned partly from reports and activities mentioned at the beginning of this section.

1. It seems feasible, and perhaps more efficient, to reduce the number of participants in the safeguard discussions. Perhaps a plausible approach would be to have merely a few like-minded states gather together to see if an agreement of limited geographical scope could be designed, which would preserve the rights of nonparticipants, be open for future accession to all current nonparticipants, and yet provide on a quasi-optional basis a somewhat higher degree of discipline for those who sign a resulting agreement.[120]

2. A "two-tier" approach has been suggested from time to time, and has much appeal.[121] The basic concept is that those governments who so desire would enter into a mutual agreement by which certain privileges, such as the right to avoid the obligation of "compensation," would be accorded to states by the other signatories, in only those circumstances where a series of escape-clause criteria of a higher discipline and better definition were fulfilled. It is possible to make such an agreement provide an optional second tier or second track even for the signatory participants, so that they do not give up their right to go the normal GATT "undisciplined" route if they so desire, and do not want the additional privilege of relief from the compensation bill. One possible legal form of such an agreement would be for signatories to "waive" their GATT compensation rights vis-à-vis another signatory in those cases only where the higher discipline was fulfilled. It seems that this could be accomplished without any action of the Contracting Parties (although nonsignatories would still have their GATT rights to pursue, so the new agreement would need to include all important trading nations).

3. Such an agreement might begin with an extensive set of obligations for "transparency." These obligations could well consist of two types:

a. a definitive requirement of full reporting of all safeguard measures, especially export-restraint measures. The reporting obligation should fall not only on the importing country, but also on the exporting country, and certain criteria or indicia should be specified as to the specificity of the report (product definition, estimated amount of trade involved, level of export, degressivity, time period, countries involved, degree of formality, country and/or industry participants).

b. In addition, each signatory might be required to table an annual report, which listed the safeguard measures in effect, and made some estimate of the percentage of their trade affected by the safeguard measures as compared to the total trade. Thus, countries who seem to be overutilizing or "abusing" safeguard measures might be noticed more rapidly.

4. The agreement might recognize or impose a responsibility in the GATT secretariat or some other international cadre to independently report on all safeguard measures which are discovered through the press or other means.[122]

5. A requirement of adjustment assistance or a structural adjustment promotion might be considered a necessary prerequisite for the privileges of the agreement. Thus, governments might be appropriately asked to prove retraining benefits, and perhaps certain types of early retirement, or at least to table in an international committee the program that they have established for the purpose of facilitating structural adjustment.

6. Regarding the prerequisites for a safeguard measure, namely increasing imports and related serious injury to the competing domestic industry, a number of the difficult ambiguities described in sections 7.2 and 7.3 of this chapter should be addressed. For example, a time period for import restraint could be specified. Possibly percentage-increase thresholds as well as import-penetration thresholds could be devised (at least for "normal" cases).

7. Likewise, some of the ambiguities concerning the "remedy," such as the time period for degressivity, the nature of the remedy (emphasizing price-tariff) could be specified. It might not always be feasible to have a single norm for each of these details, but a preferred option could be stipulated, with deviation only upon showing good cause.

8. Finally, careful thought must be given to the international institutions necessary to make such a system operate effectively. At a minimum, this would require a committee of signatories, or a safeguards committee, charged with receiving reports, meeting periodically and examining reports, and questioning national practices. Further (perhaps after a transition period), such an international body might be given authority to determine whether the prerequisites for the privileges of the agreement (such as relief from the compensation obligation)

have in fact been fulfilled. If a negative determination in this regard were made, then the privileges of the agreement — such as relief from the compensation obligation — would be denied.

It is difficult at this juncture to evaluate the potential for progress on safeguards discipline in the near future. Nevertheless, it does appear that the lack of substantial progress on this matter poses risks in an increasingly interdependent world. One can only hope that mistakes of the 1920s and 1930s can be avoided.

8 National Treatment Obligations and Non-Tariff Barriers

8.1 The Policies and History of the National Treatment Obligation

The second major obligation of nondiscriminatory treatment, after MFN, is the national treatment obligation (expressed primarily in Article III of GATT).[1] Whereas MFN requires equal treatment among different nations, the national treatment obligation requires the treatment of imported goods, once they have cleared customs and border procedures, to be no worse than that of domestically produced goods. Obviously, an important policy behind this rule is to prevent domestic tax and regulatory policies from being used as protectionist measures that would defeat the purpose of tariff bindings. It should be noted, however, that this obligation applies to all products, not just to bound products. Thus, this rule assists the general goal of reducing restraints to imports.

A "national treatment" obligation can be found in many treaties, some dating back to earlier centuries.[2] The scope of the obligation may vary from treaty to treaty, however, and may apply to various activities, not only to products. For example, a common application of national treatment obligations is in relation to criminal procedures when applied to foreign citizens. Another example is national treatment obligations for the "right of establishment," so that a foreign business can set up branches and offices in another country.[3]

The national treatment obligation is often a source of complaint or dispute among nations.[4] Since it refers to domestic regulatory and tax measures, it is intimately related to various governmental measures which are based on legitimate policies not necessarily designed for purposes of restraining imports. In some cases the domestic measures will overreach or be shaped to significantly and unnecessarily restrain imports. In other cases legitimate policy goals, including those mentioned in the article on general exceptions to GATT (Article XX), will prevent a measure from being inconsistent with GATT obligations.[5] The temptation of legislators and other government officials to shape regulatory or tax measures so as to favor domestic products seems to be very great, and proposals to do this are constantly suggested.[6] This clash of policies raises some of the broader issues described in chapters 10 and 14, about whether a "harmonization" or "interface" approach is preferable.[7]

8.2 The Contours and Application of the GATT Obligation

Article III of GATT sets out the national treatment obligation pertaining to treatment of imported products. The first paragraph is a general statement of policy, but it includes an important phrase obligating contracting parties to avoid using taxes or regulations "so as to afford protection to domestic production."[8]

The second paragraph of Article III requires that internal taxes on imported products shall not be in excess of those applied to domestic goods, and expressly refers to the general goal of paragraph 1. The fourth paragraph of this article imposes essentially the same obligation (although without reference to paragraph 1) with respect to regulations and other "requirements affecting ... [the] internal sale ..." of imported products. Paragraphs 5 and 7 prohibit the use of mixing requirements to favor domestic products. Other paragraphs, however, provide some exceptions to the general national treatment rule, the most notable of which is the exception for government purchases (to which we return in section 8.6).

A 1958 dispute-panel report, concerning Italian government measures relating to the sale of tractors, provides a fundamental interpretation for the national treatment clause. In this case the United Kingdom complained about an Italian banking measure that provided more favorable loans to farmers buying domestically made tractors than to farmers buying imported tractors. The panel report, accepted by the CONTRACTING PARTIES,[9] stated that "... the intent of the drafters was to provide equal conditions of competition once goods had been cleared through customs ..." and particularly stressed the fact that "... the assistance by the State was not given to producers but to the purchasers of agricultural machinery...."[10]

Thus, once the imported goods have entered the internal stream of commerce, no government regulatory measure should assist the purchase of the domestic goods without likewise doing the same for imported goods. Even though the domestic *producer* may be subsidized under the GATT rules (there is an explicit exception for such subsidy in paragraph 8(a) of Article III of GATT), when the subsidy has the effect of directly affecting the purchaser's choice, it is inconsistent with the GATT.

The problem of "domestic content" rules has been troublesome. As a condition of certain regulatory or license permissions such as might be required in order to build a new factory or to invest in a country, some nations have required formal or informal commitments that products produced in the new plant or assembled from imported parts be comprised of a certain minimum percent of domestic "value added." The United States brought a complaint against the Canadian government Foreign Investment Review Act (FIRA) partly on these grounds, arguing a violation of GATT Article III:4 and 5. The U.S. argued that the necessity of a commitment to the purchase of Canadian goods, when "competitively" or otherwise available from Canadian suppliers, as a requirement for investing in Canada violated GATT Article III:4. The panel report in 1984 supported this view even when the requirement was "informal."[11]

A separate complaint was made by Canada against a United States law and practice under it, known as "Section 337."[12] This law provides a procedure whereby an American industry can complain about "unfair trade practices" of foreign parties shipping goods to the U.S. market. These practices might be infringement of copyright or patents, or attempts to monopolize, etc. Canada alleged that the 337 procedure, when compared to similar U.S. domestic procedures for attacking unfair trade practices (through the Federal Trade Commission [FTC] or through patent or copyright domestic procedures) in effect discriminated against imports. A 1983 GATT panel report concluded that GATT Article XX general exceptions, which allowed "necessary" differences in treatment of imports in order to secure compliance with patent, copyright, and certain other laws, was applicable.[13] The report then went on to determine whether the 337 measures were either a "disguised restriction on international trade" or an "arbitrary or unjustifiable discrimination," and concluded again in the negative. The report, however, did not give the U.S. section 337 an entirely clean bill of health, noting that in cases with different facts, it could not exclude the possibility that "there might be cases . . . where a procedure before a United States court might provide . . . an equally satisfactory and effective remedy."[14]

In an action brought under the so-called New Commercial Policy Instrument, Akzo, a Dutch supplier of high-technology fibers, complained to the European Commission of the EC concerning a section 337 ban requested by the U.S. company DuPont.[15] The section 337 action alleged infringement by Akzo of patents held in the U.S. by DuPont. The commission brought a GATT panel proceeding arguing that section 337 subjected imported goods to a separate and distinct procedure by virtue of their non-U.S. origin, and that such discrimination could not be justified as "necessary" under Article XX(d) of the GATT. The panel reported in January 1989, agreeing with a number of the EC arguments.

8.3   De Facto or Implicit Discrimination

One of the more difficult conceptual problems of GATT rules has to do with the application of the national treatment obligation in the context of a national regulation or tax which *on its face* appears to be nondiscriminatory, but which, because of various circumstances in the marketplace or elsewhere, has the effect of tilting the scales against the imported products. As sophistication about GATT rules has increased among various national officials, the number of these "implicit discrimination" cases has seemed also to increase.

A classic example of this situation occurred in U.S. taxation of alcoholic beverages. A U.S. law (predating GATT and therefore benefiting from grandfather rights) provided for a tax of $10.50 on "each proof gallon or wine gallon when below proof." This taxing phrase applied to domestically produced as well as imported alcoholic beverages. A wine gallon is simply a gallon of the beverage, no matter how diluted the alcohol. A "proof gallon," however, is a gallon of liquid which is 100 proof, or 50 percent alcohol, by volume. If a producer can have his liquid taxed while at full proof, then later when the liquid is diluted to the percentage of alcohol used in the beverage sold at retail, (e.g., 86 proof or 43 percent for certain whiskies), the effective tax per gallon of liquid sold at retail is $9.03, rather than $10.50. Domestic producers were able to achieve this. Their concentrated whisky was kept in cask under bond, and tax was paid on that basis. Only after the tax was assessed, was the liquid diluted and bottled for retail sale. Importers, however, preferred to import the whisky bottled at their home place of production, and the tax was assessed at the time of importation at the wine gallon rate; thus, effectively taxing the imported whisky more per retail bottle. The importer *could* import the concentrated beverage, but then could not advertise it as "bottled in Scotland." Also, the bottling process might be more expensive in the United States.

In several interesting cases, foreign producers challenged this U.S. tax law as a violation of certain bilateral treaties.[16] Since the U.S. law was "grandfathered" under GATT, the GATT language was not directly involved.[17] A U.S. court held that since the tax law applied equally to domestic and imported products, the national treatment clauses of the treaties were not violated. However, those clauses did not have the language found in GATT Article III paragraph 1, prohibiting taxes arranged "so as to afford protection." Partly because of this language, under the GATT it can be strongly argued that even though a tax (or regulation) appears on its face to be nondiscriminatory, if it has an *effect* of affording protection, and if this effect is not essential to the valid regulatory purpose (as suggested by Article XX), then such tax or regulation is inconsistent with GATT obligations.

This brings to mind a number of hypothetical or not-so-hypothetical measures. One type of taxing proposal that has been considered is structured as follows. A uniform "excise" or sales tax (or value-added tax) is imposed on the sale of a product, for example automobiles (whether domestic or imported). Then the company paying this tax is allowed to credit the amount paid against U.S. employment taxes that it would otherwise pay on behalf of its employees (such as social security taxes). Again, on its face, the provision appears neutral. Only when we learn that importers have very little liability for U.S. employment taxes, and thus have little opportunity to use these "credits," do we see that the effect can be essentially discriminatory.[18]

As another example, suppose a nation's tax laws provide for accelerated depreciation deduction allowances for capital purchases when the materials or machinery purchased are produced domestically, but not when they are imported. It appears clear that this is even *explicit* discrimination. But suppose the law instead provides that the deduction is allowed only when the goods are made by persons who are paid more than an average of $25,000 per year. Again, it is clear that this is not a very well disguised discrimination. The GATT obligation does not allow for differential treatment based on characteristics of the production process rather than of the product itself.[19]

A more subtle case is that in which a regulation for standardization or safety is used to effectively discriminate against imports. In section 8.5 we take up this question.

8.4   Border Tax Adjustments

One of the more perplexing trade-policy problems, related to the national treatment obligation but also to several other GATT obligations, is the subject of border tax adjustment (BTA). Under GATT, upon importation a nation may charge a tax (in addition to other tariffs) equivalent to a like internal tax imposed on domestic products of the same type. With respect to trade in the opposite direction (i.e., exports), a nation is allowed to *rebate* the amount of any internal tax imposed on the exported goods. Thus, in theory, the goods travel in international trade "untaxed," and are taxed at their destination under whatever rules apply there to domestic as well as imported goods. It sounds equitable and reasonable, but these measures have been the source of considerable acrimony in international trade relations, and were considered by the Supreme Court of the United States in one of the few cases in which that court has ever considered an international trade issue.[20]

First, it is useful to examine the legal structure of GATT which provides for the measures described in the preceding paragraph. The language calling for this treatment is sprinkled through a number of GATT clauses. On the import side, Article II, paragraph 2(a) grants an exception from the rule limiting border charges to the amount of the scheduled tariff binding, for "a charge equivalent to an internal tax imposed consistently with the provisions of paragraph 2 of Article III. . . ." It is important to note that both Article III and the remainder of this language of Article II refers to taxes on *products*.

On the export side, matters are a bit more complex. An interpretative note to Article XVI, paragraph 4 states that a rebate of internal taxes on products shall not be considered a "subsidy" for purposes of the obligation against export subsidies.[21] In addition, a clause in Article VI likewise states that such a product tax rebate shall not be the basis of either an antidumping duty nor a countervailing duty in the country of import. Again one can note that the taxes involved are those on *products*.

These product taxes (such as a sales tax, excise tax, or tax on a product at each stage of production) are often called "indirect taxes," to distinguish them from income or corporate taxes or other taxes imposed on a firm (not on a product). The latter are, thus, often called "direct taxes." Although an argument might be made to the contrary, the value-added taxes, such as those in the European Economic Community, have for a long time been considered by GATT to be "indirect": i.e., taxes on products, and thus eligible for border-tax-adjustment treatment. Since these taxes are often as much as 20 percent or more, this obviously has considerable potential effect on imports and exports when border adjustments are applied.

In countries (like the United States) which do not generally have significant "product taxes," but instead rely heavily on income taxes for their revenue, border tax adjustments are either not used, or are relatively insignificant. Income or "direct" taxes are *not* eligible for border tax adjustment, and this has been the source of considerable criticism by political and business leaders in the United States who see this disparity of treatment as unfair to the U.S.[22] What is (or was) the rationale for this special approach of GATT toward border tax adjustments? Probably when these rules were drafted there was not too much thought given to their potential impact in the future, since at that time tariffs themselves were relatively much more important. The BTA question, like so many others involving non-tariff measures, was in early GATT years not the focus of much attention. As tariffs declined, however, these alternative methods of affecting trade flows become much more significant.

One theory supporting the BTA system is that taxes on products (indirect taxes) tend to be effectively borne by the purchaser or consumer of those products. It is thus said that such a tax burden is "shifted forward" to the purchaser, or is a "destination" approach. By contrast, it was thought that income or "direct" taxes were borne primarily by the suppliers of capital investment (i.e., were shifted "backward," or were "origin" based). Thus it seemed fair to impose the product taxes at the destination, on a basis equal to that imposed there on like domestic products. Certainly domestic producers in the importing country would perceive unfairness if the imported products were not taxed equally to their products.

To leave the products subject to the product taxes of the exporting country, however, would mean that products moving in international trade would be double-taxed: at the place of production, and again at the place of purchase or consumption. Therefore it was thought necessary to exclude the products from the product taxes of the exporting countries, by allowing a rebate of those taxes if necessary.

The problem, as any economist can demonstrate, is that both types of taxes place some burden on both the purchaser and the provider of capital, depending often on particular characteristics of the market structure. For example, if competition is keen, a product tax may mean that a producer will find it necessary to charge less than he would otherwise (to partly offset the tax effect on purchasing demand). In such a case, profitability will be lowered, and thus the return to capital will be less (i.e., investors bear part of the burden of the tax). Likewise, an income tax affects the net after-tax return to capital and (if the market permits) induces the producer to charge a higher price to purchasers so as to offset the income-tax effect on net profit. Thus the purchaser bears part of the burden of the income tax. There is no simple way to find the dividing line, or to know the percentage of each type of tax borne by the various participants for any particular product. The division probably differs from product to product.[23] Some economic comment suggests that even for a corporate tax, up to 20 percent of the burden is shifted forward to the consumer in the short run, and as much as 60 to 75 percent will be shifted forward eventually. Evidence of this (if it exists) would provide substantial arguments that income taxes should receive some border tax adjustment treatment also. Without such treatment for income taxes, those countries which depend much more on such taxes argue that goods from countries with substantial border tax rebates have not shouldered their share of the costs of government, and therefore are in essence subsidized.

How to resolve this problem? There seems to be no good way. First of all, it is very unlikely that the GATT will be changed. Even if it could be changed, it is hard to state a rule that would be more accurate. Perhaps the present rule is as good a rough approximation of equity as can be found, and it is at least administrable. In a floating exchange-rate world, at least where the product taxes are generally uniformly applied to all products, it can be argued that the exchange rate adjusts to any border tax adjustment so that over a few years (at least), most distortion effects of the BTA are neutralized. Another approach, for the "income tax" nations, is to shift to a value-added or product tax for a much larger portion of revenue, and then to apply a border tax adjustment. It seems much like the "tail wagging the dog" to change an otherwise desirable tax system to try to achieve some uncertain and perhaps dubious advantage for the international trade, but if such a product tax system has other merit to commend it, it doesn't hurt that a by-product might be lessened concern about perceptions of unfairness of the international trade rules.[24]

The issue of "pass-through" of indirect taxes was raised in a recent case before the CIT[25] in which a U.S. producer challenged, *inter alia*, the assumption of the Commerce Department that an indirect tax would be completely passed through to the eventual purchaser. Commerce argued that it knew of "no reasonable method" for accurately measuring the incidence of a tax. The CIT rejected this approach, stating that "a conclusion that full pass-through occurred in all cases is not supported by substantial evidence," and remanded back to Commerce. In a later administrative review,[26] Commerce continued to work on the assumption that full pass-through occurred, and stated that the government was considering an appeal against the decision of the CIT.

8.5 Technical Standards and the Tokyo Round Code

Implicit discrimination against imports is often found in the context of so-called "product standards." Examples are numerous. A nation which uses metric measures for tools and small fasteners might require all such products to be marked in metric measures. There may be a valid domestic consumer protection policy supporting such a requirement, but it might also be introduced because troublesome import competition stems from products which are measured in other units, such as inches or feet.[27] Likewise, in chapter 5 I mentioned one nation's requirement that packages of food products be in its own language *and no other*. While there seem to be ample policy grounds to require the labels to have the language of the country of import, to require that no other language appear on the label is to prevent the use of a cost-saving multilingual label.

Sometimes it is alleged that agencies or industry groups which set standards consciously try to "gerrymander" those standards to make it comparatively more difficult for foreign producers to comply. In such a way a market for electronic components might be protected for domestic producers by certain quality or standards specifications. Likewise drug or cosmetic standards might be "shaped" to allow domestic manufacturers to accommodate them easily.

The process of obtaining clearance of a product subject to inspection, for health or safety reasons, may also add enough of a burden to the importation of goods as to "afford protection" to domestic manufacturers. Even though the country of export may test and examine goods which are exported, the importing country might require this to be done again. In some cases it may have good reason to do so. The exporting nation's tests may be unreliable, or may not require as high a standard as that of the importing nation. If the exporting nation's tests are specifically for exports (and not for domestically consumed products also), that nation may not have a strong incentive to provide stringent testing, by contrast with the nation whose consumers will purchase the good.

On the other hand, delay and costs of processing tests in the importing nation, whether due to understaffing of the testing agency or to a tacit understanding by that agency that "slowness helps the balance of trade," clearly are contrary to the liberal trading policies of the international system.

Much of the controversy and, indeed, anger about Japan's apparent unwillingness to import focuses on practices such as those just mentioned. The Japanese government has responded with various programs designed to prevent such measures from inhibiting imports and to mute the criticism leveled at Japan for taking these measures.[28]

Because of the risk that these various problems become increasing sources of protectionism and conflict among nations, the GATT contracting parties negotiated in the Tokyo Round a new code designed to address these questions. This Agreement on Technical Barriers to Trade may expand the GATT Article III obligations, stating:

Parties shall ensure that technical regulations and standards are not prepared, adopted or applied with a view to creating obstacles to international trade. Furthermore, products imported from the territory of any Party shall be accorded treatment no less favorable than that accorded to like products of national origin and to like products originating in any other country in relation to such technical regulations or standards. They shall likewise ensure that neither technical regulations nor standards themselves nor their application have the effect of creating unnecessary obstacles to international trade.[29]

To what degree this language now requires national governments to justify standards with scientific evidence, going beyond the mere "nondiscrimination" requirement of Article III, is yet unclear.

Beyond this general "national treatment"-type obligation, there are few substantive rules in this Tokyo Round code, but the agreement specifies a number of obligations regarding the *procedure* by which product standards are developed in each of the signatory nations. Under the code, governments must, to the extent possible (recognizing that many product standards are developed by nongovernment groups), ensure that foreign nations and their producers with an interest in exporting shall have the opportunity to be heard and to present facts and arguments to standards-making bodies during the formulation of standards. In addition, the Code calls for "transparency" of standards, which is adequate notice and opportunity to comply. It urges the development of international standards, and urges parties to recognize testing which has been appropriately done in the country exporting products. It also contains a preference for performance rather than design specifications.

Some consider this Code to be one of the more successful results of the Tokyo Round, since it has the largest number of acceptances of any of the codes (thirty-six, including both developing and nonmarket economies).[30] (The U.S. has implemented the Code in Title IV of the 1979 Trade Agreements Act.[31]) Its operation in practice, and the activity of its Committee of Signatories, seems to have engendered satisfaction among governments and businesses. At least one dispute brought formally under this Code's dispute-settlement mechanism has been satisfactorily resolved.[32]

My discussion here has focused on the standards for products themselves. Another important problem is that of standards relating not to products but to the manufacture or processing of products, and its impact on the environment, on safety of workers. This subject we take up in chapter 9.[33]

8.6 Government Procurement

The most important exception to the national treatment obligation in GATT Article III itself is that found in paragraph 8, relating to government procurement. The language provides some interpretative difficulties but generally exempts, from Article III national treatment obligations, purchases by "governmental agencies of products purchased for governmental purposes . . ."[34] Since the Article I MFN obligation of GATT makes reference to the obligations of Article III, paragraphs 2 and 4, it is argued that government procurement is also an exception to MFN rules.[35]

Early preparatory drafts of the ITO charter and GATT would have included government procurement in the discipline of those instruments, but government negotiators objected, so the final drafts included explicit exclusions.[36] Apparently government procurement was too close to sovereignty to permit regulation at that time. Since military procurement would have been exempted in any event, the drafters worried that any attempt to draw lines between exempt and included government procurement would be too difficult.

There are several important reasons why this exception had become very troublesome by the 1970s. First, there had been some trend of increasing the government sector of a number of economies, so that in some nations over 40 percent of the gross national product had passed through government budgets.[37] Where major industry sectors such as steel or utilities were nationalized, an increasing amount of economic activity was beyond the reach of the GATT rules. U.S. manufacturers of heavy electrical equipment (such as turbines) saw great exporting potential if foreign restrictions on government purchases of imports could be softened. The problem of nonmarket economies could potentially become even more troublesome in this regard.

A second important (and related) reason for concern was the difficulty of finding an agreed definition of either "government agency" or "governmental purposes." Nations have a wide variety of ideas as to what is the appropriate sphere of government activity. In some countries it is assumed that the government should own and run railroads, telephone systems, all electricity generation, travel bureaus, airlines, and many other activities which private enterprise conducts elsewhere. Some countries have added to the list basic "smokestack" industries, including steel and coal, as well as major related service sectors, such as banking. Such an important exception from the GATT trading rules would clearly diminish the liberalizing effects of those rules.

Thus it was that another code came out of the Tokyo Round: the Agreement on Government Procurement. This Code is interesting because of the apparently far-reaching rules included in it. The general rule is stated in Article II, paragraph 1, as follows:

With respect to all laws, regulations, procedures and practices regarding government procurement covered by this Agreement, the Parties shall provide immediately and unconditionally to the products and suppliers of other Parties offering products originating within the customs territories (including free zones) of the Parties, treatment no less favorable than: (a) that accorded to domestic products and suppliers; and (b) that accorded to products and suppliers of any other Party.[38]

The Code outlines detailed rules to implement this general principle, including rules governing the bidding procedures to be followed. These regulate the types of technical specifications which can be required in bids: the tendering procedures, including public announcement, qualification of bidders, time limits, tender documents, etc. Foreign bidders are entitled to obtain a statement of reasons why their bids were rejected, and a dispute-settlement mechanism is established to follow through on complaints. Several cases have already been processed through this procedure.[39]

Although the Code requirements may seem far-reaching, the important limitation of the Code is that it only applies to the governmental "entities" on a list appended to the Code for each signatory. The scheme has characteristics very similar to that of tariff bindings in GATT. Each country specifies by name to which entities the Code applies, as part of a process of reciprocal negotiation among the Code signers. The basic goal of the draftsmen was to have the Code establish a framework for truly effective discipline against governmental discriminatory purchasing, recognizing that such stringent requirements would make governments somewhat hesitant to include entities on their list. Once the Code came into existence, with reciprocal negotiated lists of entities, later negotiations were contemplated for additions of more entities to the list. Some later negotiations have been held,[40] and more are contemplated.

The scope and coverage of the Government Procurement Agreement additionally depends on certain other clauses in it. Although it explicitly applies (interestingly enough) to most "services incidental to the supply of products," a minimum threshold for covered contracts was set at "SDR 150,000 " (later changed).[41] Exception is also provided for national security, and in a qualified way, for national measures to protect public morals, order, safety, health, and similar goals.[42]

As of January 1989, thirteen nations have accepted this agreement, and it has been reported that in 1983 over $38 billion worth of trade was covered by it.[43] Telecommunications has been a large issue in connection with the agreement, and this issue has figured prominently between the United States and Japan. In the U.S., telecommunications has not been government owned, and even its monopoly power has been diluted by the trend to "deregulation." Thus, the U.S. argues that foreign suppliers have the opportunity to sell telecommunication equipment in the U.S. market. On the other hand, most other nations have a government-owned telecommunications monopoly, although several have recently decided to "privatize" or deregulate also. From the end of the Tokyo Round onward, the U.S. and Japan have negotiated strenuously over U.S. demands that U.S. companies have better opportunity to sell products to the Japanese telephone monopoly. From the U.S. perspective, these negotiations have had only moderate success. On the other hand, in at least one case, the Japanese demonstrated that a U.S. telephone company, A.T.&T., refused a purchase of Japanese fiber optics equipment (which was the low bid in a competition), for "Buy American" reasons.[44] What effect the Japanese "privatization" of NTT will have is yet unclear.

In the United States, there are many "Buy American" regulations, both at the federal and at the state level.[45] A 1979 International Trade Commission study found some twenty-five instances of regulatory preferences for U.S. goods at the federal level alone.[46] The United States is not unique in requiring preferences for domestically produced goods.[47]

The best example of U.S. law is the Buy American Act,[48] which essentially requires acquisition of domestically produced articles for "public use." In an important exception, the law authorizes the federal authorities to deviate from this rule if the cost of foreign-produced articles is lower by specified amounts.[49]

Although federal procurement policies now limit Buy American provisions in order to open government markets in accordance with the MTN agreement, state Buy American statutes have proliferated during recent years. Thirty-six states now have some form of Buy American legislation, compared with twenty-three a decade ago. Interestingly enough, the United States was prepared to consider making the Code applicable to governmental subdivisions, but other nations were opposed.[50]

9

Competing Policies and Their Relation to Trade Liberalization

9.1 Protecting the Value of Tariff Concessions and Competing Policies

In chapters 5 through 8 we have examined some of the most important of the regulatory principles affecting contemporary international trade. In chapters 10 and 11 we will explore more such principles, but mostly in the context of permitted national government unilateral responses to certain so-called "unfair" practices of exporting nations. In this chapter we take up several regulatory principles which can be quite important, but which can be treated more briefly. Two basic threads run through most of the sections in this chapter: the existence of important policies competing with those of comparative advantage and liberal trade, and the desirability of protecting the value of tariff and other trade rules by plugging "loopholes" and preventing the protectionist use of a variety of ingenious import restraints.

As I have already noted, the ingenuity of man in devising import restraints which skirt the formal rules of international trade seems boundless[1]. Nevertheless, there are a number of situations in which import-restraining activity is required by legitimate government goals.

9.2 National Security

One of the exceptions to liberal-trade policies which has always been recognized by economic theorists and statesmen is that of national security. Here the competing policy of protecting a nation's continued existence is obviously more important than economic welfare or other potential benefits of comparative advantage. On the other hand, it is not always clear that the best way to protect a nation's national security is by using import restraints or other trade-distorting measures. In a world where some wars could be over in minutes, traditional notions of the need for production facilities are not always applicable. In another context, the overall economic well-being of a nation, and such subtle attributes as the scientific advancement of its research and the technical proficiency of its work force, are to some observers more important as longer-term protections of national security than traditional shorter-term goals of stockpiled war material or factories.[2]

Even if one acknowledges the importance of having viable and working production facilities in some sectors of the economy, some economists suggest that import restraints to protect such facilities from decline due to import competition may be the wrong approach. Such a policy can let the domestic sector slide into noncompetitiveness and lack of productivity which can worsen its position and even render it unfit for an emergency. On the other hand, alternative measures, if some protection from competition is deemed necessary, may work better in the economy. One such alternative to applying import restraints is to subsidize the sector or some of its facilities, as a way to keep it viable. "Mothballing" may be one type of subsidy, but another might stem from government purchases, and yet another technique would be direct payments possibly tied to particular activities needed for national security which might not otherwise be compensated in the marketplace. For example, certain equipment might need to be much more reliable if used for military rather than for civilian purposes.

Despite these various considerations, nations still occasionally feel the national security need to use border restraints or other measures not consistent with international trade rules. The GATT recognizes this in Article XXI, which provides for a general exception to all GATT obligations with respect to disclosure of national security information, regulation of fissionable materials, regulation of traffic in arms, and action in pursuance of UN Charter obligations relating to maintenance of international peace and security. Article XXI also has a catch-all clause that allows action which a contracting party "considers necessary for the protection of its essential security interests . . . taken in time of war or other emergency in international relations."[3]

This language is so broad, self-judging, and ambiguous that it obviously can be abused. It has even been claimed that maintenance of shoe production facilities qualify for the exception because an army must have shoes![4] Because of this danger of abuse, contracting parties have been very reluctant to formally invoke Article XXI, even in circumstances where it seems applicable. Thus there have been only a few reported cases regarding Article XXI in GATT's history.[5] In general, the GATT approach to Article XXI is to defer almost completely to the judgment of an invoking contracting party.

There have been a number of occasions in GATT when the United States has severed trading relations (and therefore GATT relations) with certain contracting parties. In 1951 the U.S. Congress required the non-application or withdrawal of application of MFN treatment for communist countries, and at that time one communist country—Czechoslovakia—was a GATT contracting party, so the U.S. had to terminate the application of the GATT between it and that country. There is no explicit authority in GATT for doing this,[6] but the CONTRACTING PARTIES adopted a "declaration" authorizing the two countries to suspend GATT obligations toward each other, and this action could be interpreted as a "waiver."[7] Several other comparable situations are recorded in GATT.[8] In 1985 the United States president decreed an embargo on trade between the U.S. and Nicaragua, and Nicaragua challenged the U.S. action in GATT.[9] The U.S. position in the GATT process was that since the U.S. was invoking Article XXI and since that Article deferred to national judgments about national security, GATT had no business discussing this matter further.[10]

The United States has a number of domestic trade law measures based on "national security" considerations. The most often used of these are the export control laws, under the Export Administration Act.[11] The U.S. tries to prevent all shipments to certain countries of products which it has included on a list of products which have some strategic importance. These include advance computers, various electronic devices, certain weapons and their technology, and similar items. In addition, the act gives certain powers to the president to limit exports for reasons of foreign policy or short supplies.[12]

On the import side, the U.S. has a law on its books—Section 232 of the 1962 Trade Expansion Act[13]—which permits the executive to limit imports of products when necessary to do so for national security purposes. As of mid-1988, eighteen petitions to use this statute had been received. In only three cases—all involving petroleum products—was the authority actually used, although a 232 petition led to 1986 "voluntary" export restraints on machine tools. Under this statute, citizens can petition their government to apply import restraints, and the government must respond within one year (with a few exceptions), with action restricting imports, or the reasons for not doing so must be published. In practice, the U.S. government looks at a wide variety of factors to determine whether or not import restrictions, for national defense reasons, are justified.[14]

9.3   The General Exceptions and Legislation for Health and Welfare

A very broad list of exceptions to GATT obligations is found in Article XX, and is entitled "General Exceptions." It includes governmental measures undertaken in order to effectively implement policies such as those to protect or promote:

- public morals
- protection of human, animal or plant life or health
- gold or silver trade
- customs enforcement
- monopoly laws (antitrust)
- patents, trademarks, and copyrights
- preventing deceptive practices
- banning products of prison labor
- protecting national treasures
- conserving natural resources
- carrying out an approved commodity agreement
- export restrictions to implement a price-stabilization program[15]

Most of these measures might be thought of as falling within the general "police powers" or "health and welfare powers" of a government. Article XX thus recognizes the importance of a sovereign nation being able to act to promote the purposes on this list, even when such action otherwise conflicts with various obligations relating to international trade.

Consider how many of these measures relate to the national treatment obligations of Article III. Take, for example, a government regulation imposing a minimum standard of purity for certain drugs. If this regulation applies equally to domestic and imported goods, then there is no need to invoke Article XX: the national treatment standard is fulfilled (unless there is implicit or *de facto* discrimination as described in section 8.3). On the other hand, it may be the case that a nation would find it necessary, in order to achieve the objective of protecting consumers against impure drugs, to impose some special regulations to take care of imports. Perhaps the manufacture of imported goods cannot be readily inspected because of the cost of sending inspectors to a foreign country. In such a case it might be reasonable for the importing country to require that the drug imports be subjected to some tests at or after importation. Article XX contemplates this possibility and allows it to occur without breaching GATT.

Many of these exceptions are quite general; for example, "public morals" or "human health." Obviously, clever argumentation could be used to justify practices which have as their secret goal preventing import competition. This article therefore includes some clauses designed to protect against such abuse. Its opening paragraph allows an exception to all GATT obligations for items on the list, provided that "measures are not applied in a manner which would constitute a means of arbitrary or unjustifiable discrimination between countries where the same conditions prevail, or a disguised restriction on international trade . . ."[16]

These phrases may be characterized as "softer" obligations of MFN and national treatment. They allow departure from the strict language of Article I (MFN) and Article III (national treatment) to the extent necessary to pursue the goals listed in Article XX, but not to the extent of non-MFN discrimination or protection of domestic production, if either is not necessary to pursue those listed goals.

Various disputes have been brought to GATT concerning this language. For example, a 1982 GATT panel ruled that a U.S. embargo on imports of tuna and tuna products from Canada was inconsistent with GATT Article XI obligations and not justified by Article XX.[17] The U.S. had argued that its action was taken as an enforcement measure to ensure proper conservation and management of certain fish stocks. The panel noted, however, that Article XX(g) required complementary domestic conservation measures which appeared to be missing in this case. The history of the case suggested that the U.S. was using trade measures to enforce its view of a disputed sea boundary.

As I have mentioned elsewhere,[18] section 337 of U.S. law, a measure most often applied to imports that offend patent rights, has several times been challenged, raising the question under GATT Article XX(d) of whether 337 is "necessary to secure compliance" with patent protection.

In general, the question of the protection of intellectual property rights has become prominent in trade policy discussions. The U.S. in particular has passed many motions to control counterfeiting and violation of patents and copyrights by firms within its borders. The U.S. has used section 337 (described in section 10.7 below) and section 301 (described in chapter 4) to apply pressure on these issues. The 1988 Trade Act has a number of measures relating to this concern. Most prominently, the Act (1) specifically mentions lack of protection of intellectual property rights as 'unreasonable' in its definitions under the section 301 amendments,[19] and (2) changes U.S. section 337 law so that an "injury test" is no longer a necessary prerequisite for an order excluding imports which abuse intellectual property rights.[20] In addition, the Uruguay Round negotiations include consideration of new rules regarding intellectual property.[21]

Several legitimate domestic policies pose particularly difficult conceptual problems for trade policies. We take up two of these in the next two sections, namely the problem of pollution from the manufacturing process and the problem of restrictive business practices and monopolies policies.

9.4 Pollution and Regulation of the Manufacturing Process

If an imported product has the effect when used of creating a health or pollution hazard, the Article III and XX rules make it relatively easy for a nation to take measures to deal effectively with this problem. A nondiscriminatory regulation can be adopted, applying to domestic and imported products alike and requiring certain standards. For example, a law could prohibit automobiles from issuing more than a certain amount of pollutants; or it could prohibit the use of materials in home building which are inflammatory or tend to issue noxious gas when burning.

The more difficult conceptual problem develops from the impact on the competitiveness of industry when a government imposes a requirement of pollution prevention, safety, or health protection on the manufacturing process. Take, as an example, the production of a certain type of plastic toy. The toy itself, let us suppose, is perfectly safe, poses no health hazard, and cannot burn or emit gases. Thus, neither the domestic nor the imported models of this toy will constitute a hazard to be guarded against. However, assume that the manufacture of these toys can be quite hazardous, perhaps because the processing of chemicals to make and mold the plastic involves noxious fumes, danger of explosion, or inhalation of carcinogenic gases.

Likewise assume that the domestic factory producing this toy emits noxious smoke, affecting the environment. In such a case governments will impose requirements to protect health and safety of the workers and the environs on the manufacturing company, and these will have costs that must be included in the price of the product. Now suppose that imports of identical toys occur from a country which is not so careful about the health of its employees or environs and imposes no such regulation. The imports, all other things being equal, can be priced cheaper and could cause competitive distress to the domestic producers. Is this fair? What can be done about it? Could the importing nation take a countermeasure such as (1) impose a ban (or limitation) on imports of goods which are manufactured by processes which cause health, safety, or environmental problems; or (2) impose an additional charge at the border on the imported goods, to equal the amount of the cost which domestic producers incur through compliance with health, safety, or environmental standards; or (3) impose a tax on all goods, domestic and foreign, related to the cost of the regulation; then rebate that tax to domestic manufacturers or subsidize them so as to offset their costs of compliance?

Arguably the importing nation may not do any of these, since the national treatment requirement of Article III of the GATT imposes the obligation to treat "like products" equally, and the products may be considered "like." The article does not allow discrimination on the basis of differences in the country of export or its manufacturing environment.[22] Indeed, to a certain extent, this is what comparative advantage is all about: differences in environments of production, including the environment of government regulation.[23]

Article XX does not seem to help here either. The language prohibits actions which are a "disguised restriction on international trade," and allows exceptions for human health, safety, etc. Although the language is not explicitly restricted to health and safety of the *importing* country, it can be argued that that is what Article XX means. It allows exceptions from GATT obligations, which in general apply to "like products," implying a focus on the product itself, and not on the production process (unless that process affects the *product*).[24] It might be possible to argue the contrary, but I am not aware of any such arguments which have been made in the GATT, although the issue has apparently not been squarely posed.

In addition, some measures could also be inconsistent with MFN requirements of Article I of GATT. For example, suppose country A imports the toys from countries B and C. B regulates the production just as A does, but C does not, and goods from C are therefore cheaper. If A imposed a "regulatory equalization tax" on goods from C and not from B, then an MFN objection could be raised. C would argue that the products are "like products," that Article I requires equal treatment of like products, and that it makes no allowance for unlike production processes.[25] One approach might be to apply a uniform border tax on all imported products, to provide *on the average* for imports to carry the same regulatory cost burden as domestic products, but this, of course, would effectively penalize those countries who do apply such regulatory costs. The products from those countries would be doubly burdened, and this measure would have the perverse effect of providing an incentive to avoid such regulation.

Of course, if the manufacturing process in the exporting country itself causes hazard or pollution in the importing country, such as from smoke or gases which drift across the border, there may be other ways to approach the problem. This is a problem similar to that faced by the U.S. and Canada in connection with acid rain. One solution is a bilateral or multilateral treaty dealing with the problem. Another, less likely to be successful, is a direct international law proceeding arguing wrongdoing in the nature of an "international tort."[26] In some cases (such as Rhine water pollution) there may already exist regional treaties which may be relied upon.[27]

Whether an importing nation could use border restrictions or taxes to equalize the price of imported goods with domestic costs of health and safety regulation is as yet an unresolved issue for the world trading system. It is an issue fraught with dangerous potential. If this principle were extended to many types of government regulation—for example, minimum wage or other labor regulations—it could be the basis of a rash of import restrictions, often defeating the basic goals of comparative advantage. Government regulations vary so greatly that the already difficult conceptual questions of the world's rules on subsidies[28] would pale into insignificance beside the problems which the cost of regulation equalization would create.

Alternatively, to never allow such equalization measures might appear somewhat callous. At one time, Brazil allegedly argued that its capacity to absorb pollution was a feature of its comparative advantage in the production of paper and pulp products. Yet, more recently, Brazilians have realized that even they cannot ignore the environmental effects of some of their factories. The tourism industry is often an important counter-lobby against the manufacturers on this point. Perhaps the best approach is at least temporary "benign neglect," with the possibility that over time many of these problems will sort themselves out as the necessity of health and safety regulation becomes more apparent to more nations.[29]

9.5   Restrictive Business Practices

The international law rules generally apply only to nations, not to individual citizens or business firms. There are growing exceptions to this principle, particularly in the areas of responsibility for war and treatment of prisoners, and of human rights.[30] Nevertheless, most economic international rules, certainly including those of GATT, apply almost exclusively to nations. The wording of GATT, or the IMF charter, and of most FCN treaties[31] reinforces this approach. Article XVII of GATT, applying to state trading enterprises, could be a modest exception, but even there the language requires that "each contracting party undertakes that if it establishes or maintains a State enterprise, . . ." that contracting party will do certain things. In some clauses the contracting party is obligated to require or ensure that the trading enterprise follow certain rules, but the obligation itself does not appear to fall on the enterprise. Most enterprises contemplated by Article XVII would anyway be subject to the control of the national government.

In chapter 13 we will see the difficulty that GATT principles pose for those economic systems which rely extensively on state trading agencies or monopolies. The language of most GATT obligations does not easily stretch to such nonmarket economies and their practices which affect trade. However, in market economies there is an important group of practices which can defeat the underlying purposes of the world trading rules and which are not reached by the GATT language. These are various restrictive business practices.

For example, several nations may assiduously apply all GATT rules, allowing trade to flow freely among them. But a large corporation in one nation may, for purposes of its own, decide that it will buy only domestically produced parts for its products. If the corporation's purposes are not based on efficient economic principles, their effect is to undo the governmental liberal trade policies. Perhaps the corporation is owned by a parent which also owns parts producers, and mandates (or "encourages") purchases from the sister company. Perhaps the domestic product preference is the result of informal pressure from employees, or a mutual back-scratching pact among various domestic industries. Perhaps the domestic buyers rely on domestic producers for a majority of their parts inputs, and those domestic producers have conspired together to prohibit sales of their parts to any domestic buyer who also buys imported goods (a "loyalty rule," sometimes encouraged by a "loyalty rebate," might have this effect).[32]

Many of these practices raise questions of government antitrust or restrictive business practice policies. There is a very large range in the degree to which governments regulate so as to minimize such practices. The United States, for example, is often thought to have one of the most stringent antitrust laws in the world, strongly reinforced by treble damage awards to diligent complainants (sometimes called "private attorneys general"). Yet even in the United States there have been well-publicized instances of private "buy domestic" attitudes.[33]

The draft Havana Charter for an ITO[34] contained an entire chapter devoted to the problem of restrictive business practices (RBP), recognizing the important link between these practices and liberal-trade policies generally. When the ITO failed, the GATT had to step into the trade regulation role. However, the GATT contains nothing addressed to the RBP problem, and when a suggestion was made in 1954 to bring this subject under GATT, the GATT CONTRACTING PARTIES decided only to provide for consultations on the subject and not bring it within the procedures of GATT Article XXIII (on disputes).[35]

Thus, to a certain extent there has been a missing pillar of the world trade regulation system. Perhaps some of this missing pillar is now supplied by several voluntary codes that have been developed to address the problem, including the 1976 *OECD Guidelines for Multinational Enterprises*[36] and the 1980 *UNCTAD set of Multilaterally Agreed Equitable Principles and Rules for the Control of Restrictive Business Practices.*[37]

The problem of restrictive business practices has been raised in recent years in another GATT context. It has been argued (usually in the U.S. where strong RBP laws exist) that toleration by a foreign government of RBPs which tend to exclude imported goods amount to unfair trade practice or a "subsidy" to the local business. In the 1988 Trade Act, for example, section 1301, which amended section 301, includes in the definition of "unreasonable" acts to which section 301 refers the "toleration by a foreign government of systematic anticompetitive activities by private firms or among private firms in the foreign country that have the effect of restricting . . . access of United States goods to purchasing by such firms.[38]

The measure once again points out the gaps in the international trade rules due to the absence of RBP such as those in the ITO Charter. The problem with the U.S. approach, of course, is that it is not tied to an internationally agreed standard for RBP rules. Governments and societies differ greatly in their notion of the appropriate level of RBP rules, and few governments view the rules in the United States as the best approach. Yet the U.S. law now seems to imply that the United States could take unilateral action to "retaliate" against countries who do not measure up to the U.S. view of appropriate RBP rules.

9.6 Balance-of-Payments Exceptions and Currency Obligations

When GATT was drafted, balance-of-payments (BOP) problems were severe for both developing countries and those countries faced with postwar reconstruction. For many years, economists spoke of the "dollar shortage," which reflected the relative strength of the U.S. economy and the need of many nations to buy capital goods from the U.S. One of the purposes of the International Bank for Reconstruction and Development ("World Bank"), which was created at the Bretton Woods Conference along with the International Monetary Fund Charter, was to assist postwar reconstruction of devastated countries. The IMF provided a series of obligations to prevent currency restrictions and manipulations from becoming important barriers to trade, while recognizing that BOP considerations would necessitate short-term exceptional governmental interference with currency transactions.[38] The original IMF charter obligated its member nations to pursue policies to support fixed par values for their currencies.

In the light of these conditions, the GATT draftsmen recognized the necessity for some exceptions from the other GATT obligations in the face of a severe balance-of-payments crisis. In GATT Articles XII, XIII, and XIV they authorized certain trade restrictions when a need due to BOP conditions could be demonstrated. The restrictions they authorized were quotas, and not tariffs. It is interesting to speculate why, in the face of a general policy preference for the "price mechanism" approach of tariffs, the GATT preparers opted instead to allow quantitative restrictions. One possibility was that in many nations, quotas (at least temporary ones) were under the control of executive branches of the government which could act without parliamentary approval. The contrary was normally true for tariffs, which legislatures preserved as their prerogative. Thus the draftsmen (representatives of executives) may have seen the practical advantage of quotas, particularly since a BOP crisis often requires swift action and confidentiality before such action is taken.

History has dealt with this subject differently, however, and has posed one of the persistently most difficult jurisprudential questions for GATT. In fact, many contracting parties in the face of BOP difficulties have resorted to tariff "surcharges." (A tariff surcharge is an across-the-board *ad valorem* tariff on all imports, added to the tariff otherwise charged on imports.) In general, a surcharge is supposed to be applied uniformly to all goods, and to apply to otherwise nondutiable goods as well as those which otherwise are subject to duties. A 10 percent surcharge, for instance, would apply this additional amount of tariff to all goods. Those already subject to 5 percent tariff would now be subject to 15 percent. Those otherwise duty-free goods would now be subject to the 10 percent surcharge.[40]

In some cases waivers have been given for the application of such a surcharge, but in other cases the surcharge has been used without any GATT legal cover.[41] Since a surcharge inevitably results in a tariff charged on most goods which exceeds the tariff binding of that country's GATT schedule, it is in those cases quite clearly inconsistent with GATT obligations. On the other hand, the economic policies would support the tariff surcharge as preferable to the use of quotas.[42] Thus, the GATT BOP rules are anomalous. It has been argued that the GATT rules should be changed. On the other hand, an argument against changing the rule has been made that by keeping the GATT rule as it is, the CONTRACTING PARTIES, while (to a certain extent) tolerating the use of surcharges, have more "leverage" to urge the withdrawal of the surcharge than they would have if it were technically legal. This is an interesting but troublesome argument, and it usually overlooks the subtle longer-term damage done to the fabric of the legal structure involved.

One of the major BOP tariff surcharges was that imposed by the United States president in August 1971. The level was set at 10 percent, although some exceptions were made, particularly because the basic tariff statute had lower tariffs and under the U.S. Constitution the president did not have authority to go above these statutory limits. The surcharge was part of a broader program designed to correct a serious currency crisis for the United States. Other parts included the closing of the "gold window": i.e., ceasing to buy dollars with gold at a set price; the introduction of the Domestic International Sales Corporation (DISC) legislation;[43] and the imposition of internal price controls on certain products.[44] All of these measures had serious domestic and international legal problems. The "gold-window closing" essentially left the dollar to float in world markets, and was a violation of U.S. government obligations under the IMF. Subsequently, the IMF charter was amended to accommodate floating, which had been strongly recommended by many economists for more than a decade. The DISC was challenged in GATT.[45] Domestic price controls were authorized by very broad ambiguous language in a statute which the president had not sought and had early intimated he would never use.[46] All parts of this program except the DISC were challenged in court litigation in the United States, but ultimately all were upheld.[47]

In a world with floating exchange rates, it has been suggested that there is no longer any justification for the use of trade restrictions for balance-of-payments reasons.[48] In theory, the exchange rate is supposed to shift and cause automatic adjustment in the balance of trade and payments. The GATT BOP language, which allows use of the quota exception, tends to tie the exception to decline or need for increase in monetary reserves. However, with floating exchange rates, reserves are no longer such a central feature of the world economic system, and it can be argued that almost never will the GATT criteria be met. On the other hand, the experience of more than a decade of floating leaves many questions unanswered, and there are many voices articulating the need for trade measures because of the misfunctioning of the exchange-rate system.[49]

As a result of the Tokyo Round, the CONTRACTING PARTIES adopted an "Declaration on Trade Measures Taken for Balance-of-Payments Purposes."[50] The first article of this declaration states the following:

The procedures for examination stipulated in Articles XII and XVIII shall apply to all restrictive import measures taken for balance-of-payments purposes. The application of restrictive import measures taken for balance-of-payments purposes shall be subject to the following conditions in addition to those provided for in Articles XII, XIII, XV and XVIII without prejudice to other provisions of the General Agreement.[51]

Although this language in its own terms does not modify the GATT, the language nevertheless seems to contemplate measures other than quotas, so arguably it gives some "legal comfort" for the use of surcharges. As is the case with many GATT rules, the ambiguity appears studied and intentional!

United States law regarding the use of a tariff surcharge is also interesting. The president was challenged in court for imposing the 1971 surcharge, but ultimately the courts upheld him under the emergency powers of the U.S. Trading with the Enemy Act.[52] The Congress was sufficiently disturbed, however, about presidential encroachment on its tariff domain, that it included in the 1974 Trade Act a section designed to clarify the president's authority in this regard.[53] This section gives him explicit authority to impose a surcharge, but limits it in amount and duration unless Congress approves differently. The section also calls upon the president to "seek modifications in international agreements aimed at allowing the use of surcharges in place of quantitative restrictions . . ." in BOP cases, and some authorities of this enactment are tied to international obligations.[54]

Developing countries can often argue that the BOP exceptions of GATT (Article XVIII contains some which are targeted to such countries) permit them to use quotas, since many of these countries are perennially in BOP difficulties. This exception to GATT therefore has been a major "legal cover" for many developing countries acting without the normal disciplines of international trade rules,[55] and is a source of scrutiny and potential negotiation in the Uruguay Round of trade negotiations.[56]

10

Unfair Trade and the
Rules on Dumping

10.1 The Level Playing Field and the Policies of Managing Interdependence: The "Interface" Concept

Unfair Trade Rules and the Policies of International Trade

Other than import restraints, there are a number of policies of firms or governments which are designed to influence international trade flows. In particular, both governments and enterprises may wish to promote exports through the use of discriminatory pricing or subsidies. For decades, many versions of these practices have been considered by the international system and many national systems to be unfair. To such practices the international rules have permitted certain responses from the importing nations, such as antidumping duties or countervailing duties.[1]

In this context there has long been an understood distinction between responses to "fair trade" and those to "unfair trade." The escape clause, for example, allows import-restraining responses regardless of whether imports have benefited from unfair practices. Responses to dumping or subsidies, however, are based on a totally different theory. In these and other cases, the basic idea is that the response of importing nations is designed partly to offset the effects of the unfair actions, and perhaps to go further and have a sort of "punitive" effect to inhibit such actions in the future.[2] However, the distinction between fair and unfair trade has become increasingly blurred in recent years, partly because of some fundamental disagreement about what should be called unfair. Arguments in fair cases, such as escape-clause proceedings, often include reference to unfairness; while invocation of some of the unfair trade proceedings sometimes occurs in circumstances where it is reasonably clear that the petitioners seek a sort of safeguard relief, even though there is not clear agreement among nations that the practices they complain about are unfair.[3]

A commonly expressed goal of trade policy in connection with "unfair" practices is that of the "level playing field."[4] This evokes the notion of economic activity as a game, and the notion that the competition in this game should be played according to a set of rules which all participants share. Unfortunately, it is often very difficult to carry this analogy too far. Societies and their economic systems differ so dramatically that what seems unfair to members of one society may seem perfectly fair to those of another society.

The Interface Question[5]

Many of the unfair trading practices that we will examine have been considered unfair because they interfere with or distort free-market-economy principles. GATT, of course, was largely based upon such principles. It is not surprising, therefore, that it is often difficult to apply GATT's trading rules to nonmarket economies. In addition, even among the relatively similar western industrial-market economies, there are wide differences to do with the degree of government involvement in economy, in the forms of regulation or ownership of various industrial or other economic segments. As world economic interdependence has increased, it has become more difficult to manage relationships among various economies. This problem is analogous to the difficulties involved in trying to get two computers of different designs to work together. To do so, one needs an interface mechanism to mediate between the two computers. Likewise, in international economic relations, particularly in trade relations, some "interface mechanism" may be necessary to allow different economic systems to trade together harmoniously.

These problems will become clear in this and the next chapter. We will see that part of the definition of dumping is selling for export at below-cost prices. But in nonmarket economies are there meaningful costs and prices? In the case of subsidies, it may be easy to identify cash payments to an exporter, but there are myriad government policies that affect the competitiveness of a business. If the goal is really to achieve a "level playing field," does that imply that all governments must adopt uniform policies? If not, how will it be possible to analyze the effect of different policies? Besides, isn't trade to some degree based on differences between countries (as I indicated in chapter 1)?

In some cases, the problem involves questions of preventing or inhibiting what are deemed unfair practices, such as dumping or export subsidies. As the subject of unfair practices develops, however, it becomes clear that it reaches deeply into matters of domestic concern to governments, and the questions of unfairness become more controversial. In many cases of subsidies, for example, the government providing such subsidies feels that they are an essential and praiseworthy tool of government, sometimes useful to correct disparities of income or to help disadvantaged groups or regions. With respect to dumping, it is argued that such a practice—a form of "price discrimination"—actually has beneficial effects on world and national prosperity, encouraging competition. The rules for responding to some unfair trade practices allow use of import restrictions, such as added duties (and also quantitative measures applied pursuant to settlements of dumping or countervailing cases), which can be anticompetitive and can be detrimental to world welfare. In some cases, exporting nations feel bitterness toward these import restrictions on their trade, and argue that the rules on unfair trade are being manipulated by special interests for effectively protectionist reasons.

An example of the "interface" problem and the difficulties of defining unfairness can be seen in the following problem, which focuses on so-called variable-cost analysis. It may arise in the context of two economies who differ only slightly in their acceptance of basic free-market economic principles. As the problem demonstrates, even given such similarities, there may be differences between the ways the respective economies operate over the course of the business cycle that may create situations that are considered unfair, even though these differences may not have resulted from any consciously unfair policies or practices.

Take an industrial sector (such as steel) in two economies (such as the United States and Japan) with the following characteristics:

Society A is characterized by:

1. Worker tenure (no layoffs of workers)

2. Capitalization with a high debt-equity ratio (e.g., 90 percent debt)

Society B is characterized by:

1. No worker tenure (wages for workers are therefore variable costs)

2. Capitalization with low debt-equity ratio (e.g., less than 50 percent; dividends can be skipped)

In times of slack demand, economists note that it is rational for a firm to continue to produce as long as it can sell its product at or above its short-term variable costs. This is true because it must in any event pay its fixed costs. Of course, this is true only for limited periods; presumably, over the regular course of the business cycle, the firm must not incur losses in the long term.

An analysis of the short-term variable costs of firms in societies A and B can be detailed as follows:

Costs of a firm (per unit of production)

	Society A	Society B
Plant upkeep	$ 20. fixed	$ 20. fixed
Debt service	$ 90. fixed	$ 50. fixed
Dividends (cost of capital)	$ 10. variable	$ 50. variable
Worker costs	$240. fixed	$240. variable
Cost of materials	$240. variable	$240. variable
Total "costs" (per unit of production)	$600.	$600.
Fixed	$350.	$ 70.
Variable	$250.	$530.

I use the word "cost" to include use of capital, which some may dislike, but it makes the point.

Thus, total average "costs" in both societies are the same, but as noted here, it will be rational for producers in society A to continue production so long as they can obtain a price of $250, while producers in society B need to receive a price of $530. Thus, in a period of falling prices and demand, the producers in society A can be expected to garner, through exports to society B, an increasing share of society B's market. Suppose this happens, and the firms in society B go out of business. Are society A's exports to society B unfair?

There are no easy answers to such questions. Indeed, they are much more complicated than the foregoing case indicates. For example, whatever general rules exist, it is argued that special considerations should apply to developing countries.[6] In addition, it must be recognized that economic structural characteristics vary from sector to sector within a country, and that advantages that tilt one way for one sector might tilt in the opposite direction for another sector. Furthermore, these differences may alter across time, and the direction of the tilt might reverse. One of the questions I pose in section 10.6 is whether the antidumping rules of trade policy are actually performing an "interface" or buffering role, rather than a role of response to "unfairness."

10.2 The Policies of Antidumping Rules

What Is Dumping?[7]

For almost 100 years international trade policy rules have recognized that "dumping" is a practice which "is to be condemned," and have allowed an importing country to take certain countermeasures, at least when the dumped goods cause "material injury" to competing industries in the importing country.[8]

The definition of dumping, as described in GATT and elsewhere,[9] is often expressed as the sale of products for export at a price less than normal value, where normal value means roughly the price for which those same products are sold on the "home" or exporting market. In other words:

$$\text{home market sales price} \quad \text{export sales price} \quad = \quad \text{margin of dumping}$$

When that margin is greater than zero, there is "dumping" in the sense used in international trade policy.

So defined, the concept of dumping is relatively simple. However, as applied, it is anything but simple. Each term of the equation involves complex calculations. A threshold question is, What level of trade should be used to judge price—e.g., wholesale or retail? Presumably whatever is used should be the same for both home-market and export sales.[10] Then, with respect to the home-market sales price, how is it to be calculated? Often an "average" of prices at which the product is offered in the home market is used, but a complex series of adjustments may be necessary to align that price with comparable prices for exports. Suppose, however, the goods are not sold in the home market, or too few are sold to use as the basis of a valid home market average price. Then laws may call for comparison to one of several other measures of "normal value," such as comparison to prices for sale to other countries (third markets), or to a "constructed price" composed of an evaluation of cost plus reasonable profit.

Whenever a "constructed cost" calculation is required, however, matters can become extremely complex. A foreign country may have different accounting systems, the firm involved may produce many products whose costs will have to be allocated, a foreign language is often involved, and methods of doing business vary greatly. Under some national laws, home-market prices which do not represent full recovery of cost plus a reasonable profit must be excluded from the home-price average. In such cases a "constructed cost" methodology must be followed to determine which home-market sales to exclude from the average, and this methodology introduces virtually all the same complexities of constructed cost computations in the absence of home-market sales.

Likewise, finding the "export sales price" can become very complex. Often a number of adjustments to the transaction price actually used in an export sale will be necessary to try to keep comparisons with home prices fair. Adjustments might include packaging, advertising costs, warranty services, etc.

Under most national systems of dumping law, after (or while) there is a finding of dumping (or in U.S. law, Less Than Fair Value [LTFV] sales), a separate determination is made regarding whether the requisite "injury" has been caused by the dumping. If both dumping and injury findings are affirmative, then duties will be applied at the border up to the amount of the margin of dumping.

Why Do Enterprises Dump? Profit Maximizing and Marginal Costs

Let us explore for a moment some of the motives of an enterprise in pursuing a pricing policy which is generally called "dumping." Why would enterprises dump?

In fact, there are understandable "profit maximizing" reasons why a firm might want to engage in such "discriminatory" pricing. Suppose, for example, a firm produces one million radios per year from a single plant which operates only a day shift. Suppose that it prices those radios on its home market at the equivalent of $20 each, and makes about $4 profit each. Suppose further that the variable or "avoidable" costs of those radios (workers' wages, cost of materials, etc.) are about $10 each, thus suggesting that the fixed or unavoidable costs (capital equipment, the plant, etc.) are about $6 each. Since the firm is making a $4 profit per unit with its one million sales per year, it has apparently covered *all* of its fixed costs with those sales. It could now sell more radios at anything above its variable costs of $10, and make an additional profit.[11]

For example, suppose the firm could add a night shift and produce another million radios per year. The plant and equipment costs are presumably already covered by the first million radios produced. If it could somehow sell another million without affecting the price it is receiving for its first million, then any price above the $10 variable costs will add to the firm's total profit. If it sold the night production at $14, for example, it would add $4 million to its previous profit of $4 million per year—i.e., doubling its profits. The catch, of course, is not to affect the price received for the first million produced. This implies somehow segmenting the available market, or, in other words, seeking a totally different market for the firm's night production. But, in addition, the new market must be such that buyers there cannot easily ship back to the home or first market; otherwise, the price of the day production will be undercut.

How can this segmenting be done? One way is to charge different prices in different geographical areas, in circumstances such that the return shipment costs will inhibit buyers in the lower price region from reselling into the higher price region. In some respects this method evokes normal "discriminatory pricing" questions discussed within a national boundary, such as those connected with the U.S. law known as the Robinson–Patman Act, which may prohibit such dual pricing behavior. In fact, at present, the U.S. government apparently does not enforce the Robinson–Patman Act,[12] and there is considerable economic policy literature which urges the repeal of this act; many respectable economists do not see anything wrong with discriminatory pricing as such.[13]

The Policies of International Antidumping Rules

With respect to the core idea, export sales at prices lower than those of home market sales, what is the underlying policy that has led the international trading community for more than a century to consider dumping as an action which is somehow "unfair"? That is a question that is not easy to answer. The original focus on the "price difference" can be described as a focus on "price discrimination." There seems to be a notion that sales at different prices to different persons is somehow unfair. Perhaps some of this is left over from medieval notions of "fair price."[14]

The differences can go either way, however. The person charged more can be just as aggrieved as those (usually the competing sellers) who complain that some persons have been charged less. Clearly part of the worry has to do with monopoly or competition policy. This is true not only for international but also for domestic transactions, as the U.S. Robinson–Patman Act bears out. Discussion about the formulation of laws relating to price discrimination often include concerns about large and economically powerful firms using market leverage to drive small concerns out of business, thus reducing competition so the predatory larger firms can then raise prices and reap monopoly profits.[15] This is often called "predatory behavior," or "predation." If the seller prices his goods in a particular market so as to drive out the competition, with a view to later raising his prices (which he can do when the competition has exited), this may be "monopolistic" behavior of a type which is condemned by other laws.[16] Economists, including Jacob Viner in his classic 1923 work,[17] tend to be skeptical of the predation argument, however, because they doubt that the chances for success of predation are very good. If a number of firms are producing for a market, they would need to collude in order to raise prices later. They would also need to keep out potential new producers, and if prices go up this can be very difficult.

One complaint about dumping is that government-imposed barriers may exist at the border to prevent reshipment of the goods into the home market. Thus, if there is a 40 percent tariff on imported radios, the night production can be shipped abroad at a price as low as $12, without much fear that foreign buyers would try to reintroduce those radios into the home market to undercut the home-market price. Therefore it has been argued that international trade dumping depends heavily on import barriers of the exporting country, and that this is unfair.[18] A counter-argument is that the problem in such a case is the import barriers, *not* the dumping as such, and that the sanctions against dumping are an inefficient way to get at the true problem.[19]

In section 10.4, we consider certain questions about sales below costs. Apart from predation, economists note that there are several incentives for a firm to sell at a price that may be below costs.[20] One incentive arises when production has had to be scheduled before prices are known, and when prices become known production costs are already "sunk" (e.g., the crop is planted). A second incentive is the one in which the enterprise somehow rewards market share rather than profit, perhaps because of historical patterns or internal policy struggles. A third incentive is the one in which a firm finds it advantageous to build market share (e.g., to increase volume and thus to reduce unit costs: the "learn by doing" argument). In all these cases, economic policy suggests that overall welfare is improved by the below-cost sales, and so these practices should not be punished, whether in domestic or in export trade. Total consumer welfare is greater than the loss to producers caused by the new competition. Thus, such policies would counsel against the use of antidumping duties.

Of course, if government decision makers are more responsive to producers than to consumers (as is often the case), the loss to competing *producers* may be given more weight in government policy. In this connection a meaningful safeguards policy to limit imports can be justified.[21] However, for "safeguards" the fact that imports are or are not dumped is mostly irrelevant. If antidumping duties are used, it is for "safeguard" reasons, and not because those practices are "unfair" or damaging to the economic welfare of the importing nation.

10.3 Antidumping Rules and Their Sources

History and Origins

The concept of "dumping" in international trade has a long history. Jacob Viner reports mention of "bounty" practices by Adam Smith. Likewise, Viner notes statements by Alexander Hamilton in debates in the U.S. in 1791 warning about foreign country practices of underselling competitors in other countries, thus to "frustrate the first efforts to introduce [a business] . . . into another by temporary sacrifices, recompensed, perhaps by extraordinary indemnifications of the government of such country . . ."[22] Other allegations of dumping by British manufacturers into the new American market are reported, and public discussion of this problem as well as various legislative attempts to deal with it were reported during most of the nineteenth century.[23] Indeed, one of the first United States laws relating to international trade was concerned with practices we might identify as dumping.[24]

Viner reports that during the early twentieth century, dumping was most widespread by firms in Germany.[25] During and after World War I, the U.S. Congress enacted several antidumping statutes.[26] During the 1930s the U.S. embarked on its reciprocal trade agreements program, negotiating about thirty bilateral treaties for the mutual reduction of tariff barriers. Many of these agreements recognized the "problem" of dumping, and allowed national government treaty partners to use antidumping duties to offset dumping.[27]

The International Rules: GATT and the Codes

Given the long history of national and international concern with dumping, it is not surprising that when the GATT was negotiated in 1947, special provision was made for cases of dumping. Article VI of

GATT allows GATT contracting parties to utilize antidumping duties to offset the margin of dumping of dumped goods, provided that it can be shown that such dumping is causing or threatens to cause "material injury" to competing domestic industries.[28] Today this is still the core international rule regarding dumping.

As time passed, however, some countries in GATT began to feel that other countries, in applying their antidumping laws, were doing it in such a way as to raise a new barrier to trade. Some believed that anti-dumping procedures, such as delay, or certain calculations of dumping margins, certain applications of the injury test, etc., were causing restrictions and distortions on international trade flows, sometimes by creating a period of risk and uncertainty to traders in a particular product. Thus, during the Kennedy Round of GATT trade negotiations (1962–1967), the GATT contracting parties negotiated an "Anti-dumping (AD) Code," which set forth a series of procedural and substantive rules regarding the application of antidumping duties, partly due to the desire to limit antidumping duty practices and procedures of governments which were damaging international trade.[29]

In the United States (ironically, since the U.S. was a major proponent of the AD Code), this Code caused a major constitutional problem. The Code, as an international treaty, had been signed by authority of the president, but there was no participation of the U.S. Congress, either through the constitutional Senate advice-and-consent procedure, or by statute adopted by the Congress as a whole. The president's officials argued that the Code could be accepted within the existing constitutional and statutory powers of the president, but the Congress disagreed with him. The Congress enacted legislation that prohibited the executive and the then Tariff Commission (later the International Trade Commission) from following the rules of the GATT AD Code in certain circumstances.[30] Although the U.S. consistently argued that the internal measures it took were an adequate compliance with the Code, many other nations did not agree.[31]

Although at the outset of the Tokyo Round negotiation in 1973 the subject of dumping was not on the agenda, a rather sudden turn of events late in that negotiation[32] caused the negotiators to take up the dumping subject; and, partly to provide symmetry with the drafting which was occurring in the negotiations for the subsidies Code, the GATT parties developed a new antidumping Code, which came into effect in 1979, replacing the 1967 AD Code.[33] This new Code has twenty-five signatories, and among them this Code prevails over any prior agreements on dumping, including the 1967 Code.[34] As of January 1989, all 1969 Code signatories but Malta and Portugal[35] have signed the new Code, and Portugal's entry into the EC causes it to be bound to the new Code through the EC acceptance.[36]

Thus the international commitments concerning dumping are now set forth in the GATT, particularly Article VI, and in the 1979 Tokyo Round Antidumping Code, officially titled "Agreement on the Implementation of Article VI of the General Agreement on Tariffs and Trade."[37] These commitments can be briefly over summarized as follows:

First, nothing in these agreements obligates nations or firms to refrain from practices that are construed as dumping, as such. The GATT Article VI language does say that dumping ". . . is to be condemned if it causes or threatens material injury to an established industry," but the wording is far short of a binding obligation to prevent dumping.[38] Of course, these international treaties do not apply to private persons or firms; rather, they apply to nations who accept the treaties. But the wording of obligations does not require nations themselves to refrain from dumping, nor does it require nations to see to it that firms refrain from dumping. This contrasts with the international obligations concerning subsidies and countervailing duties, which do have some commitments against certain types of uses of subsidies. This difference has sometimes been overlooked or misrepresented by political leaders or diplomats.[39]

On the other hand, the GATT and Code language do provide for a permitted response to dumping in certain circumstances. This permitted response is the "antidumping" duty, (which otherwise might be prohibited by GATT commitments on tariff maximums and MFN treatment). The treaty obligations specify three type of obligations constraining the use of such duties: (1) detailed rules about what facts constitute "dumping"; (2) detailed rules about the "injury requirement"; and (3) detailed rules about the procedures under which governments determine and apply these antidumping duties.

The basic overall pattern of antidumping law, derived from these rules and the national implementations of them, is that dumping requires a certain comparison of export price with "normal" price (usually home-market price). For responding duties to be permitted, there must also be found "material injury" or threat occurring to the competing domestic industry in the importing country (or preventing the establishment of such an industry). If, and only if, these two conditions are found to exist (dumping plus injury), then the importing country may apply antidumping duties. That country is, however, obligated to see to it that its procedures and provisional remedies for dumping are kept consistent with a number of international rules in the GATT and the Code.

The National Rules: The United States and its Procedures

Although the GATT reports indicate that as many as twleve countries have used antidumping laws from time to time,[40] it is commonly understood that four nations are the principal users of antidumping laws: the United States, the EC, Canada, and Australia. These four countries account for the vast majority of antidumping cases brought in the world, although there are some signs that other countries are "learning this game," and may increasingly use antidumping laws as a means of inhibiting imports.[41]

In the United States, antidumping laws were enacted in 1916 and 1921.[42] The 1916 act, however, was primarily patterned after U.S. antitrust acts, and provides a private right of action by domestic producers who feel they are harmed by dumped imports, provided that a certain predatory intent can be proven. There has never been a case in the United States which has been successful under this statute. In 1970, a landmark case was brought under the 1916 act, but in the end, after much litigation (some of it mingled with antitrust litigation), the U.S. courts determined that the case had not been made for recovery under the 1916 act.[43] Although there have been proposals to enhance the possibility of 1916 act litigation,[44] as of this writing those proposals have not become law.

The principal U.S. law regarding antidumping which has in fact been applied is the 1921 Antidumping Act.[45] It is this law which provides for application of antidumping duties by federal government authorities when it is ascertained that imported goods have been dumped and are causing injury in the United States. It will be noted that there is a two-part test (as required under international law), namely the determination of "dumping," and then the determination of "injury." The injury test is the same as that for subsidy cases, and I will describe that in section 10.5 of this chapter.[46]

Since the introduction of the new antidumping regime in 1979, there have been nearly 420 petitions accepted by the Commerce Department. Seven have resulted in suspension agreements (an eighth was later revoked and the case withdrawn), and material injury was finally determined to exist in about 120 cases. Of the 300 remaining cases, approximately half were withdrawn and the remainder were pending as of September 1988.[47]

Prior to 1974, the laws of dumping in the United States were sufficiently vague that they allowed the administrating authorities considerable discretion. In addition, it was not clear that there would be an
opportunity to appeal to the courts to overturn administrative determinations. In the 1974 Trade Act, the Congress took its first steps to remedy
what it perceived to be an improper mode of implementation of antidumping laws. Thus, in this statute, the Congress provided time limits
and judicial review.[48]

By the mid-1970s, the pressures of domestic interests for a more diligent application of antidumping duties were becoming very strong,
partly because other major trade barriers, particularly the tariff, had
been substantially dismantled since 1948 under the GATT rules. Thus
considerably more attention was focused on the antidumping rules
(and, as we shall see in the next chapter, on the subsidy and countervailing duty rules). Some of these pressures had been building for years,
and were responsible for the congressional antagonism to the U.S. participation in the 1967 AD Code.

In 1979, as a result of the Tokyo Round negotiations which led to a
new international antidumping code, the Congress embodied in the
Trade Agreements Act of 1979 (implementing the Tokyo Round results)
a new statutory framework for U.S. antidumping law. This new statute,
in the context of implementing the new international Code, substantially overhauled the U.S. rules for antidumping duties.[49] These rules
will be addressed in later sections, but a brief overview of the procedural
steps of an antidumping case may be useful.

Under the current United States law, antidumping cases (as well as
subsidy and countervailing duty cases) are handled by at least two
administrative agencies of the United States.[50] A complaint must be filed
simultaneously with the Commerce Department and with the International Trade Commission (ITC). The Commerce Department is responsible for examining whether dumping exists: i.e., whether there is a
margin of dumping. The ITC is responsible for examining whether the
dumping or dumped goods are causing "material injury" of the competing
industry within the United States. A fairly elaborate series of procedural
steps is mandated by the statute, roughly outlined as follows:

1. Filing of the complaint with both Commerce and the ITC.

2. Within forty-five days, an ITC preliminary determination of whether
there is any reasonable chance of finding injury (a negative finding
would halt the procedure).

3. A preliminary determination by the Commerce Department of whether dumping margins exist. If this determination is affirmative, customs-entry "liquidations" are suspended on the goods, and all imports of these goods thereafter are subject to the ultimate antidumping duties which are applied. There are also provisions for retrospective application to earlier imports. The preliminary determination is followed by a fairly elaborate additional "verification," undertaken by investigators who travel abroad to ascertain various facts, such as the foreign-market price.

4. A final determination by the Department of Commerce of whether a margin of dumping exists. If this is negative, the case ceases. If it is affirmative, the case then proceeds to the ITC.

5. ITC final determination of the existence of "material injury" caused by the dumped imports.

6. If both the Commerce Department final determination and the ITC injury determination are affirmative, then the Commerce Department will issue an antidumping order which must be implemented by the Customs officials at all the ports of entry into the United States with respect to the goods from the sources stipulated in the antidumping order.

The original complaint procedures, undertaken by administrative agencies, and the antidumping order, can apply either to specific producers abroad, or to all producers in a particular country.[51] In order to ascertain the necessary facts, it is useful to have the cooperation of foreign producers. Needless to say, such producers do not have an overwhelming incentive to cooperate, except for the fact that U.S. law allows the administrators, in the absence of cooperation, to use "best evidence." Sometimes best evidence is little more than the allegations of the complaint brought by the competing domestic U.S. interest, and thus can operate to the substantial detriment of the foreign producers. All this induces considerable cooperation from foreign producers.[52]

Once the antidumping order has been issued, then a very intricate set of procedures is put in place, which can only be briefly suggested here. Essentially, each customs entry of goods from the producer sources or producer country identified in the antidumping order, must be compared to see whether the price of the goods in that transaction is less than some benchmark price determined to be the fair market price (i.e., the home-market price in the foreign producing market.) In some countries, by way of contrast, a flat antidumping duty amount is assessed on all goods from the identified sources. In the United States, however, an attempt is made to match each entry with the fair market price which has been ascertained through part of the procedure; although for administrative reasons, certain annual determinations are made and certain estimates are utilized in the process. In addition, there is an annual review process of outstanding antidumping orders, and in some circumstances the antidumping orders can be repealed, renewed, or a different level of fair market price set.[53]

Although there have been a fairly large number of signatories to both the 1967 and 1979 Codes, very few nations have regularly used their antidumping legislation. Since 1980, nine countries have notified the initiation of actions to GATT. Of these, the so-called "Big Four" notified almost 98 percent. Since 1982 Australia has notified approximately 220 actions, and since 1980 Canada has notified about 225, the European Community about 215, and the United States about 240.[54] There are also indications that other countries are becoming interested in the use of antidumping laws, in particular Japan and Mexico.[55]

10.4 Dumping Margins and LTFV

Introduction

To find "dumping," we have noted that the rules compare the price for export with some "fairness" benchmark. At one time this was essentially a price discrimination test—a comparison of the price for export with the price on the home (exporting) market. However, there was always allowance for the case where the home price was not comparable, either because there were no home market sales, or for other reasons. The traditional approach for such cases has been to turn to comparisons with sales to third markets, or to a "constructed cost" method of arriving at a "fair" home price.

During recent decades, however, more attention has been focused on the "cost" of the goods produced abroad, for reasons we shall soon explore, so that there has been a shift from exploring potential "price discrimination" to a determination of whether the exported goods have been sold at a price which is "below cost."

In this section we will briefly examine some of these concepts, looking first at the determination of "export price," and then to the prices used for comparison. In U.S. law this is called the Less Than Fair Value (LTFV) determination, which is carried out by the Commerce Department. As previously noted, this determination process can be extremely complex, partly because of the large number of potential "adjustments" that can be made either to the export price figures or to the comparable home-market price in order to arrive at what is deemed a fair comparison. In this chapter we can only scratch the surface and suggest general approaches, leaving to specialized treatises the lawyer's details of how these computations and comparisons are made.[56]

In U.S. law, however, a curious legal aspect might be noted. The language of the statute speaks of "less than fair value," but does not define it.[57] Under the U.S. law, if it is determined that LTFV sales exist, then the authorities determine a "margin of dumping" by making the comparison we will study later. This margin can, if injury is found, determine the amount of the antidumping duty to be applied at the border. For this reason it is often assumed that the LTFV determination is essentially the task of determining the margin of dumping. It seems possible under the statute for the authorities to find a dumping margin but to rule that there is no LTFV. In at least one case this may have been done.[58]

U.S. authorities have also generally refused to proceed with cases when the dumping margin is less than *de minimis*, and have defined that to mean 0.5 percent or less.[59] This concept relates to the injury test. Some would argue that the *de minimis* level should be substantially raised—e.g., to 3 percent or 4 percent—and then the technique of determining injury and its cause could be different. We will return to this issue in Chapter 11, with its discussion of countervailing duties.

The Price Comparison: Export Sales Price ("United States Price") and the Home-Market Price

The price of the goods exported is the starting point of the analysis. The U.S. law specifies that this shall be the "export sales price" or the "purchase price," whichever is appropriate. Basically, the transaction price is the beginning figure. Other adjustments are necessary also. Essentially the rules aim at an FOB or ex factory price, at the wholesale level, in the country of export.[60] This price, under U.S. law, must exclude the freight. Supposedly, shipping costs are responsible for part of the natural comparative lack of advantage of imported goods, so it is deemed unfair to allow them to be considered part of the price for comparison purposes. Likewise, the price must not include duties paid in the United States.

The figure to compare is the home-market price, or as U.S. law specifies, the "Foreign Market Value." This is the price normally offered for sale in the usual wholesale quantities. There is, however, an important difference between the two prices compared. For the export sales price, a *single* price can be matched to see if dumping or LTFV exists. The foreign market value, however, is an average. If prices on the home market vary over some time span — e.g., if ten sales are at an average price of $95 but range from $90 to $100 — then the foreign market value is this average. Yet ten *export sales* may be at exactly the same distribution of prices, averaging $95 but ranging from $90 to $100, and in this case about half of the export sales will be at a price below the foreign-market value; and thus dumping or LTFV has been established.[61] This disparity of treatment in U.S. law (and in laws of other countries) has been criticized, and it is one of the reasons why it is sometimes argued that the antidumping laws are "tilted" against imports.

Many attorney hours are spent on numerous potential adjustments to each of the prices to be compared.[62] For example, if the exported goods benefit from a superior warranty, or from better after-sale service than the home-market goods receive, adjustments will be made to make the prices comparable. Differences of quality or financing assistance must be taken into account. A troublesome and perplexing issue during recent years has been the difference of treatment of sales expenses and commissions for goods sold by the exporter to an independent importer compared to those sold by that exporter to a subsidiary.[63]

If there are no comparable home-market prices, for example, on a product sold only for export (the classic case of golf carts from Poland), then the rules provide alternative benchmarks. One of these is to look to comparable sales in third markets as an indication of the "home-market price."[64] Again, care must be taken to establish comparability. The goods may differ in quality, or type, or other characteristics, which may make them hard to compare.

If third-market sales are not to be used to determine the dumping comparison, then the traditional rules allow a "constructed cost" approach. In this situation the export sales price will be compared to a price that is "constructed" as the "fair" or "home-market" price. This constructed price is developed by examining the costs of the product and then adding to it a profit amount to establish what shall be deemed the "home-market" price.[65] It is not hard to see how difficult this can sometimes be.

In addition, U.S. law since the 1974 act has added another wrinkle. That act now requires that even if home-market sales are found, in establishing the average home-market price that will be the "benchmark" for comparison, all sales that are at a price below cost plus profit must be excluded from the average.[66] This will tend to raise that average and thus make it more likely that a dumping margin will be found. For example, if, in our specific case above with an average price of $95, the costs plus profits of the product are deemed to be, say, $92, then the home-market "average" price will be the average of sales excluding those below $92. Thus the average is likely to move up to $96, and more export sales will be found to be under that level—ergo, dumped.

There certainly is logic to support this shift in average, if there is some reason to think that below-cost sales are somehow unfair also, and if (a big "if") the methods of computing the constructed costs are "fair." We will now turn to some problems about that.

Constructed Cost and Its Conceptual and Practical Difficulties

There are many difficulties of computing the constructed cost of a product, and some of these difficulties raise questions about the administration of antidumping laws of various countries. To begin with, investigators of the importing country must explore in considerable depth the accounting and data of foreign firms to establish benchmark figures. This means a considerable intrusion into a foreign society and into foreign firms. Reluctant cooperation is obtained by rules of the importing country such as the "best evidence available." In addition, we have noted that differences in language and accounting methods make the investigators' tasks formidable and cast some doubts on the validity of the process. But besides these practical administrative problems, there are some very worrisome conceptual problems also.

If a firm produces multiple products, it may be very difficult to allocate costs among products. This difficulty may be compounded if the product for the export market differs slightly (for marketing and customer acceptance reasons) from the products sold at home. More significant, however, is the extremely difficult problem of selecting which longer-term costs to include in a "constructed cost."

As we noted at the beginning of this chapter, firms can reasonably sell products at a price that is only slightly larger than so-called short-term variable cost. This is because the firm must pay the longer-term fixed "costs" (debt service, etc.) regardless of whether it produces goods. Thus, if it is able to produce at slightly more than a short-term variable cost, it has incentive to do so. Unfortunately, however, the U.S. law regarding the calculation of the foreign-market price does not seem to recognize this. The current practice of the U.S. Commerce Department is to base a constructed cost computation on fully allocated average costs, including all longer-term fixed costs as well as the short-term variable costs.[67] Thus, in times of slack demand, the U.S. Commerce Department acts as if the foreign enterprise must price for export at a level that includes all of these long-term costs, even when it would be rational for the enterprise to price at a much lower level both at home and abroad. In addition, the United States statute requires that the constructed costs include a minimum figure of 10 percent for administrative overhead, and 8 percent for profit, to arrive at the comparable home-market price.[68] Discussions with attorneys suggest that the 10 percent figure is not much of a problem, since actual costs reach or normally exceed that amount. However, in times of slack demand, imposing an 8 percent profit requirement for the computation of price can be quite unrealistic, when profit margins may only be 1 or 2 percent. Indeed, this provision of the United States statute is very likely inconsistent with United States international obligations, since those obligations require that a realistic method be used to compute the constructed cost and prices based on constructed cost.[69]

The 1974 Trade Act, which introduced the requirement that below-cost sales be discarded from the information on which the average home-market price is based, speaks of prices being based on figures which "permit recovery of all costs within a reasonable period of time in the normal course of trade. ..." One could expect that "reasonable period of time" should be interpreted in a manner consistent with normal business practice. Thus recovery of costs should here mean shorter-term variable costs, with an understanding that over a business or product cycle the firm should demonstrate that it can recoup all costs, including fixed ones. During a period of slack demand this would mean that prices for export need not be based on full average cost recovery. Nevertheless, the U.S. administration of its antidumping laws seems to ignore these economic realities, and to impose on foreign producers an obligation to price at a higher level than, for example, competing domestic producers within the United States would find necessary in the same circumstances.

Needless to say, these and other peculiarities of the antidumping law render it suspect in many ways. When politicians rail against "dumping prices," one has to be wary of what they are talking about, since prices which are deemed "dumping" under U.S. law may really be bsed on artificial and arbitrary accounting concepts. It is not coincidental that such arbitrary concepts tend to restrict imports more than would be the case if the concepts were more genuinely attuned to economic and accounting practices.

Finally, we need only mention how difficult these concepts are in relation to nonmarket economies. That is a subject to which we will return in chapter 13.

10.5   The Material Injury Test

Both antidumping duties and countervailing duties require, under international rules, fulfillment of the "material injury test."[70] The basic idea is that in the case of imported dumped or subsidized goods, the importing country is not authorized to respond with the antidumping or countervailing duties (as an exception to other obligations in GATT), unless it can be established that the imported goods have caused "material injury" to the competing industry of the like product in the importing country. The rules concerning this injury test are fundamentally the same as those concerning dumping and subsidies. However, there is no inherent reason why they need to be. The policies concerning a permitted response to dumped goods are substantially different from those concerning subsidized goods. One might easily think of a separate set of material injury rules for each of these subjects, each set being more carefully tuned to the policies of each subject.

The basic overall approach is that when goods which are dumped or subsidized are imported, in order to respond the importing country must show their harmful impact on the total industry producing the like product in the importing country. This is not just a matter of harm to a particular firm, but of "material injury" to the industry as a whole. If the industry is generally thriving, even though several firms are going out of business, arguably there is not material injury.

Trade law and policy are full of a number of different kinds of injury tests, and in previous chapters we have already encountered some.[71] Although the phraseology of the tests differ (e.g., for the escape clause it is "serious injury"), the definitions of the various injury tests are not very precise. Thus it is difficult in an abstract way to compare the tests. However, it is generally thought that the "serious injury" test of the escape clause and safeguards is the most stringent, in the sense that it is hardest to show that it is fulfilled. This approach accords with the general policies that the safeguards questions are addressed to fair trade.

On the other hand, the "material injury test" of dumping and subsidies is thought to be somewhat easier to fulfill than the serious injury test, and one rationale offered is that in the case of "unfair trade practices," the competing domestic industries ought to find it easier to obtain a response (antidumping duties or countervailing duties).[72]

United States law concerning the material injury test for both the antidumping and the countervailing duty cases has not always been completely consistent with the GATT rules. The original GATT (Article VI) called for the material injury test in antidumping and subsidy cases, and the language of this test has been carried over in the three codes concerning antidumping and countervailing, namely the two anti-dumping codes (1967 and 1979) and the subsidies countervailing duty code of 1979. U.S. law on dumping, prior to 1979, merely specified an "injury" test, without the additional word "material."[73] U.S. law concerning countervailing duties had no injury test prior to the 1974 Trade Act.[74] Since these United States laws preceded the GATT, the United States benefited from grandfather rights with respect to injury test matters.[75]

In connection with dumping, the U.S. grandfather rights could only carry the United States argument so far. Since the United States accepted the 1967 AD Code, which reiterated the material injury test, the U.S. could claim no grandfather rights to avoid its international obligations under that code. Thus, from 1967 until 1979, the U.S. statute was phrased in a manner different from its material injury obligations under the international Code. As I related in a previous section, the 1967 Code was accepted with presidential authority only, and was not referred to Congress; and this angered Congress. One of the reasons for its anger was its belief that the president did not have authority to accept the material injury test, thereby relinquishing the grandfather rights (which allowed a softer test). After 1967 the U.S. was annually pilloried in the GATT Antidumping Code Committee because its statute did not live up to the material injury wording of the Code. The response of the United States was to claim that even though the statute did not include the word "material," in fact when it applied the statute the U.S. government was fulfilling the requirements of material injury.[76] This was an interesting argument, because it is very difficult for a foreign nation to refute. A refutation would require not only an examination of what in fact was obligated by the phrase "material injury," but a difficult factual inquiry into each of the specific cases brought in the United States, to see whether the facts of those cases lived up to the Code's material injury standard. At one point in the U.S. dumping administration, the then

Tariff Commission (now the ITC) was apparently applying a fairly soft definition of injury, sometimes termed *"de minimis."* The theory of this, propounded by the ITC commissioners,[77] was that any injury more than *"de minimis"* fulfilled the U.S. statutory injury requirement. It seems to me likely that such a *de minimis* test did not fulfill the material injury test of U.S. international obligations.

When the Antidumping Code was revised during the Tokyo Round, and a new code put forth for signature and implementation, the matter was revisited before Congress in connection with the adoption of the 1979 Trade Agreements Act. During the preliminary deliberations by the appropriate congressional committees, those committees seemed inclined to retain the older U.S. statutory language, which omitted the word "material." An interesting facet of the diplomacy that occurred on trade laws at this time was a protest that was registered by the European Community and transmitted to the congressional committees. The EC argued that the failure to include the word "material" in the U.S. implementing statute for the Tokyo Round results would be considered by the EC to be inconsistent with U.S. obligations under the Tokyo Round agreements. The congressional committees acquiesced in this viewpoint, and reluctantly added the word "material" to the U.S. statute, so that the current version of the statute on the injury test (for both antidumping and countervailing) reads "material injury." Nevertheless, the Congress proceeded to define "material injury" as "harm which is not inconsequential, immaterial, or unimportant." The committee reports on this matter went further and said that it was the understanding of the committees that the phrase "material injury" meant the same level of injury standard as that which had been applied during the preceding five years in the Tariff Commission. The committee reports, however, did explicitly reject the *"de minimis* test" of an earlier period.[78] Thus, the view of the U.S. Congress was that material injury should be understood to be a level of injury that can be induced from the injury cases that actually occurred before the Tariff Commission during the period from 1974 to 1979.[79]

In discussing the matter with practitioners who must appear on these issues before the ITC, it is very difficult to try to generalize as to the meaning of the material injury test. Indeed, some practitioners seem to think that it depends more on who the particular ITC commissioners are, at any given time, than on any statutory formula or committee attempt to define that formula.[80]

The current state of international obligations regarding the material injury test (for both antidumping and countervailing) is not very satisfactory. Prior to the Tokyo Round, the GATT Article VI definition of material injury was embellished by the 1967 AD Code. In the context of the Tokyo Round negotiations for a subsidy code, the injury test was elaborately changed. The treaty language defining material injury was extended, and it can be argued that it was made much "looser" with excess verbiage. Although this treaty language was worked out in the context of the negotiations on rules of subsidies (as I have previously indicated), late in the Tokyo Round negotiations it was decided to redraft the antidumping code, and this subsidies injury-test language was also included in the new code.[81]

This language is very broad indeed. For example, it calls for an examination of both "the volume of subsidized imports and their effect on prices in the domestic market for like products and . . . the consequent impact . . . on domestic producers. . . ." The language then goes on to add considerable explanation for "volume" of subsidized imports, "either in absolute terms or relative to production or consumption in the importing signatory." A long list of factors is suggested, including potential decline in output, sales, market share, profits, productivity, return on investments, or utilization of capacity. Included in the language is the explanation of effect on prices, which directs the investigating authorities to "consider whether there has been a significant price undercutting by the subsidized imports . . . or whether the effect of such imports is otherwise to depress prices to a significant degree or prevent price increases, which otherwise would have occurred, to a significant degree." Arguably, any competition, including import competition, should have some of these effects. Consequently, if a particular nation wished to push toward the outer limits of the permissible range of definition for "material injury" such national authorities would find comfort in this extremely broad and permissive language of the new GATT codes.

In the U.S., of course, the matter is constrained by the U.S. statutory test,[82] which is more precise and controlled than that of the international treaty obligation. Fortunately, at present there is no evidence of any important trend on the part of national authorities to move to the outer limits of this permissive international language regarding the material injury tests, but some potential for that exists and presumably should be guarded against, possibly by some attention to it in new GATT rounds of negotiation.

Several other important issues have arisen in connection with the injury test. First, it must be recognized that the injury test also includes the concept of "threat of material injury." In evaluating whether "threat" exists, the national authorities have much more leeway than in the case of existing injury, since they are expected to evaluate trends for the future, which in many cases are not clear.

In addition, two issues have been particularly troublesome in connection with the way the United States applies its material injury tests in these types of cases. These are the issues of cumulation and "margins analysis."

Cumulation is the proposition that when dumping and/or subsidization has occurred in several different countries which export to the United States, then these various cases can be lumped together for purposes of evaluating the presence of material injury. Thus, suppose countries A, B, C, and D each import into the U.S. a fairly small quantity of goods, let us say 5 percent of the U.S. market for each. If each of these four countries is determined to be dumping, then the cases go to the ITC for determination of injury. It might well be that the ITC would decide that no single country's dumping could be the cause of material injury to the competing U.S. industry. However, when dumping of all four countries is combined, the products now take 20 percent of the U.S. market, and it would be much easier for the ITC to make an affirmative injury determination. Prior to 1984, the ITC cumulated in some cases, but had the discretion to refrain from doing so. It had developed some general guidelines for when to cumulate.[83] The Congress, with the 1984 Tariff and Trade Act, imposed a requirement on the ITC to use cumulation in almost all cases.[84] The result of this has in some ways been insidious.

Let us take, for example, a situation in which two or three larger exporting countries ship significant quantities of goods to the United States and are found to be dumping. In addition, assume that two other countries ship very small quantities to the U.S., but are also found to be dumping. These latter two countries will be lumped together with the larger countries to determine material injury, thus exposing the very small traders in the latter countries to the vicissitudes of a dumping finding. This means a much greater exposure to the costs and burdens of a U.S. unfair trade practice case for start-up entrepreneurs who desire for the first time to try to invade the U.S. market. Obviously this can have a considerable restraining effect, apart from the underlying policies of the AD or CV rules, on world trade. One solution might be to have some sort of *de minimis* cut-off to eliminate from such exposure the truly small cases.[85] One of the troublesome aspects about the small cases is that in some situations the amount of trade does not warrant paying for the attorney and other costs which it would require to defend against an antidumping or countervailing duty case, even when a defense would almost certainly prevail. Recently, there has also been raised the question of whether the imports which are dumped should be cumulated with imports that are subsidized for an even greater cumulation effect in determining material injury.[86]

A second troublesome direction in the U.S. application of its unfair trade laws in connection with the injury test is usually discussed under the rubric "margins analysis" or "imports analysis." Prior to 1982, the ITC tried to show the causal connection between the extent of dumping or the extent of subsidization (the so-called margins), on the one hand, and the material injury on the other hand. It was not enough merely to show that there was material injury in the United States: it had to be shown that this injury was caused not only by the imported goods which had been dumped or subsidized, but by the amount of the dumping or the subsidization. Thus, if the dumping margin were determined to be 5 percent, whereas the price undercutting caused by the imports were 15 percent, it could be argued that the dumping was not the cause of the material injury, since the imports would easily undersell domestic producers in the U.S. market anyway. If the purpose of unfair trade law is to eliminate the effect of the unfair action, policy would seem to support a "margins analysis."

In 1981–82, pursuant to some memoranda coming from the ITC General Council's Office,[87] the ITC began to consider a different approach. It was urged upon the commissioners that they should not try to show a causal relationship between the margin of dumping or margin of subsidy, on the one hand, and material injury on the other hand. Rather, the only causal relationship that need be shown was that between the dumped or subsidized *imports* as a whole. Thus the ITC could enjoy the luxury of ignoring the extent of the margin of dumping or subsidization, and could look merely at the amount of imports which were tainted by the dumping or subsidization and connect those to the injury.[88]

The argument in favor of this approach seems to hinge primarily upon the language of the 1979 act in defining material injury, which speaks of "imports of the merchandise" rather than more specifically about a margin. However, the counter argument is the long-established practice to the contrary (some have challenged whether this was a consistent practice).[89] In the absence of any expression of congressional intent to change that practice, it is argued that no change was intended. In addition, the GATT Subsidies Code explicitly states, "It must be demonstrated that the subsidized imports are through the effects of the subsidy, causing injury within the meaning of this Agreement."[90] This would seem to establish an international obligation to pursue a causal connection that would relate to the actual subsidization—i.e., the margin. A similar clause exists in the Antidumping Code.[91] A counter argument has been raised in connection with footnotes to these clauses. These footnotes refer to paragraphs 2 and 3 in a way that have led some to argue that the notion of an obligation to use margin analysis has softened. However, such a conclusion appears to me somewhat improbable.

Thus, it can be argued that the United States government is obligated to use a "margins analysis" in evaluating the material injury resulting from dumping or subsidization, and that at the very best the U.S. statute is ambiguous enough that the general principle[92] in U.S. jurisprudence, that calls upon the statutory interpretation to be consistent with international obligations when it is possible to do so, comes into play.

10.6   Remedy and Reflection on Dumping Rules and Policies

The discussion in the preceding section should amply demonstrate that even if there is some underlying validity to the notion of the international and national antidumping rules when properly managed, as actually managed currently it is fair to express considerable doubt about the policy soundness of the implementation of some of these rules. There seems to be a considerable "tilt" against imports, and any close observer of the processes of governments, whether of the United States, the European Community, Canada, or Australia (the four principal users of the antidumping law), can observe the considerable pressures brought by competing domestic producer groups so as to influence the governmental implementation of the antidumping laws in order to limit import competition.[93]

United States law, in particular, is especially vulnerable to these type of criticisms, partly because the Congress has made that law so mandatory, limiting the discretion involved in government implementation. In the European Community, the antidumping rules grant to the Community officials a discretion "in the interests of the Community" to refrain from applying antidumping duties; and they also give the Community officials discretion to apply an antidumping duty which is lower than that of the margin of dumping, if such lower duty will "eliminate the injury."[94] Indeed, this concept has been written into the Antidumping Code, which states that such lower duties are "desirable."[95] U.S. law does not permit this amount of discretion, a fact which reflects congressional suspicion of executive-branch implementation of these laws, as well as the pressures of domestic producers who are seeking to use the antidumping laws as a way to limit the importation of competing goods.[96]

Another aspect of the unfair trade laws (both dumping and subsidies) is the advantage they tend to give to the larger economic entities in the world. By allowing a unilateral national response (antidumping duties or countervailing duties), the more economically powerful nations can have a considerable impact on smaller trading nations, while the reverse may not be true. For example, for Canada, exports to the United States are an extremely significant portion of the Canadian economy, while in reverse, exports from the U.S. to Canada are only a small part of the U.S. economy.[97] Thus, the United States finds that it can more easily apply antidumping duties to Canadian products without a worry of retaliation or symmetrical application by the Canadians of such duties on U.S. products. This is because when the Canadians apply the duties, they have only a very small effect on the U.S. economy or U.S. producers. Thus, part of the frustration of other countries of the world, particularly those smaller than the big three (the U.S., Japan, and the EC), is the feeling that there is a lack of symmetry about the application of unfair trade laws. When this lack of symmetry is combined with relative freedom for unilateral sovereign definitions and determinations, it effectively grants considerable trade-policy power to the larger trading entities.

Finally, an additional aspect might be mentioned. Some political leaders liken antidumping laws to criminal or tort statutes, and argue that the statutes should provide a penalty for dumping.[98] This obviously misconceives the very nature of the antidumping rules under international and even national laws. We have seen, from an examination of the policies of dumping and antidumping duties, that these policies reflect a certain tentativeness about declaring the "wrongfulness" of dumping. Thus, it is not dumping, but dumping that causes injury, for which the international system allows the permitted response of antidumping duties.

Nevertheless, pursuing concepts of wrongfulness, some parties advocate that domestic competing producers in the importing country should be given a "private right of action" under which they could sue the foreign exporting producers who are dumping and recover damages which would go directly to the "harmed" interests in the importing country.[99] Indeed, sometimes it is argued, by way of analogy to the terms of the U.S. antitrust statutes, that the recoverable damages should treble those of the actual harm. Clearly such proposals would dramatically change the trade policy impact of the antidumping (and subsidy) rules, and would substantially increase the risk of exporting to markets which introduce such "private rights" laws. Indeed, unless there were a comparable domestic statute allowing domestic producers to seek similar recoveries from domestic producers who engage in the pricing activities comparable to dumping, these private-right-of-action proposals would most surely be in violation of GATT.[100]

Despite all the policy hesitations that can be expressed about antidumping laws, nevertheless there does not appear to be any realistic probability that those laws will be either abolished or substantially overhauled in the foreseeable future. Consequently, it seems advisable that additional attention be given to the shape and implementation of the antidumping rules of the world, in the context of a multilateral trade institution such as the GATT and its trade round negotiations.[101]

Finally, it is both interesting and potentially provocative to suggest the possibility that for all its faults, the system of antidumping rules may be performing a useful function in world trade, *not* as a response to so-called unfairness, but rather as an "interface" or buffer mechanism to ameliorate difficulties such as those discussed in section 10.1, caused by interdependence among different economic systems. Could it be that the antidumping rules are acting as a crude or blunt instrument to cause different economic systems to more equitably share the burdens of adjusting to shifts of world trade flow? If so, perhaps we should view antidumping rules as part of the subject of "safeguards" (described in chapter 7) rather than as part of a subject of "unfair trade."

10.7   Beyond Dumping and Subsidies

What is Unfair?

Dumping and certain types of subsidies have been deemed by international trading governments for almost a century to be "unfair" exporting measures, and thus vulnerable to permitted responses from importing countries and subject to certain types of international rule constraints. But in addition to those activities there are a number of other actions which have been challenged — if not by the international rules, then at least by one or more importing nations — as "unfair" when involved in international trade.

The most prominent category of other practices are those related to "restrictive business practices," described in section 9.5. Closely related to those are a group of practices deemed "unfair" by domestic law when they are undertaken with respect to domestic trade. Such activities as patent, copyright, or trademark infringement, deceptive business practices, or other monopolistic actions can be challenged in some countries on the basis of common-law rules or statutory provisions designed to reinforce "fairness" in trade. It would therefore seem natural to apply such concepts to imported goods, although this practice poses some difficult procedural problems. The United States has probably been the most aggressive country in developing a procedure (its "Section 337") to handle these situations, and consequently we will explore that further.

Apart from the section 337 responses to "unfair" trade, there are a number of other possible importing nation counterattacks upon certain types of trade practices. Focusing just on the United States, for example, we find various relatively unknown laws which are designed for this purpose.[102] One dramatic example is a provision of U.S. law potentially connecting certain unfavorable income-tax treatment of a company to foreign-nation practices affecting exports. As we noted in section 4.5, the U.S. law of section 301 has language allowing the potential of unilateral U.S. definition of what is "unfair" as a trigger for possible retaliatory actions.

In the current rapidly changing world, with the problems that economic interdependence has created, it is not surprising that many political leaders have a number of candidates to bring within national and international disciplines on "unfair actions" in international trade. One general category of potential new rules, suggested for a new round of trade negotiations in GATT, is that of international trade in services. Another subject which has been much discussed is called "targeting."[103] By this is meant the practice of some countries of using various government favors and "guidance" to encourage some industry sectors and discourage others. This practice is closely related to "industrial policy" ideas.[104] Somehow the possibility of this type of government "interference" with market processes seems to have struck a chord of fear in the hearts and minds of some political leaders, and these leaders suggest that certain aspects of these practices should be deemed "unfair" under trade rules, and should trigger certain import-restraint responses. The issues raised are extraordinarily complex, and they go to the heart of some of the trade-policy dilemmas of today. They also raise questions about the validity of the traditional comparative-advantage theories, suggesting the idea of "dynamic comparative advantage."[105]

It should be recognized that we cannot in this book cover all possible international trade policies, rules, responses, or restraint techniques. There is almost an infinite variety of subjects which relate to the flow of trade across borders. I have selected for inclusion here those issues which normally are considered to be a part of "international trade policy," but the reader should not overlook other issues which can also have a strong influence on international trade. Product liability issues, for example, pose considerable difficulties for the interdependent world.[106]

U.S. Law Section 337 Actions

A 1922 statute, modified and reenacted as section 337 of the Tariff Act of 1930 and amended in the Trade Act of 1974 and the Omnibus Trade and Competitiveness Act of 1988, provides an important remedy for certain types of "unfair trade practices" involved with imports into the United States. Since the 1974 amendments, this remedy has become increasingly invoked and its importance has been growing. Over 260 cases have been brought during that time, and remedies have been directed against imports in approximately sixty of those cases.[107]

The statute provides a remedy against "unfair methods of competition and unfair acts in the importation of articles into the United States, or in their sale . . . , the effect or tendency of which is to destroy or substantially injure an industry, efficiently and economically operated, in the United States, or to prevent the establishment of such an industry, or to restrain or monopolize. . . ."[108] The 1988 act added a provision so that an "injury" test is no longer required when the unfair practices involve intellectual property rights, such as patents, trademarks, and copyrights.[109] The ITC carries out the procedure, with appeal being directly to the Court of Appeals for the Federal Circuit.

Unfair acts within this statute are most often deemed to be violations of intellectual property rights, such as patent or copyright or trademark infringements. In addition, though, monopoly or other actions against competition can be the basis of remedy under this statute. All of these unfair actions have counterpart remedies in the courts of the United States, and in some instances are also the subjects of regulatory actions by the Federal

Trade Commission. Thus, it can be argued that there is no discrimination regarding imports due to the 337 remedy, since counterpart remedies exist in domestic U.S. law when domestic goods are involved. However, a big difference is in the procedure. The 337 remedy is *"in rem"* — a lawyer's term which means that the procedure is against the goods (imports) themselves, rather than against firms or individuals for actions relating to the goods. The advantage of this is that difficult procedural problems of service or process, or of carrying out a court's judgement, are avoided. The 337 remedy can be an "exclusion order," preventing further importation of the goods.

Complaints to initiate this procedure are directed to the ITC, which then has a strictly limited time (twelve to eighteen months) within which to complete its process. Normally an "ALJ" (administrative law judge) will "try" the case and report to the commission, which must then make the final determination. An interesting facet is that after the commission's ruling, the law provides an opportunity for the president of the United States to "veto" or overrule the commission (and he has done so in approximately five cases), for various reasons he deems sufficient.

The essential elements of a complaint (other than in intellectual property cases) include: (1) unfair acts or methods of competition, (2) the importation of goods, (3) effect to destroy or injure, (4) a U.S. industry, which (5) is efficiently and economically operated. The ITC cases provide a certain amount of interpretative exegesis for each of these elements. The injury test here, for example, is clearly not as stringent as tests in the escape clause or in AD or CV cases.[110] On the other hand, the requirement that the industry be "efficiently and economically operated" imposes a burden on the domestic industry. The ITC must also consider whether an exclusion order would have an effect on the "public health, welfare or competitive conditions" of the U.S. economy.[111]

This U.S. law has been challenged several times in GATT, as I described in chapter 8, because it is argued that section 337 effectively discriminates against imports compared to domestic goods, and therefore, concerning national treatment, is inconsistent (at least) with GATT Article III.[112]

11

The Perplexities of Subsidies in International Trade

11.1 Introduction: The Policies

At the beginning of chapter 10, I outlined some of the general policies regarding so-called "unfair trade practices" in international trade.[1] Other parts of chapter 10 dealt with the problem of dumping and antidumping duties. In chapter 11, we now turn to the partner of dumping: namely, the problem of subsidies and the response of countervailing duties.[2]

Both of these unfair trade practices depend, under international rules, on an injury test. Thus, in order for a nation to be permitted under GATT rules to respond to subsidized imports by imposing a countervailing duty, that nation must show that the subsidized imports are causing "material injury" to the domestic industry of the like product. As I noted in section 10.5,[3] the rules regarding the injury test are virtually the same for dumping as for subsidies, although there is no inherent policy reason why this should be so. Perhaps this is partly for purposes of symmetry and simplicity. Indeed, during the Tokyo Round, when a number of new provisions and criteria were worked out for injury in the context of subsidies and countervailing duties, the negotiators decided late in that negotiation to bring the antidumping injury rules into basic conformity with those of the subsidy rules.[4] For these reasons, I will not repeat the description of injury in this chapter, but will concentrate here on the substantive issues of subsidies: how they are identified, and what are the policies regarding them with respect to international trade.

Discussions of subsidies in international trade begin by drawing the distinction between "export subsidies," on the one hand, and "domestic," "production," or "general" subsidies on the other hand. Export subsidies are those which are granted to products only when they are exported. Some people view export subsidies as particularly pernicious,[5] and indeed it has been argued that, because export subsidies are such an obvious attempt to impose burdens on other countries (burdens which are more political or producer-oriented than they are economic in a broader sense), perhaps there should not even be an injury test as a criterion for responding with countervailing duties in such cases. Indeed, if this logic is followed, it might even be argued that an importing country should have the obligation to counter export subsidies by imposing countervailing duties on the products concerned.

Domestic or production subsidies, on the other hand, are subsidies that are granted for the benefit of products regardless of whether those products are exported or not. These are clearly the most perplexing, because they involve a vast range and number of government policies, many of which are perfectly justifiable as exercises of sovereign activity within a country.

It should be noted that, by way of contrast with dumping matters, in the case of subsidies we are almost always talking about government action, rather than to individual enterprise action. Thus, issues of subsidies and countervailing duties are often significantly more visible and involve a higher level of government-to-government diplomacy than do many other trade policy matters. If an importing nation decides to counter a foreign subsidy, it is acting rather confrontationally toward a foreign sovereign's act. It can certainly be expected that the foreign sovereign will not be pleased to have this reaction from another nation.

Apart from the different types of subsidies mentioned above, it should be noted that there are at least three effects of subsidies. For example, subsidies of country A can enhance the exportability of products into an importing nation, country B. In such a case, nation B may wish to respond with countervailing duties. Second, subsidies from country A can enhance the exportation of its products to a third country, C, where they compete with similar products that are exported from country B. In such a case, country B does not have easy recourse to a response. Its own countervailing duties are not effective. It may not wish to competitively subsidize its exports. Thus it must somehow induce the importing country, country C in this case, to respond to the subsidized imports. However, country C may be quite happy to receive such subsidized goods. Consequently, country B's grievance against country A may have to be aided by some other technique, such as recourse to an international forum like the GATT.

A third effect of subsidies can be to restrain imports into the subsidizing country. Thus, if country A subsidizes its bicycles even when all of those bicycles are sold in its home market, one effect is to make it harder for other countries such as B or C to export bicycles to country A. The subsidy in this situation has become an import barrier, and economists can demonstrate that the effect is in some ways similar to a tariff.[6] Once again, countervailing duties will not provide a remedy, since the country which is "harmed" is not receiving subsidized imports.

In the next section, we will look at the overall landscape of national and international rules which affects subsidization in international trade. Basically, there are two sets of such rules: those regarding the use of countervailing duties and those providing certain substantive international obligations against the use of subsidies that may affect international trade. With respect to the use of countervailing duties, it should be noted that at the present time the United States is the principal user of this response to subsidized goods. Although several other countries have had a few countervailing duty cases, and more have a law on their books which permit them,[7] the U.S. is the only country in the world that has extensively used countervailing duties. The number of countervailing cases in the U.S. since 1979 is more than 300.[8]

As is the case with dumping and antidumping duties, the economic and other policies concerning the use of subsidies in international trade, and the permitted responses to those subsidies, are perplexing and controversial.[9] Particularly focusing on whether an importing nation should use countervailing duties to respond to imports which are subsidized, there is a considerable amount of economic literature which would suggest that such response is unwise. The basis for this view is that if a foreign government wishes to subsidize the exports to an importing country, the importing country — or at least its consumers — should be grateful for the gift which has been sent to it. The appropriate response in such a case, so it is said (tongue in cheek), is to send a "thank-you note" to the subsidizing nation. Although certain subsidies may correct, rather than distort, the most efficient allocation of resources, a reasonably careful economic analysis[10] suggests that in the case of a subsidy — whether an export subsidy or a domestic subsidy (on products exported) — the country who does the subsidizing loses in net national economic welfare, while the rest of the world gains. The particular distribution of the gains within the rest of the world may not always be predictable, although certainly the consumers in the importing countries usually benefit sufficiently to offset the harm to producers in the same countries. And in net exporting countries and elsewhere in the world where that is not the case, consumers gain sufficiently to offset the harm to their own producers. This has been the rationale of many economists who have urged that all countervailing duty laws should be abolished.

However, economists recognize that there are certain types of situations, sometimes called "strategic," for which an import restraint such as a countervailing duty might have a welfare-enhancing effect for the importing country. However, they will further say that this effect is unrelated to whether the goods are subsidized or not. The effect usually arises because of the market power of the importing country. If this country is large enough that by restraining imports it causes a reduction in the world price of the commodity (an "optimum tariff" concept[11]), then there are certain situations in which the tariff (including countervailing duty) can enhance the overall welfare of the importing country.

However, the basic problem with all of these views, it seems, is that they focus on too narrow a perspective—that of the importing country. When one moves to a worldwide perspective—i.e., in order to explore which actions will enhance or decrease worldwide net welfare—then a stronger case can be made for providing some kind of international or national disciplines on the use of subsidies of internationally traded goods. The economists would apparently admit that in such circumstances some subsidies tend to distort international production and trading patterns, and reduce efficiency and thus reduce world welfare.[12] This is, however, a rather peculiar argument to use within an importing nation for the application of countervailing duties. It is certainly not the basis of most of the arguments heard. Most of the arguments originate from competing producer groups, and they are most interested in their own welfare, and not in that of the world in general. On the other hand, it can be argued that if such relatively parochial or selfish motivations result in the use of measures, such as countervailing duties, which coincidentally in the long run tend to inhibit a practice (subsidization) which reduces world welfare, then why not take advantage of such parochial/selfish motivations? This argument would support the use of countervailing duties.

Other arguments have been used concerning the traditional international trade policies of countervailing duties. One of these arguments notes the adjustment costs when new subsidies are put in place. For an importing nation, the subsidies may dramatically shift the competitive relationship between its domestic products and the imports, and cause domestic industry to go out of business or to "adjust outward." If subsidies are short-lived, there may soon come a time when the reverse adjustment will occur. Adding up the two adjustment costs (in and out) may establish that the adjustment costs are greater than the net welfare addition to the importing country. Thus, in the case of short-lived subsidies, there may be some special arguments for using countervailing duties at the very beginning. If one believes that subsidies are inherently unstable, because they show favoritism by the public fisc of the subsidizing country, which will stimulate opposing political forces to get rid of them, one might think that this argument has some weight. However, observers note that subsidies are often very long term and very stable. Thus, this argument of "in and out adjustment costs" is relatively weak.

Another possible argument is very similar to that made in the case of dumping. It can be argued that subsidies can be used for "predatory purposes," to enable a subsidizing nation's industry to obtain market share abroad to the point where it has sufficient monopoly power that it can then raise prices, reduce the subsidy, and extract "monopoly rents."[13] There are some curious dimensions to this argument. For one, it will be noted that subsidization is primarily a government activity, so this argument is essentially accusing a foreign government of predatory intent. That accusation seems not too polite from a sovereign's viewpoint, but of course it may nevertheless be deserved. On the other hand, since a government is likely to have the broadest impact on its own firms and to be a single decision-making entity, it may have greater opportunity to actually effectuate a predatory intent than would a sector of economic activity in which there existed a number of firms, each suspicious of the other. We studied these problems in the context of dumping, and it will be recalled that many economists are skeptical of predatory intent because of the difficulty of "succeeding."[14] In the case of subsidies, a single relatively powerful economic national government can more easily "succeed." Thus, if predation can in fact be proven, this fact may also be an argument against subsidies and in favor of such policies that would tend to prevent the effectiveness of subsidies (including countervailing duties). Some of these arguments may relate to the notion of "targeting" which has been much discussed during recent years.

Of course, there may be some policies relating to subsidies which are relatively unrelated to the question of total economic net welfare. For example, national defense policies may suggest that an importing nation must defend itself against the competition of subsidized imports in certain sectors.[15] Likewise, income-distribution arguments can be made, and there are also some short-term arguments with respect to various governmental fiscal and budgetary considerations, or political considerations (e.g., maintaining a majority in the parliament by avoiding unemployment in certain districts). These arguments, however, can also be made about subsidized imports.

Finally, there may be some policies that relate to subsidization which are connected to a national government's general approach to its economic system. Entrepreneurs in a market economy, such as that of the U.S., often say that they can compete against "fair imports," but they cannot compete against a foreign government's treasury. What they mean, partly, is that there is an additional layer of risk involved in competing in a world trade environment when other than market and profit-maximizing considerations of foreign firms are motivating those firms' exports. If the motivation is some set of policies carried out by the foreign government, the importing country's entrepreneurs say that this is unfair, and that it tends to reduce the efficacy of the importing country's economic system when that system is geared toward a free-market orientation. In short, it is fair to worry about escalating competitive subsidization that would be occasioned by strong political pressures within an importing country when its entrepreneurs feel aggrieved by foreign government subsidies. Such competitive subsidization would tend to change the economic system within the importing country, and arguably the importing country ought not be put to that choice. Thus, a "buffering response," such as countervailing duties on the imports which are subsidized, might be appropriate as a way to assist the importing nation to maintain the relative purity of its free-market economic system. This argument is so vague, it is even hard to articulate, much less prove. Nevertheless, it certainly appeals in a visceral way to entrepreneurs, who would argue that the entrepreneurial spirit is important to the free market economy.

The reader may now detect that there is great controversy about economic policies with respect to subsidies in international trade. It is not possible at this point in time, nor in this book, to resolve these issues. One thing is clear: for more than a century, the international trade rules, and some national systems, have been established on the basis of the proposition that imports which are subsidized by foreign governments are somehow "unfair." The politicians, perhaps because they respond more to the arguments and pressures of producer groups than to those of consumer groups, constantly repeat these notions. Thus it is all too likely that whatever may be the underlying economic merits of these cases, these are not clear enough to establish movement toward radical change, and that the countervailing duty regimes of the world (currently mostly in the United States, but probably to be emulated by other countries soon) will continue.

Sometimes, in arguing against the use of countervailing duties in the United States, persons have noted that the world perspective, which might justify unilateral national government actions which generally could help to inhibit the use of subsidies worldwide, is not persuasive because the U.S. does not have that much impact on the world. However, discussions and experience with specific cases, and with specific individuals and foreign governments, suggest that through its trade policies the United States does indeed have a very great impact on the world. Canada, for example, during the 1970s and '80s has been shocked by its own vulnerability to what Canadians often call "contingent protectionism" of the United States, which means the application of United States antidumping and countervailing duty laws. Some would say that the very large and important U.S. countervailing duty cases against lumber from Canada were a major motivation leading the Canadians to seek a bilateral free-trade agreement with the United States.[16] Comparable instances of U.S. countervailing duty law impact on other government policies can be noticed.[17] Thus, if one believes that the world would be better off if there were a general reduction of the use by governments of subsidies relating to products that flow in international trade, one could argue that the U.S. policies, motivated for entirely different reasons, may fortuitously or coincidentally be having a salutary effect on the world economy.

11.2 The Rules on Subsidies and Countervailing Duties in National and International Law

Those national rules which provide a response from the importing country to imports which have been subsidized by foreign governments can be traced back to the nineteenth century.[18] Indeed, certain generalizations about unfair trade seem to fuse together the concepts that we now separate into "dumping" and "subsidization," and some of these concepts can be traced back much further than the 19th century.[19] In the United States, the original countervailing duty statute is taken to be that of 1897.[20] A number of treaties, particularly bilateral treaties, touched on this subject,[21] including general wording in some of the U.S. bilateral reciprocal-trade-agreement treaties of the 1930s and '40s.[22]

But the elaborate development of multilateral international rules concerning subsidized trade began primarily with the GATT. In the original GATT agreement of 1947, there was very little discipline on the question of subsidizing, except for the permitted response of countervailing duties. There was a fairly general reporting requirement in Article XVI of the original GATT, plus a general obligation in Article II, paragraph 4 against the use of new subsidies to inhibit imports into the subsidizing country when that country had "bound" its tariff on the product concerned.[23] But there were no other substantive international rules on subsidy practices.

The 1955 review session amendments to the GATT introduced the first substantive obligations regarding subsidies into the GATT (paragraphs 2 through 5 of Article XVI).[24] However, this portion of GATT related only to export subsidies and did not apply to general, production, or domestic subsidies. Even then, the discipline of GATT was attenuated. In addition, the GATT rule was divided between applications to "primary" and "nonprimary" products. With respect to primary products, GATT Article XVI, paragraph 3 admonished countries to "seek to avoid" their use for exports and stated that they should not be applied "in a manner which results in that contracting party having more than an equitable share of world export trade in that product . . ." This "equitable share" language has been troublesome for its ambiguity ever since.[25]

In addition, paragraph 4 of Article XVI of GATT provided that "from 1 January 1958 or the earliest practicable date thereafter," contracting parties should cease to grant subsidies on exports of nonprimary goods, when the subsidy resulted in a sale at a price for export lower than that for the domestic market. This obligation thus had two significant conditions: a date before which it would not apply, and the "bi-level pricing" test, which has also proved troublesome in subsequent developments.[26] Because of the structure of this amendment to GATT, the paragraph 4 obligation for nonprimary goods would not come into effect until there was some additional action taken by countries concerned. For some years, the GATT CONTRACTING PARTIES adopted an annual standstill declaration, but finally, in 1962, a declaration applying the paragraph 4 obligations was opened for signature.[27] However, partly because of the differentiation of treatment between primary and non-primary goods, many developing and primary-goods countries felt that the GATT was discriminating against their trade. Consequently, not all countries were prepared to adopt the declaration implementing paragraph 4 of Article XVI; and to this day, this paragraph has been accepted only by the industrialized contracting parties of GATT and not by the developing contracting parties.[28]

Article VI allows governments to impose duties on imported products otherwise subject to GATT obligations in cases of dumping and subsidization. However, this "exception" to GATT obligations only operates when imports cause material injury to the competing domestic industries of the importing country.

The U.S. countervailing duty law anteceded the GATT, and thus, according to the Protocol of Provisional Application, which applied "grandfather rights" to Article VI of GATT, the U.S. 1897 statute[29] that provided for countervailing duties against subsidized goods without the necessity of showing "material injury" did not technically violate U.S. obligations under GATT.

As tariffs declined under GATT, domestic producing interests in a number of GATT countries began to search for other ways to inhibit import competition, and more attention was devoted in the United States to the U.S. antidumping and countervailing duty laws. Thus, during the 1960s and early 1970s, new attention was given to countervailing duties and a higher risk that such duty cases in the United States would succeed. Since the U.S. law was relatively short and sketchy, considerable discretion was exercised by the U.S. administrative agency that applied it (then the Department of the Treasury), and the application of U.S. countervailing duty laws was relatively hesitant.[30] This hesitancy, however, angered the domestic interests and the Congress. Partly because of this anger, Congress in 1980 succeeded in obtaining the transfer of jurisdiction of countervailing and antidumping duties from the Department of the Treasury to the Department of Commerce.[31]

At the beginning of the Tokyo Round of GATT negotiations, in 1973 and 1974, the U.S. government developed a statutory framework for the U.S. negotiating position, and in that statute the Congress demanded a tightening of the countervailing duty laws.[32] This resulted in specific time limits being applied to the administrating agency's consideration of complaints, the opportunity for judicial review of those decisions, and a tightening of the criteria for the mandatory application of countervailing duties on subsidized goods. In addition, in this statute, the executive branch and the Congress agreed to extend the application of countervailing duties to nondutiable goods. Prior to this point in time, countervailing duties in the United States only applied to dutiable goods. This change reflected the fact that an increasing amount of trade was entering the United States duty-free, and that a new generalized system of preferences for developing country trade would extend duty-free treatment to much more trade in the future.

However, the reader will note that U.S. grandfather rights (allowing the U.S. to avoid applying a material injury test) only applied to the pre-GATT existing statute that covered dutiable goods. Therefore, in a careful exercise of obedience to international obligation, the Congress enacted the 1974 statute with an injury test imposed for those subsidy cases where the goods could be entered duty-free.[33] Thus, for the first time the United States established an injury test in connection with countervailing duties on subsidized goods.

The U.S. was much criticized at this time for its lack of a general injury test in its countervailing duty statute, and so the U.S. indicated to its trade-negotiating partners in the Tokyo Round that it was prepared to put that issue on the table, provided that other nations in the world would join with the U.S. in establishing a new international discipline on the use of subsidies in international trade. Negotiations leading to a "code" concerning subsidies and countervailing duties were begun in the Tokyo Round, resulting in 1979 in an agreement on that subject. This agreement, the Subsidies Code,[34] was the first general comprehensive multilateral discipline of the use of subsidies in international trade and the first elaboration of the subsidy rules since the 1955 GATT amendments. In addition, in the Code were placed the first international obligations of a multilateral character that explicitly concerned so-called "domestic subsidies," not just export subsidies.[35]

The 1979 GATT Subsidies Code has its substantive obligations essentially in two parts, sometimes called "Track I" and "Track II." Track I deals entirely with countervailing duties, establishing international rules on what national governments can do in implementing their countervailing duty rules (including constraints on the procedures for those cases) and rather elaborate definitions of material injury. The one thing that is lacking, however, is any definition of "subsidy" in the context of national countervailing duty rules. This means that unless this lack is corrected in a new negotiation, national governments can and often will enjoy a considerable amount of latitude in defining "subsidy" for countervailing duty purposes. There has not been any definitive panel or other case in GATT that would suggest how this relative freedom of definition would be constrained by the international rules.

Track II of the Code is devoted to the substantive obligations under international law regarding how governments should refrain from granting subsidies that affect goods in international trade. Some of these rules are further elaborations of Article XVI of GATT, and apply only to export subsidies. The Code's Track II reiterates the obligation to avoid the use of export subsidies on primary products (defined slightly differently) when the result would be "larger than an equitable share" of the world market. Regarding nonprimary goods, the Code is more stringent than the GATT, although the Code purports merely to be interpreting the GATT. For this category of goods, the Code flatly prohibits the use of export subsidies, and does not repeat the bilevel pricing test found in Article XVI of GATT.

The important additional feature of Track II of the Subsidies Code, however, is found in Article 11, entitled "Subsidies Other Than Export Subsidies." It is this article which contains the first general multilateral treaty discipline on government use of domestic subsidies which have an impact on international trade. The language of the article is relatively tortured and ambiguous, clearly because there was not much agreement among the negotiating countries regarding this subject. The language notes that domestic subsidies "are widely used for the promotion of social and economic policy objectives," and that the Code does not "intend to restrict the right of signatories to use such subsidies to achieve these and other important policy objectives which they consider desirable." On the other hand, the language of the article recognizes that the use of subsidies "may cause or threaten to cause injury" to the domestic industry of other signatories, or "serious prejudice to the interests," or "may nullify or impair benefits" to the other signatories. Then the language imposes the obligation on signatories to "seek to avoid such effects through the use of subsidies." Needless to say, it is not surprising that the Subsidies Code has had a very difficult history subsequent to the completion of the Tokyo Round, since its very language reflects considerable ambivalence about its obligations.

An interesting feature of the Code is that, with respect to export subsidies, it contains an annex which lists a series of practices entitled "Illustrative List of Export Subsidies." This annex is a revision of a 1960 GATT document resulting from a working party study which also listed practices which would be deemed to be export subsidies.[36] Thus, for purposes of Track II language which applies to export subsidies, the Illustrative List is an important source of interpretive material for defining "export subsidies." It does not, of course, apply to domestic subsidies. In addition, the United States has taken the position[37] that the Illustrative List of Export Subsidies is only useful in interpreting a definition of subsidies for purposes of Track II of the Code and does not in any way constrain national sovereigns in their definition of "subsidy" for purposes of Track I (countervailing duties). This position is, needless to say, somewhat controversial, but certainly the structure of the Code can be interpreted to support it. Thus we have the outlines of the international rules regarding the use of subsidies in international law, and some of the intertwining of those rules with at least one nation's national rules (those of the United States).

The United States implemented this Code through its 1979 Trade Agreements Act (which generally implemented the results of the Tokyo Round[38]). In that statute, the Congress wrote the specific rules of United States law regarding subsidies and countervailing duties, doing so in a way that the Congress felt fully implemented U.S. obligations under the new Subsidies Code of the Tokyo Round. As I have noted elsewhere, the Congress explicitly indicated that the Code would not be "self-executing," and that therefore it would not be part of domestic U.S. law.[39] Rather, the statute implementing the Code is the source of definitive law in the domestic legal structure of the United States. Furthermore, the Congress specified that the full benefits of the Code obligations, and most particularly the implementation of the injury test in United States law for dutiable goods, would apply only to products of any other nation of the world who became "a country under the agreement." This was defined to mean a country which had accepted the Tokyo Round's Subsidies Code and its obligations, or a country which had generally accepted the obligations of the Code even though it did not sign the Code.[40] As of January 1989, twenty-four countries have ratified the Subsidies Code, of which fourteen are industrial countries and ten are developing countries.[41]

One particularly troublesome wrinkle of the United States law, in light of this selective application of U.S. implementation of the Subsidies Code, is what has been called the "commitments policy." Because of the phrasing of the United States statute, the executive branch has interpreted circumstances of the accession of developing countries to the Code to be not in themselves sufficient, under United States law, to persuade the United States to extend the Code privileges including the material injury test—to such developing countries. This is because the Code has a rather generally worded exception for developing countries (which, some argue, allows developing countries to escape the disciplines of the Subsidies Code), and therefore mere code acceptance should not be sufficient to entitle those countries to the benefit of code treatment (i.e., the material injury test) under U.S. law. The U.S. executive branch, pursuing this logic, has required developing countries who wish for full U.S. Subsidies Code treatment to enter into a separate bilateral "commitment" to the United States and to undertake a certain level of discipline regarding their subsidies.[42] Each of these bilateral commitments has been negotiated separately, so they vary somewhat from country to country. Developing countries have argued that this approach of the U.S. is inappropriate and contrary to U.S. obligations under the Code, but U.S. negotiators have counterargued that they had warned developing countries during the Tokyo Round that this would be the U.S. approach.[43] In an interesting case in 1980, India challenged the United States on this point. In particular, India, which had been refused the injury test treatment for some of its products then subjected to U.S. countervailing duties, joined the Code, and at about the same time brought a complaint against the United States in GATT, arguing that the United States had not fulfilled the MFN obligation of GATT.[44] Although the case was referred to a panel, it was settled before the panel made any determinations, the settlement being a redrafted bilateral commitment between India and the United States which the latter accepted as satisfactory. Thus, the issue of the international law status of the United States commitment policy remains undecided, although it is perhaps "precarious."

11.3 Defining Subsidies and "Actionable Subsidies"

The definition of "subsidy" has always perplexed policymakers, partly because the word "subsidy" can mean so many things and be so generic. If the term "subsidy" is defined in a rather broad way, as is sometimes the case, it can include an enormous range of government activities. For example, if an economic definition of subsidy contends that it is deemed to mean a "benefit conferred on a firm or product by action of a government,"[45] then the concept of subsidy could include such typical and universal governmental activities as providing fire and police protection, roads, and even schools or education. Highly effective fire and police protection would obviously reduce the insurance costs of producing firms, and thus reduce part of their costs of production. Likewise, other types of societal infrastructure can reduce the costs which are "internalized" in the accounting of a firm evaluating the price of its goods.[46] The problem is that if such a broad definition were used, and international rules permitted governments to respond with countervailing duties against such subsidies, the whole system of post-World

War II GATT liberal trade (including the reduction in tariffs) would be undermined: governments would be able to impose many countervailing duties, since virtually every product would benefit from these kinds of governmental assistance.

Therefore, the problem becomes one of defining "subsidy" in such a way as to avoid these broad, damaging effects on international trade. This problem is primarily connected to the use of countervailing duties by unilateral national government actions. Of course, these definitional problems occur with respect to the substantive international obligations against the use of subsidies (such as in Track II of the Code); but in that context generally there is an international procedure, and governments do not have as much unilateral scope or freedom to define subsidy. Furthermore, the international obligations, and particularly those in Track II of the Code, have a number of definitions or illustrative instances which are part of the definitional process, such that the definitions can be there restrained.[47] So this section will focus on defining subsidy in the context of countervailing duties by national governments.

My basic approach is to recognize that there is a vast universe of governmental activity which can be called "subsidy" under broad definitions, but to recognize that the international system should not be concerned about all of the contents of this vast universe. Rather, the international system should be trying to define a subset of a certain type of "subsidy" with which it will be concerned. This subset of "subsidy" could be called "actionable subsidy": a typical "lawyer's phrase" implying that only subsidies of this kind should trigger attention or "action" on the part of the international discipline regarding subsidies. Henceforth, I will use this phrase, "actionable subsidy," to identify the subset of broadly defined subsidies which should come under the international discipline of the GATT and its Code, including applications of countervailing duties.[48]

Next, we must turn to the question of how we should define "actionable subsidy." It must also be recognized that there may be different grades or levels of "actionable subsidy." For example, a proposal discussed during the Tokyo Round negotiations was to have a "three basket" or "red, green, and yellow light" approach.[49] The basic concept was that the myriad subsidy practices should be separated into three categories by negotiators: (1) a category of subsidies which should not trigger any international concern (green light); (2) a category of subsidies which should always trigger an international concern or permitted national-government response (countervailing duties) (red light); and

(3) an intermediate category of subsidies which should trigger international or national concern in certain cases (such as when the injury test has been established) (yellow light). This approach did not get very far in the Tokyo Round negotiation, perhaps because negotiators despaired of their ability to develop any sort of consensus on what should be the contents of these three baskets. Nevertheless, a further elaboration of the current and future GATT negotiations of an international discipline for subsidies might well consider the advisability of setting up an institutional framework (perhaps based on independent and impartial panel determinations) for putting subsidies into these different categories, so as to give guidance to governments and policymakers about the potential response of other nations or of the international system to subsidy practices.[50]

Behind all this it must be recognized that subsidies are an exceedingly important, even crucial, tool of national governments in order to act in their sovereign capacities to promote legitimate governmental policies to serve their constituents. There is no way that a government can "give up subsidies" under any broad definition of the term "subsidies." One needs only to recall a variety of different kinds of subsidies to realize this, including: aid to the poor, aid for technological development, special aids for education, aid to handicapped persons, aid to disadvantaged groups and regions, aid to offset certain disadvantages that have been created by other government policies, national security policies, etc.[51]

Although many subsidies, particularly the so-called production or general subsidies, have legitimate government policies behind them, as implemented these subsidies may transgress on foreign governments' legitimate aspirations on behalf of their own producing interests. Thus we may have a clash of competing policy goals: on the one hand, governments have legitimate reasons for implementing subsidies; on the other hand, importing nations have legitimate reasons for being concerned about the importation of subsidized goods when those goods cause distress to their own industries. The basic problem is how to balance these competing interests. It is in this connection that the material injury test is crucial: it acts as a sort of "mediating principle" to help governments accommodate these diametrically opposed competing interests. If the subsidized goods are not harming or causing material injury in the importing country, then why bother with any response? On the other hand, if the subsidized imports create sufficient distress in the importing country to rise to some threshold level of "material injury," perhaps at that point a response such as a countervailing duty is justified (although at this point the economic policies outlined in section 1 of this chapter may introduce reasons why, even in cases of material injury, countervailing duties may be inappropriate).

The whole conceptual structure of these policies is very intricate and very confused, and as I noted in the first section of this chapter, we are not going to be able to solve these problems in this book; nor is it likely that they will be solved in the near future.

With these caveats in mind, we can turn to some of the concepts which are currently being used to constrain the breadth of a definition of "actionable subsidy," and also think a bit about other concepts that could be likewise used.

An initial question is sometimes asked by policy-makers, namely: Does the subsidy impose a cost on the granting government, and/or a benefit on the production of a particular product which moves in international trade? According to one approach, in order for a subsidy to be "actionable" under the GATT rules, it must be established that the government has incurred a cost. According to a different viewpoint (that prevailing in the United States administration), "cost" is not the relevant consideration. Instead, the key question is whether the subsidy activity has conferred a benefit on a firm, compared to what that firm would receive under normal market conditions without the government intervention.

In order to illustrate this difference in approach, an example will be useful. Suppose that the government is prepared to make special loans to a particular industry sector, at a cost of 8 percent interest. Suppose, at the same time, the government can borrow its own funds at a cost of about 6 percent. On the other hand, suppose that the normal private-market lending would require an interest rate of 10 percent. In this situation, it might be argued that there has been no cost to the government for its 8 percent loans, since the government receives its funds for 6 percent. It will be further noted that the recipient firm is receiving a benefit because it obtains the loan at 8 percent, instead of the market rate of 10 percent. Under United States administration of its countervailing duty law, it is very clear that the benefit approach is being used and that the loan would be considered a "subsidy."[52] It seems to me that the United States approach is the correct one, if one of the basic policies of the international discipline on subsidies is to prevent "distortions." The benefit conferred on the firm by a lower interest rate than that of the market induces that firm to produce goods that it might not otherwise produce, and induces a certain allocation of resources that is not "fine tuned" to economic principles and to the needs of society or the world.[53]

Of course, if one wanted to push the frontiers of this concept, it would be possible to note that when the government lends at 8 percent (even though it borrows at 6 percent), it has incurred an "opportunity cost" by giving up a portion of the interest it *could* obtain. If the "cost approach" includes this "opportunity cost," then we see the opposing approaches converge. Perhaps this is another reason why the benefit approach seems to be preferable.

Another approach to trying to develop some parameters for a definition of "actionable subsidy," is to look at whether the subsidy "distorts" economic activity by comparison with some notion of "normal free market" conditions. This comparison obviously is very tricky, and indeed some writers would suggest that there is no such thing as "normal market activity."[54]

It does seem possible, however, to use the "distortion test," at least to some extent, for ascertaining some guideposts for our problem of defining "actionable subsidy." However, it seems to me that not just any "distortion" should suffice for the international system to take action. In some sense, every governmental action that impinges on the economy creates a "distortion." The economists will show, with their graphs and deadweight triangles, that many of these subsidy activities will reduce overall national welfare.[55] However, it is a legitimate choice for a national sovereign to accept lower economic welfare in order to promote certain societal and governmental objectives (such as redistribution of income, or support for the handicapped). As long as the government's actions are taken in such a way that the costs are borne only by that society, it seems inappropriate for other nations in the world to complain.[56] It is when the government's subsidy activity not only creates distortions within its own economy, but also significantly distorts the economies of other societies, that the international system has a legitimate concern.

A hypothetical example will partly illustrate this point. Suppose in a country, say Italy, private entrepreneurs would gladly invest in the production of a glass factory in a port city. The object would be to produce both for the home and the export market. Suppose, in addition, the government of Italy prefers that the factory be located in a depressed area in the mountains, so as to uplift that area economically. Suppose, further, that the government is prepared to pay a subsidy to the firm just equal to the additional costs of locating in the mountain region rather than in the port. In such a case, presumably the government's subsidy will distort economic activity within its national boundaries, and will somewhat lower its overall national economic welfare. However, it has a legitimate reason for wanting to do this and for bearing the costs of doing it. If the subsidy, however, is no more than enough to offset the additional costs of the factory's more remote location, it can be argued that there will be no change in the amount of glass exported and thus no distortion outside the borders of the country. In such a case, it can be further argued that the international system should not be concerned about this "regional aid" subsidy. (Nevertheless, the U.S. law currently requires that the U.S. apply countervailing duties even in this case.[57])

Although the current international and national rules do not approach the "actionable subsidy" issue this way, it would seem that it would be wise to develop the notion that there should be a prerequisite to bring actions within the concept of "actionable subsidy," namely that there be "distortion across the border." Of course, administering this concept may not be easy. That process could require a fairly detailed and sophisticated economic analysis of each case. In addition, it would have to be recognized that in the interdependent world of today, there is no clean case in which there is zero distortion across the border; instead, some sort of concept of a minimal threshold of distortion across the border would have to be developed, as an outer limit for the definition of "actionable subsidy."

To some extent, certain ways to apply the material injury test could measure this distortion across the border. The problem with relying on the injury test is two-fold. First, as I noted in chapter 10, there are certain methods of employing the injury test which venture considerably beyond the distortion caused by the foreign subsidy. Second, the injury test tends to be applied in a later stage of a CVD investigation, thus requiring the foreign exporter to undergo considerable procedural costs. If a "distortion across the border" test could be applied as part of the process of defining an "actionable subsidy" (or at least a "preliminary injury" determination that recognized the need to show a causal relation between the injury and the subsidy), then a certain number of cases could be easily disposed of.

Another very important concept that is increasingly being used in connection with defining "actionable subsidy" is the concept of "specificity." This is explicit in the United States countervailing duty statute, but not necessarily in the laws of other nations. To some degree, the specificity concept is the reverse side of the coin of what has in the recent past been called "general availability."[58] The basic idea is that when there is a foreign government subsidy that affects exports, in order for an importing country to respond with countervailing duties it must be established that the subsidy is "specific" and not one which is so "generally available" that everyone in the exporting society can use it.

United States law defines "subsidy" (what I am calling "actionable subsidy") with the following words: "The following domestic subsidies, if provided or required by government action to a specific enterprise or industry, or group of enterprises or industries, whether publicly or privately owned . . ."[59] This is the source of the "specificity test," which has been an important and pivotal concept in the U.S. administration's application of countervailing duties, and on which there is considerable jurisprudence both at the administrative level and in court appeals from administrative determinations.[60] There is considerable doubt, however, whether the international rules currently require the same approach. There is nothing in GATT or in the Subsidies Code which so explicitly focuses on a "specificity test," although in the Code at Article XI, paragraph 3, there is reference to "the aim of giving an advantage to certain enterprises."

Whether the concept of specificity, is sufficiently alluded to in the GATT Code that a Code or GATT panel could conclude that it constrains national governments, as a matter of international law, is not yet determined. Perhaps negotiators' attention in the new GATT round could be directed to this issue and better clarification obtained. In any event, it must be remembered that the words in the Code alluded to above appear in the context of Track II, and not of Track I (the latter regarding countervailing duties). The sum of this is that in the current state of play, United States law constrains the United States government in the use of countervailing duties — which, in this particular context, constitutes more constraint than the international rules mandate. The risk here is that if other governments began to emulate the United States by using more countervailing duties, they may not limit themselves with some of the constraints which limit the United States under its own laws.

What are the policy arguments supporting a "specificity test"?[61] It seems that there are probably two. First, there is an economic argument that could be made that if a subsidy is generally provided across the board to all of society and all of the producing sectors of society, it does not "distort." This argument has to be made with some caution, of course, although it might be modified simply to say that the distortions are quite minimal in such cases. Furthermore, in the context of a floating-exchange-rate world, given a moderate time for adjustment of exchange rates, the *international* distorting effects of a generally available subsidy may normally be quite minimal. Thus some economic argument can be used to buttress the notion that generally available subsidies – i.e., non-specific subsidies – should not be "actionable."

But these economic arguments can probably go only part of the way toward explaining a rationale for the specificity test. If we recognize the need to eliminate from the subset of subsidies called "actionable" the general activities which all governments undertake, such as the societal infrastructure of police, fire protection, roads, schools, etc., the specificity test can offer a very useful method of doing so. Thus, it can be argued that part of the rationale for the specificity test is that it is useful as a tool of administration (albeit sometimes blunt) to get rid of a number of cases which really ought not to be brought into a countervailing duty or other international rule process.

However, a specificity test is not itself free of problems. An immediate question that arises is the difference between *de jure* and *de facto* specificity. A government subsidy may be worded so that it appears to offer a benefit to everyone in society, or at least to offer benefits broadly to many sectors of the producing part of society. Yet, the underlying reality may be such that only a few producers or sectors can really take advantage of it. For example, Canadian provinces offer "stumpage," which gives to firms the right to remove trees from government property, to use them as a material input in production of a variety of goods. In theory, this offer is open to all comers. In practice, obviously there may be only a more limited set of industries which can profitably utilize the privilege.[62] Likewise, the Mexican government may ostensibly offer to all comers the opportunity to have ammonia at a very favorable price compared to the world market price, but it may be that only fertilizer makers are really interested in taking up such an offer.[63] Thus United States jurisprudence, at both the administrative and the court levels, has pushed the concept of specificity to a "*de facto* test,"[64] such that in order for the specificity test to be fulfilled, it must be demonstrated that not only as a legal matter are the benefits available, but also that in fact a broad segment of the economy is able to take advantage of the benefits.

Problems still remain, of course. Probably no "non-specific subsidy" is uniformly applied across all of society. For example, in the income tax law an accelerated depreciation privilege could be offered to all who can take advantage of it, but in fact it will likely benefit those firms which use more capital goods than other firms (such as service firms) which do not. Yet, it seems generally understood that such a tax measure would be "nonspecific," and therefore not "actionable."[65] Likewise, is something which is available to the entire agricultural sector nonspecific because there are number of subsectors of agriculture (grains, beef, etc.) and thus agriculture is broad enough to be considered "nonspecific"?[66] What other perimeters can be placed around the concept?

In approaching these questions, it seems that the issue is not so much an abstract one of what is or is not "specific," but is one that must be understood as an administrative tool which can assist even low-level officials to determine "actionability," in the light of some of the economic and "administrability" principles that have been outlined above. National government administrators need some leeway in making these determinations, which will allow them to provide some guideposts for lower-level officials. Otherwise, the processes become so expensive that they themselves are "non-tariff barriers" to liberal world trade.

11.4 Perspectives and Reflections on the Subsidies Subject

From the previous sections, it may be seen that the whole area of subsidies activity in international law, including the rules designed to constrain the use of subsidies and the other rules designed to allow national governments the unilateral privilege of responding to subsidies with countervailing duties, is not only extremely complex but holds the potential, if misapplied, of undermining the basic policy goals of the post-World War II liberal trade system. On the one hand, governments can use subsidies to evade a liberal trade system by subsidizing so as to inhibit imports, or by subsidizing so as to enhance exports. On the other hand, responses to subsidies, particularly the unilateral national government response of countervailing duties, can be implemented in such a way as to undermine liberal trade policies. The countervailing duty becomes, in a sense, a substitute for the older normal tariff. Indeed, the processes of determining the appropriate application of countervailing duties can become so convoluted and expensive themselves that they play into the hands of domestic producing interests in an importing country.[67]

These troublesome aspects are being worked out in a series of specific issue contexts, such as natural resources, "upstream subsidies," etc.[68] The lack of consensus on what is an "actionable" subsidy for purposes of countervailing duties is very troublesome, as is the lack of consensus about the definition, particularly, of "domestic" subsidy, in the context of the substantive international obligations on subsidization (Track II of the Code). Clearly this is one of the reasons that has motivated the negotiators in the new GATT negotiation (Uruguay Round) to include subsidies as a major item on the agenda for future international deliberations.[69] Such deliberations are clearly needed. A number of the points mentioned in the previous sections should be addressed in those deliberations.

Perhaps a brief inventory of a series of concepts which should be considered, in my view, would be useful. The remainder of this section will be devoted to this inventory. The following are a series of principles that could be entertained by negotiators or national-policy leaders in connection with the further elaboration of the international subsidy rules.[70]

1. National governments should recognize the principle of "generalizability" of what they do in the context of their countervailing duty laws. When a government, such as the United States, begins to apply countervailing duties to a particular subsidy practice, it must recognize that this will aid and comfort other governments who wish to emulate that approach. But in addition, countries which have substantially greater economic power in the world should recognize that they owe the world trading system an additional obligation of responsibility not to use that power merely because they can get away with it.

2. The specificity test seems to be very useful, and very important, as a way to differentiate in many cases between subsidies for which there should be no international concern and other subsidies which we call "actionable." Further elaboration of the specificity test would seem wise, and it would also seem wise to be sure that it is firmly established in international rules.

3. There ought to be developed a prerequisite test for "actionability," requiring the subsidy to have some kind of "cross border effect" that is not merely insubstantial.

4. It may be possible, and would assist "administrability," to define certain types of subsidy practices as "*per se* violations," or at least as "presumptive violations" of both international rules and countervailing-duty triggering rules. To a certain extent this has begun with the annex to the Subsidies Code, relating to export subsidies.[71] It may be possible to further elaborate this annex, and also to establish that this annex should be considered in the process of subsidy definition for countervailing duty purposes. (U.S. law incorporates by reference this annex as part of its countervailing-duty definition of subsidy, but U.S.

law does not limit or constrain the notion of "subsidy" with this annex).[72] It might even be the case that certain kinds of *"per se* violations" should be subject to countervailing duties without an injury test. This might be done by explicitly excepting the injury test, or by providing that in certain kinds of subsidy practices, a material injury will be "presumed," perhaps subject to offsetting evidence.

5. A *"de minimis"* cutoff seems very wise in the practical administration of countervailing duties. In United States administrative practice, it is now considered that if the total subsidies for a product amount to less than 0.5 percent of the price of that product, the *de minimis* threshold has not been met and the case will be dismissed.[73] A number of commentators believe that this threshold is too low, and that it ought to be raised to 3 percent or 4 percent or even 5 percent, as a way to get rid of "nuisance cases" and cases which are brought primarily to harass importers because of the cost of the process. It would have to be recognized that for certain kinds of products, a lower *de minimis* threshold may make sense. This would be true for products that are highly fungible (such as grains) and have a relatively high price elasticity of demand.[74] In these conditions, even a small subsidy could have a substantial impact on competitive conditions. The way to handle this, perhaps, is to have a higher *de minimis* as *prima facie,* and to allow those industry sectors who feel that their particular products deserve a lower *de minimis* to make a case for that.

6. The injury test, as I have stated, is an important mediating principle to help balance the clash of policy goals particularly with reference to the so-called domestic subsidies. This test must be preserved, and its implementation probably needs some attention. As mentioned in the previous chapter, several aspects of the current evolution of the injury test in United States law give cause for concern, particularly: (a) the cumulation test; and (b) the possible decline of the "margins analysis."

7. Constant efforts must be made to reduce the procedural costs of applying a countervailing duty system. There is already much commentary on the fact that those costs are getting out of hand.[75] To some extent these costs are necessary in order to provide a more liberal trading system than would otherwise be available. However, when the costs become very high compared to the value of imports of certain commodities (exacerbated by the cumulation test in the injury determinations[76]), then domestic competing interests are tempted to bring processes simply to impose those costs on foreign imports, and thus to inhibit foreign

imports. In addition, there is an effect on foreign exporters that will lead them to hesitate in attempting to penetrate a market, when they feel there is great vulnerability to process costs (as in countervailing duty cases).

8. In general, countervailing duty procedures ought *not* to be based on practices that have occurred far in the past. To open up the possibility of countervailing-duty suits against subsidies which have ceased ten or fifteen years ago or more, simply because there is a "continuing effect," is very dangerous indeed, since it would expose a great deal of international trade to the costs of such processes. A corollary to this, however, would seem to be that the rules ought to be able to look better into the future. Thus, the "threat of material injury" may become more significant. In addition, it may be that certain kinds of countervailing-duty type procedures should be allowed even before imports actually occur.[77]

9. Some special deference to the particular needs of developing countries of the world needs to be worked out. In some cases, there is an argument that subsidy practices, even export subsidies, can be justified for various economic reasons, such as "infant industry arguments," or to offset other disadvantages imposed on the goods (such as a distorted exchange rate). We are not able to resolve these issues here, but they do merit more attention and explicit elaboration in the international and national rules.

By way of conclusion, it can of course be asked again whether there is any rational justification for the countervailing duty rules of the GATT system, or even for the substantive obligations regarding subsidies in the GATT system. I asked those questions at the beginning of this chapter, and I noted that we would not be able to resolve those issues or answer those questions in any satisfactory way. I think the reader can now readily see why that is so. Consequently, a reasonable prediction based on empirical observation of the world and the many conflicting interested parties in it suggests that both the international subsidy system and the national government countervailing duty systems will continue for many years, and probably will see a greater number of national governments using countervailing-duty actions. Thus, even though it may not be the optimal approach for an international system regarding subsidies, it seems wise to continue the process of elaborating the rules of this system, particularly in the context of international agreements developed either in GATT negotiating rounds or elsewhere. Indeed, it may be wise to develop some explicit institutional mechanisms in the context of the GATT Code and the GATT itself, which could be charged with elaborating the rules, perhaps defining whether a particular subsidy practice should or should not be "actionable" over time, as experience is obtained. In this regard, the provisions in the free-trade agreement between Canada and the United States, signed in January 1988, are very interesting. They provide not only for a special international bilateral tribunal to determine certain appeals from cases regarding antidumping and countervailing duties, but also for joint work through negotiations to try to better elaborate the rules regarding these matters. It can only be hoped that this bilateral effort can be generalized somewhat to a multilateral one, so as to provide greater stability in this connection for world trade.[78]

12

Developing Countries and World Trade Rules

12.1 Economies That Do Not Well Fit the Rules of the World Trading System

In this and the next chapter we take up several types of national economies that for one reason or another do not well fit the post-World War II Bretton Woods world trading system. In the next chapter we deal with the perplexing problems of nonmarket economies and state trading. In this chapter, we will focus on the problems of developing countries—i.e., countries which have low living standards. However, since this subject has been extensively treated elsewhere, and generally involves the expertise of economists rather than lawyers, we will be relatively brief. Indeed, the GATT system "legal rules" concerning developing countries are remarkably vague and "aspirational" in approach.

Throughout the forty years of GATT history, there has been much discussion and considerable perplexity about the position of developing countries in world trade. The economics literature is extensive[1] and a number of different problems can be posed or debated. Here I will only address a few problems.

The first is the question of whether the world trading rules are fair to developing countries. At various times it has been alleged that these rules operate in such a way as to disadvantage the nonindustrial countries. Indeed, some of the controversy during the GATT drafting process and at the Havana conference in 1948 turned on this question. After the Havana conference, a number of developing countries, particularly Latin American countries, were sufficiently dismayed by the rules that had evolved that they opted to stay out of the GATT system for years and even decades. (Mexico, for example, only recently joined the GATT.[2]) In 1958, the GATT commissioned a special study by a group of eminent experts, headed by Gottfried Haberler, to comment on the application of the world trading rules regarding trade of developing countries.[3] The GATT itself has only two provisions that explicitly allow differential treatment for developing countries—namely, Article XVIII and the articles in part IV of GATT. For the most part, the GATT rules do not otherwise distinguish between trade of developing and developed countries.

A number of the 1979 Tokyo Round codes have special provisions for developing countries, some of which have provoked troublesome policy responses.[4] In addition, one "understanding" resulting from the Tokyo Round explicitly contemplates industrial-country actions favoring developing countries, while noting the possibility of improving the capacity of those countries to "participate more fully in the framework of rights and obligations under the General Agreement."[5] In addition, there are some special arrangements between certain groups of countries (sometimes permitted by a GATT waiver or justified as a free trade area under GATT Article XXIV), which are designed to benefit developing countries. The most prominent of these is the EC's "Lome" agreements with over fifty African, Caribbean, and Pacific (ACP) nations.[6] The U.S. "Caribbean Basin Initiative" can also be mentioned as an example.[7]

The question of whether the rules operate fairly for developing countries, however, is a complex one involving several levels of analysis.[8] The first level of analysis asks which rules of GATT explicitly discriminate against the trade of developing countries. The answer to this question is generally none. The GATT rules tend not to explicitly distinguish between trade of developing and developed countries, except to give benefits to developing countries.

A slightly deeper layer of analysis would look at whether the nominally nondiscriminatory rules of GATT and the trading system in fact have a discriminatory effect, given the facts and circumstances of the real world. Attention could be given to the way the rules apply to different kinds of trade; as I have noted, some of the GATT rules distinguish between primary and nonprimary goods,[9] and insofar as this distinction might adversely affect developing countries, some case could be made that a problem exists.

An even deeper analysis might look at the institutional structure of the trade-rule system, to ascertain if some countries are put at a disadvantage in that system. Here it could be argued that since the GATT does not have a very effective enforcement mechanism,[10] large and powerful economic countries can "get away with more" than can the weaker countries. Since the developing countries tend to be weakest economically, they might argue that they are at some disadvantage in this process.

Against all this, however, would have to be balanced the observation that many developing countries are able to take advantage of either explicit or implicit exceptions in GATT so as to to pursue almost at will any form of trade policy they wish. For example, the balance-of-payments rules of Article XII and XVIII of GATT give a claim of legitimacy to many measures implemented by developing countries, including quantitative restrictions, despite the nominal prohibitions in GATT against such measures.[11]

Another approach would be to analyze certain patterns that lead to what is called the "effective tariff rate" problem, whereby developing countries can sometimes demonstrate that industrial importing countries' tariff structures impose little tariff on raw materials, but increasingly higher tariffs as one goes up the scale of processing. One result of this, it has been alleged, is to discourage developing countries from developing downstream value-added industries, and therefore to inhibit their economic development.[12]

Of course, any appraisal of the effects of the world trading rules on developing countries must also recognize the danger of some alternative possibilities. For example, flawed as the rules are, the MFN clause does extend many privileges to developing countries (without reciprocal obligations) which might not be available otherwise.[13] A trade "deal" between two large economic entities will often, through MFN, give benefits to economically smaller entities. In addition, the dispute settlement procedures, although also flawed, do occasionally give some added leverage to the trade diplomacy of weaker nations,[14] compared to what they would have when acting unilaterally or bilaterally. This has been one of the motivations for GATT entry or for participation in specific Tokyo Round codes.[15]

A second issue of considerable importance in the GATT-Bretton Woods world trading system, is whether there are valid reasons to give special privileges to developing countries. There are two different questions raised by this broad general one, namely: What is the moral basis for favorable discrimination toward developing countries? Is favorable discrimination actually helpful, or does it merely perpetuate undesirable policies in the developing countries?[16]

These questions lead into a third general policy issue which has been highly debated in recent years, namely whether the more advanced developing countries should now be required to accept more fully the general nondiscriminatory discipline of the GATT and trade rules. This is the so-called "graduation" issue.[17] Recently, for example, the United States has been vigorous in pushing the idea of graduation, partly at the behest of Congress. One manifestation of this has been a U.S. disposition to revoke the benefits of its GSP (Generalized System of Preferences) program for certain key developing countries.[18]

Finally, the whole question of debt must be noticed. Developing-country debt is an obvious and extraordinarily difficult problem, and of course it relates to trade and the trade rules. Insofar as the rules tend to inhibit the ability of developing countries to export in such a way as to obtain the necessary foreign exchange to service their debt, those rules can be deemed faulty.[19]

To works that are more focused on the economic considerations of world trade, I will leave the task of sorting out these and many other questions. However, the legal structure of the generalized system of preferences merits a bit more exploration here.

12.2 The Generalized System of Preferences in International Law

At the first United Nations Conference on Trade and Development (UNCTAD I) in 1964, the secretary general of that United Nations organization shepherded through the adoption of a report designed to focus international attention on the need for special rules for the trade of developing countries. In particular, the report promoted the idea of lower tariff rates for imports into industrial countries from developing countries. This idea of preferences clearly was inconsistent with the GATT MFN principle.[20] Thus it was necessary to develop a new legal exception to MFN for the benefit of developing countries.

This exception was developed in a variety of international institutions.[21] However, it was recognized that the final legal authority for a GSP program would have to be taken in GATT, in the form of a GATT waiver to the MFN clause. This waiver was granted in 1971 for a ten-year period.[22] The waiver authorized each industrial country to establish its own GSP program, providing that each of those programs benefitted all "developing countries." However, it was left to each industrial country to define what was a "developing country" for purposes of benefitting from the GSP program. Thus, although the GATT waiver established the GSP framework, a great deal of individual discretion was left to each of the sovereign industrial nations implementing it. There was no international law requirement to grant GSP, and no particularly detailed requirements as to what should be the shape and framework of GSP. As actually put into effect, each country's GSP program has its own features. Furthermore, different countries implemented their programs at different times, the United States being the last major nation to implement GSP.[23] (The United States program is described in the next section). Some countries granted lower tariffs or zero tariffs, but hedged them with quota limits.

The degree to which these programs provided actual benefits to developing countries is somewhat controversial. Various estimates come up with various results.[24] Nevertheless, the programs have been highly popular among developing countries, who view them as an important part of the evolving world trading system.

Since the GATT waiver was limited to a ten-year period, it technically expired in 1981. However, as part of the Tokyo Round negotiations, the CONTRACTING PARTIES developed and adopted a declaration entitled "Differential and More Favourable Treatment, Reciprocity and Fuller Participation of Developing Countries."[25] In this declaration, adopted as a "decision" of the CONTRACTING PARTIES but not explicitly labeled a "waiver," it was stated that "CONTRACTING PARTIES may accord differential and more favorable treatment to developing countries, without according such treatment to other Contracting Parties . . . ," notwithstanding the provisions of the GATT MFN clause. This declaration or decision has been called the "enabling clause" and is seen by some essentially to perpetuate the authority for GSP. This decision, however, does speak of the possible improvement of the ability of developing countries to make "contributions or negotiated concessions" under the provisions of GATT. This oblique language, in the minds of some, constitutes a potential "graduation requirement."[26]

However, the whole legal situation is one of extraordinary ambiguity, probably reflecting not only a lack of precision on the part of the negotiators, but also a lack of agreement among them on many of the details.

12.3 GSP and the U.S. Law

Originally the United States was generally opposed to any concept of special or general preferences of developing countries, and it was not until 1967 that the United States president announced a shift in U.S. policy toward being more favorably inclined to a GSP program.[27] Although the GATT waiver of 1971 authorized GSP programs, the United

States was the last to implement it, and it did so in Title V of the 1974 Trade Act.

Under the act, the Congress provided authority to the president that was very broad and gave him much discretion, both to determine the countries which would benefit from the program and in many cases to determine when the benefits could be withdrawn. The Congress also had a number of ideas for attaching strings to these benefits, including, for example, prohibiting GSP benefits to countries who expropriated property without compensation or nullified existing contracts with U.S. citizens, or to communist countries unless they received MFN treatment from the U.S. and were members of GATT and the IMF.[28]

Countries who are members of OPEC or are engaged in activities to "withhold supplies of vital commodity resources" so as to increase prices are also excluded from the U.S. GSP program.[29] The Congress also exempted certain "import sensitive articles" from the application of its GSP program.[30]

Essentially the U.S. GSP provided a zero tariff on all articles except those excepted, for the countries who were designated as beneficiary countries. The U.S. law had something called a "competitive need formula," though.[31] Under this provision, when a particular GSP beneficiary country was shipping a quantity of an eligible article to the U.S. market in an amount that exceeded a certain threshold either in dollars ($25 million, adjusted for inflation) or in a percentage of total imports of that article (e.g., 50 percent), then GSP treatment for that product would be withdrawn for that country. The basic idea was that when such a threshold was reached, the GSP beneficiary country no longer could claim that its industry was "infant" and needed such special privileges. Another idea was that by removing the GSP privileges from the more advanced industries of the third world, the lesser developing countries would be better able to take advantage of the program.[32]

Overall, under the United States program 140 countries have at one time or another been eligible under the GSP program, and at its peak the system covered upwards of $13 billion worth of imports.[33] However, this figure only represented around 3 percent to 4 percent of imports.[34]

The U.S. statute was limited to ten years and so needed renewing in 1984.[35] The Congress enacted the renewal in the 1984 Tariff and Trade Act, but a number of modifications were made: in particular, a policy of graduation was specified. Under these provisions and subsequent evolution of the system, the United States has taken significant steps to graduate both countries and products from its GSP program.[36]

As this is written, the program still covers approximately 140 countries (including associations of countries) — providing for a zero tariff for all beneficiary countries, with a number of specific exceptions, some of which result from an annual process of review. The total trade coverage under current GSP (1987) was $13 billion.

The graduation policy and annual reviews provide domestic producers and other lobbies opportunity to petition for the withdrawal of GSP status. For example, in December 1987, the president withdrew the GSP status from Chile because Chile had not taken steps to afford workers internationally accepted rights.[37]

13

State Trading and Nonmarket Economies

13.1 State Trading and the GATT System

The post-World War II international trading system is obviously based on rules and principles which more or less assume free market-oriented economies. The rules of GATT certainly were constructed with that in mind.[1] Yet important parts of the world do not have economies based on these principles, and even in market economies there are many institutions which do not operate under free-market principles, such as state trading agencies or monopolies, government-owned industries, and the like. These circumstances pose some difficult conceptual problems for the GATT trading system. Can that system continue to exist and improve if it embraces economies and institutions which do not follow the assumed economic structure of free markets? Should that system remain primarily one that consists of economies which are relatively "market oriented"? Should major nonmarket economies, such as China or the Soviet Union, be incorporated into this system? If so, on what terms? Likewise, can this system accommodate, without increasing tension and rancor, a situation in which current participants have major portions of their economies essentially outside the normal GATT rule discipline because these portions are government owned or operated? In this chapter we will explore these questions.[2]

First, let us examine how the GATT rules fail to accommodate the state trading or nonmarket situation.

An hypothetical case will illustrate the problem. Suppose that the government of Xonia maintains a state trading monopoly for the importation of bicycles. No bicycles can be imported except through this state trading enterprise. Suppose further that this government has accepted a binding in GATT for tariffs of 5 percent on bicycles. In addition, it will be remembered that GATT prohibits the use of quantitative limitations on the importation of bicycles (or any other goods). Thus, exporting nations may think they have an opportunity to sell bicycles to Xonia.

Instead, however, Xonia may, as a matter of proprietary direction, inform the bicycle trading enterprise that during the next year it shall purchase for import no more than one million bicycles. With such an order, Xonia evades the impact of Article XI of GATT, prohibiting the use of quantative restrictions. In addition, suppose that Xonia directs the state trading enterprise that, when they are resold on the domestic market the mark-up on all imported bicycles must be 100 percent. Likewise, part of the effect of this order is to evade the tariff binding, since the mark-up can partly operate like a tariff. Article II, paragraph 4 of GATT does provide that when a government maintains a monopoly on importation of a product which has been bound, the operation of this monopoly should not "afford protection on the average in excess of the amount of protection provided for . . ." under the binding. Nevertheless, this has been a difficult measure to police.[3] In addition, many products may be unbound.

GATT Article XVII addresses the problem of state trading enterprises, but its provisions are not very rigorous. Arguably, the activity mentioned in the hypothetical case above is completely consistent with GATT, even though it undermines two of the fundamental obligations of GATT: the tariff binding and the rule against quantitative restrictions. Article XVII requires state trading enterprises to "act in a manner consistent with general principles of non-discriminatory treatment prescribed in this agreement. . . ." This obligation has been deemed by some interpretations of GATT to apply only as a sort of MFN measure. Such an approach argues that there is no "national treatment" Article III-type obligation with respect to how state trading enterprises operate. There is an alternative view, which was mentioned in a recent GATT panel report.[4] Nevertheless, the general thrust of Article XVII of GATT is weak as it relates to the possibility of governments using state trading measures to evade the other obligations of GATT. Needless to say, if an entire economy is based primarily on state trading principles—such that we would call it a "nonmarket economy"—then most of the economic activity of this economy evades the effective responsibilities and policies of GATT, even though this economy may be in complete conformity with the technical rules of GATT.

Thus, there are several important problems facing GATT. Perhaps the most serious problem is how to manage the acceptance into the GATT system of major nonmarket economies. We will take that up in the next section. In addition, however, there has been considerable criticism of the current GATT as it applies to current contracting parties, since it allows many contracting parties to evade the GATT discipline through the use of government-owned industries and state trading monopolies. Some proposals for legislative revision of United States law would attempt to impose greater disciplines on state trading of other countries in connection with the GATT obligations, and the whole state trading question is one of those which is to be addressed during the Uruguay Round of GATT trade negotiations.[5] Whether it will be possible politically to tighten the discipline of GATT concerning state trading is questionable. It is very difficult to amend the text of GATT,[6] and how one would design a separate code on state trading and induce countries to accept such discipline (without any apparent advantage or quid pro quo) is not clear.

In recent years there has been a fair amount of comment about the problem of countertrade.[7] Countertrade describes a situation in which governments or enterprises barter and exchange products rather than simply pay a price for goods. Some forms of countertrade can be accomplished through state trading enterprises or other government monopolies or regulations. In some cases these are set up under bilateral treaty frameworks. Of course, countertrade can also be carried on purely by private enterprises in a free-market context, in which case the GATT may have rules which apply. However, countertrade mandated by governments may be inconsistent with certain GATT obligations,[8] such as MFN, or with obligations prohibiting the use of quotas, or with national treatment.

13.2 Nonmarket Economies and the GATT: China and the U.S.S.R.

For various historical and other reasons, the GATT has always had a few nonmarket economies as Contracting Parties. In some cases, these were nations that were Contracting Parties to GATT before they shifted to a nonmarket economy structure (such as Czechoslovakia or Cuba). In other cases, the GATT has explicitly accepted into membership certain nonmarket economies under special provisions or protocols (such as Poland, Hungary, Romania, and Yugoslavia[9]). Sometimes it is said that because of these precedents GATT should have no problem accepting new nonmarket economies. However, commentators are quick to note that the Contracting Parties who are nonmarket economies in GATT are relatively small in terms of their impact on trade. Furthermore, relations between the GATT and its nonmarket Contracting Parties have always been troublesome.[10] Arguably, the trading relationship does not work well, but the other members of GATT are willing to tolerate the situation because they either have special arrangements of their own with the countries concerned, or the amounts of trade are small. Neither of these circumstances would apply in the case of a country like China or the Soviet Union, both of which are very large and therefore very significant in terms of potential trade impacts in the GATT context.[11]

On the following page is a chart of the contracting parties in GATT that might be deemed "non-market oriented," although there is much difficulty about the definition of "non-market." Some countries would argue that they have a substantial portion of their economies which operates under market- and price-oriented systems, and some would argue that the trend is more in that direction, so that they should not be branded with the label "nonmarket." Commentators point out, furthermore, that even in so-called "market-oriented" economies, such as those in Europe or in certain developing countries (e.g., India and Brazil), a very large proportion of the economy resources of such nations may be owned and controlled by government operation, either through state trading enterprises or directly through government-owned industrial complexes.[12] Nevertheless, the countries listed here are those which are deemed to be "more nonmarket" than the other members of GATT. The chart indicates the date of their entry into GATT, and a short phrase describing the nature of the protocol of entry.

As mentioned in this chart, in some cases trade relations between these countries, and between certain contracting parties of GATT, are handled under bilateral regimes, some of which include quota measures (which may not be technically consistent with GATT obligations). This seems to be particularly the case for the European Economic Community.[13]

In some cases, special "safeguard measures" have been designed to try to address the conceptual difficulties of a GATT relationship with nonmarket economies. In the United States, for example (as we will see in the next section) this approach has been taken. In particular, such special safeguard measures tend to be "selective" — i.e., targeted just at the particular nonmarket economy and thus not consistent with the general notions of Article XIX of GATT and its MFN requirement.[14]

State Trading Contracting Parties to GATT

Name	Date of GATT entry	Nature of protocol
Cuba	1948	Original entrant
Czechoslovakia	1948	Original entrant
Hungary[15]	1973	Normal schedule of concessions in accordance with Article XXXIII. Article XIX may be used against Hungary on a non-MFN basis. Withdrawal of concession granted to Hungary possible after negotiations.
Poland[16]	1967	Undertook to increase imports at an annual rate of 7 percent. Article XIX may be used against Poland on a non-MFN basis. Withdrawal of concession granted to Poland possible after negotiations.
Romania[17]	1971	Undertook to increase imports from Contracting Parties at a rate not smaller than growth of total imports, as provided in Five-Year Plans. Article XIX may be used against Romania on a non-MFN basis. Withdrawal of concession granted to Romania possible after negotiations.
Yugoslavia[18]	1966	Normal accession process

China poses some particularly interesting questions, both legal and economic, for the GATT. China was one of the original twenty-three contracting parties of the GATT when it came into force under the Protocol Provisional Application at the beginning of 1948, and so the current government in Beijing argues that China continues to be a contracting party and merely needs to resume its position. However, the legal situation is somewhat more cloudy.[19] During the early years of GATT, China was in the midst of a civil war. In about 1950, the GATT headquarters received a cable from a Chinese government then located on the island of Taiwan, which purported to withdraw China from GATT membership. Since that time, there has been no China that has acted as a Contracting Party in GATT, although a government located on Taiwan took an observer position in GATT from 1965 to 1971. The current government of Beijing argues, however, that the 1950 cable to GATT was null and void, because it did not originate from the government which was then in control of "China." It also argues, by analogy with credentials actions taken in other international organizations such as the United Nations and the International Monetary Fund, that the mainland Chinese government of today is the beneficiary of the various memberships of China in international organizations.[20]

As of mid-1988, the matter of Chinese membership in GATT had not been resolved, but the GATT has accepted that the mainland Chinese government will negotiate[21] for membership in GATT, either as a new contracting party or, more likely (this appears to be acceptable to most GATT members), as a resumption of the contracting party position for China. Even in the later case, however, it is recognized by all parties, including China, that a negotiation will proceed in GATT about the terms of this resumption, and that the negotiation generally will be guided by the procedures for new members under Article XXXIII of GATT.[22]

In fact, a pure "resumption" approach would probably be satisfactory neither to existing GATT Contracting Parties nor to the Chinese government. From the Chinese government's perspective, the following problems would exist:

1. There would arguably be some back "dues" for years for which contributions have not been made. (This is probably the least important of the potential issues.)

2. The original Chinese tariff schedule of 1948 is totally out of date and inappropriate in the modern context, and would need to be revised.

3. There might be some issues of "grandfather rights" under the Protocol of Provisional Application, but arguably there would be no grandfather rights because current Chinese statutes are all subsequent to the original date of the Protocol Provisional Application (January 1, 1948).

4. Article XXXV "opt out" issues are in question. The right to opt out of a relationship with an existing GATT member only occurs at the time of

first entry into GATT, but it appears that the current Chinese government would want such opt-out rights with respect to several Contracting Parties of GATT. Likewise, some current members of GATT (particularly the United States) may find it necessary to exercise "opt out rights" in connection with certain legislative problems existing in their law. (I will take this up in the next section.)

As of this writing, the negotiation for Chinese re-accession has been proceeding in the manner typical for new entrants under Article XXXIII. Thus, the GATT has established a working party to consider the Chinese entry; the Chinese have presented a statement about their economic and trading systems to the working parties; GATT members of the working party have formulated a series of questions (numbering more than four hundred!) for the Chinese government; the Chinese government has prepared answers to those questions; and discussion on them is continuing.[23]

The assimilation of China into GATT is a formidable task. Not only has China been a non-market-oriented economy (although it has argued that it is now evolving more toward price and market orientation), but China can claim the status of a developing country with special privileges in GATT. Many producers, both in the industrialized western countries and in other major developing countries, are eyeing potential Chinese competition with considerable apprehension. The method by which China could be drawn into a satisfactory GATT relationship is not easy to foresee. In all probability, it will involve a number of different measures embodied in a protocol of resumption. Many of these measures may not be entirely consistent with the traditional habits of GATT policymakers, and may involve departures from some of the generally accepted norms of GATT which apply primarily to market- and price-oriented economies. For example, it is quite easy to conceive of special safeguard rules for Chinese products. In addition (as I will discuss in section 13.4), certain special rules regarding the so-called "unfair trade practices" will likely be necessary. With respect to China's importing regime, other GATT members will undoubtedly want some assurances from China beyond its mere acceptance of GATT and of a tariff schedule. Already suggested have been such measures as requiring China to: accept an obligation to unify its national customs rules and institutions; accept some of the Tokyo Round codes, such as the codes on licensing procedures and customs valuation; and publish its import regulations and other "transparency measures."

The China negotiation for resumption, of course, is important not only because China is important, but also because the rules for accommodation that are worked out in the China context will set an important precedent for future similar activities of the GATT, including the possible accession of the Soviet Union, and revisions of Article XVII relating to state trading.

The issue of the Soviet Union cannot be entirely ignored, despite the fact that some GATT members would like to do so. So far, Soviet overtures to the GATT have been rebuffed, and the United States has taken a fairly strong position against Soviet membership or even observer status in GATT. The argument is that the Soviet Union has an economy that is too different from that contemplated by the GATT rules, and that therefore to admit the Soviet Union would do too much damage to the fabric of the GATT system. This raises important long-term policy issues for the GATT and the world trading system.[24]

It is my view that it will be very difficult in the long run to deny membership in the GATT to any important nation of the world. Since the GATT is the principal world trading institution, strong arguments can be made that it must be a universal institution, for both political and economic reasons. Politically, it must be recognized that an important goal of the economic institutions is the preservation of peace and the prevention of tensions which could lead to war or other conflict.[25] An international institution which accepted all nations of the world into an endeavor to try and accommodate respective interests would seem to be an important part of that general policy. In addition, economic considerations suggest the possible enhancement of world welfare through the additional trading opportunities, economies of scale, and comparative advantage of general inclusion of all important trading blocs of the world.[26]

Should the GATT, however, be preserved as a more purely "market oriented" institution? Given the lack of alternative universal trade organization, the question then becomes how to "interface" the different economic systems of the world into one universal organizational structure.[27] Although some are tempted to use GATT membership as a bait to try to force different national economic systems to change, it can be argued strongly that the GATT has a responsibility to change and to figure out an appropriate way to accommodate the different economic systems. This might involve buffering mechanisms, such as some of those just suggested in the case of China. Once again, buffering mechanisms might involve a number of measures which are not very "pure" in the eyes of market-oriented economic policies. It is also important

that these mechanisms adequately protect the market-oriented economies from abuse by the fact that nonmarket economies and state trading
agencies can too easily evade the disciplines of the GATT rules and
policies. All this is a tall order, but it is certainly not an impossible one.

One possible way to develop an "interface mechanism" for nonmarket economies in GATT, while at the same time accommodating the
possibility that portions of such economies might move toward a market orientation, would be to establish a "two track" safeguard system. A
protocol of accession/resumption would first likely provide for transparency (publication of regulations and administration of customs),
procedural fairness, and a working party or other committee established under the protocol to meet annually to review problems of the
relationship (with the review clearly able to look in both directions —
that is, not only to compliance with obligations by the nonmarket economy, but also to compliance of other GATT members in their trade
relations with the nonmarket economy). All the other obligations of
GATT would be assumed.

In addition, however, a two-track safeguard system could be provided to operate roughly as follows: The first track would be normal
GATT procedures, which would *prima facie* apply to all trade from the
state trading economy to other GATT members. In the absence of an
explicit invocation of a second track, the GATT would apply in all respects similarly to the way it applies to other countries.

Provision would also be made, however, for a second track, whereby
the government of an importing country would be allowed to set up a
procedure by which industry sectors could specially petition their government to allege that the imports from the country covered in the protocol are "state trading exports." When this allegation is received, it would
automatically proceed toward a second track, which would first require
consultation between the importing government and the exporting government. During this consultation phase, the factual circumstances of the
exports would be explored to see whether they were sufficiently "state
trading" in nature that the second track should be followed. Certain
criteria could be set out in the agreement, but for practical political
purposes it would likely be necessary to defer on this issue to the decision of the importing country (possibly offering it some chance to appeal to the committee or working party set up under the accession/
resumption protocol). If the criteria were fulfilled so that the second
track were followed, then the importing country would apply a "serious
injury test," and if the importing country's industry were "seriously

injured," and it could be demonstrated that this was causally related (under specified causal tests) to the imports from the state trading sector, then the importing country would be authorized to apply selective safeguards (import restraints) on those imports.

However, part of the protocol for the exporting country would be a set of restraints on the use of such selective safeguards, including a shorter time limit (e.g., three years), and possibly some quantitative prerequisites (such as the need to show that the state trading imports constituted a certain percentage of all like-product imports, as well as a certain percentage of consumption of those products in the importing country). In addition, requirements might be imposed that the imports from the state trading sector be increasing absolutely (and not just relatively, as permitted under the current GATT system) and that appropriate "adjustment measures" be taken in the importing nation. Finally, appeal on these issues would be permitted to the GATT committee established by the protocol of accession/resumption.

Clearly, such measures are not entirely consistent with their liberal trade economic arguments. But they might furnish a fairly pragmatic way for the GATT to accommodate the state trading countries in a manner that would minimize the suspicions and tensions that could otherwise occur. Furthermore, the two-track system has the advantage of accommodating evolution in the economic system of the state trading country. At that point in time when such a country becomes truly a "market system," obviously the second track will not be invocable. In between, if certain sectors of the state trading country achieve sufficient "market orientation," they will be eligible for the full regular GATT treatment instead of the second track.

13.3   The United States and Nonmarket Economies

The United States has a special and sometimes unfortunate legal regime for its trading relationship with communist countries. This legal regime poses certain problems in connection with the accommodation of nonmarket economies into the GATT system. It stems principally from a congressional impetus during the early 1950s, as a reaction to the Cold War. In 1951, the U.S. Congress enacted a law which prohibited the United States from granting MFN status to countries controlled or dominated by world communism.[28] With respect to the contracting parties then part of GATT, only Czechoslovakia was really affected, but the result of the U.S. enactment was to require the U.S. government to cease to apply the GATT, at least as a *de facto* matter, to Czechoslovakia. When Czechoslovakia complained to the GATT about this, the GATT approach was to adopt a resolution that merely recognized this state of affairs between the United States and Czechoslovakia.[29] By 1960, political relations between the United States and some Eastern Bloc nations were such that the United States was willing for Poland to enter the GATT, and was willing to establish trading relationships with Yugoslavia.[30]

In 1972 the United States negotiated a bilateral trade agreement with the Soviet Union, with the understanding that the Congress would have to approve key actions to be taken under that agreement. When the executive branch began to draft a potential trade bill during the early 1970s,[31] part of the bill authorized the president to enter into bilateral trade agreements, including the extension of MFN treatment, with communist countries under certain conditions. At this point, however, an important movement in the Congress, generated by U.S. citizens interested in promoting the opportunity for emigration (particularly of Jewish persons) from the Soviet Union led to the "Jackson–Vanik amendment." Under these statutory proposals, which were included in the trade bill versions voted on by the House and later the Senate, a communist country would be entitled to receive MFN treatment from the U.S. only if it permitted free emigration, with the possibility of being granted a waiver if the president determined that certain progress toward the goal of free emigration was being achieved. This waiver was to be subject to various checks and actions by the Congress.[32] After prolonged negotiations between the executive and congressional branches of the U.S. government, measures to this effect were finally included in Title IV of the Trade Act of 1974.[33] One result of this series of events was the rejection by the Soviet Union of the trade agreement, since it announced that it was not prepared to conform to the U.S. Congress measures included in the act.[34]

Thus, the United States is constrained in terms of how it can enter into trade relations with communist countries. This constraint prevents the United States from fully accepting new members of GATT when such members are communist countries. Indeed, because of the legislation, the United States is required to exercise its Article XXXV opt-out of a GATT relationship with a contracting party which is communist. The United States may then be prepared to enter into a bilateral trade agreement with such a country—which trade agreement will incorporate GATT treatment but also the essential clauses mandated by U.S. legislation, including the review of the trade relationship which must occur annually before the Congress. Needless to say, this is not an entirely satisfactory state of affairs for the countries concerned.[35]

Another feature of Title IV of the Trade Act of 1974 is section 406, regarding "market disruption," which is a special escape-clause channel that applies only to communist countries. To a certain extent, section 406 is partly based on a recognition of the difficulty of applying normal unfair trade laws, such as antidumping and countervailing duties, to the cases of nonmarket economies.[36]

The following countries have come under this special regime of bilateral arrangement with the United States,[37] subject to Title IV of the Trade Act of 1974[38]:

Country	Date of signing	Dates of renewal
Romania[39]	1975	1981 1984 1987 1988 [suspended]
Hungary[40]	1978	1981 1984 1987
China[41]	1979	1982

The potential membership of China in GATT raises some of these same issues for the United States administration, which would like to support such a role. In all likelihood, the United States is required under U.S. statutes to opt out of a GATT relationship between it and China and establish such a relationship by means of a bilateral agreement subject to the provisions of the statute. This could be one reason why the United States is apparently not (in early 1989) prepared to accept a "resumption" legal theory for China entry into GATT (since the "opt out" is only available to new entrants). Perhaps, however, when the negotiations have proceeded further, it may be possible for the United States executive branch to obtain some sort of explicit change in the statute by the Congress which would permit a more regular GATT relationship with China.

The Omnibus Trade and Competitiveness Act of 1988 contains a rather intriguing provision relating to this subject.[42] Section 1106 of that act, entitled "Accession of State Trading Regimes to the General Agreement on Tariffs and Trade," provides that before any major country with significant state trading enterprises can enter the GATT, the U.S. president must determine whether trade between the U.S. and that country is significant and unduly burdens the U.S. If so, the act provides that the GATT rules will apply between the U.S. and that country only if the state trading enterprises are conducted on a commercial basis, or (and this is perhaps the most interesting feature) if the extension of

GATT rules is approved by Congress under "fast track" procedures. This implies the possibility that, in a relatively comprehensive settlement agreement between a potential nonmarket entrant into GATT and U.S. interests, the Congress might be willing to alter or soften some of the existing measures of United States law that make it difficult for the U.S. to enter into a full GATT relationship with nonmarket economies.

Clearly, a potential Soviet Union membership in GATT raises these issues also.

13.4 Unfair Trade Practice Laws and the Nonmarket Economies: Antidumping and Countervailing Duties

The rules regarding antidumping duties and those regarding countervailing duties are difficult (some say impossible) to apply in the cases of nonmarket economies. With respect to responses to subsidized goods and the determination of subsidies in nonmarket economies, the matter is so difficult that the U.S. administrating authority, ultimately backed by the courts on appeal, finally determined that the U.S. countervailing duty law did not apply to products from nonmarket economies. This was based partly on the failure of the U.S. countervailing duty statute to mention any special regime for applying countervailing duties to nonmarket economies (in contrast to the antidumping laws, which did so mention).[43] Here I will describe how each of these laws relates to nonmarket economy trade, and then will offer briefly some proposals for handling the problem.

Take first the problem of dumping. Dumping requires a comparison of the price for export with the home-market price to see if the former is lower than the latter so that there is a "margin of dumping."[44] However, what is the "price" in the home market of a nonmarket economy? Almost by definition, since such an economy is not based on pricing principles, the nominal price of goods may bear little relation to prices that would be set by enterprises in a market/price-oriented economy. The prices may be set by a state planning commission, and may vary according to end user. Furthermore, the prices may bear little relation to the costs of an enterprise, or "profitability."

Thus in United States application of its antidumping law, the practice has developed of seeking to compile a "constructed cost" method of establishing the home-market price, while using information from market economies. In particular, as established in the landmark Polish golf cart case,[45] and embellished by later cases,[46] the U.S. procedure became the following: In a case involving alleged dumping from a nonmarket economy, the U.S. authorities would examine the product in the non-market economy, and determine all the various input components (parts, labor, overheads, etc). Then the U.S. authorities would seek a "surrogate country," who would be a market-oriented country at approximately the same level of economic development as the allegedly dumping nonmarket economy. The U.S. authorities would take the list of inputs, a sort of "shopping list," to the surrogate country, and price each of those inputs on the market of the surrogate country. With this information it would then compile an overall constructed cost, and by adding the statutorily mandated amounts for administration and profit (the latter being 8 percent), the U.S. authorities would find the "home market price," which would be compared to the export price, to establish whether dumping had occurred.

Needless to say, this process is very cumbersome. First, a great deal can depend on which country is chosen as a surrogate. Second, any country selected to be a surrogate has very little incentive to cooperate or to allow U.S. investigators to enter its territory and investigate prices there. Neither the surrogate country nor any of its enterprises are, after all, parties to the procedure. (It is even alleged that in one case a surrogate country later found it was the object of a dumping investigation in the U.S., which investigation may partly have relied on the information ascertained during the surrogate procedure![47]) Also, it is argued that a fair amount of manipulation of the data can occur, giving a wide latitude to administrative discretion so that its decisions can become biased, depending upon the antidumping procedure. In any event, many feel that the process is not satisfactory.

With respect to countervailing duties and responses to subsidized goods, the matter has been somewhat different. There has never been (so it is claimed) an application of countervailing duties in United States law to products imported from a nonmarket economy. Until the fall of 1983, no such case had been brought.[48] Then the U.S. textile industry brought a case alleging that textile imports from China were subsidized and therefore should be subject to countervailing duties. Partly for reasons relating to the general evolving political relationship of the United States and China, the U.S. administration was very concerned about this case. Furthermore, the Chinese had formally intimated their distaste for the process and indicated the possibility of counter responses of China (such as a reduction in the purchase of grains from U.S. farmers) if the United States actually applied countervailing duties. The matter was further complicated because of the U.S. laws that require insulation of the administrators of antidumping and countervailing duty laws from the diplomatic and other political arms of U.S. government. In the end, a settlement was obtained and the case was withdrawn, but not before considerable comment and concern.[49]

The next filed case concerning nonmarket economies concerned steel wire rod from Czechoslovakia.[50] In a preliminary determination the U.S. administration suggested that the countervailing duty law should not apply to nonmarket economies, and in a final determination the administrators made this definitive. On appeal to the U.S. court, the CIT overruled the Commerce Department, but was later overruled by the Court of Appeals for the Federal Circuit.[51] The result, therefore, was a precedent in U.S. jurisprudence that the countervailing duty laws did not apply to nonmarket economies. Various legislative proposals to change this state of the law have been made in the Congress, but have not been adopted.[52]

The rationale for nonapplication of countervailing duty law to non-market economies bears some similarity to arguments in dumping cases. It was argued by the Commerce Department that the concept of subsidization has no real meaning in an economy which is not market- or price-oriented in the first place. In some sense, one could argue that everything is subsidized in such an economy. In any event, there was no benchmark against which to compare the activities of economic entities, government or otherwise, in order to ascertain what was the level of subsidization.[53] Since the U.S. statute and legislative history was silent on the question of whether it applied to nonmarket economies,[54] the administrators found it possible simply to rule that the law did not apply.

The conceptual problems of these and similar international trade policies as they relate to nonmarket economies are clearly not resolved. Various proposals have been made as to how to handle these questions. Many of these proposals can be lumped under the rubric "benchmark approaches."[55] The basic concept of the benchmark proposals is that the imports from a nonmarket economy will be compared to some sort of benchmark price, and whenever the imports are priced below the benchmark, they will be presumed to have been dumped or subsidized and a duty equal to the difference between the price and the benchmark will be applied. In some proposals the presumption is conclusive; in others it can be rebutted. In any event, the critical question is how to set the benchmark. It was on this question that the House Ways and Means Committee of the U.S. Congress floundered in trying to make a concrete legislative proposal in 1984.[56]

One proposed benchmark is simply the average price in the U.S. market of U.S.-produced goods. Obviously this tends to be more restrictive of imports. Another benchmark proposal is to look toward the price of imports from market economies. Still another is to look at the home-market prices of like products in market economies. An approach that seeks some intermediate level of restrictiveness for trade is to set the benchmark equal to the lowest average price of a substantial quantity of imports of like products from a market economy. All of these approaches, of course, to a certain extent undermine the concepts of comparative advantage, and make it harder for a nonmarket economy to compete on the world market, at least in price. On the other hand, the purpose of these approaches is to assure competing producers in importing market economies that they do not have to face competition which is deemed "unfair" under long-established traditional international trade policies. There is no easy solution, and some sort of benchmark approach may be the "least worst" solution to the problem, if the benchmark is chosen with great care.

14 Conclusions and Perspectives

14.1 The "Trade Constitution"

What we have explored in the preceding chapters can be characterized as the "constitution" for international trade relations in the world today. It is a very complex mix of economic and governmental policies, political constraints, and above all (from my perspective) an intricate set of constraints imposed by a variety of "rules" or legal norms. It is these legal norms which provide the skeleton for the whole system. Attached to that skeleton are the softer tissues of policy and administrative discretion. Even the skeleton is not rigid or always successful in sustaining the weight placed upon it. Some of the "bones" bend and crack from time to time. And some of the tissues are unhealthy.

This "constitution" imposes different levels of constraint on the policy options available to public or private leaders. Some of its "rules" are virtually immutable. Others can be changed more easily. Part of the complexity of the whole system is this variety of constraints, which limit the realistically available options for solving problems. In addition, there are different contexts or levels for these constraining rules. Some of these constraints come from national or sovereign-state governmental systems (e.g., the Constitution of the United States, or the statutes of a GATT member country). Other rules come from the international system and its treaty mosaic, centering for our purposes on the GATT system, but also influenced by other elements of the Bretton Woods system and indeed the entire structure of international law (weak as it may be).

Some of these "constitutional" constraints are sources of great annoyance both to decision-makers and to economists. The rules, they will sometimes say, too often "get in the way." Indeed, with respect to the "trade constitution," they are probably right. As I will explain, there is considerable reason to be discontented with that "constitution" as it exists today, and to worry about its weaknesses and defects in the context of the type of interdependent world with which we are faced.

However, some of the constraints are the result of important and necessary principles, resulting from competing policy goals of the total system (not just those of international trade). For example, there is no doubt that the U.S. constitutional "separation of powers" principles are the source of great annoyance for decision-makers, who must struggle with the constant tensions of the executive–Congress power struggles. Yet the great genius of the draftsmen of this Constitution was their understanding of the need to disperse power so as to avoid its abuse. Thus, in a broader context, the separation-of-powers principle can be seen to have greater importance than the needs for short-term solutions to disagreeable international economic and trade problems.

Likewise, a rule-oriented structure of the portion of the skeleton devoted to international treaties for trade (GATT) is often a source of annoyance and aggravation. Yet that rule structure itself, as outlined in chapter 4, has potential value for creating greater predictability, redressing unfair power imbalances, and preventing escalating international tensions. In some instances it is more important that international disputes be settled quietly and peacefully than that they conform to all correct economic policy goals, although the long-term impact of a "settlement" on the rule structure must also be considered.

Like almost all government activity, the international trading system and its constitution contain conflicting and competing policy goals. Thus, like most government institutions, methods of resolving or "compromising" these competing goals are crucial to the potential long-range success of the system. For example, the worthy objectives of liberal trade (based on economic principles such as comparative advantage) will often conflict (at least in the short run) with goals of protecting poorer or weaker parts of a society's citizenry. Thus, as we saw in the chapter on safeguards, the "pureness" of liberal trade policies is relaxed somewhat to accommodate some competing goals of helping those who are poorer to adjust. (Of course, the constitutional structure of the system sometimes perversely also assists the more privileged of the world's producers to perpetrate that privilege at the expense of others — merely illustrating one of the many imperfections in the system.) The "conservative social welfare function" so ably described by Max Corden[1] realistically explains the approach of many national governments in today's world. Even if Corden and his admirers (including me) do not always think that this function is wisely administered, yet it can be defended in some circumstances as an appropriate governmental goal which also competes with purer versions of liberal trade policy.

With these observations we can now see some approaches to solutions for the puzzles posed in chapter 1. How vulnerable is a small country to blocking by other nations of the small country's exports? As we have seen, at the moment almost the only recourse or inhibition of such an action by importing nations is the GATT system. Defective as it is, it nevertheless plays a crucial role in constraining some of the more rampant national governmental actions which would otherwise restrict trade and defeat important expectations of small (and large) exporting countries.

Likewise, one puzzle was that faced by the investor who needed some long-term dependability of export markets in order for his new plant to be a viable investment. Again, in such cases the GATT system is crucial (and not necessarily too comforting!). Without this system, the degree of predictability would be even considerably less.

Why do governments choose fourth-best economic policy options? It should now be clearer. The intricate interplay of international rules and national constitutions and norms gives us the necessary clues. National executives prefer to avoid going to Congress or parliaments in order to obtain the necessary authority for certain approaches, and this may rule out some options. The international rules provide in some circumstances the onus of "compensation" or rebalancing of negotiated benefits, which impose constraints. Thus governments may pursue "informal" measures or other approaches which are less advantageous in economic terms in order to avoid some of the national or international rule-imposed "costs" of particular actions. The use of export-restraint arrangements particularly comes to mind.

14.2 How the System Works

We can now summarize, or at least characterize, how the world's "trade constitution" works, such as it is. As the previous section noted, this system is a complex interplay of both national and international norms, institutions and policies. It cannot be understood if only the international part is studied, nor can it be understood if only the sovereign national states are studied. The linkages are extremely significant: the GATT is what it is at least partly because of the U.S. constitutional structure and, more recently, because of the structure of the European Community. U.S. law is what it is at least partly because of the GATT. To explore how to achieve certain policy options, one must know not only the GATT procedures for rule formulation or treaty change, but also the similar procedures of at least some of the key nation-state GATT members.

Within major GATT trading nations, a cardinal principle of the administrating (executive) authorities is often to avoid seeking legislation from the legislature. Thus the constitutional allocation of powers, embellished by existing legislation, often produces significant constraints on policy selection.

A core part of the system is the vast body of GATT tariff bindings, made significant and relatively enforceable because of the GATT and its institutional makeup. An additional part of the system (perhaps less effective) is the code of conduct established by the many other GATT rules and for at least some nations extended by the various "side codes" of the GATT (described elsewhere in this book.)

Important additions to the system come from national government laws and institutions, particularly those relating to "unfair trade practices." In many cases national procedures provide for initiation of complaints by private entrepreneurs, and various nations have rules that differ in the extent to which government officials are "mandated" to carry out certain actions, or have discretion to choose among various possibilities. We have seen that, at least for dumping and subsidy countermeasures, the U.S. Congress has strongly pushed the U.S. law in the direction of mandatory import restraints, and this is posing certain threats to the liberal trade policies of the system. Part of the congressional impetus for this approach is the distrust by the Congress of executive-branch handling of trade policy in the past, but also some of the impetus stems from the natural proclivity of members of Congress to please particular constituents.

All in all, however, the system does work; or perhaps it would be better to say that the GATT system operates better than anyone had reason to expect, given the uncertain beginings and the various gaps in this "trade constitution."

14.3 Weaknesses of the "Trade Constitution"

Although it works (sort of), there is plenty of reason for much of the concern expressed about this system, as we have now seen. What are these concerns?

Most fundamental (and perhaps most difficult to remedy) is the basic constitutional infirmity of the GATT as a treaty and an organization. It was never intended to be what it has become, and as we have seen the GATT has become what it is largely through an evolutionary and pragmatic adaptation to the role thrust upon it when the ITO failed to come into being. This has meant that:

• changes in the trade rules are hard to achieve; amending the GATT is almost impossible, and so the trading nations have turned to other measures such as "side codes" (which have some troublesome side effects) to establish changes in the trading rules

• the GATT membership is changing and expanding; different types of societies are entering the GATT fold, and some are still left out

• loopholes or lacunae in the GATT rules have been troublesome, partly because of the difficulty of changing GATT rules

• the GATT has not yet manifested its ability to house amicably under its single roof vastly different economic systems, including those called "nonmarket"

• problems of agricultural trade have so far been intractable

• some urge the GATT approach to be extended to areas of international economic endeavor (such as trade in services) not heretofore covered by the GATT system

• rule implementation has sometimes been troublesome in GATT, as a number of nations avoid GATT rules by subterfuge, exploiting lacunae in the rules, or merely exercising their power

• the procedures for dispute settlement have been heavily criticized and need attention

• subsidy rules in particular have been a source of great confusion, disagreement, and dissatisfaction

• the GATT as an organization has probably not developed sufficiently to accomplish all the responsibilities heaped upon it; in particular the secretariat may be inadequate

Not only the GATT can be criticized, however. The laws and procedures of national governments leave much to be desired. For example, in the United States there is much ambiguity and potential for troublesome delay in situations when a GATT dispute-settlement panel and procedure rules that the United States is obligated to change its law because of

GATT rules. The Congress or the administration does not always efficiently implement such international rulings, a fact which tends to induce other countries also to resist such rulings and to generally reduce the respect for and predictability of the rules of the trading system.

In the United States there is some concern about the inefficiency of the U.S. national laws and procedures relating to "unfair trade practices," particularly those involving dumping or subsidies. This concern includes worry that the procedures are cumbersome, slow, and very costly, in some cases becoming themselves barriers to liberal trade among nations.

In addition, there is general concern about the functioning of the U.S. Congress. Its vulnerability to narrow local constituency interests and to certain powerful lobbies, especially in the absence of strong presidential leadership, is a worry expressed by many about the U.S. Constitution. The performance of the Congress in trying to shape a trade bill during 1985, 1986, 1987, and 1988 must be seen as evidence of the weakness of some of the congressional processes, confirming those worries.

Concerns may also be expressed about the trade laws of other governments. The European Economic Community is in the process of an agonizing constitutional evolution which sometimes renders its relations to the GATT system less than satisfactory from the points of view of other nations.

Likewise, the influence of approaching national elections (and when is there none?) on international trade policy and negotiations, especially in Europe, often raises worries similar to those about the U.S. Congress.

More could obviously be said, but we need to turn to some key policy questions.

14.4 Some Fundamental Policy Questions

Clearly the implications of the preceding section are that considerable attention to the basic constitutional structure of GATT is warranted. New mechanisms for rulemaking and rule evolution would be welcome, and these may require some sort of "steering group" or other institution. Perhaps sometime governments will even be bold enough to consider a new OTC-type charter—i.e., a brief treaty of only institutional measures (not covering substantive obligations), such as that tried unsuccessfully during the mid-1950s.[2]

The dispute-settlement procedures are also under close scrutiny, as I have indicated.[3] The critical question of whether such procedures should be tilted toward a "rule orientation" or a "power orientation" (or what should be the appropriate intermediate orientation) is still unresolved. To what extent are governments today willing to submit to "rules" and to rule-implementing procedures which effectively reduce the discretion of national officials? How far will governments trust dispute-settlement panels with "big issues" of trade policy? Can a rule system at least partly serve to replace the hegemonic system which many commentators suggest has been lost, as U.S. relative economic power has declined?[4]

A particularly fundamental question, not often discussed, is the issue of what techniques are appropriate to "manage interdependence." Several alternative approaches can be suggested[5]:

• Harmonization, a system that gradually induces nations toward uniform approaches to a variety of economic regulations and structures. An example would be standardization of certain product specifications. Another example would be uniformity of procedures for applying countervailing duties or escape-clause measures.

• Reciprocity, a system of continuous "trades" or "swaps" of measures to liberalize (or restrict) trade. GATT tariff negotiations follow this approach.

• Interface, which recognizes that different economic systems will always exist in the world and tries to create the institutional means to ameliorate international tensions caused by those differences, perhaps through buffering or escape-clause mechanisms.

Obviously a mixture of all these techniques is most likely to be acceptable, but that still leaves open the question of what is the appropriate mixture. For example, how much should the "trade constitution" pressure nations to conform to some uniform "harmonized" approaches, or is it better simply to establish buffering mechanisms that allow nations to preserve diversity but try to avoid situations in which one nation imposes burdens (economic or political) on other nations?

Closely connected to this previous point is an issue which may be loosely characterized as similar to federalism. This is the issue about the appropriate allocation of decision-making authority to different levels of government. Each federal nation faces this question—i.e., What is the appropriate allocation of power between the national government and subordinate state or municipal governments? The international system broadly, and the international trade system particularly, also face this question. As interdependence drives nations to more concerted action, there also arises the question of whether a gradual drift of decision-making authority upward to international institutions is always best for the world. How much power do we want to delegate to such international institutions? In what instances do we wish to preserve local or subordinate government control on the ground that such government is closer to the affected constituents? To what degree does a "harmonization" approach to managing interdependence unduly interfere with these federalist principles of maintaining decision-making closer to affected individuals and firms?

One very perplexing issue is that of the appropriate linkage of international economic policies and measures to "noneconomic" policies such as human rights, or to geopolitical considerations. Many enterprises and their leaders (at least in the U.S.) have been arguing against any such linkage. They argue that measures such as trade boycotts, or removing MFN privileges, often tend to be self-defeating and only allow competing nations and firms to move in with trade to fill the gap. Yet national leaders of powerful states cannot easily eschew the use of economic measures, particularly since the use of more "active" or military approaches have become less and less feasible. Economic measures are often the sole usable instruments of diplomacy.

No one denies that if a nuclear war can be avoided by the use of an economic trade measure, such action is appropriate. But that type of causal connection is never clearly presented. But if the "trade constitution" were to provide for a more effective channel of concerted economic actions to encourage better human rights treatments in some states, or to discourage risky national military moves or terrorism, to what degree should such economic actions be allowed or encouraged?

Clearly there are some causal connections between economic measures and other policy goals, even though in many instances it appears that the economic measures do not work very well.[6] Enlarging the EC to include Greece, Spain, and Portugal had a large component of noneconomic policy in it. Other examples can be readily cited. It has been argued that economic interchange and discourse can play an important role in promoting understanding among nations and their citizens, and that it can also build constituencies for identity of interests which cross national boundaries and thus discourage resort to force.

There is an important policy issue in connection with the "trade constitution's" principles of nondiscrimination, particularly the MFN principle described in chapter 6. It must be recognized that MFN policies have some costs as well as benefits. Thus the question arises, in connection with many trade measures, whether MFN principles should be observed or not. Closely related but not identical is the question of multilateralism versus bilateralism. Which of these approaches best promotes the long-term interests of the system?

Within national governments there are also a number of fundamental policy issues closely linked to the international "trade constitution." One of these is the degree to which a legalistic and adversarial system (such as the U.S. antidumping and countervailing duty systems) of administrating trade laws is best. A more legalistic or litigious approach has its costs, including attorney and consultant fees, time delay, and government costs. On the other hand, it may in some situations provide better information to decision-makers, allow interested parties to make their cases and give them the feeling that they have had their "day in court", and avoid corruption through transparency.[7]

Also pertaining to national governments is the question of the appropriate distribution of power to courts and administrative officials. What is the appropriate role of courts in reviewing trade measures undertaken by administration officials? Should the courts exercise great deference toward the administrators on the grounds of the courts' relative lack of expertise and information-gathering techniques? Or will such deference result in increasing abdication of judicial responsibilities to maintain fairness and completeness of decisions, as interdependence extends to more human endeavors?

14.5 Prospects and Worries

More than forty years after the current world "trade constitution" was launched as part of the immediate post-World War II Bretton Woods system, we still find that the central institution of this constitution is an organization which was not intended to be an organization, a treaty that is yet only "provisionally" in force, and an incredibly complex, tangled web of international agreements and provisions modifying, explaining, or escaping those agreements. That it works at all is truly surprising. Yet this GATT system does work, and as I have said, it works considerably better than anyone had reason to expect at the end of the 1940s.

But clearly it is defective. As the world becomes increasingly interdependent, and increasingly vulnerable to rapidly changing and rapidly transmitted economic forces, it is impossible not to worry about the question of whether the "trade constitution" can stand up to the stresses it is likely to face during the next few decades. One of the negotiating topics listed on the agenda for the Uruguay Round of trade negotiations is the "functioning of the GATT system," or FOGS for short.[8] Whether this or other endeavors can succeed in time to bring into effect sufficient improvement in the "trade constitution" as to avoid a worldwide economic disaster, no one can say for certain. Yet the reasonable but surprising success of the past few decades, based largely on pragmatic and evolutionary problem-solving techniques, does give us some reason to be optimistic. Let us hope, therefore, that the world's economic diplomats will be able to continue to keep the system functioning. Let us also hope, however, that they can begin to develop changes that will move the trade constitution, even if slowly, toward a system that is not so vulnerable to short-term ad hoc "fixes," but instead can establish the framework for mutual international cooperation in a manner creating both the predictability and stability needed not only for solid economic progress, but also for the flexibility necessary to avoid floundering on the shoals of parochial special national interests.

Notes

Chapter 1

1. "The OECD Member Countries," *OECD Observer* 145 (1987), 22–23.

2. Thurow, "America, Europe, and Japan: A Time to Dismantle the World Economy," *Economist* 297 (1985) 21. See also statement of Canadian Ambassador Gotlieb, *International Trade Reporter* 4 (1987), 655: "The diplomacy of interdependence, characterized by compromise and mutual concessions, is profoundly unsatisfying to national feeling. It is unable to strengthen governments against their political opponents or attract popular support. In an international negotiation, a concession will always attract more attention than an advantage it is designed to deliver. It will be perceived by the media and electorate as a sign of weakness and betrayal of the national interest."

3. See Cooper, "U.S. Position on International Economic Relations," *Department of State Bulletin* 77 (1977), 696, 698; McCracken, "Economic Policy in the U.S.," *Wall Street Journal* 198 (August 27, 1981), 18. See also Shultz, "National Policies and Global Prosperity" *Department of State Bulletin* no. 2099 (1985), 26.

4. See supra note 3.

5. Feldstein, "American Economic Policy and the World Economy," *Foreign Affairs* 63 (1985), 995–1008. See also Blumenthal, "The World Economy and Technological Change," *Foreign Affairs*, 66 (1988), 529.

6. See Jackson, "Transnational Enterprises and International Codes of Conduct: Introductory Remarks for Experts," speech delivered to the International Bar Association in Berlin, August 27, 1980. Reprinted in *Law Quadrangle Notes* 25 (1981), 19.

7. Commission of the European Communities, *Completing the Internal Market: White Paper from the Commission to the European Council* (Brussels: Commission of the European Communities, 1985). See also subsequent annual reports (COM [86], 300 [Brussels: Commission of the European Communities, 1986] and COM [87] 203, [Brussels: Commission of the European Communities, 1987].

8. C. Fred Bergsten, *Managing International Economic Interdependence: Selected Papers of C. Fred Bergsten, 1975–1976* (Lexington, Mass.: D.C. Heath, 1977).

9. See generally John H. Jackson, *World Trade and the Law of GATT* (Indianapolis: Bobbs-Merrill, 1969); John H. Jackson and William Davey, *Legal Problems of International Economic Relations* (St. Paul: West, 2d ed., 1986); and John H. Jackson, Jean-Victor Louis, and Mitsuo Matsushita, *Implementing the Tokyo Round* (Ann Arbor: University of Michigan Press, 1984).

10. Paul Samuelson, *Economics* (New York: McGraw Hill, 11th ed., 1980), 651. See also Kenen, infra note 18, and Jagdish Bhagwati, *Protectionism* (Cambridge, Mass.: MIT Press, 1988).

11. *Trade Policies for a Better Future: Proposals for Action* (Geneva: GATT, 1985), 23 (also called The Leutwiler Report).

12. History of the Committee on Finance, Sen. Doc. 91–57, 91st Cong., 2nd sess., 1970.

13. *United States International Economic Policy in an Interdependent World, Report to the President Submitted by the Commission on International Trade and Investment Policy* (Washington, D.C.: USGPO, 1971), vol. I, 11.

14. Cooper, R.N., 1987. Trade Policy as Foreign Policy. In *US Trade Policies in a Changing World Economy*, R. M. Stern (ed.) Cambridge, Mass.: MIT Press, pp. 291–336.

15. Hawkins, *U.S. Department of State, Commercial Policy Series* 74 (Pub. no. 2104, 1944), 3. See also Jackson, supra note 9, 38.

16. United States Proposals, *U.S. Department of State, Commercial Policy Series* (Pub. no. 2411, 1946), 1–2.

17. For example, *Trends in International Trade* (Geneva: GATT, 1958) (also called The Haberler Report). See also Jackson, supra note 9, Section 25.4.

18. Peter Kenen, *The International Economy* (Englewood Cliffs, NJ: Prentice Hall, 1985), 1.

19. Ibid., 6.

20. Ibid.

21. Ibid., 7.

22. As observed by the author.

23. Samuelson, P.A., 1949. Gains from International Trade Once Again. Reprinted in *International Trade: Selected Reading*, Jagdish N. Bhagwati (ed.) Cambridge, Mass.. MIT Press, 1981, pp. 1–161. See also Kenen, supra note 18, chapters 2, 3, and 4.

24. See Deardorff, A. V., 1984. Testing Trade Theories and Predicting Trade Flows. In *Handbook of International Economics*, Ronald Jones and Peter Kenen (eds.) Amsterdam: North Holland, pp. 487–517. See also infra note 34 .

25. See, for example, *International Trade 1983/84*, 2 (Table 1). See also Kenen, supra note 18, chapter 6.

26. See *Economic Effects of Export Restraints* (332-TA-117), USITC Pub. 1256 (1982). See also Peter Morici and Laura Megna, *U.S. Economic Policies Affecting Industrial Trade* (Washington, D.C.: National Planning Association, 1983); "The Consumer Costs of U.S. Trade Restraints," *Federal Reserve Bank of New York Quarterly Review* (1985), 1–12; David Greenaway and Brian Hindley, *What Britain Pays for Its Voluntary Export Restraints* (London: Trade Policy Research Centre, 1985); c.f. Bhagwati and Brecher, 1987, "Voluntary Export Restrictions versus Import Restrictions: A Welfare-theoretic Comparison" in *Protection and Competition in International Trade*, H. Kierzkowski (ed.) Oxford: Basil Blackwell, pp. 41–53.

27. Norton, "Industrial Policy and American Renewal," *Journal of Economic Literature* 24 (1986), 1.

28. Ibid., 3.

29. Ibid., 27.

30. Stern, "Tariffs and Other Measures of Trade Control: A Survey of Recent Developments," *Journal of Economic Literature* 11 (1973), 857.

31. See, for example, Krugman, P., 1987. Strategic Sectors and International Competition, and Dixit, A., 1987. How Should the U.S. Respond to Other Countries' Trade Policies? Both in *U.S. Trade Policies in a Changing World Economy*, R.M. Stern (ed.). Cambridge, Mass.: MIT Press, 1987.

32. See Deardorff, "Gains from Trade In and Out of Steady Stage Growth," *Oxford Economic Papers*, 25 July (1973), 173.

33. See Kenen, supra note 18, 526–527. See also Zysman and Cohen, "Double or Nothing: Open Trade and Competitive Industry," *Foreign Affairs* 61 (1983), 1113.

34. Deardorff, A.V. 1985, Major Recent Developments in International Trade Theory. In *International Trade and Exchange Rates in the Late 1980s*. Theo Peeters, Peter Praet, and Paul Reding (eds.) Amsterdam: North Holland, chapter 1, Deardorff, "General Validity of the Law of Comparative Advantage," *Journal of Political Economy* 88 (1980), 941.

35. See in general the so-called "Stolper-Samuelson" model. For more recent analyses of the problems, see *Handbook of International Economics*, supra note 24.

36. W. Max Corden, *Trade Policy and Economic Welfare* (Oxford: Clarendon Press, 1974). See also W. Max Corden, *The Theory of Protection* (Oxford: Clarendon Press, 1971).

37. Ibid., 107.

38. Ibid., 107–108. See also Corden, "Market Disturbances and Protection: Efficiency versus the Conservative Social Welfare Function," Discussion Paper No. 92, Centre for Economic Policy Research, Australian National University.

39. See, for example, Ambassador Yeutter speaking after his nomination as USTR, where he declared that he supports "free and open, but fair trade, on a level playing field" (*International Trade Reporter* 2 [1985], 510). The concept has

also arisen in certain presidential statements; see *Federal Register* 49 (1984), 36813, where in refusing import relief, the president said:

The Administration's hope is that this combination of actions, taken without protectionist intention or effect would enable one of the United States' most basic and vital industries to return to a level playing field, one in which steel is traded on the basis of market forces, not government intervention, and one in which the market would seek a return to a more normal level of steel imports, or approximately 18.5 per cent, excluding semi-finished steel.

40. See infra chapters 10 and 11.

41. See Kenen, supra note 18, 169–172; Charles P. Kindleberger, *International Economics* (Homewood, Ill.: Irwin, 5th ed., 1973), 126.

42. Adam Smith, *The Wealth Of Nations* (1776), book IV, chapter 2. See also Kenen, supra note 18, 169–172.

43. See Kenen, supra note 18, 171; Kindleberger, supra note 41, 126–127.

44. See Robert Reich, *The Next American Frontier* (New York: Times Books, 1983), 235. For arguments that certain industries ought to be preserved for national security reasons, see Daniel Okimoto, Henry Rowen, and Michael Dahl, *The Semiconductor Competition and National Security*, Special Report of the Northeast Asia–United States Forum on International Trade Policy, Stanford University, December 1987. See also *Washington Post*, January 30, 1986, C26 (steel), and *Washington Post*, November 21, 1985, A23 (textiles).

45. Of course, such choices may be rationalized as reflecting merely one aspect of the preferences of consumers and laborers, but the question remains: Does the market create efficiently the environment most of its citizens would choose to live and work in?

46. See Kenen, supra note 18, 213; Kindleberger, supra note 41, 113.

47. See infra chapter 12.

48. See Kindleberger, supra note 41, 113.

49. See, for example, Gerard Curzon, *Multilateral Commercial Diplomacy* (London: Michael Joseph, 1965), 187–191, 206 for a discussion of the role of the Farmers' Union in the Swiss decision to retain agricultural protectionism.

50. See Pieter Verloren Van Themaat, *The Changing Structure of International Economic Law* (The Hague: Martinus Nijhoff, 1981). See also Jackson, J.H., 1985. Economic Law, International. In *Encyclopaedia of Public International Law* Amsterdam: North Holland, 1985. Dominique Carreau, Patrick Juillard, and Thiebaud Flory, *Droit International Economique* (Paris: Pichon et Durand-Anzias, 2d ed., 1980); Paolo Picone and Georgio Sacerdoti, *Diritto Internazionale Dell'Economia* (Milan: Franco Angeli, 1982).

51. Carreau, Juillard, and Flory, supra note 50, 3–22.

52. Concerning a "GATT for Investment," see Kindleberger and Goldberg, 1970, Toward a GATT for Investment: A Proposal for Supervision of the International Corporation," in *Multinational Excursions* Cambridge, Mass.: MIT Press, 1984, pp. 202–231, and Kindleberger, A GATT for International Direct Investment: Further Reflections, ibid., 247–265. On a "GATT for Services," see U.S. National Study on Worldwide Trade in Services, A Submission by the United States Government to the General Agreement on Tariffs and Trade, Prepared Under the Direction of the U.S. Trade Representative. Pr Ex 9.2: T 67/4 (1984).

53. See supra note 52.

54. Louis Henkin et al., *International Law* (St. Paul: West, 2d ed., 1987) 37–68; Ian Brownlie, *Principles of Public International Law* (Oxford: Clarendon Press, 3d ed., 1979) 4–9.

55. See Henkin, supra note 54, 37–68; Brownlie, supra note 54, 4–9.

56. See Schwarzenberger, "The Principles and Standards of International Economic Law," *Receuil des Cours* 117 (1966), 14; Jackson and Davey, supra note 9, 261.

57. See American Law Institute, *Restatement of the Law (Third): Foreign Relations Law of the United States*, 1987, § 712. See also Robinson, "Expropriation in the Restatement (Revised)", *American Journal of International Law* 78 (1984), 176; Schachter, "Compensation for Expropriation", *American Journal of International Law* 78 (1984), 121; Schachter, "Compensation Cases—Leading and Misleading", *American Journal of International Law* 79 (1985), 420.

58. See American Law Institute, *Restatement of the Law (Third): Foreign Relations Law of the United States* (1987), §511c. Brownlie, supra note 54, 183–186; Henkin, supra note 54, 1244.

59. See infra chapter 6.

60. See, for example, Schwarzenberger, "Equality and Discrimination in International Economic Law," *Yearbook of World Affairs* 25 (1971), 163. See also infra section 6.1.

61. For example, the abduction of Adolf Eichmann in 1960, described in detail in Louis Henkin, *How Nations Behave: Law and Foreign Policy* (New York: Council on Foreign Relations/Columbia University Press, 2d ed., 1979), 269–278. See also Maier, et al., "Appraisals of the ICJ's Decision: Nicaragua v. United States (Merits)," *American Journal of International Law* 81 (1987), 77.

62. See Henkin, supra note 61, 49–68; Roger Fisher, *Improving Compliance with International Law* (Charlottesville: University Press of Virginia, 1981), 12–16.

63. See infra chapters 4 and 14.

64. Maitland, "Prologue to a History of English Law," *Law Quarterly Review* 14 (1898), 13.

65. See supra discussion in section 1.1.

66. Ibid.

67. For example, see the Trade Act of 1974, Pub. L. 93–618, 121, 123, and 126, 88 Stat. 1986 et seq. Section 121(b) (19 USC §2131 [1980 and Supp. 1988]) directs the president *inter alia* to make trade agreements conform with GATT principles; section 123 (19 USC §2133 [1980 and Supp. 1988]) permits the president to grant new concessions or to modify existing agreements in order to compensate for any trade restrictions increased by the U.S.

Chapter 2

1. See generally John H. Jackson, *World Trade and the Law of GATT* (Indianapolis: Bobbs-Merill, 1969); John H. Jackson and William Davey, *Legal Problems of International Economic Relations* (St. Paul: West, 2d ed., 1986); and John H. Jackson, Jean-Victor Louis, and Mitsuo Matsushita, *Implementing the Tokyo Round* (Ann Arbor: University of Michigan Press, 1984). See also Robert Hudec, *The GATT Legal System and World Trade Diplomacy* (New York: Praeger, 1975); Kenneth Dam, *The GATT: Law and International Economic Organization* (Chicago: University of Chicago Press, 1970); Edmond McGovern, *International Trade Regulation* (Exeter: Globefield Press, 2d ed., 1986); Gerard Curzon, *Multilateral Commercial Diplomacy* (London: Michael Joseph, 1965); Thiebaut Flory, GATT, *Droit International et Commerce Mondial* (Paris: Librairie Générale du Droit et Jurisprudence, 1968). See also, for example, Tumlir, J., 1986. GATT Rules and Community Law. In *The European Community and GATT*, Meinhard Hilf, Francis Jacobs, and Ernst-Ulrich Petersmann (eds.) Deventer: Kluwer, pp. 1–22.

For an overview of GATT's troubled history, see William Diebold, *The End of the ITO* (Princeton, NJ: Princeton University Press, 1952); Richard N. Gardner, *Sterling-Dollar Diplomacy* (Oxford: Clarendon Press, 1969); William A. Brown, *The United States and the Restoration of World Trade* (Washington, D.C.: Brookings Institution, 1950); Clair Wilcox, *A Charter for World Trade* (New York: Macmillan, 1949).

2. Charles H. Alexandrowicz, *World Economic Agencies* (London: Stevens, 1962); Charles H. Alexandrowicz, *The Law-Making Function of the Specialized Agencies of the United Nations* (Sydney: Angus and Robertson, 1973); Henry Schermers, *International Institutional Law* (Rockville, MD: Sijthoff & Nordhoff, 2d ed., 1980); Marcel A. G. Van Merrhaeghe, *International Economic Institutions* (Boston: Martinus Nijhoff, 4th ed., 1985); Don Wallace and Helga Escobar (eds.), *The Future of International Economic Organizations* (New York: Praeger, 1977); Guiseppe Schiavone, *International Organizations: A Dictionary and Directory* (Chicago: St. James Press, 2d ed., 1986).

3. See Joseph Gold, *Legal and Institutional Aspects of the International Monetary System: Selected Essays* (Washington, D.C.: IMF, 1984). See also John K. Horsefield (ed.), *The International Monetary Fund, 1945–1965* (3 vols.) Washington, D.C.: IMF, 1969); Margaret Garritsen de Vries, *The International Monetary Fund, 1966–1971: The System Under Stress* (Washington, D.C.: IMF, 1976); Richard W. Edwards, *International Monetary Collaboration* (Dobbs Ferry, NY: Transnational Publishers, 1985).

4. See Edward Mason and Robert Asher, *The World Bank Since Bretton Woods* (Washington, D.C.: Brookings Institution, 1973); Roberto Lavalle, *La Banque Mondiale et Ses Filiales* (Paris: Librairie Générale de Droit et de Jurisprudence, 1972); Aart van de Laar, *The World Bank and the Poor* (The Hague: Martinus Nijhoff, 1980).

5. Union of International Associations, *Yearbook of International Organizations* (Munich: K. G. Saur, 24th ed., 1987/88).

6. The International Bank for Reconstruction and Development (the World Bank) is a sister organization to the IMF, all members of the bank being obliged to be members of the IMF. The Articles of Agreement of the IBRD as amended in 1965 are found in 16 UST 1942, TIAS 5929, 606 UNTS 294. The IBRD has two affiliates, the International Development Association (IDA) (11 UST 2284; TIAS 4607; 439 UNTS 249) and the International Finance Corporation (IFC)(as amended 24 UTS 1760; TIAS 7683; 563 UNTS 362). See Edwards, supra note 3, 44–48.

7. See OECD, Annual Reports; Ohlin, "The Organization of Economic Cooperation and Development," *International Organization* 22 (1968) 231; Van Meerhaeghe, supra note 2, chapter 8; OECD, *OECD at Work* (Paris: OECD, 1969); Henry Aubrey, *Atlantic Economic Cooperation: The Case of the OECD* (New York: Praeger, 1967); Miriam Camps, *"First World" Relationships: The Role of the OECD* (New York: Council on Foreign Relations, 1975).

8. Cordovez, "The Making of UNCTAD," *Journal World Trade Law* 1 (1967), 243; Gardner, "The United Nations Conference on Trade and Development," *International Organization* 22 (1968), 99; Kamal Hagras, *United Nations Conference on Trade and Development* (New York: Praeger, 1965); Branislav Gosovic, *UNCTAD Conflict and Compromise* (Leiden: Sijthoff, 1972); Walters, "UNCTAD: Intervenor Between Poor and Rich States," *Journal World Trade Law* 7 (1973), 527; Ramsey, "UNCTAD's Failures: The Rich Get Richer," *International Organization* 38 (1984), 387.

9. For some references that show ECOSOC's relationship with the UN, see the *United Nations Journal of the Economic and Social Council* 1, (1946), 7. See generally Walter Sharp, *The United Nations Economic and Social Council* (New York: Columbia University Press, 1969); Ali Syed Amjad, *The Record and Responsibilities of the Economic and Social Council* (New York: United Nations, 1952).

10. On the FAO, see documents relating to the Food and Agriculture Organization of the United Nations, 1 Aug.–14 Dec., 1944 (1945); Gove Hambidge, *FAO, Food and Agriculture Organization of the United Nations, Cornerstone for a House of Life* (Washington, D.C.: FAO, 1946).

On the ICAO, see ICAO, *Memorandum on ICAO* (12th ed., 1984); Stanley Rosenfield, *The Regulation of International Commercial Aviation: The International Regulatory Structure* (Dobbs Ferry, NY: Oceana, 1984); Peter Haanappel, *Pricing and Capacity Determination in International Air Transport: A Legal Analysis* (Boston: Kluwer, 2d ed., 1984); Thomas Buergenthal, *Law-Making in the International Civil Aviation Organization* (Syracuse, NY: Syracuse University Press, 1969).

On the ILO, see Anthony Alcock, *History of the International Labor Organization* (New York: Macmillan, 1971); David Morse, *The Origin and Evolution of the ILO and Its Role in the World Community* (Ithaca, NY: Cornell University Press, 1969).

On the International Maritime Organization, see Samir Mankabady (ed.), *The International Maritime Organization* (London, NH: Croom-Helm, 1984).

11. See Eric Stein, Peter Hay, and Michel Waelbroeck, *European Community Law and Institutions in Perspective: Text, Cases and Readings* (Indianapolis: Bobbs-Merrill, 1976) (with supplement, 1985); P.S.R.F. Mathijsen, *A Guide to European Community Law* (London: Sweet and Maxwell, 3d ed., 1980). However, also note U.S.–Canada Free Trade Agreement, *International Legal Materials* XXVII (1988), 281. See *The Canada–U.S. Free Trade Agreement Synopsis* (Ottawa: Canadian Department of External Affairs, 1987). See also Robert Stern, Philip Trezise, and John Whalley (eds.), *Perspectives on a U.S.–Canadian Free Trade Agreement* (Washington, D.C.: Brookings Institution, 1987); William Diebold (ed.) *Bilateralism, Multilateralism, and Canada in U.S. Trade Policy* (Cambridge, Mass.: Ballinger, 1988).

12. Frederick Meyer, *The European Free Trade Association: An Analysis of "The Outer Seven"* (New York: Praeger, 1960); Victoria Curzon, *The Essentials of Economic Integration: Lessons of EFTA Experience* (New York: St. Martin's Press, 1974); Robert Middleton, *Negotiating on Non-Tariff Distortions of Trade: The EFTA Precedents* (London: Macmillan/TPRC, 1975).

13. See Van Meerhaeghe, supra note 2, 350.

14. On commodity agreements, see Charles Johnston, *Law and Policy of Intergovernmental Primary Commodity Agreements* (Dobbs Ferry, NY: Oceana looseleaf, 1976); Fiona Garden-Ashworth, *International Commodity Control: A Contemporary History and Appraisal* (London: Croom-Helm, 1984); Ervin Ernst, *International Commodity Agreements: The System of Controlling the International Commodity Market* (Boston: Martinus Nijhoff, 1982); Kabir-ur-Rahman Kahn, *The Law and Organization of International Commodity Agreements* (Boston: Martinus Nijhoff, 1982). See also Wassermann, "UNCTAD: International Agreement on Jute and Jute Products, 1982," *Journal World Trade Law* 18 (1984), 173; Wassermann, "UNCTAD: International Tropical Timber Agreement," *Journal World Trade Law* 18 (1984), 89; Stubbs, "The Natural Rubber Agreement," *Journal World Trade Law* 18 (1984) 15; Smith, "Prospects for a New International Sugar Agreement," *Journal World Trade Law* 17 (1983), 308.

15. For example, the International Tin Council ceased trading in 1985 and the resulting upheaval brought about a number of interesting cases in the U.K. courts. See Cheyne, "The International Tin Council," *International and Comparative Law Quarterly* 36 (1987), 931–935.

16. 22 UST 320, TIAS No. 7063, 157 UNTS 129. The CCC published a revised nomenclature and a set of explanatory notes in 1955. Both are updated and supplemented regularly. See *Customs Cooperation Council, Nomenclature for the Classification of Goods in Customs Tariffs* (5th ed., 1976); *Customs Cooperation Council, Explanatory Notes to the Brussels Nomenclature* (2d ed., 1966). For a discussion

of the history of efforts to develop a uniform classification system, see Friedenberg, *The Development of a Uniform International Tariff Nomenclature: From 1853 to 1967 with Emphasis on the Brussels Tariff Nomenclature* (U.S. TC Pub. No. 237 [1968]). See also the "International Convention on the Simplification and Harmonization of Customs Procedures (Kyoto Convention)." Done at Kyoto, May 18, 1973. Entered partially into force in U.S., January 28, 1984. The convention is under the auspices of the CCC, and attempts to harmonize customs procedures.

17. See infra section 5.3.

18. 21 UST 1749, TIAS No. 9964, 828 UNTS 3. See United International Bureau for the Protection of Intellectual Property, *Intellectual Property Conference of Stockholm, Documents* (1967). See generally Joseph Ekedi-Samnik, *L'Organization Mondiale de la Propriété Intellectuelle* (Brussels: Bruylant, 1975); Georg Roeber, *Das Stockholmer Vertragswerk zum Internationalen Urle Berrecht* (Munich: Verlag Dokumentation, 1969).

19. TS 548. See Charles Bevans, *Treaties and Other Agreements of the United States of America, 1776–1949* (Washington, D.C.: U.S. Department of State, 1974), vol. 12, 319–327. See generally Louis Bloomfield and Gerald Fitzgerald, *Boundary Waters Problems of Canada and the United States* (Toronto: Carswell, 1958).

20. See *Military Occupation of the Rhine*, Sen. Doc. 75, 66th Cong., 1st sess., Military Occupation of the Rhine (1919). See also generally Ernst Fraenkel, *Military Occupation and the Rule of Law; Occupation Government in the Rhineland, 1918–1923* (London: Oxford University Press, 1944).

21. Youngquist, "United States Commercial Treaties: Their Role in Foreign Economic Policy, Studies in Law and Economic Development," *George Washington University International Law Society*, vol. 2, study no. 1 (1967).

22. See generally Pattison, "The United States–Egypt Bilateral Investment Treaty: A Prototype for Future Negotiations," *Cornell International Law Journal* 16 (1983), 305; Bergman, "Bilateral Investment Projection Treaties: An Examination of the Evolution and Significance of the U.S. Prototype Treaty," *New York University Journal International Law & Policy* 16 (1981), 1; Comment, "The BIT Won't Bite: The American Bilateral Investment Treaty Program," *American University Law Review* 33 (1984), 931; "Recent Development, Developing a Model Bilateral Investment Treaty," *Law and Policy in International Business* 15 (1983), 273. A list of bilateral investment treaties as of October 1, 1982 appeared in *International Legal Materials* XXI (1982), 1208.

23. See Youngquist, supra note 21.

24. See Schermers, supra note 2, 681–683.

25. For example, GATT and many UN bodies. See van Meerhaeghe, supra note 2.

26. See Pieter Verloren Van Themaat, *The Changing Structure Of International Economic Law* (Boston: Martinus Nijhoff, 1981); Pieter Van Dijk (ed.), *Supervisory*

Mechanisms in International Economic Organizations (Deventer: Kluwer/TMC As-
ser Institute, 1984); Schwebel (ed.), "The Effectiveness of International Decisions" (Papers and Proceedings of a Conference of the American Society of
International Law [1971]).

27. See generally Jackson, supra note 1; see also McGovern, supra note 1, 3 et seq.

28. VerLoren von Themaat (infra note 30, at p. 1) makes the history begin in the
Middle Ages, in the Hansa context, citing Erler, infra note 31.

29. Edmund Heward, *Lord Mansfield* (Chichester: Barry Rose, 1979), 99–105.

30. See Verloren van Themaat, P., 1987. In *Restructuring the International Legal
Order: The Role of Lawyers*, Peter van Dijk, Fried van Hoof, Alfred Koers and
Kamiel Mortelmans (eds.) Deventer: Kluwer, pp.1. See also Sir Charles Petrie,
Earlier Diplomatic History, 1492–1713 (London: Hollis and Carter, 1949), chapter 23.

31. See George Erler, *Grundprobleme des Internationalen Wirtschaftsrecht* (Gottin-
gen: Schwartz, 1956). See also Schwarzenberger, "The Principles and Standards
of International Economic Law," *Recueil des Courts Academies de Droit International* [1965/1] 1. On FCN-Treaties, see Youngquist, supra note 21. As of 1986, the
United States was a party to forty-eight FCN treaties, of which twenty-five have
come into force since the end of World War II. See U.S. Department of State,
Treaties in Force (Washington, D.C.: USGPO, 1986).

32. See infra chapters 6 and 8.

33. See Amos Peaslee and Dorothy Xydis, *International Governmental Organizations: Constitutional Documents* (The Hague: Martinus Nijhoff, 2d ed., 1961), 1506.

34. Congress on the Regulation of Customs Procedure, Paris 1900; Congress of
Chambers of Commerce, Prague, 1900; Geneva Conference on International
Trade, May 1922; Congress of International Chamber of Commerce, held at
Rome, March 1923. See League of Nations Economic Committee, International
Conference on Customs Formalities, LN Doc. C.D.I.2. (Sales No. 1923-II.18),
(Oct. 15, 1923); International Economic Conference held at Geneva, 1927; Inter-
national Conferences with a View to Concerted Economic Action, Geneva
1930–1931; Monetary and Economic Conference held at London, 1933. See Au-
fricht, *Guide to League of Nations Publications* (New York: Columbia University
Press, 1951), 217–30.

35. See Jackson, supra note 1, 441.

36. Ibid., 37.

37. See, for example, Cooper, R. N., 1987, Trade Policy as Foreign Policy In U S
Trade Policies in a Changing World Economy, R. M. Stern (ed.) Cambridge, Mass.
MIT Press pp. 291–336.

38. The conference was held from July 1–22, 1944, at Bretton Woods, New
Hampshire. See Jackson, supra note 1, 40.

39. See United Nations Monetary and Financial Conference (Bretton Woods, NH, July 1–22, 1944), Proceedings and Documents 941 (U.S. Department of State Pub. No. 2866, 1948).

40. See "Act to Extend the Authority of the President" under section 350 of the Tariff Act of 1930 as amended, and for other purposes, July 5, 1945, Pub. L. 79–130., 59 Stat. 410.

41. 1 UN ECOSOC Res. 13, UN Doc. E/22 (1946).

42. Estimate based upon examination of the documents. GATT headquarters in Geneva, of course, has a practically complete collection. In the United States, the UN Library in New York and the U.S. Department of State in Washington also have fairly complete collections. Most of the records are also available on microfiche.

43. For example, if a tariff commitment for a maximum 10 percent tariff charge were made, nevertheless a country might decide to use a quantitative restriction to prevent imports and thus would evade the trade liberalizing effect of the tariff commitment.

44. See GATT, Article XXV, and Jackson, supra note 1, 126.

45. See infra chapter 5.

46. See GATT, Article XXIX. Cf. Jackson, supra note 1, chapter 2.4.

47. See infra chapter 7. See also Jackson, supra note 1, 20 et seq., 48–49.

48. See the works of Diebold, Gardner, and Wilcox, supra note 1.

49. U.S. Department of State, *Analysis of General Agreement on Tariffs and Trade* (Washington, D.C.: U.S. Department of State, 1947), 112–125, 147–171.

50. See Jackson, supra note 1, 62; UN Doc. EPCT/TAC/7, 3 (1947).

51. See supra note 40. The act expired on June 12, 1948. See Jackson, supra note 1, 37.

52. See UN Doc. EPCT/TAC/4, 8 (1947).

53. 55 UNTS 308 (1947).

54. See infra chapter 3.

55. See Jackson, supra note 1, section 3.3.

56. See Vermulst and Hansen "The GATT Protocol of Provisional Application: A Dying Grandfather?" to be published in volume 27, 1987, of the *Columbia Journal of Transnational Law.*

57. See infra chapter 11.

58. GATT, BISD 31 Supp. 74–94 (1985).

59. See supra note 56.

60. See Jackson, supra note 1, 92, and Appendix D. Under the Annecy Protocol, Denmark, the Dominican Republic, Finland, Greece, Haiti, Italy, Nicaragua,

Sweden, and Uruguay acceded, and under the Torquay Protocol, Austria, Federal Republic of Germany, Peru and Turkey did so.

61. See Jackson, supra note 1, 154.

62. Ibid., chapter 6.

63. GATT, BISD 14 Supp. 17 (1966).

64. See Jackson, supra note 1, 51; see also Dam, supra note 1, 337–8.

65. See Jackson, supra note 1, Section 6.3; see also Dam, supra note 1, 339–40.

66. See "Securing the Foothold," *Time* 91 (17 May 1968), 92; "The Kennedy Round: The Sick, Sick, Six," *The Economist* 223 (1967), 367; "The Politics of the Success," *The Economist* 223 (1967), 814. See also John W. Evans, *The Kennedy Round in American Trade Policy: The Twilight of GATT* (Cambridge, Mass.: Harvard University Press, 1971), 235 and 272.

67. Protocol Amending the GATT to Introduce a Part IV on Trade and Development, GATT, BISD 13 Supp. 2 (1965).

68. See infra sections 5.4, 8.5, and 8.6, and chapters 10 and 11.

69. *The Tokyo Round of Multilateral Trade Negotiations: Supplementary Report by the Director-General of GATT* (Geneva: GATT, 1980), 6–7.

70. *United States International Economic Policy in an Interdependent World, Report to the President Submitted by the Commission on International Trade and Investment Policy* (Washington, D.C.: USGPO, 1971), volume 1, 627.

71. GATT Article XXX.

72. On the basis of the Protocol of Provisional Application to the General Agreement on Tariffs and Trade, Oct. 30, 1947, 61 Stat. pts. 5, 6, TIAS No. 1700, 55 UNTS 308. See generally Jackson, supra note 1, section 3.2.

73. Cf. Jackson, supra note 1, Section 9.2.

74. GATT Article XXX. Cf. Jackson, supra note 1, chapter 3.6.

75. See infra chapter 11 and Jackson, supra note 1.

76. GATT Article XXV:5. This waiver authority has been used more than fifty times. See Jackson, supra note 1, chapter 22.

77. GATT Article XII and XVII (for developing countries). See Jackson, supra note 1, chapter 18; Jackson and Davey, supra note 1, chapter 11.4(b).

78. See Jackson, supra note 1, chapter 26.

79. See Jackson and Davey, supra note 1, section 9.4. See also Petersmann, "Grey Area Measures and the Rule of Law," *Journal of World Law* 22/2 (1988), 23.

80. Sampson and Snape, "Identifying the Issues in Trade in Services," *World Economy* 8 (1985), 171; Stern and Hoekman, "Issues and Data Needs for GATT Negotiations on Services" *World Economy* 10 (1987), 39; Diebold and Stalson, 1983, Negotiating Issues in International Services Transactions, in *Trade Policy in*

the 1980s William Cline (ed.) Washington, D.C.: Institute of International Economics, p. 582; Ascher and Whichard, 1987, Improving Service Trade Data, in *The Emerging Service Economy*, Orio Giarini (ed.) Oxford: Pergammon Press, pp. 255–281.

81. See Wolfgang Friedmann, *The Changing Structure of International Law* (New York: Columbia University Press, 1964), chapter 4; Ian Brownlie, *Principles of Public International Law* (Oxford: Clarendon Press, 3d ed., 1979), section 2.4 and chapter 24; Louis Henkin et al., *International Law* (St. Paul: West, 2d ed., 1986), section 5.6.

82. Cf. Jackson, supra note 1, chapters 14 and 1. See also infra section 4.6 and section 13.2.

83. See infra section 9.5.

84. F. G. Jacobs (ed.), *The Effect Of Treaties On National Legislation* (London: Sweet and Maxwell/KCCCL, 1987). See also Pescatore, "The Doctrine of 'Direct Effect': An Infant Disease of Community Law," *European Law Review* 8 (1983), 155; Bebr, "Agreements Concluded by the Community and Their Possible Direct Effect: From International Fruit Company to Kupferberg," *Common Market Law Review* 20 (1983), 35; Bellis, "The Interpretation of the Free Trade Agreements Between the EFTA Countries and the European Community," *Swiss Review International Competition Law* 23 (1985), 21; Bourgeois, "Effects of International Agreements in European Community Law: Are the Dice Cast?", *Michigan Law Review* 82 (1984), 1250; Hartley, "International Agreements and the Community Legal System: Some Recent Developments," *European Law Review* 8 (1983), 383; Maresceau, "Current Issues in World Trade Law: The European Community and the GATT, the GATT in the Case Law of the European Court of Justice," King's College London Centre of European Law (10 December 1984); Petersmann, "Application of GATT by the Court of Justice of the European Communities", *Common Market Law Review*, 20 (1983), 397; Petersmann, E.U., 1983, Participation of the European Communities in the GATT: International Law and Community Law Aspects, in *Mixed Agreements*, David O'Keeffe and Henry Schermers, eds. Deventer: Kluwer, pp. 167–198, 191 et seq.; Petersmann, "The European Communities and GATT on the Economic and Legal Functions of GATT Rules," *Legal Issues of European Integration* [1984/1] 37, 46 *et seq.* (1984); Petersmann, "International and European Foreign Trade Law: GATT Dispute Settlement Proceedings Against the EEC," *Common Market Law Review* 22 (1985), 441, 452–465; Riesenfeld, "The Doctrine of Self-Executing Treaties and Community Law: A Pioneer Decision of the Court of Justice of the European Community," *American Journal of International Law* 67 (1973), 504; Schermers, "The Direct Application of Treaties with Third States: Note Concerning the Polydor and Pabst Cases," *Common Market Law Review* 19 (1982), 563; Schermers, H. G., 1982, The Internal Effect of Community Treaty-Making, In *Essay in European Law and Integration*, David O'Keeffe, and Henry Schermers (eds.) Deventer: Kluwer, 167; Stein, E, with Henkin, L., 1985, Towards a European Foreign Policy? The European Foreign Affairs System from the Perspective of the United States Constitution, in *Integration Through Law*, Mauro Cappelletti, Monica Seccombe, Joseph Weiler

(eds.) New York: Walter de Guyter, vol. 1, book 3, 3, 51; VerLoren van Themaat, "The Impact of Case Law of the Court of Justice of the EC on the Economic World Order," *Michigan Law Review* 82 (1984), 1422; Voelker, "The Direct Effect of International Agreements on the Community's Legal Order," *Legal Issues European Integration* [1983/1], 131; Waelbroeck, "Effect of GATT Within the Legal Order of the EEC", *Journal World Trade Law*, 8 (1974) 614. The ECJ has denied direct effect to GATT provisions on several occasions; e.g., see International Fruit Co. v. Produktschap, Cases 21–24/72, [1972] ECR 1219; SIOT v. Ministero delle Finanze v. SPI, [1983] ECR 731.

85. See generally Jackson, "The General Agreement on Tariffs and Trade in United States Domestic Law," *Michigan Law Review* 66 (1967), 249; Hudec, R.E., 1986, The Legal Status of GATT in the Domestic Law of the United States, in *The European Community and GATT*, Meinhard Hilf, Francis Jacobs, and Ernst-Ulrich Petersmann (eds.) Deventer: Kluwer, pp. 187–249.

86. Jackson, supra note 85, 297–311. See also Jackson, Louis, and Matsushita, supra note 1, 142 et seq. See also Jackson and Davey, supra note 1, section 3.6 and Hudec, supra note 85.

87. GATT Doc. SR.7117 (1952); GATT, BISD 1st Supp. 86 (1953). Cf. Jackson, supra note 1, chapter 22, especially section 22.3, and chapter 5, especially section 5.6.

88. See, for example, the 1955 U.S. agriculture waiver, Waiver to the United States Regarding the Restrictions under the Agricultural Adjustment Act, GATT, BISD 3 Supp. BISD 32 (1955); and the 1971 waiver allowing developed countries to depart from MFN to the extent necessary to grant tariff preferences to developing countries, Generalized System of Preferences Waiver, Decision of 25 June 1971, GATT, BISD 18 Supp. 24 (1972).

89. At their thirty-eighth session, the Contracting Parties agreed to examine the issue of services (GATT, BISD 29 Supp. 21 [1983]) and set up a procedure to examine the issue. A report on the matter was presented in 1985 (GATT, BISD 32 Supp. 70 [1986]). The matter was formally adopted by the Contracting Parties at Punta del Este. See Ministerial Declaration, GATT, BISD 33 Supp. 19 (1987); GATT/1396, 25 September 1986, part 2, 11. See also John H. Jackson, *The Constitutional Structure for International Cooperation in Trade in Services and the Uruguay Round of GATT* (Washington, D.C. Institute for International Economics, 1988), and bibliography contained therein.

90. Jackson, supra note 1, section 20.3.

91. Ibid., section 20.2, 520, 521

92. See, for example, GATT Article XVI.3 and Article 10 of the 1979 Subsidies Code (GATT, BISD 26 Supp. 56 [1980]).

93. Jackson, supra note 1, Section 27.6.

94. See waiver request of the U.S. regarding the restrictions under the Agricultural Adjustment Act, supra note 88.

95. The Punta del Este Declaration supra note 89 contained language arguably calling for the elimination of farm subsidies. A number of proposals have been tabled, the two most notable being those of the so-called "Cairns Group" (for details, see *International Trade Reporter* 4 (1987), 696) and those of the U.S. (for details, see *International Trade Reporter* 4 (1987), 884).

96. The Multifibre Arrangement (MFA), signed originally in 1973 (25 UST 1001, TIAS 7840), was extended on July 31, 1986 for five more years. See Henry Zheng, *Legal Structure of International Textile Trade* (New York: Quorum Books, 1988). See also symposium "Perspectives on Textiles," *Law and Policy in International Business* 19 (1987), 1–271.

97. Eighteen GATT contracting parties have no current GATT schedule. See GATT, *Status of Legal Instruments* (GATT: Geneva: looseleaf). Each of these members acceded under the Article XXVI:5(e) procedure. See Jackson, supra note 1, sections 4.5 and 10.1.

98. See infra chapter 12.

99. See generally Jackson supra note 1, section 4.6. It was felt that it would be unreasonable to force a nation to accept an agreement with another nation when it may have compelling political reasons not to enter into such a relationship with another country. As of June 6, 1988 thirteen contracting parties were exercising such an option (see GATT L/6361 [1988]).

100. See Jackson, supra note 1, 98–102.

101. All but three of the 1979 MTN arrangements had measures permitting non-application of the rights and obligations between signatories. The three that contained no such waiver provision were the Arrangement Regarding Bovine Meat (GATT, BISD 26 Supp. 84 [1980]), the International Dairy Arrangement (GATT, BISD 26 Supp. 91 [1980]), and the Agreement on the Implementation of Article VII (GATT, BISD 26 Supp. 116 [1980]). See also infra chapter 11 on subsidy law in the U.S. The U.S. operates what is referred to as a "commitments" policy. Under section 701 of the 1979 Trade Agreements Act (Pub.L. 96–39; 93 Stat. 151; 19 USCA §1671[b] [1980 and Supp. 1988]), a "country under the Agreement" was defined to include "a country which has assumed obligations with respect to the U.S. which are substantially equivalent to obligations under the Agreement." This has proven to be a controversial aspect of U.S. trade law. See Jackson and Davey supra note 1, 776.

102. See Jean Groux and Phillipe Manin, *The European Communities in the International Order* (Brussels: European Commission, 1985), part 2, chapter 1; see also Petersmann, E. U., Participation of the European Communities in GATT: International Law and Community Law Aspects, in *Mixed Agreements*, David O'Keeffe and Henry Schermers (eds.) Boston: Kluwer, pp. 167–198; Petersmann, 1986, The EEC As a GATT Member: Legal Conflicts between GATT Law and European Community Law, in *The European Community and GATT*, Meinhard Hilf, Francis Jacobs and Ernst-Ulrich Petersmann (eds.) Deventer: Kluwer, pp. 23–71.

103. See Li, "Resumption of China's GATT Membership," *Journal of World Trade Law* 21 (1987), 25; Herzstein, "China and GATT: Legal and Policy Issues Raised by China's Participation in the General Agreement on Tariffs and Trade," *Law and Policy In International Business* 18 (1986), 371. See infra section 13.2.

104. China became a signatory to the GATT MFA on December 15, 1983, the agreement having effect on 18 January 1984 (*Status of Legal Instruments*, supra note 97, chapter 12: "Textiles").

105. For example, Hong Kong has brought an action before a GATT panel, although the request for the establishment of the panel was placed by the U.K. (see GATT, BISD 30 Supp. 129 [1984]).

106. See GATT/1384, 24 April 1986.

107. See supra section 2.2.

108. See GATT Article XXV.1.

109. See Jackson supra note 1, sections 4.6, 5.6, and 22; see also Jackson and Davey supra note 1, section 5.4(g), and Edmond McGovern, supra note 27, section 1.153.

110. See Jackson supra note 1, chapters 6 and 7, and McGovern supra note 27, chapter 1.14. See also GATT, INF/236 (1987), "List and Index of Documents Issued by Bodies" (especially "Index of Documents by Bodies," which lists the committees of GATT).

111. See, for example, *Department of State Bulletin* 86 (July 1986), 1, and 87 (August 1987), 1; *International Trade Reporter* 4 (1987), 784 on the Venice Summit. See also Robert Putnam and Nicholas Bayne, *Hanging Together: The Seven-Power Summits* (Cambridge, Mass: Harvard University Press, 1984).

112. See infra subsection d.

113. See, for example, GATT, BISD 32 Supp. 44 (1986).

114. See Gilbert Winham, *International Trade and the Tokyo Round Negotiations* (Princeton, NJ: Princeton University Press, 1986), 97–101. See also L. A. Glick, *Multilateral Trade Negotiations: World Trade After the Tokyo Round* (Totowa, NJ: Rowman & Allenheld, 1984), 12–14. See also Jackson, supra note 1, Chapter 10.

115. See Decision of 28 January 1987, GATT, BISD 33 Supp. 31, 34–5 (1987); GATT/1405, February 5, 1987.

116. See Jackson, Louis, and Matsushita, supra note 1. See Winham supra note 114, chapters 6 and 9. See also Symposium on the Multilateral Trade Agreements II, *Law and Policy in International Business* 12 (1980), 1–334, in particular Jackson, "The Birth of the GATT-MTN System: A Constitutional Appraisal," 21. See also McRae and Thames, "The GATT and Multilateral Treaty Making: The Tokyo Round" *American Journal of International Law* 77 (1983), 51; the contributions in *Cornell International Law Journal* 13 (1980) 145–290; and the MTN Studies commissioned by the Senate Finance Committee, 96th Cong., 1st sess., 1979, Comm. Prints 96–11 to 96–15.

117. See infra sections 4.3 and 4.6.

118. The Arrangement Regarding Bovine Meat (GATT, BISD 26 Supp. 84 [1980]) and the International Dairy Arrangement (GATT, BISD 26 Supp. 91 [1980]) both have provisions referring to decision-making by consensus. The Agreement on the Implementation of Article VII (GATT, BISD 26 Supp. 116 [1980]) also has an explicit voting provision in Annex II relating to the Technical Committee on Customs Valuation. The other MTN agreements do not explicitly refer to formal decision-making powers.

119. See infra section 3.4. See also Jackson, "The Birth of the GATT-MTN System: A Constitutional Appraisal," *Law and Policy in International Business* 12 (1980), 21; Jackson, Louis, and Matsushita, supra note 20, 36 et seq.

120. Jackson, supra note 1, 74 et seq.

121. See Jackson, supra note 1, 216–238.

122. Jackson, supra note 119, 40.

123. Ibid., 44.

124. Ibid., 40. See also infra chapter 4.

125. See supra note 89. See also *Results of the GATT Ministerial Meeting held in Punta del Este, Uruguay: Hearings Before the Subcommittee on Trade of the Committee on Ways and Means*, 99th Cong., 2nd Sess., 1986, 17–23. See also the comments of USTR Yeutter to the U.S. Congress, 3–11; and *International Trade Reporter* 3 (1986), 1151 and *International Trade Reporter* 3 (1986), 1182.

126. See Deardorff and Stern, *An Economic Analysis of the Effects of the Tokyo Round on the United States and Other Industrialized Countries*, Senate Finance Committee, 96th Cong., 1st sess. III-IV, 1979, Comm. Print 96–15. See also R. E. Baldwin, R. M. Stern, and H. Kierzkowski, *Evaluating the Effects of Trade Liberalization* (Leiden: Sijthoff, 1979).

127. See Jackson, supra note 1, Chapter 10.

128. See Jackson and Davey, supra note 1. Cf.Peter Kenen, *The International Economy* (Englewood Cliffs, NJ: Prentice Hall, 1985), 232–50.

129. *Agreement on the Implementation of Article VI of the General Agreement on Tariffs and Trade* (GATT, 15th Supp. BISD 74 (1968). See infra chapter 10.

130. See infra chapter 10.

131. *Agreement on the Interpretation of Article VI of the General Agreement on Tariffs and Trade* (GATT, BISD 26 Supp. 171 (1980).

132. See Thomas Curtis and John Vastine, *The Kennedy Round and the Future of American Trade* (New York: Praeger, 1971), chapters 9 and 10; Evans, supra note 66, 90–2, 227–9, 285–6. See also Jackson and Davey, supra note 1, 385.

133. See supra chapter 2.2.

134. The texts of the agreements and understandings can be found in GATT, BISD 26 Supp. (1980). See also Jackson, Louis, and Matsushita, supra note 1; Winham, supra note 114; Glick, supra note 114.

135. See Robert Stern, John H. Jackson and Bernard Hoekman, *An Assessment of the GATT Codes on Non-Tariff Measures* (Brookfield, VT: Gower, 1988). See also Jackson, supra note 119.

136. The United States left the International Dairy Agreement at the end of 1984 after the EC had made sales of subsidized butter to the U.S.S.R. (see *International Trade Reporter* 2 [1985], 12). Austria followed suit in March of 1985 (*International Trade Reporter*, 2 [1985], 429).

137. GATT, BISD 26 Supp. 201 (1980).

138. See especially *Declaration on Trade Measures Taken for Balance-of-Payments Purposes* (GATT, BISD 26 Supp. 205 [1980]) and *Decision on Differential and More Favorable Treatment, Reciprocity and Fuller Participation of Developing Countries* (GATT, BISD 26 Supp. 203 [1980]).

139. See *Action by the Contracting Parties on the Multilateral Trade Negotiations* (GATT, BISD 26 Supp. 201 [1980]).

140. See infra section 6.5.

141. See supra section 2.4.

142. The United Kingdom accepted a number of agreements on behalf of Hong Kong. On 23 April 1986 Hong Kong was deemed to be a member of the GATT in accordance with Article XXVI:5(c). Hong Kong, having declared its intentions to accept those agreements, became a party thereto on 23 April 1986. See GATT, *Status of Legal Instruments*, supra note 97, chapter 16.

143. For example, Botswana, which was not a member of GATT, accepted the Customs Valuation Code; similarly, Bulgaria accepted the International Dairy Arrangement and the Bovine Meat Arrangement, and Guatemala signed the Bovine Meat Arrangement.

Chapter 3

1. Wolfgang Friedmann, *The Changing Structure of International Law* (New York: Columbia University Press, 1964), chapter 3; Friedmann, "National Sovereignty, International Co Operation and the Reality of International Law," *U.C.L.A. Law Review* 10 (1963), 739.

2. See supra section 2.2.

3. See John H. Jackson and William Davey, *Legal Problems of International Economic Relations* (St. Paul: West, 2nd ed., 1986), section 10.2(b), 3. See also infra chapter 10.

4. See infra Section 3.4.

5. See John H. Jackson, Jean-Victor Louis, and Mitsuo Matsushita, *Implementing the Tokyo Round* (Ann Arbor: University of Michigan Press, 1984), 164.

6. Ibid., 35 et seq.

7. 299 U.S. 304, 57 S. Ct. 216, 81 L. Ed. 255 (1936).

8. Berger, "The Presidential Monopoly of Foreign Relations," *Michigan Law Review* 71 (1972), 1; Levitan, "The Foreign Relations Power: An Analysis of Mr. Justice Sutherland's Theory", *Yale Law Journal* 55 (1946), 467; Fulbright, "American Foreign Policy in the Twentieth Century Under an Eighteenth-Century Constitution," *Cornell Law Quarterly* 47 (1981), 1; Borchard, "Treaties and Executive Agreements: A Reply," *Yale Law Journal* 54 (1945), 616; Lofgren, "United States v. Curtiss-Wright Export Corporation: An Historical Reassessment," *Yale Law Journal* 83 (1973), 1; Schlesinger, "Congress and the Making of American Foreign Policy," *Foreign Affairs* 51 (1972), 78; Henkin, "Foreign Affairs and the Constitution," *Foreign Affairs* 66 (1988), 284.

9. U.S. Constitution, Art. I, sec. 8, cl. 3.

10. See, for example, Trade Reform Act of 1974, S. Rep. No. 1298, Senate Finance Committee, 93rd Cong., 2nd sess., 1974, 14.

11. 343 U.S. 579, 72 S. Ct. 863, 96 L. Ed. 1153 (1952).

12. United States v. Guy W. Capps, Inc., 204 F.2d 655, (4th Cir. 1953). See also Jackson and Davey, supra note 3, 88–92.

13. However, see Koh, "Congressional Control on Presidential Trade Policy-making after INS v. Chadha," *New York University Journal of International Law and Politics* 18 (1986), 1191; Franck and Bob, "The Return of Humpty-Dumpty: Foreign Relations Law After the Chadha Case," *American Journal of International Law* 79 (1985), 912. See also infra note 66.

14. See supra section 2.1(b).

15. The American Law Institute, *Restatement of the Law (Third); Foreign Relations Law of the United States*, 1987, §§ 301–308; Jackson, J. H., The Application of International Conventions in Domestic Law of the United States, in *The Effect of Treaties in Domestic Law*, Francis G. Jacobs (ed.) London: Sweet and Maxwell, 1987; McDougal and Lans, "Treaties and Congressional-Executive or Presidential Agreements: Interchangeable Instruments of National Policy," *Yale Law Journal* 54 (1945), 181; Berger, supra note 8.

16. See *Restatement*, supra note 15, §308.

17. See, for example, Connell, "External Affairs Power and the Domestic Implementation of Treaties," *Australian Foreign Affairs Record* 54 (1983), 9:492; Joutsamo, "The Direct Effect of Treaty Provisions in Finnish Law," *Nordisk Tiddskrift for International Ret* 52 (1983), 34; see also Jackson, Louis, and Matsushita, supra note 5, 78–95. See also supra note 15.

18. See Jackson, supra note 15; Iwasawa, "The Doctrine of Self-Executing Treaties in the United States: A Critical Analysis," *Virginia Journal of International Law* 26 (1986), 627.

19. Jackson, Louis, and Matsushita, supra note 5, 198–210.

20. Jackson, supra note 15.

21. The use of the term 'presidential' is intended to extend to all acts of the executive branch.

22. See supra note 12. See also Jackson and Davey, supra note 3, section 3.2(b).

23. Bernard Schwartz, *Super Chief: Earl Warren and His Supreme Court: Judicial Biography* (New York: New York University Press, 1983), 165–66.

24. 506 F.2d 136 (1974), cert. denied, 421 U.S. 1004, 95 S. Ct. 2406, 44 L. Ed. 2d 673 (1975). See also Jackson and Davey, supra note 3, 92–104.

25. Section 607 of the Trade Act of 1974. See Jackson and Davey, supra note 3, 615.

26. See Metzger, "The Mills' Bill: Domestic Implication and Foreign Repercussions," *Journal of World Trade Law* 5 (1971), 235.

27. See Cooper, R. N., 1987. Trade Policy as Foreign Policy. In *U.S. Trade Policies in a Changing World Economy*, R. M. Stern (ed.) Cambridge, Mass.: MIT Press, pp. 291–336. See also I. M. Destler, *American Trade Politics: System Under Stress*, (Washington, DC: Institute for International Economics, 1986), 9–10. Cf. Barry Eichengreen, *The Political Economy of Smoot Hawley* (Washington, D.C.: NBER Working Paper No. 2001, 1986).

28. Omnibus Trade and Competitiveness Act of 1988, Pub. L. 100–418, 102 Stat. 1107 et seq. See Bello and Holmer, "The 1988 Trade Bill: Is It Protectionist?" *International Trade Reporter* 5 (1988), 1347; Bello and Holmer, "The Heart of the 1988 Trade Act: A Legislative History of the Amendments of Section 301," *Stanford Journal of International Law* 25 (1988) 1. The enactment of the 1988 Act met with a great deal of criticism from foreign nations. For example, the EC protested the passing of the Act at the September GATT Council meeting (*International Trade Reporter* 5 [1988], 1302), and on September 26, 1988, the EC Council of Ministers released a statement concerning "serious concern" about the Act (*European Community News*, No. 24/88). Japanese officials also expressed concern over the Act: see "New US trade bill raises fears in Asia and Europe," *Financial Times*, August 5, 1988, 1, and "Japan Fumes at US Steps in Trade Bill," *Wall Street Journal*, August 9, 1988, 24. See also "New US Trade Bill Dismays France," *Journal of Commerce*, October 6, 1988, 5A.

29. As to the effects of such programs in general, see David Tarr and Morris Morkre, *Aggregate Costs to the United States of Tariffs and Quotas on Imports: General Tariff Cuts and the Removal of Quotas on Automobiles, Steel, Sugar and Textiles* (Washington, D.C.: FTC, 1984). See also Savage and Horlick, "United States Voluntary Restraint Agreements: Practical Considerations and Policy Considerations," *Stanford Journal of International Law* 21 (1985), 281–298. Regarding

textiles in particular, see Henry Zheng, *Legal Structure of International Textile Trade* (Westport, CT: Quorum Books, 1988).

30. See Morkre and Tarr, supra note 29. See also Michael Levine, *Inside International Trade Policy Formulation: A History of the 1982 U.S.–EC Steel Arrangements* (New York: Praeger, 1985).

31. See Morkre and Tarr, supra note 29; Jackson and Davey, supra note 3, Section 9.4(d). See also Crandall, "The Effects of U.S. Trade Protection for Autos and Steel," *Brookings Papers on Economic Activity* (1987), 271–298.

32. Schechter v. United States, 295 U.S. 495, 79 L. Ed. 1570, 55 S. Ct. 837 (1934).

33. J. W. Hampton & Co. v. United States, 276 U.S. 394, 409; 72 L. Ed. 624; 48 S. Ct. 348 (1928).

34. Amalgamated Meat Cutters & Butcher Workmen of North America, AFL-CIO v. Connally, 337 F. Supp. 737 (D.D.C. 1971).

35. Trade Act of 1974, Pub. L. 93–618, § 101a , 88 Stat. 1983, 19 USCA §2111 (1980 and Supp. 1988). Note the breadth of the authority contained therein. See also Jackson and Davey, supra note 3, sections 3.2(c), 3.4, 3.5.

36. See infra Section 3.2(e) and (f).

37. See, for example, the Curtiss-Wright case, supra note 7. See also Jackson and Davey, supra note 3, 79–84.

38. Chicago v. Southern Air Lines, Inc. v. Waterman S.S. Corp., 333 U.S. 103, 68 S. Ct. 431, 92 L. Ed. 568 (1948).

39. Ibid., 11.

40. Haig v. Agee, 453 U.S. 280, 101 S. Ct. 2766, 69 L. Ed. 2d 640 (1981) at 291, citing Zemel v. Rusk, 281 U.S. 1, 17 (1965).

41. See infra chapter 14.

42. See infra chapter 10.

43. See infra chapter 11.

44. Missouri v. Holland, 252 U.S. 416, 40 S. Ct. 382, 64 L. Ed. 641 (1920). See also Jackson, Louis, and Matsushita, supra note 5, 142–145.

45. See, for example, Baldwin-Lima-Hamilton Corp. v. Superior Ct., 208 Cal. App. 2d 803, 25 Cal. Rptr. 798 (1962); Bethlehem Steel Corp. v. Board of Commrs., 276 Cal. App. 2d 221, 80 Cal. Rptr. 800 (1969); Territory v. Ho, 41 Hawaii 565 (1957); American Institute for Imported Steel v. County of Erie, 58 Misc. 2d 1059 (Sup. Ct. 1968); KSB Technical Sales Corp. v. North Jersey Water Supply Commission, 75 N.J. 272, 381 A. 2d 774 (1977), appeal dismissed, 435 U.S. 982 (1978); Armstrong v. Taxation Division Director, 5 NJ Tax 117 (Tax Ct.) aff'd 6 NJ Tax 447 (S. Ct. App. Div.); Association of Alabama Professional Numismatists v. Eagerton, No. Civ. 4259-X, Court of Appeals of Alabama, 25 April 1984. See also Jackson, "The General Agreement on Tariffs and Trade in United States Domestic Law," *Michigan Law Review* 66 (1967), 249, 297–311; Hudec, R. E. 1986; The

Legal Status of GATT in the Domestic Law of the United States, in *The European Community and GATT*, Meinhard Hilf, Francis Jacobs and Ernst-Ulrich Petersmann (eds.) Deventer: Kluwer, pp. 187–249, 221–225.

46. *Agreement on Government Procurement*, GATT BISD 26 Supp. 33–55 (1980).

47. See L. A. Glick, *Multilateral Trade Negotiations: World Trade After the Tokyo Round* (Totowa, NJ: Rowman and Allenheld, 1984), 31.

48. In 1987, Premier Mulroney and some of the provincial heads expressed differing views as to the role of the provinces in the implementation process (see, for example, *International Trade Reporter* 4 [1987], 1503, 1505), and there were indications that a constitutional challenge might be brought if the federal government tried to implement the FTA without prior approval of the provinces (*International Trade Reporter* 5 [1988], 296). The Canadian Senate's Foreign Affairs Committee suggested that the federal government had the sole right to implement the FTA, and this opinion may have some influence (*International Trade Reporter* 5 [1988], 693).

49. See Jackson, Louis and Matsushita, supra note 5, 21–23; Weiler, J.H.H., 1980. The European Parliament and Foreign Affairs: External Relations of the European Economic Community. In *Parliamentary Control Over Foreign Policy*. A. Cassese (ed.) Germantown, MD: Sijthoff and Nordhoff, 151, 156. See also infra section 3.4.

50. See supra section 3.2.

51. Jackson and Davey, supra note 3, 130–131, quoting from remarks before July 18, 1985 conference on The Export Administration Amendments Act of 1985, reported in *International Business Review*, 4 (1985), 3.

52. See Jackson and Davey, supra note 3, section 3.4, especially fn. 21.

53. Jackson and Davey, supra note 3, 144. See generally John H. Jackson, *World Trade and the Law of GATT* (Indianapolis: Bobbs-Merrill, 1969).

54. Jackson and Davey, supra note 3, 145, fn. 38.

55. See supra note 28.

56. Senate Rep. No. 258, 78th Cong., 1st sess., 1943, 47, 48. See Jackson and Davey, supra note 3, 145.

57. Trade Act of 1974, Pub. L. No. 93–618, 88 Stat. 1978.

58. Trade and Tariff Act of 1984, Pub. L. 98–573, 98 Stat. 2948.

59. See supra note 55.

60. See supra sections 2.1 and 2.2(b), (c), and (d).

61. On the Trade Act, see Jackson and Davey, supra note 3, Section 3.4(d). See also Jackson, Louis, and Matsushita, supra note 5, 146–149.

62. See supra note 57. See also Senate Report No. 93–1298, 93d Cong., 2nd sess., 1974. Reprinted in *U.S. Code Congressional and Administrative News* 4 (1974), 7186, 7253. See also Jackson, Louis, and Matsushita, supra note 5, 146–149.

63. See Jackson, Louis, and Matsushita, supra note 5, 162–169.

64. Ibid., 163.

65. See Barbera Hinkson Craig, *Chadha* (New York: Oxford University Press, 1988).

66. Immigration and Naturalization Service v. Chadha, 462 U.S. 919, 103 S. Ct. 2764, 77 L. Ed. 2d 317 (1983). See Elliot, "INS v. Chadha: The Administrative Constitution, the Constitution and the Legislative Veto," *Supreme Court Review*, (1983), 125; Tribe, "The Legislative Veto Decision: A Law by Any Other Name?," *Harvard Journal on Legislation* 21 (1984), 1; Breyer, "The Legislative Veto After Chadha," *Georgia Law Journal* 72 (1984), 785; Levitas and Brand, "Congressional Review of Executive and Agency Actions After Chadha: The 'Son of Legislative Veto' Lives On," *Georgia Law Journal* 72 (1984), 801; Spann, "Reconstructing the Legislative Veto," *Minnesota Law Review* 68 (1984), 473; Cutler, "The Right to Intervene, *Foreign Affairs* 64 (1985), 96, 97. See also Jackson, Louis, and Matsushita, supra note 5 162–168. See also supra note 13.

67. See, for example, section 203 of the Trade Act 1974 as amended by the Tariff and Trade Act of 1984, Pub. L. 98–573, Title II, §248(a), 98 Stat. 2998, codified at 19 USC §2253(c)(1) and (2) (1980 and Supp. 1988).

68. After the Senate Finance Committee proved hostile to the use of "fast track" (see below), Canadian Finance Minister Michael Wilson said, "At this point in time we are not withdrawing our proposal" (*International Trade Reporter* 3 [1986], 497). The next week, in the Senate Finance Committee, George Mitchell (D-Maine) said that Canada had too much to lose if it were to pull out of the FTA simply because of lack of "fast track." John Chaffee (R-RI) disagreed, stating that Canadian Premier Mulroney had put himself on a limb over the proposal and was unlikely to renew the FTA talks if the Senate disapproved "fast track" (*International Trade Reporter* 3 [1986] 530 and 721).

Cf. Negotiation of United States–Canada Free Trade Agreement, S. Hrg. 99–743, Senate Committee on Finance, 99th Cong., 22d sess., 1986. Eventually the Senate Finance Committee approved the use of the "fast-track" procedure (*International Trade Reporter* 3 [1986], 565).

69. See text accompanying note 55 supra. See also, for example, "The Plant Closings Debate," *Journal of Commerce* 377 (July 6, 1988), 8a.

70. See Jackson, Louis, and Matsushita, supra note 5, 55–56.

71. Jackson and Davey, supra note 3, section 4.9. See also Jackson, supra note 45, 285–6.

72. Proclamation 2761A, *Federal Register* 12 (1947), 8863. See Jackson, supra note 71, 293–294; and Hudec, supra note 45, 201.

73. Jackson, Louis, and Matsushita, supra note 5, 169–172.

74. Ibid. See also *Restatement of the Law, Foreign Relations Law of the U.S.*, supra note 15, §135; Jackson, "The Application of International Conventions in Domestic Law of the United States," supra note 15.

75. See Senate Report No. 249, 96th Cong., 1st sess., 1979, 4, 36; House Report No. 317, 96th. Cong. 1st. Sess., 1979, 26, 41. See also Jackson, Louis, and Matsushita, supra note 5, 167, text accompanying note 153; Jackson and Davey, supra note 3, 151–55.

76. See *Restatement of the Law, Foreign Relations Law of the U.S.*, supra note 15, §134.

77. Trade Agreements Act of 1979: Statements of Administrative Action, H. R. Doc. No. 153, 96th Cong., 1st sess, pt. 2, 1979. Reprinted in *U.S. Code Congressional and Administrative News* (1979), 665.

77a. Senate Report No. 249, supra note 75, 6.

78. "But these roles have been cut back somewhat compared to former times." See the annual *United States Government Annual*, (Washington, D.C.: USGPO). See also Jackson, Louis, and Matsushita, supra note 5, 172–173.

79. For the statutory basis of the Office of the USTR, see section 141 of the Trade Act of 1974 (19 USCA §2171[c] [1980 and Supp. 1988]) as amended by section 1601 of the Omnibus Trade and Competitiveness Act of 1988 (supra note 28). See also Jackson and Davey, supra note 3, 157–160.

80. For a general discussion of the ITC, see Robert Baldwin, *The Political Economy of U.S. Import Policy* (Cambridge, Mass.: MIT Press, 1985), chapter 3. The ITC has varying functions in the administration of section 201 (the "escape clause," see infra section 7.2), section 404 (the "market disruption clause," see infra section 13.3), section 337 (see infra section 10.7), the antidumping (see infra chapter 10), countervailing (see infra chapter 11) and tariff schedules, advice concerning trade negotiations, the GSP (see infra section 12.3), and East-West Monitoring System.

81. See Jackson, Louis, and Matsushita, supra note 5, 203 et seq.

82. For example, in the United States, section 301 of the Trade Act of 1974 (19 USC §2411 [1980 and Supp. 1988]) and in the EC, the so-called "New Commercial Policy Instrument," Council Regulation (EEC) 2641/84 on the strengthening of the common commercial policy with regard in particular to protection against illicit commercial practices, O. J. [1984] L. 252/1. See infra section 4.5.

83. See infra section 10.1 and chapter 14.

84. See Jackson, Louis, and Matsushita, supra note 5; Hans Smit and Peter Herzog, *The Law of the European Economic Community* (New York: Matthew Bender, 1976, looseleaf); Eric Stein, Peter Hay, and Michel Waelbroeck, *European Community Law and Institutions in Perspective: Text, Cases and Readings* (Indianapolis: Bobbs-Merrill, 1976) (with supplement, 1985); Megret, Waelbroeck et al., *Le Droit de la Communauté Economique Européene*, (Brussels: Presses Universitaires de Bruxelles, 1970).

84a. Figures derived from Table A2 of *International Trade 1986–87*, (Geneva: GATT, 1987), 156–7.

85. GATT, *The Tokyo Round of Multilateral Trade Negotiations*, volume II, Supplementary Report of the Director-General, chapter IV. See also John W. Evans, *The Kennedy Round in American Trade Policy: The Twilight of the GATT?* (Cambridge, Mass.: Harvard University Press, 1971), sections 4 and 12; Gilbert Winham, *International Trade and the Tokyo Round Negotiation* (Princeton, NJ: Princeton University Press, 1986), 146–155, 156–158, 247–255.

86. The three basic treaties that establish the European Communities are the treaty establishing the European Coal and Steel Community (ECSC) — the Treaty of Paris (1951); the treaty establishing the European Economic Community — Treaty of Rome (1957); and the treaty establishing the European Atomic Energy Community (Euratom) (1957). The 1965 "Merger Treaty" established a single Council and Commission for the European Communities. Treaties of accession were signed in 1972 with Denmark, Eire, and the U.K., in 1980 with Greece and in 1985 with Spain and Portugal. See Jackson, "United States–EEC Trade Relations: Constitutional Problems of Economic Interdependence," *Common Market Law Review* 16 (1979), 453.

87. The Single European Act was negotiated as a result of the Stuttgart Solemn Declaration of 19 June 1983. The Act itself was negotiated at an Intergovernmental Conference in accordance with Article 236 of the Treaty of Rome. The negotiations took place in Luxembourg in September 1985, again in February 1986, and in the Hague in February 1986. For the text of the Act, see *Bulletin of the European Communities*, Supp. 2/86. See also the *Common Market Law Review* 24 (1987), 9–64, and Ehlermann, "The Internal Market Following the Single European Act," *Common Market Law Review* 24 (1987), 361.

88. The goal of the completion of the internal market by 1992 was based upon a European Commission White Paper, *Completing the Internal Market: White Paper from the Commission to the European Council* (Brussels: European Commission, 1985).

89. Under the amendments to Article 149 of the Treaty of Rome, the European Parliament is now able to amend and in some circumstances to reject legislation.

90. See Title III of the Single European Act.

91. See Part Five, Title I, Chapter I, Section 3 of the European Economic Treaty, as amended by the Merger Treaty and Accession Treaties.

92. See "A Crisis Overcome," *Bulletin of the European Communities* 15 (5–1982), 7. See also Evans, "The 'Veto' in EEC Law," *Public Law* [1982], 366.

93. Article 189 of the European Economic Community (EEC) Treaty.

94. See Part Five, Title I, chapter I, section 4 of the European Economic Treaty, as amended by the Accession Treaties.

95. Article 113 of the European Economic Community (EEC) Treaty.

96. See Stein, E., with Henkin, 1985. Towards a European Foreign Policy? The European Foreign Affairs System from the Perspective of the United States Constitution. In *Integration Through Law*, Mauro Cappeletti, Monica Seccombe and Joseph Weiler (eds.) New York: Walter de Gruyter, vol. 1, book 3.

97. Article 229 of the Treaty of Rome states that it shall be for the Commission to ensure the maintenance of appropriate relations with GATT. Because of the exclusive competence of the Community in commercial relations, the community tends to represent the interests of the Member States in the GATT. However, some debate exists as to the exclusive power of the Community to sign agreements under the auspices of the GATT. In the Tokyo Round, the Community felt it had exclusive competence to sign all the multilateral and bilateral agreements. Some debate arose as to whether Community competence extended to standards and to trade in aircraft. So, largely as a political gesture, the Member States were allowed to sign the Civil Aircraft Agreement and the Standards Code. The Member States also signed the Tariff Protocols with respect to products covered by the ECSC. For an excellent discussion of this process, see Jackson, Louis, and Matsushita, supra note 1, chapter 2.

98. See Jackson, Louis, and Matsushita, supra note 5, 47–61; Ehlermann, C. D., 1986. Application of GATT Rules in the European Community. In *The European Community and GATT*, Meinhard Hilf, Francis Jacobs, and Ernst-Ulrich Petersmann (eds.) Deventer: Kluwer, 1986, pp. 187–249, 201; Petersmann, "Application of GATT by the Court of Justice of the European Communities," *Common Market Law Review* 20 (1983), 397–437.

99. See Chalmers Johnson, *MITI and the Japanese Miracle* (Stanford: Stanford University Press, 1982), 47–49.

100. See Jackson, Louis, and Matsushita, supra note 5, chapter 3.

Chapter 4

1. See supra section 1.4.

2. See, for example, William B. Lockhart et al., *Constitutional Rights and Liberties* (St. Paul: West, 6th ed., 1986), 815–921, 1138–1186 and Gerald Gunther, *Constitutional Law*, (Mineola, NY: Foundation Press, 11th ed., 1985, supplement 1987) 586–642, 855–968. For a historical look at the problem, see Richard Kluger, *Simple Justice* (New York: Knopf, 1st ed., 1976).

3. See Louis Henkin, *How Nations Behave* (New York. Council on Foreign Relations, 2d ed., 1979), 38–88.

4. Examples include the change of U.S. law on *DISC (Domestic International Sales Corporation)*. In reference to GATT, a compromise was reached between the parties leading to the rather vague and contradictory Council statement (GATT, BISD 28 Supp. 114 [1982]). In 1984 the U.S. replaced the DISC system by the FSC system (26 USC §§921–7). See also the 1986 Customs Users' Fee case: During the congressional consideration of the 1986 Tax Reform Act, certain committees

decided to impose a customs users fee to add to tariffs at the border in order to partially fund the U.S. Customs Service. The initial proposal were clearly contrary to GATT bindings and obligations. As a result of committee staff members' criticisms, the proposals were redrafted so as to tie the amount of revenue raised to the total expenditure of the Customs Service. This would have allowed the U.S. to claim that the measures was consistent with Article VIII of the GATT. However, the provisions were challenged and a GATT panel held the provisions were incompatible with GATT obligations (see *International Trade Reporter* 4 [1987], 1450). Also, in 1982, at the request of the European Community, a GATT Panel was established to consider the compatibility with the Agreement of the U.S. "manufacturing clause" (17 USC § 601). The panel reported in May 1984 (GATT, BISD 31 Supp. 74 [1984]), concluding that the clause was inconsistent with Article XI and that its extension beyond July 1, 1982 was not excused by U.S. grandfather rights. In 1986 a bill (S 1822–HR 4696) was introduced which attempted to make the clause a permanent feature of U.S. copyright law. In the hearings in the House, Ambassador Yeutter said that:

...we have to be concerned about the fact that the manufacturing clause has been declared GATT illegal. Here we are attempting to strengthen the GATT, respond to the criticisms of the GATT that exist throughout the world, including in this subcommitee, appropriate critcisms in my judgment, but how do we go about reaching that objective, which all of us share, if we patently violate GATT ourselves.

We have a definitive GATT decision against the United States on this clause. We have no defence whatsoever for the continuation of the manufacturing clause. How can we possibly go to other countries and say don't violate the GATT, if we cavalierly and flagrantly violate it ourselves.

(Hearing on HR 4696, House Ways and Means Committee, 99th Cong., 2nd sess. 1986, 2). However, the bill did not pass, and the legislation lapsed.

5. See infra chapters 10 and 11.

6. See Trimble, "International Trade and the 'Rule of Law,'" *Michigan Law Review* 83 (1985), 1016.

7. See supra section 2.2 and infra section 9.6.

8. Unlike the one-nation-one-vote system in the GATT, the IMF and the World Bank both have voting weighted on the basis of total contribution to the fund, with a minimum number of votes per nation to ensure representation of developing and poorer nations. See Richard W. Edwards, *International Monetary Collaboration* (Dobbs Ferry, NY: Transnational Publishers, 1985), 32–35. See also John H. Jackson and William Davey, *Legal Problems of International Economic Relations*, (St. Paul: West, 2d ed., 1986), 273–276, 286–289; Henry Schermers, *International Institutional Law* (Rockville, MD: Sijthoff and Noordhoff, 2d ed., 1980), 681–683.

9. See, for example, Robert Triffin, *The World Money Maze: National Currencies in International Payments* (New Haven, CT: Yale University Press, 1966); Robert V.

Roosa, *Monetary Reform for a World Economy* (New York: Council on Foreign Relations, 1965); Gold, "Unauthorized Changes of Par Value and Fluctuating Exchange Rates in the Bretton Woods System," *American Journal of International Law* 65 (1971), 113.

10. Adapted from Jackson, "Governmental Disputes in International Trade Relations: A Proposal in the Context of GATT," *Journal of World Trade Law* 13 (1979), 3–4, and Jackson, "The Crumbling Institutions of the Liberal Trade System," *Journal of World Trade Law* 12 (1978), 98–101.

11. The Vienna Convention on the Law of Treaties, with Annex, done at Vienna, 23 May 1969. (Text: UNGA U.N. Doc. A/Conf. 39–27, May 23, 1969). The revised Restatement closely follows the Vienna Convention. See American Law Institute, *Restatement of the Law (Third): Foreign Relations Law of the United States*, part 3. On the Vienna Convention on the Law of Treaties, see generally Ian Sinclair, *The Vienna Convention on the Law of Treaties* (Dover, NH: Manchester University Press, 2d ed., 1984); Taslim Elias, *The Modern Law of Treaties* (Dobbs Ferry, NY: Oceana, 1974); Shabtai Rosenne, *The Law of Treaties: A Guide to the Legislative History of the Vienna Convention* (Dobbs Ferry, NY: Sijthoff, 1970); Shabtai Rosenne, *Breach of Treaty* (Cambridge, Eng.: Grotius, 1985) Mark E. Villiger, *Customary International Law and Treaties* (Boston: Martinus Nijhoff, 1985).

12. Vienna Convention, supra note 11, Article XXXII. Further preference may be made to supplementary means of interpretation, including the preparatory work of the treaty and the circumstances of its conclusion, in order to confirm the meaning resulting from the application of Article XXXI, or to determine the meaning when the interpretation according to Article XXXI: (a) leaves the meaning ambiguous or obscure; or (b) leads to a result which is manifestly absurd or unreasonable.

13. Annex I, Notes and Supplementary Provisions. Volume 4 of the *Basic Instruments* (Geneva: GATT/1969–7) contains the text of the General Agreement (of which the Annex I is an integral part) which entered into force 27 June 1966.

14. See supra section 2.5.

15. GATT, *Analytical Index, Notes on the Drafting, Interpretation, and Application of the Articles of the General Agreement*. Revisions were published in 1959 and 1966. The *Analytical Index* currently in use is the 1985–1986 looseleaf edition.

16. This is a critical question for Article XIX, concerning safeguards. See infra section 7.5.

17. John H. Jackson, *World Trade and the Law of GATT* (Indianapolis: Bobbs-Merrill, 1969), chapter 3.

18. See Ian Brownlie, *Principles of Public International Law*, (Oxford: Clarendon Pres, 3d ed., 1979), 21–23. Cf. McGovern E. 1986. Dispute Settlement in the GATT – Adjudication or Negotiation? In *The European Community and the GATT*, Meinhard Hilf, Francis Jacobs and Ernst-Ulrich Petersmann (eds.) Deventer: Kluwer, pp. 73–84, 78–79.

19. Statute of the International Court of Justice, 59 Stat. 1055, T.S. 993. Article 59 reads: "The decision of the Court has no binding force except between the parties and in respect of that particular case."

20. See GATT *Analytical Index*, supra note 15, Article I:12. See also Article I:15 (Chairman); Article I-16 (Chairman); Article II:20 (Secretariat).

21. There is even some doubt about this. See infra section 4.4.

22. Vienna Convention on the Law of Treaties, supra note 11, Article XXXI:3: "There shall be taken into account, together with the context . . . (b) any subsequent practice in the application of the treaty which establishes the agreement of the parties regarding its interpretation . . ." See also McGovern, supra note 18.

23. See, for example, *Articles of Agreement of the International Monetary Fund* (60 Stat. 1401; TIAS 1501), Article XXIX, and *Articles of Agreement of the International Bank for Reconstruction and Development* (60 Stat. 1440; TIAS 1502), Article VIII.

24. See supra section 2.2.

25. International Court of Justice, *Reports of Judgments, Advisory Opinions, and Orders.*

26. Havana (ITO) Charter Articles 92–97. See Jackson, supra note 17, section 5.5, 135.

27. See Whitt, "The Politics of a Procedure: An Examination of the GATT Dispute Settlement Panel and the Article XXI Defense in the Context of the U.S. Embargo of Nicaragua," *Law and Policy in International Business* 19 (1987), 603, 611–615. For the details of the dispute(s), see Report of the Panel, GATT, BISD 31 Supp. 67 (1984). See also *Case Concerning Military and Paramilitary Activities in and Against Nicaragua* (Nicaragua v. United States), Merits, Judgment of 27 June 1986. ICJ Reports 1986.

28. See supra note 11.

29. For texts of the 1979 MTN Agreements, see GATT, BISD 26 Supp. (1980).

30. See, for example, the *Agreement on Implementation of Article VII of the GATT* (GATT, BISD 26 Supp. 116 [1980] Article 20:5).

31. See, for example, the *Agreement on Government Procurement* (GATT, BISD 26 Supp. 33 [1980] Article VII:9).

32. See supra section 2.2.

33. See generally, Leo Gross (ed.), *The Future of the International Court of Justice* (Dobbs Ferry, NY: Oceana 1976); Partan, "Increasing the Effectiveness of the International Court," *Harvard International Law Journal* 18 (1977), 559.

34. Olivier Long, *Law and Its Limitations in the GATT Multialteral Trade System* (Dordrecht: Kluwer, 1985), 73, citing Kenneth Dam, *The GATT: Law and International Economic Organization* (Chicago: University of Chicago Press, 1970), 356.

35. Arthur Dunkel, GATT/1312, 5 March 1982.

36. See Long, supra note 34, 21: "GATT is at the same time a legal framework and a forum for negotiation." See also Hudec, "GATT or GABB?", *Yale Law Journal* 80 (1971), 1299.

37. See Long, supra note 34, 71, citing Dam, supra note 34, 335–336.

38. Statement of Harry Hawkins, representing the U.S., speaking about the proposed ITO Charter at the London meeting of the Preparatory Committee of the United Nations Conference on Trade and Employment, UN Doc. EPCT/C.II/PV.2, 8 (1946).

39. See Charter of the ITO, Chapter 8, Articles 92–97, UN, Final Act and Related Documents, UN Conference on Trade and Employment, held at Havana, Cuba, from 21 November 1947 to 24 March 1948, Interim Commission for the International Trade Organization, Lake Success, New York, April 1948. UN Doc. E/Conf.2/78. See also Clair Wilcox, *A Charter for World Trade* (New York: Macmillan, 1949), 159, 305–308.

40. See Wilcox, supra note 39, 159.

41. Ibid., 160.

42. See supra section 4.1(b).

43. GATT, BISD 14 Supp. 18 (1967).

44. GATT, BISD 11 Supp. 95 (1963).

45. Jackson, supra note 17, 167–171.

46. Ibid. Generally on the GATT, dispute-settlement procedure, see Davey, "Dispute-settlement in GATT," *Fordham International Law Journal* 11 (1987), 51; Plank, "An Unofficial Description of How a GATT Panel Works and Does Not," *Swiss Review of International Competition Law* 29 (1987), 81; McGovern, supra note 18.

47. Jackson, supra note 17, 164–166.

48. Ibid., 175.

49. An action may also be brought under Article XXIII when the attainment of any objective of the agreement is being impeded.

50. *Australian Ammonium Sulphate*, GATT, BISD Vol. II, 188 (1952). This case is sometimes called the "Marbury v. Madison" of GATT. See Hudec, "Retaliation Against Unreasonable Foreign Trade Practices," *Minnesota Law Review* 59 (1975), 46; Robert Hudec, *The GATT Legal System and World Trade Diplomacy* (New York: Praeger, 1975), 144 153; Hudec, supra note 36, 1341.

51. The *Australian Ammonium Sulphate* case (supra note 50) and the *German Sardines* case (GATT, BISD 1 Supp. 53 [1953]) both endorsed the view that the GATT should be construed to protect "reasonable expectations" of the contracting parties. See Hudec, *GATT Legal System*, supra note 50, 144–153, and Hudec, "GATT or GABB?" supra note 36, 1341. On the notion of protecting reasonable expectations generally, see Edward Allen Farnsworth, *Contracts* (Boston: Little, Brown, 1982), 19.

52. GATT, BISD 3 Supp. 224 (1955). See infra chapter 11.

53. GATT Doc. L/1222/Add. 1 (1960). See also Jackson, supra note 17, 182.

54. See Hudec, *GATT Legal System*, supra note 50, 66–96.

55. Some of this information is developed from private conversations with senior GATT officials closely associated with the early development of GATT.

56. *Understanding Regarding Notification, Consultation, Dispute Settlement and Surveillance*, GATT, BISD 26 Supp. 210 (1980), especially paragraphs 10–21.

57. *Netherlands Measures of Suspension of Obligations to the United States*, GATT, BISD 1 Supp. 32 (1953). This was one fallout result of the U.S. Congress's enactment of Section 22 of the Agriculture Act in 1951. See Jackson and Davey, supra note 8, 956.

58. The Netherlands never enforced the quota, arguably because of its ineffectiveness in removing the U.S. quota on dairy products. See Hudec, "Retaliation Against Unreasonable Foreign Trade Practices," supra note 50, 57.

59. As a result of the panel decision in the so-called Superfund case (GATT, BISD 34 Supp. 136 [1988]), the EC requested that the CONTRACTING PARTIES authorize retaliation (*International Trade Reporter*, 5 [1988], 681 and 1303–4). To date, authorization has not been granted.

60. For example, in the Citrus case, as a result of the failure of the EC to accept the findings of a 1985 GATT panel (*International Trade Reporter* 2 [1985] 162), the U.S. president authorized retaliatory measures against imports of EC pasta (Proclamation 5354 of June 21, 1985, *Federal Register* 50 [1985], 26143). However, in the light of continuing discussion between the EC and the U.S., the president issued Proclamation 5363 of August 15, 1985 (*Federal Register* 50 [1985] 33711), suspending the application of the duty until November 1, 1985. The duties became effective until August 21, 1986, when the president revoked the increased rates of duty due to a settlement of the Citrus case (*Federal Register*, 51 [1986], 30146). However, it must be noted that trade in pasta between the U.S. and the EC was itself a problem, and so retaliation against a problematic product may have had a certain added attraction.

61. See supra note 56.

62. Ibid.

63. GATT, BISD 29 Supp. 13 (1983).

64. See Ministerial Declaration, GATT, BISD 33 Supp. 19, 25 (1987) and Decision of 28 January 1987 GATT, BISD 33 Supp. 31, 44–45 (1987). See also, for example, Yeutter, "The GATT Must Be Repaired—and Fast!", *The International Economy* (March/April 1988), 44, 47–48; Address by Lamb (U.S. Department of State, *Current Policy*, No. 585 [1984]). Improvement of the dispute settlement procedures of GATT is also listed in the 1988 Trade Act (Omnibus Trade and Competitiveness Act of 1988, Pub. L. 100–418, Section 1101(b)(1), 102 Stat. 1121) as a U.S. objective under the Uruguay Round.

65. Agreement on Technical Barriers to Trade, GATT, BISD 26 Supp. 8 (1980).

66. For the texts of the MTN Agreements, see GATT, BISD 26 Supp. (1980).

67. The increase in cases partly reflected a decision by the United States to utilize the GATT dispute settlement processes more fully, and the 1974 U.S. Trade Act, Section 301, which established a presumption that cases initiated under Section 301 procedures would be taken to GATT when appropriate. See infra section 4.5.

68. See supra sections 4.1(b) and 4.3.

69. Much of the specific information and many of the statistics about GATT disputes which are contained in this section of this book are derived from my own study, based on an inventory of GATT disputes developed over a number of years and contained in a computer database. One article which describes some of this work is Jackson. J. H. 1984, Dispute Settlement Techniques Between Nations Concerning Economic Relations — With Special Emphasis on GATT, in *Resolving Transnational Disputes Through International Arbitration*, Thomas Carbonneau (ed.) Charlottesville: University Press of Virginia, pp. 39–72. In other footnotes of this section, we will refer to this research as "Jackson, GATT disputes inventory research." See also Hudec, "Reforming GATT Adjudication Procedures: The Lessons of the DISC Case" *Minnesota Law Review* 72 (1988), 1443; Hudec. R. E. 1988, Legal Issues in U.S.-EC Trade Policy: GATT Litigation 1960–1985, in *Issues in U.S.-EC Trade Relations*, Robert Baldwin, Carl Hamilton and Andre Sapir (eds.) Chicago: National Bureau of Economic Research (NBER), pp. 17–58.

70. See supra note 56.

71. See supra note 69, Jackson, GATT disputes inventory research.

72. Ibid.

73. On compliance with ICJ rulings, see Weissberg, 1976, Role of the International Court of Justice in the UN System: The First Quarter-Century, in *The Future of the International Court of Justice*, supra note 33, 137–150, 170–174.

74. See supra note 69, Jackson, GATT disputes inventory research.

75. *Agreement on Interpretation and Application of Articles VI, XVI and XXIII of the General Agreement on Tariffs and Trade*, GATT, BISD 26 Supp. 56 (1980).

76. Agreement was reached on August 5, 1987 (*International Trade Reporter* 4 (1987) 1004), and was implemented on the U.S. side by Proclamation 5712 of 30 September 1987 (*Federal Register* 52 [1987], 36895) and on the EC side by Council Decision 87/402/EEC of 7 August 1987 (OJ [1987] L.275/36). Paragraph 10 of the settlement states that agreement is without prejudice to the position of the parties on the GATT consistency of the original EC measures. The implementation of the settlement of the dispute was also enacted by section 1122 of the Omnibus Trade and Competitiveness Act of 1988, Pub. L.100–418; 102 Stat. 1143.

77. See *U.S. Export Weekly* 18 (1983), 899. See Coccia, "Settlement of Disputes in GATT Under the Subsidies Code: Two Panel Reports on EEC Export Subsidies," *Georgia Journal of International and Comparative Law* 16 (1986), 1.

78. See *U.S. Export Weekly* 19 (1983), 371; *U.S. Import Weekly* 8 (1983), 468. See Coccia, supra note 77, and Garcia Barcero, "Trade Laws, GATT and the Management of Trade Disputes Between the U.S. and EEC," *Yearbook of European Law* 5 (1985), 149.

79. See Brownlie, supra note 18, 495–505.

80. Governments do not have a duty to exercise diplomatic protection. See Charles E. Rousseau, *Droit International Public* (Paris: Dalloz, 10th ed. 1984), 116. Cf. Barcelona Traction, Light, and Power Co., Ltd. (Belgium v. Spain), [1970] L.C.J.

81. Trade Expansion Act of 1962, §252, Pub. L. 87–794, 75 Stat. 879.

82. Fisher and Steinhardt, "Section 301 of the Trade Act of 1974: Protection for U.S. Exporters of Goods, Services, and Capital," *Law and Policy in International Business* 14 (1982), 569; see also Hudec, "Retaliation Against 'Unreasonable' Foreign Trade Practices," supra note 50.

83. The enactment of the 1988 Omnibus Act met with a great deal of criticism from foreign nations, particularly the EC and Japan. The EC protested the passing of the Act at the September GATT Council meeting (*International Trade Reporter* 5 [1988], 1302) and on September 26, 1988, the EC Council of Ministers released a statement expressing "serious concern" over the Act (*European Community News*, No.24/88). Japanese officials also expressed concern over the Act: see "New U.S. Trade Bill Raises Fears in Asia and Europe," *Financial Times*, August 5, 1988, 1 and "Japan Fumes at U.S. Steps in Trade Bill," *Wall Street Journal*, August 9, 1988, 26.

84. Trade Act of 1974 (as amended through 1988), sections 301–306, 19 USCA §§2411–2416 (1980 and Supp 1988). As to application to services, see 19 USCA §2411(e)(1)(A), (1980 and Supp. 1988); as to scope of retaliation, §2411(a)(2)(A) (1980 and Supp. 1988), see also United States v. Star Industries 462 F.2d 557, cert. denied 409 U.S. 1076, 93 S. Ct. 678, 34 L. Ed. 663 (CCPA, 1972).

85. The legislative history of the 1974 Act made it clear that the President was not obliged to refer a section 301 action to the GATT, see Comm. Rpt. No. 93–1298, Senate Finance Committee, 93rd Cong., 2nd sess., 1974, reprinted in *U.S. Code Congressional and Administrative News* 4 (1974), 7186, 7304. However, the Trade Agreements Act of 1979 (§901, 93 Stat. 295, 19 USCA §§2413–2414 (1980 and Supp. 1988]) introduced a new section, section 303, which requires that the USTR refer the matter to international dispute-settlements procedures where applicable. It is clear that the dispute-settlement procedure need not be fully completed (in the GATT case the adoption on the panel report by the Council) before the USTR can recommend action.

86. 19 USCA §2411(e)(3) (1980 and Supp. 1988). See Hansen, "Defining Unreasonableness in International Trade: Section 301 of the Trade Act of 1974," *Yale Law Journal* 96 (1987), 1122.

87. 19 USCA §2411(a)(1)(B)(ii) (1980 and Supp. 1988).

88. Action 301–58. On December 30, 1986, the United States and Canada concluded an agreement under which the Department of Commerce terminated a countervailing duty case after Canada agreed to levy a 15 percent *ad valorem* duty on certain softwood exports to the U.S. (*Federal Register* 52 (1987), 229, 231, and 232). See also Holmer and Hippler Bello "The U.S.–Canada Lumber Agreement: Past as Prologue" *International Lawyer* 21 (1987), 1185; Charles Doran and Timothy Naftali, *U.S.–Canadian Softwood Lumber: Trade Disputes Negotiations* (Washington, D.C.: Foreign Policy Institute, John Hopkins University, FPI Case Study No. 8, 1987).

89. Action 301–48. Petition was filed in 1985 (*Federal Register* 50 [1985], 28866). The action resulted in the Arrangement Between the Government of Japan and the United States of America Concerning Trade in Semiconductor Products, September 2 1986, (reprinted in *International Legal Materials* XXV [1986], 1409). The section 301 action was suspended as a result in 1986 (*Federal Register* 51 [1986], 27811) but certain sanctions for breach of the agreement were imposed in 1987 (*Federal Register* 52 [1987], 13412). These were later partially withdrawn (*Federal Register* 52 [1987], 22693 and 43146).

90. See supra note 60. See also the retaliation on certain electrical products for breach of the semiconductor accord, supra note 89.

91. For legislative history of the original 1974 act, see *U.S. Code Congressional and Administrative News* 4 (1974), 7186.

92. See Fisher and Steinhardt, supra note 82, 577 et seq.

93. See supra note 87. In a Section 301 steel complaint, filed by the American Iron and Steel Institute, for example, USTR decided not to initiate an investigation (*Federal Register* 48 [1983], 8878) because *inter alia*, "the petition fails to present evidence to demonstrate that U.S. benefits under the GATT have been nullified or impaired by reason of the GATT-inconsistent measure." The petition does not include specific information relating to the impact on petitioners and on U.S. commerce arising from the alleged foreign practices.

94. In 1981, the U.S. specialty steel industry filed a Section 301 complaint, alleging that Austria, Belgium, Brazil, France, Italy, Sweden, and the United Kingdom had subsidized their specialty steel industries. The complaint placed the executive in a difficult position because it was not limited to GATT-countervailable subsidies. Therefore an affirmative determination would likely have created an uproar among U.S. trading partners. Following a USTR recommendation to that effect, the President in 1982 suspended the Section 301 proceeding, while requesting the ITC to conduct an expedited Section 201 (safeguards) proceeding (*Federal Register* 47 [1982], 51717). The ITC issued an affirmative finding and in 1983 the president decided to grant relief in the form of tariff increases and quotas (*Federal Register* 48 [1983], 31177).

95. Council Regulation (EEC) 2641/84, OJ [1984] L.252/1.

96. See Eric Stein, Peter Hay, and Michel Waelbroeck, *European Community Law and Institutions in Perspective: Text, Cases and Readings* (Indianapolis: Bobbs-Merrill, 1976, with supplement, 1985), 66 et seq.

97. Article 13 of Regulation 2641/84 supra note 95.

98. M. C. E. J. Bronckers, *Selected Safeguard Measures in Multilateral Trade Relations* (Deventer: Kluwer, 1985), 210. Cf. Bourgeois and Laurent, "Le 'Nouvel Instrument de Politique Commerciale': Un Pas en Avant Vers L'Elimination des Obstacles aux Echanges Internationaux," *Revue Trimestrielle Droit Européen* 21 (1985), 41.

99. There have been two cases formally initiated under the EEC Regulation. The first concerned a case between the Dutch company Akzo and the U.S. company DuPont and concerned aramid fibers (Notice of Initiation, OJ [1986] C.25/2; Commission Decision to refer to GATT, OJ [1987] L11/18). The case is currently before a GATT panel. The second dealt with intellectual property protection in Indonesia, and the result was a change in Indonesian policy with respect to enforcement of intellectual property rights (Notice of Initiation, OJ [1987] C.136/3; Notice of Suspension of Procedure, OJ [1987] L.335/22; and Termination of Procedure Following Undertaking by Indonesian Government, OJ [1988] L.123/51).

100. See Statements of Ambassador Yeutter, S.Hrg. 99–216, Senate Committee on Finance, 99th Cong., 1st sess., 1985,12–89; Statement of Ambassador Yeutter, Com. Ser. 99–96, House Ways and Means Committee, 99th Cong., 2d sess., 1985, 3–40.

101. See Jackson, "Governmental Disputes in International Trade Relations," supra note 10, 8–13.

102. Ibid. 15–16; see Jackson, "MTN and the Legal Institutions of International Trade, MTN Studies," Comm. Print 96–14, 96th Cong., 1st sess., 1979, 17.

103. Article 38, Statute of the International Court of Justice, 59 Stat. 1055, T.S. 993.

104. See supra section 2.4(d).

105. See, for example, the U.S.–Canada Free Trade Agreement, *International Legal Materials* XXVII (1988), 281.

106. The dispute-settlement provisions of the U.S.–Canada Free Trade Agreement (see supra note 105) contains two distinct tracks. The first, found in chapter 18, deals with general problems relating the agreement; the second (chapter 19) deals with more specific problems arising under antidumping or countervailing duty provisions.

These provisions have been seen by some as a potential model for dispute settlement in the Uruguay Round: see, for example, *Congressional Record* 134 (1988), H6626 (statement of Mr. Crane) and H6640 (statement of Mr. Bereuter).

107. See supra note 105, Article 1904. On the U.S. side the implementation of this provision was carried out by section 401(c)(g)(7) of the United States–Canada Free Trade Implementation Act of 1988, Pub. L. 100–449; 102 Stat.

108. John H. Jackson, Jean-Victor Louis, and Mitsuo Matsushita, *Implementing the Tokyo Round* (Ann Arbor: University of Michigan Press, 1984), 208–209.

109. Giorgio Malinverni, *Le Règlement des Différends dans les Organizations Internationales Economiques*, (Leiden: Sijthoff, 1974), 106, quoted in Long, supra note 34, 7.

110. See supra notes 34 and 35. See also Edmond McGovern, *International Trade Regulation* (Exeter: Globefield Press, 2d ed., 1986), 32.

111. GATT, BISD 18 Supp. 149, 158, 166 (1970–1971); 19 Supp. 97 (1972); 20 Supp. 145–209 (1973).

112. See Ministerial Declaration (GATT, BISD 33 Supp. 19; GATT/1396, 25 September 1986), part 1 (e) (i), which states that the negotiations aim to develop understandings and arrangements: to enhance the surveillance in the GATT to enable regular monitoring of trade policies and practices of Contracting Parties and their impact on the functioning of the multilateral trading system. See also Olivier Long, et al., *Public Scrutiny of Protection: A Report on Policy Transparency and Trade Liberalization* (New York: Trade Policy Research Centre, 1987).

113. See GATT, *Review of Developments in the Trading System*, a biannual survey of developments affecting international trade, issued by the GATT Secretariat.

Chapter 5

1. John H. Jackson, *World Trade and the Law of GATT* (Indianapolis: Bobbs-Merrill, 1969), chapter 10.

2. See Jackson, supra note 1, 305–308, 625–638; John H. Jackson and William Davey, *Legal Problems of International Economic Relations* (St. Paul: West, 2d ed., 1986), 366 et seq.

3. See Jackson, supra note 1, chapter 14.

4. Ibid., chapters 15 and 16.

5. Ibid., chapter 25. See also infra chapter 12.

6. Peter Kenen, *The International Economy* (Englewood Cliffs, NJ: Prentice Hall, 1985), 175–177. Charles Kindleberger, *The International Economy* (Homewood, IL: R. D. Irwin, 5th ed., 1973). See also Deardorff A.V. 1987. Safeguards and the Conservative Social Welfare Function. In *Protection and Competition In International Trade*. H. Kierzkowski (ed.) Oxford: Basil Blackwell, pp 22–40.

7. F. W. Taussig, *The Tariff History of the United States* (New York: G. P. Putnam's, 8th ed., 1931).

8. See Kenen, supra note 6, 224–232.

9. Supra chapter 2.5. See also Jackson and Davey, supra note 2, section 6.3.

10. See supra section 2.5.

11. Technical barriers to trade, see infra section 8.5. Government procurement, see infra section 8.6. Subsidies, see chapter 11. Customs valuation, see infra section 5.4. Import licensing, see infra section 5.5. Antidumping, see infra chapter 10. In addition to these treaty agreements, several understandings were developed: Decision on differential and more favorable treatment for developing country, see infra chapter 13. Declaration trade measures taken for BOP purposes, see infra chapter 9.6. Understanding regarding notification, consultation, dispute settlement, and surveillance, see supra chapter 4.3.

12. This concern was crucial among Canada's reasons for negotiating the U.S.–Canada Free Trade Agreement (*International Legal Materials* XXVII (1988), 281).

13. A. V. Deardorff and R. M. Stern, "An Economic Analysis of the Effects of the Tokyo Round of Multilateral Trade Negotiations on the United States and the Other Major Industrialized Countries," Subcomm. on International Trade, Senate Finance Comm., 96th Cong., 1st sess., 1979, III-IV (Comm. Print 96–15). See also Alan V. Deardorff and Robert M. Stern, *The Michigan Model of World Production and Trade: Theory and Application* (Cambridge, Mass: MIT Press, 1985), 54–55.

14. Articles VII-X, GATT, BISD, Vol. IV (1969):

Article VII   Valuation for customs purposes
Article VII   Fees and formalities connected with importation and exportation
Article IX   Marks of origin
Article X   Publication and administration of trade regulations

15. In October, 1982, the French government required all Japanese VCRs to be sent to a nine-person customs depot in Poitiers, where they were checked in minute detail. There was also a French language requirement. The measures aroused criticism inside as well as outside the community. For example, see *Agence Europe*, No. 3052, December 8, 1982, for details of a Commission action against the French restrictions. As to the implications of the dispute, see Hindley, "EC Imports of VCRs From Japan: A Costly Precedent," *Journal of World Trade Law* 20 (1986), 168; David Greenaway and Brian Hindley, *What Britain Pays for Its Voluntary Export Restraints* (London: Trade Policy Research Centre, 1985), chapter 2.

16. The inspections were lifted on April 29, 1983, partly as a result of successful negotiation of a voluntary export restraint between the EC and Japan. See *New York Times*, April 29, 1983, D6. Details of the VER can be found in *Agence Europe*, No. 3733, November 19, 1983 and in Hindley, supra note 15 and Greenaway and Hindley, supra note 15.

17. See generally Jackson, supra note 1, chapter 10; Kenneth Dam, *The GATT: Law and International Economic Organization* (Chicago: University of Chicago Press, 1970), 17; Gerard Curzon, *Multilateral Commercial Diplomacy* (London: Michael Joseph, 1965), 70–123.

18. Reciprocol Trade Agreements Act of 1934, Act of June 12, 1934, 48 Stat. 943, 19 USC §1351. See Jackson and Davey, supra note 2, 145, 294.

19. An *ad valorem* duty is a duty expressed as a percentage of the import price — for example, 34 percent. A specific duty is a duty expressed as a fixed amount per unit, weight or measure; for example, the duty is $0.10 per pound of fish.

20. See Jackson, supra note 1, 203 et seq.

21. This has occurred, for example, in Canada and Japan.

22. See Jackson and Davey, supra note 2, 396.

23. GATT, Article XXVIII details some of the procedures by which these renegotiations occur. See Jackson, supra note 1, 229 et seq.

24. See Jackson, supra note 1, 219 et seq.; J. W. Evans, *The Kennedy Round in American Trade Policy: The Twilight of the GATT?* (Cambridge, Mass.: Harvard University Press, 1970), 221 et seq.

25. See Jackson, supra note 1, 223 et seq; Evans, supra note 24, 140 et seq; Rehm, "The Kennedy Round of Trade Negotiations," *American Journal of International Law* 62 1968), 403. See also *Operation of the Trade Agreements Program, 19th Report*, TC Publication 287 (1967), 167–170.

26. See *Operation of the Trade Agreements Program,* supra note 25, 236 et seq.

27. See Jackson and Davey, supra note 2, 409; Albregts and van der Gevel, 1969, Negotiating Techniques and Issues in the Kennedy Round, in *Economic Relations after the Kennedy Round* Alting von Geusau (ed.) Leiden: Sijthoff, pp. 20–47; Thomas B. Curtis and John R. Vastine, *The Kennedy Round and the Future of American Trade* (New York: Praeger, 1971), 82–91.

28. See Deardorff and Stern, supra note 13. See also Deardorff and Stern, "Economic Effects of the Tokyo Round," *Southern Economic Journal* 49 (1983), 605. They estimate that the coverage tariff rate on industrial products, which was 7.8 percent 1979, will fall to 5.8 percent in 1987 when the Tokyo Round tariff cuts are all implemented.

29. *The Tokyo Round of Multilateral Trade Negotiations, Report of the Director-General of GATT* (Geneva: GATT, 1979), 46–48.

30. *The Tokyo Round of Multilateral Trade Negotiations Supplementary Report of the Director-General of GATT* (Geneva: GATT, 1980), 3–7.

31. See, for example, Article XXXVI:8 of GATT: "The developed contracting parties do not expect reciprocity for commitments made by them in trade negotiations to reduce or remove tariffs and other barriers to the trade of less-developed contracting parties."

32. See supra note 18.

33. Kenen, supra note 6, section 2.2.

34. Ibid.

35. See, for example, U.S. Tariff Commission, *Customs Valuation,* Senate Committee on Finance, 93d Cong., 1st sess., 1973. Reprinted in Jackson and Davey, supra note 2, 383–384.

36. See Trade Act of 1974, Title I, §104, 88 Stat. 1985, 19 USCA §2114 (1980 and Supp. 1988).

37. See Peter Morici and Laura Megna, *U.S. Economic Policies Affecting Industrial Trade: A Quantitative Assessment of Non-Tariff Barriers* (Washington, D.C: NPA, 1983).

38. The so-called "Danforth Bill," S. 2094, 97th Cong., 2d sess., *Congressional Record* 128, (1982) S678. There were, however, numerous other proposals; see Gadbaw, "Reciprocity and Its Implications for U.S. Trade Policy," *Law and Policy in International Business* 14 (1982), 691, 692 n.4.; see also William Cline, *Reciprocity: A New Approach to World Trade Policy?* (Washington, D.C.: Institute for International Economics, Policy Analyses in International Economics, No. 2, 1982); Hay and Sulenko, "U.S. Trade Policy and 'Reciprocity,'" *Journal of World Trade Law* 16 (1982,) 471; Bhagwati and Irwin, "The Return of the Reciprocitarians: U.S. Trade Policy Today," *World Economy* 10 (1987), 109.

39. See Trade and Tariff Act of 1984, Title III, *Barriers to Market Access*, 98 Stat. 3000 et seq., 19 USCA §2111 et seq. (1980 and Supp. 1988).

40. See infra chapter 6.

41. See supra note 37.

42. For useful secondary books on customs law, including classification, see Ruth Sturm, *Customs Law and Administration* (New York: American Importers Association, 3d ed., looseleaf, 1985); David Serko, *Import Practice: Customs Law and International Trade* (New York: Practicing Law Institute, 1985). The court with exclusive primary jurisdiction over customs matters is the Court of International Trade, whose decisions are published in the Federal Supplement. Appeals are to the Court of Appeals for the Federal Circuit, whose decisions are published in *Federal Reporter*, 2d ed.

43. See Jackson, supra note 1, section 10.3.

44. The Brussels Tariff Nomenclature is also known as the Nomenclature for the Classification of Goods in Customs Tariffs and the Customs Cooperation Council Nomenclature. The text is reproduced in Customs Cooperation Council, *Nomenclature for the Classification of Goods in Customs Tariffs* (5th ed., 1976) (supplemented from time to time).

45. The first United States tariff schedule came into being only four months after the Constitution of the United States became effective. The current tariff schedules of the United States became effective on August 31, 1963. See, in general, Jackson and Davey, supra note 2, 371 et seq.

46. The Convention on the Harmonized Commodity and Coding System was approved by the CCC on June 14, 1983, and is to enter into force on acceptance by no less than seventeen states or customs or economic unions, but in no case no *earlier* than January 1, 1987. It was submitted to Congress on June 15, 1987. See also the Geneva (1987) *Protocols relating to the Introduction of the Harmonized Commodity Description and Coding System*, GATT, BISD 34 Supp. 5 (1988).

47. The implementation of the Code was carried out by sections 1201–1217 of the Omnibus Trade and Competitiveness Act of 1988, Pub.L. 100–418; 102 Stat. 1147–1163.

48. See Curzon, supra note 17, 60, note 7.

49. GATT, BISD 28 Supp. 102 (1982). See also Jackson and Davey, supra note 2, 378.

50. A number of GATT waivers have been granted to various countries over the years to facilitate their shift from specific to *ad valorem* tariffs. See Jackson, supra note 1, sections 22.3 and 23.4.

51. An FOB price is the price of the point of shipment for the goods only, while a CIF price is the price for the goods plus an amount covering transportation and insurance to buyer's port. The statutory basis for the United States use of the FOB valuation method is 19 USC §1401a(b)(4)(A), providing that dutiable value excludes any costs, charges, or expenses, or expenses incurred for transportation, insurance, and related services incidental to the international shipment of the merchandise to the United States.

52. See supra note 35.

53. See Jackson and Davey, supra note 2, 380–381.

54. Agreement on Implementation of Article VII of the General Agreement on Tariffs and Trade, GATT BISD, 26 Supp. 116 (1980). See also *Protocol to the Agreement on Implementation of Article VII of the General Agreement on Tariffs and Trade*, GATT BISD, 26 Supp. 151 (1980).

55. Twenty-seven countries (including the European Community as one signatory) have accepted the Code. Spain withdrew in November 1987 as a result of its accession to the EC (GATT L/6212/Add.3). Turkey has signed the Code but has not accepted the Code as of the time of this writing. For detailed information on the signatories, see GATT Doc. L/6453 (1989).

56. See GATT Articles XII, XIII, XIV, and XV.

57. See GATT Article XVIII, and part IV, Articles XXXVI, XXXVII, XXXVIII. Compare the discussion of the safeguards system in chapter 7.

58. See Jackson, supra note 1, 309 et seq.

59. See Jackson supra note 1, section 26.8. See also, for example, Senate Finance Committee, *The Quantitative Restrictions in the Major Trading Countries*, Executive Branch Study No. 6, 93d Cong., 2d sess., 1974.

60. Agreement on Import Licensing Procedures, GATT BISD 26 Supp. 154 (1980).

61. Ibid., Articles 2 and 3.

62. Robert M. Stern, John H. Jackson, and Bernard Hoekmans, *An Assessment of the GATT Codes on Non-Tariff Measures* (Brookfield, VT: Gower/TPRC, 1988).

63. GATT Doc. NTM/W/6/Rev.2 and addenda. The information therein is summarized in "Quantitative Restrictions and Other Non-Tariff Measures," *Report (1984) of the Group on Quantitative Restrictions and Other Non-Tariff Barriers*, GATT BISD 31 Supp. 211 (1985). See also Jackson and Davey, supra note 2, section 6.1(d).

64. UNCTAD, *Non-Tariff Barriers Affecting the Trade of Developing Countries and Transparency in World Trading Conditions: The Inventory of Non-Tariff Barriers* (Geneva: UNCTAD, 1983).

65. Morici and Megna, supra note 37.

66. A. V. Deardorff and R. M. Stern, *Methods of Measurement of Non-Tariff Barriers*, UNCTAD/ST/MD/28 (New York: UN, 1985).

67. For example, French regulations stipulated that French inspectors must inspect the factory of any pharmaceuticals sold in France, but "French inspectors do not travel." See *U.S. Export Weekly* 20 (1984), 953. See also infra section 8.5.

68. For a general overview of the EC Common Agricultural Policy, see Hudson, *The European Community's Common Agricultural Policy in Trade Policy Perspectives: Setting the State for 1985 Agricultural Legislation*, Senate Finance Committee, 98th Cong., 2d sess., 1984 323. On the variable levy, see Edmond McGovern, *International Trade Regulation* (Exeter: Globefield Press, 2d ed., 1986), 456–458.

Chapter 6

1. See, generally, John H. Jackson, *World Trade and the Law of GATT* (Indianapolis: Bobbs-Merrill, 1969), chapter 11; John H. Jackson and William Davey, *Legal Problems of International Economic Relations* (St. Paul: West, 2d ed., 1986), chapter 7; Jackson, "Equality and Discrimination in International Economic Law (XI): The General Agreement on Tariffs and Trade," *Yearbook of World Affairs* 37 (1983), 224; Report of the International Law Commission, "Draft Articles on Most-Favored-Nation Clauses and Commentary," *Yearbook of the International Law Commission*, [1978] (vol. II, pt 2., 8); Gardner Patterson, *Discrimination in International Trade: The Policy Issues, 1945–1965* (Princeton, NJ: Princeton University Press, 1966); Gros Espiell, "The Most-Favored-Nation Clause," *Journal of World Trade Law* 5 (1971), 29; Screnson, "Most-Favored-Nation and Less Favorite Nations," *Foreign Affairs* 52 (1974), 273; Hufbauer, Erb, and Starr, "The GATT Codes and the Unconditional Most-Favored-Nation Principle," *Law and Policy in International Business* 12 (1980), 59.

2. See *The Most-Favored-Nation Provision*, Executive Branch GATT Study No. 9, 93d Cong., 2d sess., 1974, 1.

3. Ibid. Also, Jackson, *World Trade* supra note 1, section 11.1.

4. Ibid.

5. See, for example, "A Convention to Regulate the Commerce Between the Territories of the United States and of His Britannick Majesty," July 3, 1815, Article the Second 8, Stat. 228, Treaty Series 110 (reprinted in Charles Bevans,

Treaties and Other International Agreements of the United States of America, 1776–1949 12 [Washington, D.C: Department of State, 1974], 49.

6. See, for example, Schwarzenberger, "Equality and Discrimination in International Economic Law (I)," *Yearbook of World Affairs* 25 (1971), 163; Verloren van Themaat, supra note 1, chapter 1 (1981). See also Ian Brownlie, *Principles of Public International Law* (Oxford: Clarendon Press, 3d ed., 1979), chapter 23, especially section 4.

7. See infra chapter 12.

8. Cf. section 126 of the Trade Act of 1974, Pub. L. 93–618; 88 Stat. 1978; 19 USCA § 2136 (1980 and Supp. 1988), providing for "reciprocal non-discriminatory treatment." Senate Report No. 93–1298, 93d Cong., 2d Sess., 1974, 94–495, explains the rationale behind these sections. See also Hufbauer, Erb, and Starr, supra note 1.

9. Trade Agreements Act of 1979, Pub. L. 96–39; Title I, section 101, 93 Stat. 151, 19 USCA §1671(b) (1980 and Supp. 1988). See S. Rep. 96–249, Senate Finance Committee, 96th Cong., 1st. Sess., 1979, 45. See also infra section 11.2.

10. See Jackson, "Equality and Discrimination in International Economic Law (XI): The General Agreement on Tariffs and Trade," supra note 1, 225. See also Schieffelin v. United States, 424 F. 2d 1396 (U.S. CCPA, 1970).

11. See cases cited in Jackson and Davey, supra note 1, 450–452.

12. See supra note 2, 2. Cf. John T. Bill Co. v. United States, Court of Customs and Patent Appeals, 104 F. 2d 67, 26 CCPA (Customs) 67 (1939).

13. See Gerard Curzon, *Multilateral Commercial Diplomacy* (London: Michael Joseph, 1965), 67–68, quoting Evans, Director of Commercial Policy of GATT in 1956, from a speech given at the Bologna Center of the School of Advanced International Studies of Johns Hopkins University, February 20, 1956; see also Jackson, supra note 10, 231 et seq. See also supra note 2.

14. If, however, both A and X are GATT members, or for other reasons have granted each other MFN treatment, a legal issue arises, which I discuss in section 6.5.

15. This was an important issue in one of the earliest GATT cases: *German Sardines*, GATT, BISD, 1 Supp. 53–59 (1953). See also GATT, *Analytical Index, Notes on the Drafting, Interpretation and Application of the Articles of the General Agreement* (Geneva: GATT, looseleaf), paragraph I-4 et seq.

16. *Belgian Family Allowances*, GATT, BISD, 1 Supp. 59 (1953).

17. See Jackson and Davey, supra note 1, 378, and *Spanish Coffee*, GATT, BISD 28 Supp. 103 (1982).

18. Kostecki, "Export-restraint Arrangements and Trade Liberalization," *World Economy* 10 (1987), 425, 429.

19. See supra sections 5.3 and 6.2.

20. See Jackson, *World Trade* supra note 1, section 11.5; GATT, Article I:2 and 3 and Annex A-F to the agreement.

21. See infra chapter 7.

22. See infra section 6.5.

23. See supra section 2.4.

24. See supra section 2.4.

25. 1965 United States-Canadian Automotive Products Agreement, 17 UST 1372, TIAS No. 6093, discussed in Jackson and Davey, supra note 1, 467 et seq.; see also Metzger, "The United States–Canadian Automotive Products Agreement of 1965," *Journal of World Trade Law* 1 (1967), 103.

26. The Caribbean Basin Initiative was established under the Caribbean Basin Economic Recovery Act, Pub. L. 98–67; 97 Stat. 384; 19 USC §§ 2701–2706; 19 CFR §§ 10.191–10.198 (1985). Cf. GATT, BISD, 31 Supp. 20 (1985) where GATT CONTRACTING PARTIES granted the U.S. a waiver for the program. See Sawyer and Sprinkle, "Caribbean Basin Economic Recovery Act," *Journal of World Trade Law* 18 (1984), 429; Zagaris, "A Caribbean Perspective of the Caribbean Basin Initiative," *International Law* 18 (1984), 563. See also infra section 12.1.

27. *Differential and More Favorable Treatment, Reciprocity and Fuller Participation of Developing Countries*, GATT, BISD, 26 Supp. 203 (1980). See, generally, Yusuf, "Differential and More Favorable Treatment: The GATT Enabling Clause," *Journal of World Trade Law* 14 (1980), 488; Balassa, "The Tokyo Round and the Developing Countries," *Journal of World Trade Law* 14 (1980), 93. See also chapter 13.

28. See infra chapter 9.

29. See infra section 9.3.

30. See infra section 7.7.

31. See infra section 10.1 and chapter 13.

32. See infra chapters 12 and 13.

33. See infra chapters 12 and 13.

34. In a customs union, customs duties between the parties are eliminated and a common tariff with respect to third countries is adopted by all parties to the union. In a free-trade area, the parties eliminate tariffs between themselves but not do adopt a common external tariff. Free-trade areas are therefore prone to a type of trade diversion by which goods from third countries enter the free trade area at the point of the lowest external tariff and then move duty-free to their ultimate destination within the free-trade area. This can be dealt with by differential and more strict rules of origin.

35. Dam, "Regional Economic Arrangements and the GATT: The Legacy of a Misconception," *University of Chicago Law Review* 30 (1963), 615; Jackson, *World Trade* supra note 1, chapter 9.4.

36. Article XXIV of GATT, particularly XXIV, paragraph 8, which provides that a "customs union" is understood to mean the "substitution of a single customs territory for two or more customs territories, so that . . . duties and other restrictive regulations . . . are eliminated with respect to substantially all the trade between the constituent territories, . . . and, substantially the same duties and other regulations of commerce are applied by each of the members of the union to the trade of territories not included in the union."

With respect to the "free trade area," the definition in paragraph 8 of Article XXIV reads that it shall be understood to mean "a group of two or more customs territories in which the duties and other estrictive regulations of commerce . . . are eliminated on substantially all the trade between the constituent territories in products originating in such territories."

37. See GATT *Analytical Index,* supra note 15, XXIV-51 to 67. See also supra note 35; Edmond McGovern, *International Trade Regulation* (Exeter: Globefield Press, 2d ed., 1986), 262.

38. See supra section 6.1.

39. The preference-giving developed countries will also have special (law) tariff rates for certain products from developing countries. In addition, special rules of origin may apply to certain *products* — for example, textiles (see 19 CFR §§12.130–131 [1985]). See also note, "The 1984 'Country of Origin' Regulations for Textile Imports: Illegal Administrative Action Under Domestic and International Law," *Georgia Journal of International and Comparative Law* 14 (1984), 573.

40. The International Convention on the Simplification and Harmonization of Customs Procedures (signed at Kyoto, May 18, 1973, entered into force September 25, 1974).

41. The Senate gave its advice and consent to the convention on June 21, 1983 (see *Congressional Record* 129 [1983] S8803 and 8814; *U.S. Import Weekly* 8 [1983]), 535). The U.S. instrument of accession was deposited with the Customs Cooperation Council on October 8, 1983, and entered into force for the U.S. on January 28, 1984.

42. See chapter 3 of the U.S.–Canada Free Trade Agreement, *International Legal Materials* 27 (1988), 281. The rules were implemented in the United States by section 202 of the U.S.–Canada Free Trade Agreement Implementation Act of 1988, Pub.L. 100–449; *102 Stat. 1856.* For some statements critical of the rules of origin, see *International Trade Reporter* 4 (1987), 1579 and 5 (1988), 576 and 953.

43. Thus, the EC preferential rules generally focus on whether the four-digit tariff classification number of the product changes, although there are many special exceptions. On EC rules of origin, see Forrester, "EEC Customs Law: Rules of Origin and Preferential Duty Treatment," *European Law Review* 5 (1980), 167 and 257.

44. See Trade Act of 1974, supra note 8, section 503; 19 USCA §2463 (1980 and Supp. 1988); 19 CFR §§10.171–178 (1985).

45. U.S. Department of Commerce, *EEC and EFTA Rules of Origin Governing Preferential Trade* (Overseas Business Reports, OBR 74–04, 1974).

46. See chapter 6.1.

47. GATT *Analytical Index*, supra note 15, VI-25, reports: "In November 1968 . . . the Director-General was asked for a ruling on whether parties to the Agreement had a legal obligation under Article I of the General Agreement to apply the provisions of the anti-dumping code in their trade with all GATT Contracting Parties. The Director-General replied in the affirmative."

48. Action by the Contracting Parties on the Multilateral Trade Negotiations. GATT, BISD 26 Supp. 201 (1980).

49. See supra note 9.

50. See Jackson, *World Trade* supra note 1, 291, and Jackson and Davey, supra note 1, 522.

51. See supra note 9, Title IV, section 401 et seq. See also McGovern (supra note 37, 232), who suggests that the Standards Code merely restates Articles I and III.

52. See GATT Article VI and the *Agreement on Interpretation and Application of Articles VI, XVI and XIII of the General Agreement on Tariffs and Trade* (Article VI, GATT, BISD 26 Supp. 56, 64 [1980]).

53. GATT, BISD 28 Supp. 113 (1982) and GATT L/5062 (1980).

54. Briefing Materials Prepared for Use of the Committee. On the Subject of Foreign Trade and Tariffs, House Ways and Means Committee, 93d Cong., 1st sess., 1973, 189–190.

55. See supra section 6.3.

56. *Canada/United States Agreement on Automotive Products*, GATT, BISD 13 Supp., 112, 119 (1965); *United States–Imports of Automotive Products*, GATT, BISD 14 Supp., 181, 185 (1965). See also Jackson and Davey, supra note 1, section 7.4(B).

57. See supra chapter 3.

58. See supra section 6.3 and infra chapter 13. See McCulloch, "United States Preferences: The Proposed System," *Journal of World Trade Law* 8 (1974), 216, at para. 217. The original U.S. GSP Scheme was authorized by Title V of the 1974 Trade Act and most recently renewed in the Trade and Tariff Act of 1984, Pub. L. 98–573; 98 Stat. 3109; 19 USCA §2462 et seq. (1980 and Supp. 1988).

59. See infra chapter 12.3

60. See supra section 6.5 and infra section 11.2; see also John H. Jackson, Jean-Victor Louis, and Mitsuo Matsushita, *Implementing the Tokyo Round* (Ann Arbor: University of Michigan Press, 1984), 171–72.

61. See, for example, *International Trade Reporter* 2 (1985), 474. NTT purchased equipment from U.S. suppliers (see *International Trade Reporter* 3 [1986], 710). However, this purchase was not then repeated and there was some indication that NTT resumed its "buy Japanese" policy (see *Business Week*, June 13, 1988,

46). See also Curran, T. J., 1982, Politics and High Technology: The NTT Cas, in *Coping with U.S.–Japanese Economic Conflicts*, Destler and Sato (eds.) Lexington, Mass.: Lexington Books, pp.185–241.

62. In 1977, the Trade Facilitation Committee was established with the aim of assisting U.S. firms to gain access to Japanese markets. The bilateral committee was staffed by members of the U.S. Department of Commerce and the Japanese Ministry of International Trade and Industry. In September 1981, a bilateral sub-Cabinet body called the U.S.–Japan Trade Subcommittee was established to monitor and review broad-ranging trade policy issues. There are also numerous other sector-specific groups operating under the general rubric of Market-Oriented Sector Selective (MOSS). These aim to deal with specific industry issues. See also General Accounting Office, *U.S.–Japan Trade/Interim Report on Sector Selective Agreements* (Washington, D.C.: USGPO, 1987).

63. *Japanese Measures on Leather*, GATT, BISD 26 Supp. 320 (1979); see also *U.S Export Weekly* 401 (1982), 768; *U.S. Import Weekly* 8 (1983), 136.

64. S. Hrg. 99–624, Senate Finance Committee, 99th Cong., 1st sess., 1985, 11 and 41–42.

65. Remarks by the President to Business Leaders and Members of the President's Export Council and Advisory Committee for Trade Negotiations (ibid., 18, 20).

66. See *International Trade Reporter* 1 (1984), 625. See also the statements of Treasury Secretary Baker, Department of the Treasury, *Treasury News*, B-1277, 5. See also *International Trade Reporter* 5 (1988), 620.

67. Reciprocal Trade and Investment Act of 1982, amending the Trade Act of 1974, S.2094, 97th Cong., 2d sess., 1982; Reciprocal Trade and Investment Act of 1982, S. Rep. No. 97–483, Senate Finance Committee, 97th Cong., 2d sess., 1982.

68. *Heavyweight Motorcycles and Engines and Power Train Subassemblies Thereof*, 201-TA-47, USITC Pub. 1342 (1983). The president granted temporary import relief (Proclamation 5050, April 15 1983, *Federal Register* 48 [1983], 16639) but this was terminated in 1987 (Proclamation 5727, October 14, 1987, *Federal Register* 52 [1987], 38075).

69. "Tentative Steel Agreement Reached by U.S. Commerce Department and European Community Negotiators," *U.S. Import Weekly* 141 (1982), 620. For a discussion of the 1982 steel cases and the U.S.–EEC Steel Arrangement, see Michael Levine, *Inside International Trade Policy Formulation: A History of the 1982 U.S.–EC Steel Arrangements* (New York. Praeger, 1985); Bonyon and Bourgeois, "The EC–U.S. Steel Arrangement," *Common Market Law Review* 21 (1985), 305; Horlick, "American Trade Law and the Steel Pact Between Brussels and Washington," *World Economy* 6 (1983), 357; Horlick and Savage, "Steel Trade Wars: How Washington Became the Center of U.S. Steel Trade," *World Law* 1 (1984), 5.

70. Caribbean Basin Economic Recovery Act of 1983, Pub. L. 98–67; 97 Stat. 384 (1983); "Democracy and the Path to Economic Growth, Address by Secretary

Schultz," *Department of State Bulletin* 85 (1985), 1; Stokes, "Reagan's Caribbean Basin Initiative on Track but Success Still in Doubt," *National Journal* 17 (1985), 206.

71. *International Trade Reporter* 1 (1984) 540 and 624. See also the U.S.-Israel Free Trade Agreement, signed on April 22, 1985 and entered into force on August 19, 1985 (*International Legal Materials* 24 [1985], 653), implemented in the U.S. by the United States–Israel Free Trade Area Implementation Act of 1985, Pub. L. 99–47; 99 Stat. 82; 19 USC §2112b.

72. See supra note 47. See also William Diebold, *Bilateralism, Multilateralism, and Canada in U.S. Trade Policy* (Cambridge, Mass: Ballinger, 1988). Cf. *Canada Not for Sale: The Case Against Free Trade* (Toronto: General Paperbacks, 1987).

73. See supra note 9, Title XI, section 1104; 93 Stat. 310; 19 USC §2486. See, for example, the discussion of a possible U.S.–Japan FTA, *International Trade Reporter* 5 (1988), 58 and 103. With respect to Mexico, see "Mexico May Seek Series of Trade Pacts with U.S.," *Journal of Commerce*, July 5, 1988, 3a.

Chapter 7

1. See generally John H. Jackson, *World Trade and the Law of GATT* (Indianapolis: Bobbs-Merrill, 1969), 553; Wolff, A., 1983, The Need for New GATT Rules to Govern Safeguard Action, in *Trade Policy in the 1980s*, William Cline (ed.) Washington, D.C.: Institute for International Economics, pp. 363; Merciai, "Safeguard Measures in GATT," *Journal of World Trade Law* 15 (1981), 41.

2. See, in general, John H. Jackson and William Davey, *Legal Problems of International Economic Relations* (St. Paul: West, 2d ed., 1986) chapter 13. See also infra section 9.2.

3. See Jackson and Davey, supra note 2, chapter 9. See also *Report of the Drafting Committee of the Preparatory Committee of the United Nations Conference on Trade and Employment*, Lake Success, New York, E/PC/T/34, March 1947, 29–30; Committee on Finance, United States Senate, 93d Cong., 1st Sess., (1973); *GATT Provisions on Relief from Injurious Imports*, Executive Branch GATT Study No. 8, 93d Cong., 1st. Sess. (1974); Trade Reform Act of 1973, H. Rep. 93–571, House Ways and Means Committee, 93d Cong., 1st sess., 1973; Trade Reform Act of 1974, S. Rep. 93–1298, Senate Finance Committee, 93d Cong., 2d sess., 1974; *United States International Economic Policy in an Interdependent World: Report to the President Submitted by the Commission on International Trade and Investment Policy*, (Washington, D.C.: USGPO, 1971), volume I, 11.

4. See Senate Rep. No. 93–1298, infra note 14.

5. See Robert Lawrence and Robert Litan, *Saving Free Trade: A Pragmatic Approach* (Washington, D.C.: Brookings Institution, 1986), chapter 2.

6. Ibid. See also the 1982 Job Training Partnership Act, intended in part for dislocated workers, Pub. L. 97–300, 96 Stat. 1322.

7. See, for example, Mancur Olsen, *The Rise and Decline of Nations* (New Haven, CT: Yale University Press, 1982). See also Walter, I. Structural Adjustment and Trade Policy in the International Steel Industry. In *Trade Policy for the 1980s*, supra note 1, 483.

8. This argument is invoked by union representatives, such as those for the UAW. See statement of D. Fraser, UAW vice president, Trade Adjustment Assistance the House Committee on Foreign Affairs, 92d Cong., 2d sess. (1972).

9. See infra section 7.6.

10. See Joan Pearce and John Sutton, *Protection and Industrial Policy in Europe* (Boston: RIIA/Routledge and Kegan Paul, 1985); Alexis Jacquemin (ed.), *European Industry: Public Policy and Corporate Strategy* (Oxford: Clarendon Press, 1984). The literature on industrial policy in general is extensive, but the reader may be interested in William Diebold, *Industrial Policy as an International Issue* (New York: McGraw-Hill, 1980); John Zysman, *Governments, Markets and Growth* (Ithaca, NY: Cornell University Press, 1983); Ezra Vogel, *Japan as No. 1 — Lessons for America* (Cambridge, Mass.: Harvard University Press, 1979).

11. Note the structure of the 1974 Trade Act, infra note 14, where Title II deals with "fair trade" and Title III deals with "unfair trade." See sections 201, 301, 341 (88 Stat. 2011, 2041, 2053). See also infra chapter 10.1.

12. See Jackson and Davey, supra note 2, 648–650. See also infra section 10.1.

13. It is possible that the steel section 301 petition in 1983 may have been brought partly for this reason, although in the end the executive branch referred the case to the International Trade Commission under the escape clause provisions (see infra section 10.1, fn. 3.). See *Twenty-Sixth Annual Report of the President of the United States on the Trade Agreements Program, 1981–82*, 196.

14. Trade Act of 1974, Title IV, Section 406, Pub. L. No. 93–618, 88 Stat. 2062 (1975); Trade Reform Act of 1973, S. Rep. 93–1298, Senate Finance Committee, 93d Cong., 2d Sess., 1974, 210–213, reprinted in *U.S. Code Congressional and Adminstrative News* 4 (1974), 7186.

15. See infra chapters 10 and 11.

16. Amended Tariff Act of 1930: Reciprocal Trade Agreements, H. Rep. No. 73–1000, House Ways and Means Committee, 13–14 (1934).

17. Reciprocal Trade Agreement with Mexico, Dec. 23, 1942, Art. XI, 57 Stat. 833 (1943); E.A.S. No. 311 (effective Jan. 30, 1943); Hearings on the Extension of the Reciprocal Trade Act House Ways and Means Committee, 79th Cong., 1st sess., 1945, 277, 280. See Jackson, supra note 1, 663 et seq.

18. See Jackson, supra note 1, *World Trade*, chapters 2 and 23; William Diebold, *The End of the ITO*. (Princeton, NJ: Princeton University, 1952).

19. See Executive Order 9832 of February 25, 1947, 3 CFR §634 (1947). See also Trade Agreements Extension Act of 1951, ch. 141; 65 Stat. 74. For a general

history of the U.S. escape clause, see Jackson, supra note 1, 553–555, and Jackson and Davey, supra note 2, 541 et seq.

20. Ibid., 541.

21. See Jackson, supra note 1, chapter 23. See also Jackson and Davey, supra note 2, section 23.2.

22. *Avoidance of Market Disruption*, GATT, BISD, 9 Supp. 26–28 (1961).

23. The U.S. escape clause is contained in section 201 of the Trade Act of 1974, supra note 14, as amended by the Trade Agreements of 1979, Pub. L. No. 96–39, §§ 106(b)(3), 1106(a)(1)-(7), 93 Stat. 193, 312; and the Trade and Tariff Act of 1984, Pub. L. No. 98–573, §§ 248(a), 249, 98 Stat. 2998 codified in 19 USCA § 2251 (1980 and Supp. 1988). The main EEC escape clause is Council Regulation (EEC) 288/82, OJ (1982) L.35/1.

24. The only change in the language of the escape clause in GATT, Article XIX, was as follows: (1) In paragraph 1(a), "relatively" had been inserted between "such" and "increased" in the Havana Charter, but it was not included in GATT Article XIX; and (2) In the ninth session, "obligations or concessions" was substituted for "concessions or other obligations" in paragraph 3. GATT, *Analytical Index, Notes on the Drafting Interpretation and Application of the Articles of the General Agreement* (Geneva: GATT, 3d revision, 1970), 106.

25. The text of Article XIX: 1(a) reads: "If, as a result of unforeseen developments and of the obligations incurred by a contracting party under this agreement, including tariff concessions, any product is being imported into the territory of that contracting party in such increased quantities and under such conditions as to cause or threaten serious injury to domestic producers in that territory of like or directly competitive products, the contracting party shall be free, in respect of such product, and to the extent and for such time as may be necessary to prevent or remedy such injury, to suspend the obligation in whole or in part or to withdraw or modify the concession." GATT, BISD, Vol. IV, Article XIX, 1(a) (1969).

26. See infra chapters 10 and 11.

27. In contrast to U.S. administrative and judicial practice, there are very few interpretations of Article XIX in the GATT documentation. The only dispute panel reports regarding Article XIX included the following:

Hatters' Fur (Czechoslovakia–U.S., 1951);
Dried Figs (Greece–U.S., 1952);
Clothespins (Denmark–U.S., 1957);
Poultry (U.S.–EEC, 1963),
Beef (Australia–Japan, 1974);
Textiles (Hong Kong–Norway, 1978); and
Fish (Canada–Spain, 1981).

Other interpretations have resulted from references to the Havana Conference, and occasionally from certain GATT actions. See GATT, *Analytical Index*, supra note 24.

28. This is especially true of the 1980 U.S. escape clause concerning automobiles. See *Certain Motor Vehicles and Certain Chassis and Bodies Thereof* (TA-201-44), USITC Pub. No. 1110 (1980).

29. The 1974 Trade Act speaks of factors which must be considered, but is worded so as not to confine the ITC attention to the factors listed. The legislative history notes that "it is not intended that a mathematical test be applied by the Commission." S. Rep. No. 93–1298, supra note 14, 120. See also Adams and Dirlam, "Import Competition and the Trade Act of 1974: A Case Study of Section 201 and Its Interpretation by the International Trade Commission," *Indiana Law Journal* 52 (1977), 535, 539–540.

30. See supra note 28. However, the attempt by the American automobile industry to obtain protection from import competition did not end with the negative ITC determination. Legislation introduced in the U.S. Congress to authorize a VRA in the automobile sector and to impose quotas on automobile imports from Japan was not pushed after an exchange of letters between U.S. Attorney General Smith and Japanese Ambassador Okawara, whereby the Japanese government agreed to unilaterally restrain the export of cars to the U.S. (see infra notes 98 and 100). See Jackson and Davey, supra note 2, 573–584, 619–622. See also David Tarr and Morris Morkre, *Aggregate Costs to the United States of Tariff Cuts and Removal of Quotas on Imports: General Tariff Cuts and Removal of Quotas on Automobiles, Steel, Sugar and Textiles* (Washington, D.C.: Federal Trade Commission, 1984).

31. See supra chapter 3.

32. One of the significant issues in the drafting of the Trade Act of 1974 was how much discretion to give the president to depart from the findings or recommendations of the ITC. The 1974 Act tried to achieve a balance between those who wanted more and those who wanted no presidential discretion. Thus, the president was given the right to decline to order relief "in the national economic interest." However, section 203 established a legislative veto in order to check (override) the presidential decision. After the Chadha case, Congress replaced the veto with a provision that enables Congress to override the president (two-thirds of the votes of each house required) and cause the recommendation of the ITC to come into effect by adopting a joint resolution to that effect. See Jackson and Davey, supra note 2, section 9.3.

33. Information concerning such actions can be obtained from the ITC *Annual Report* and from the annual report, *Operation of the Trade Agreements Program*, also issued by the ITC.

34. *Carbon and Certain Steel Alloy Products* (TA-201-51), USITC Pub. No. 1533 (1984). The petition was brought by the United Steelworkers of America, AFL–CIO, and Bethlehem Steel Corp. on January 24, 1984. On June 12, 1984, the ITC (by a 3 to 2 decision) voted that the domestic steel industry was injured with respect to plates, sheets and strip, wire and wire products, structural shapes and units, ingots, blooms, billets, slabs, sheet, and sheet bars. They also found that the domestic industry was *not* injured with respect to wire-rods, railway-type

products, bars, pipes and tubes and blanks thereof. On July 11, 1984, the ITC recommended to the president that quotas be imposed for over a five-year period. The president rejected the proposed form of relief, and instead directed USTR Brock to negotiate VRAs with foreign governments.

35. "Steel Import Relief: Memorandum from the President, September 18, 1984," *Weekly Compilation of Presidential Documents* 20 (1984), 1307.

36. GATT, *Analytical Index*, supra note 24, XIX-27.

37. See infra section 7.7.

38. See infra section 7.7. See also the articles by Jackson, Kostecki, and Petersmann, infra note 96.

39. For details of the U.S. law resulting from administrative and court opinions on these subjects, see in particular *International Trade Reporter Decisions* (BNA, biweekly), which contains both the ITC and CIT administrative decisions. With respect to section 201, see section 58 in the Classification Guide.

40. See supra note 25 for the text of Article XIX: 1(a).

41. See supra note 39. Regarding product definition, see 58.07. Regarding limitations on relief, see 58.121.

42. See *Report on the Withdrawal by the United States of a Tariff Concession Under Article XIX of the GATT (the Hatter's Fur Case)* (Geneva, GATT/151-3, 1951); Jackson, supra note 1, 560; Jackson and Davey, supra note 2, 556.

43. Jackson, supra note 1, 563.

44. Ibid., 201–211.

45. See supra note 14. See also Jackson and Davey, supra note 2, 541–547, 559–560.

46. *Modifications to the General Agreement*, Working Party Report, GATT BISD, Vol. II, 39, 44–45 (1952); Jackson, supra note 1, 557–559; Jackson and Davey, supra note 2, 551–552; GATT, *Analytical Index*, supra note 24, 3d revision, 1970, 106.

47. The Omnibus Trade and Competitiveness Act of 1988, Pub. L. 100–418, Title I, Subtitle D, Part 1, 102 Stat. 1225–1241; H. Rpt. 100–40, Pt. 1, House Ways and Means Committee, 100th. Cong., 1st sess., 1987; S. Hrg. 100–419, Pt. 1, Senate Finance Committee, 100th Cong., 1st sess., 1987. See also *Proposals to Reform the Escape Clause*, S. Hrg. 99–898, Senate Finance Committee, 99th Cong., 2d sess., 1986. For a brief commentary, see Holmer and Bello, "The 1988 Trade Bill: Is it Protectionist?" *International Trade Reporter* 5 (1988), 1347, 1350–1.

48. See *United States International Economic Policy in an Interdependent World*, supra note 3, volume I, 49. See also *Administration Analysis of the Proposed Trade Reform Act of 1973*, House Ways and Means Committee, 93d Cong., 1st sess., 1973; *Press Release and Other Materials Relating to the Administration Proposal Entitled the "Trade Reform Act of 1973," Including the Message of the President, Text, Summary, and Section-by-Section Analysis of the Proposed Bill*, HR 6767, 70–72 (1973); Jackson and Davey, supra note 2, 541–547.

49. See supra note 14, section 201(b)(1), (4), 19 USC §2551(b)(1), (4). See, for example, *Certain Motor Vehicles* (TA-201-44), USITC Pub. No. 1110 (1980); *Heavyweight Motorcycles* (TA-201-47), USITC Pub. No. 1342 (1983); *Non-Rubber Footwear* (TA-201-50), USITC Pub. No. 1545 (1984); *Non-Rubber Footwear,* (TA-201-55), USITC Pub. No. 1717 (1985).

50. See *Certain Motor Vehicles* and *Heavyweight Motorcycles,* supra note 49.

51. Jackson, supra note 1, 566–567; Jackson and Davey, supra note 2, 541–547.

52. Other injury tests in United States law include: the "market disruption" phase in the Trade Act of 1974, supra note 14, Title IV, Section 406(e)(2); the original provision for trade adjustment assistance, "contributed importantly," in the Trade Act of 1974, supra note 14, Title II, Section 222; and the provisions of Section 337 which use, "to destroy or substantially injure an industry," supra note 14, Title III, Section 341(a). See also the "material injury" standard in antidumping and countervailing duty proceedings, infra chapters 10 and 11.

53. See supra note 14, Title II, Section 201(a)(2)(A), which mentions the significant idling of productive facilities in the industry, the inability of a significant number of firms to operate at a reasonable level of profit, and significant unemployment or underemployment within the industry. This list is not exhaustive.

54. See generally Jackson, supra note 1, chapter 23; Jackson and Davey, supra note 2, section 9.3.

55. See supra note 25 for the full text of GATT Article XIX(1)(a).

56. See Jackson, supra note 1, section 10.6; Jackson and Davey, supra note 2, 405 et seq.

57. See infra chapter 7.5.

58. See *Norwegian Restrictions on Hong Kong Textile Imports,* GATT, BISD, 27 Supp., 119, 125 (1981). For United States escape-clause cases where quotas were imposed, see *Clothespins,* (TA-201-36), USITC Pub. No. 933 (1978); "Clothespins Imports," Proclamation 4640, *Weekly Compilation of Presidential Documents* 15 (1979), 325; *Heavyweight Motorcycles* supra note 49; "Imports of Heavyweight Motorcycles," Proclamation 5050, *Weekly Compilation of Presidential Documents* 19 (1983), 550; *Stainless Steel and Alloy Tool Steel* (TA-201-48), USITC Pub. No. 1377 (1983); "Imports of Specialty Steel," Proclamation 5074, *Weekly Compilation of Presidential Documents* 19 (1983), 1023.

59. See supra note 14, section 203.

60. See supra note 47, Title I, Subtitle D, Part 3.

61. Charles P. Kindleberger, *International Economics* (Homewood, Ill: Irwin, 5th ed., 1973), 107–110, 122–123; Bronckers, "The Non-Discriminatory Application of Article XIX GATT: Tradition or Fiction?", *Legal Issues of European Integration,* (1981/2), 39; Bronckers, "Reconsidering the Non-Discrimination Principle as Applied to GATT Safeguard Measures: A Rejoinder," *Legal Issues of European*

Integration (1983/2), 114. See generally Bo Sodersten, *International Economics* (New York: St. Martin's Press, 2d ed., 1980).

62. GATT, *Analytical Index*, supra note 24, 3d revision, 1970, 107. In 1983, Brian Hindley ("Voluntary Export Restraints and the GATT's Main Escape Clause," *World Economy* 3 [1980], 313, n. 25) pointed out that a West German restriction under Article XIX was still in force even though it was begun in 1958.

63. See supra note 14, section 203(h)(1).

64. See Jackson, supra note 1, 565–566; Jackson and Davey, supra note 2, 606–607.

65. See infra section 7.8 and OECD, *Policy Perspective for International Trade and Economic Relations* (Paris: OECD, 1972) 81–84 (the "Rey" Report).

66. Supra note 23, section 123. See also M. C. E. J. Bronckers, *Selective Safeguard Measures in Multilateral Trade Relations* (Boston: Kluwer, 1985), chapter 3. See also *U.S. Import Weekly* 9 (1983), 305.

67. See Trade Expansion Act of 1962, and other negotiating authorities. See supra section 5.2.

68. See supra note 14. See also Jackson and Davey, supra note 2, 607–608.

69. See supra chapters 1 and 3.

70. See *Article XIX — Action by the United States — Specialty Steel — Extension of Time-Limit* (as to Austria, Korea, Brazil, Sweden, and Japan), GATT L/5524/Adds. 44–49 (1985); *Article XIX — Action by Canada — Footwear, other than Footwear of Rubber or Canvas*, GATT L/4611/Add. 50 (1985). See also GATT *Analytical Index*, supra note 24.

71. *Fair Practices in Automotive Products Act of 1982*, H. R. 5133, 97th Cong., 2d sess., 1982; *Fair Practices in Automotive Products Act*, H. R. Rep. 97–842 Committee on Energy and Commerce, House of Representatives, 97th Cong., 2d sess., 1982.

72. See Bronckers, supra note 66; Bronckers, "The Non-Discriminatory Application of Article XIX GATT: Tradition or Fiction?", supra note 61; Koulen, "The Non-Discriminatory Application of GATT Article XIX(1): A Reply," *Legal Issues of European Integration*, (1983/2), 89; Bronckers, "Reconsidering the Non-Discrimination Principle as Applied to GATT Safeguard Measures: A Rejoinder," supra note 61; cf. Petersmann, "Economic, Legal and Political Functions of the Principle of Non-Discrimination," *World Economy* 9 (1986), 113. See also Corbet, "Reform of the GATT Provision for Emergency Protection," *EFTA Bulletin* 27 (1986), 1; Wolff, supra note 1; Kumer, "Critical Issues in the Talks on Emergency Protection," *World Economy* 5 (1982), 241; Merciai, supra note 1; Tumlir, "A Revised Safeguard Clause for GATT," *Journal of World Trade Law* 7 (1973), 404.

73. Section 1102 of the Trade Act of 1974, supra note 14 authorized the president to sell import licenses at public auction. This applied *inter alia* to the section 201 procedures. Section 1401 of the Omnibus Trade and Competitivness Act of 1988, supra note 47 amends section 203 to include at section 203(a)(3)(F) the optional

auction of quotas as an explicit presidential remedy. For the arguments for the use of such auctions, see C. Fred Bergsten, K. Elliott, J. Schott, and W. Takacs, *Auction Quotas and U.S. Trade Policy*, Policy Analyses in International Economics No. 19 (Washington, D.C.: Institute for International Economics, 1987). Cf. Palmeter "Turkeys Masquerade as Peacocks," *Journal of Commerce* (June 10, 1988). See also Deardorff, A. V., 1987. Safeguards Policy and Conservative Social Welfare Function. In *Protection and Competition in International Trade*, H. Kierzkowski (ed). Oxford: Basil Blackwell, pp. 22–40.

74. See *Heavyweight Motorcycles and Engines and Power Train Subassemblies Thereof*, supra note 49; "Imports of Heavyweight Motorcycles," supra note 58; Bronckers, "Reconsidering the Non-Discrimination Principle As Applied to GATT Safeguard Measures: A Rejoinder," supra note 61, 117–120; Bronckers, supra note 66.

75. Of course, the problem of distinguishing "fair" and "unfair" trade, discussed supra chapter 7.1, is part of this question. See also infra section 10.1.

76. See articles, supra note 72, in particular the debate between Bronckers and Koulen, published in *Legal Issues of European Integration*, [1983/2].

77. Havana (ITO) Charter, Interpretative Note, ad art. 40, at 65. See Jackson, supra note 1, 564, fn. 6.

78. GATT L/76 (1953); Bronckers, "Reconsidering the Non-Discrimination Principle As Applied to GATT Safeguard Measures," supra note 61, 114–117.

79. See supra note 72. Regarding the concerns of the developing countries, see *The Tokyo Round of Multilateral Trade Negotiations: Report of the Director-General of GATT* (Geneva: GATT, 1979), 90–95; *The Tokyo Round of Multilateral Trade Negotiations: Supplementary Report of the Director-General of GATT* (Geneva: GATT, 1980), 14–15. See also Gilbert Winham, *International Trade and the Tokyo Round Negotiation* (Princeton, NJ: Princeton University Press, 1985), 243–247.

80. Bronckers, "Reconsidering the Non-Discrimination Principle As Applied to GATT Safeguard Measures," supra note 61, 130.

81. See supra note 74; *Artificial Fibers from the United States*, Commission Regulation (EEC) 388/80, OJ [1980] L45/5; Commission Regulation (EEC) 388/80, OJ [1980] L45/7; *Norwegian Restrictions on Hong Kong Textiles Imports*, GATT, BISD, 27 Supp. 119 (1981). See also Commission Regulation (EEC) 539/83, OJ [1983] L63/15 (EEC restricted imports of certain textile products from Turkey, based on bilateral preferential agreement).

82. For example, in 1977, the United Kingdom introduced an annual quota on the import of portable television sets from South Korea (see GATT L/4613 [1977]). According to the GATT Secretariat at the time, "this case is the only one in the history of the GATT in which Article XIX action has unilaterally been taken on a discriminatory basis with regard to a simple source of supply in a fully transparent manner." (GATT L/4679, 10 et seq [1978])

83. See *Norwegian Restrictions on Hong Kong Textile Imports*, GATT, BISD, 27 Supp. 119, 125 (1981). Note that the panel report was adopted by the Contracting Parties "in principle." See GATT, C/M/141, 11 (1980). This could cast some moderate doubt on the binding character of the panel report. See also Bronckers, supra note 66.

84. See *Twenty-Eighth Annual Report of the President of the United States on the Trade Agreements Program, 1984–5* (Washington, D.C.: Office of the USTR, 1986), 50–51.

85. Louis Henkin et al., *International Law* (St. Paul: West, 1st ed., 1982), 64–66; Ian Brownlie, *Principles of Public International Law* (Oxford: Clarendon Press, 1979), 8–12.

86. See Bronckers, supra note 66, chapter 3. Cf. Petersmann, supra note 72.

87. Grey, R., 1979. A Canadian Comment on the Tokyo Round. In *Aides et Mesures de Sauveguarde en Droit International Economique* Seminaire de la Commission Droit et Vie des Affaires de l'Université de Liège, Paris: Feduci Editions du Moniteur, pp. 286–287.

88. See supra Section 7.1.

89. See generally Gary C. Hufbauer and Howard F. Rosen, *Trade Policies for Troubled Industries* (Washington, D.C.: Institute for International Economics, Policy Studies in International Economics No. 15, 1986); see also Lawrence and Litan, supra note 5; Richardson, Worker Adjustment to U.S. International Trade, 1983, in *Trade Policy in the 1980s* Cline (ed.) Washington, D.C. Institute for International Economics, pp. 393–424; *United States International Economic Policy in an Interdependent World* supra note 3, 47–49, and Stanley Metzger, vol. I, 319; Bratt, "Issues in Worker Certification and Questions of Future Direction in the Trade Adjustment Assistance Program," *Law and Policy in International Business* 14 (1982), 819; Bratt, "Assisting the Economic Recovery of Import-Injured Firms," *Law and Policy in International Business* 6 (1974), 1; Jackson and Davey, supra note 2, 623–627; Jacques Steenbergen, Guido de Clerq, and René Foque, *Change and Adjustment: External Relations and Industrial Policy of the European Community*, (Deventer: Kluwer, 1983).

90. See Richardson, "Worker Adjustment" supra note 89.

91. The working party was set up by the GATT Council (GATT, C/M/144, 21 (1980)) as a result of the Report of the Consultative Group of Eighteen. The Working Party Report (L/5120 [1981]) was presented in 1981.

92. *Ministerial Declaration of 29 November 1982*, GATT, BISD 29 Supp. 9, 41 (1983).

93. Working Party on Structural Adjustment and Trade Policy, *Report to the Council*, GATT L/5568 (1983); Council of Representatives, *Report on Work Since the Thirty-Ninth Session — Addendum*, GATT L/5734/Add. 1, 21–24 (1984).

94. See John Williamson (ed.), *IMF Conditionality* (Washington, D.C.: Institute for International Economics, 1983).

95. See supra note 47.

96. See generally Reinhard Quick, *Exportselbstbeschraenkungen und Artikel XIX GATT* (Cologne: Carl Hegmans Verlag, 1983); Hindley, supra note 66; Bronckers, "Private Response to Foreign Unfair Trade Practices: U.S. and EEC Complaint Procedures," *Northwestern Journal of International Law and Business* 6 (1985), text accompanying notes, 168–184. See also Petersmann, "Gray Area Measures and the Rule of Law," *Journal of World Trade* 22/2 (1988), 23; Kostecki, "Export Restraint Arrangements and Trade Liberalization," *World Economy* 10 (1987), 425; Jackson, "The GATT Consistency of Export Restraint Arrangements," *World Economy* 11 (1988), 485.

97. See Jan Tumlir, *Protectionism: Trade Policies in Democratic Societies* (Washington, D.C.: American Enterprise Institute, 1985), chapter 3, esp. 39–55; Consumers Union v. Kissinger, 506 F. 2d 136, 146–152 (1974), cert. denied, 421 U.S. 1004 (1975); *Safeguards*, Chairman's Report, GATT, BISD, 30 Supp. 216, 217–218 (1983); *Committee on Safeguards: Minutes of Meeting of 2 April 1982*, GATT Doc. L/5310 (1982).

98. See Jackson and Davey, supra note 2, 617–622. See also Davidow, "Cartels, Competition Laws and the Regulation of International Trade," *New York University Journal of International Law and Politics* 15 (1983), 351, 366–375.

99. Trade and Tariff Act of 1984, Title VII, section 805, Pub. L. No. 98–573, 98 Stat. 2948, 3045 (1984); Steel Import Stabilization Act, H.R. Rep. No. 98–1089, House Ways and Means Committee, 98th Cong., 2d sess., 1984; Trade Act of 1974, supra note 14, Title II, section 201. See also section 607 of the Trade Act of 1974, supra note 14, which contains a congressional grant of immunity from antitrust laws with respect to voluntary arrangements of steel.

100. See the exchange of letters, supra note 98. See also Applebaum, 1983, The Antitrust Implications of Trade Law Proceedings, in *The Trade Agreements Act of 1979: Four Years Later*, New York: Practising Law Institute, pp. 33; OECD, *Competition and Trade Policies: Their Interaction* (Paris, OECD, 1984).

101. See exchange of letters, supra note 98; Consumers Union v. Kissinger, 506 F. 2d 136, 146–152 (1974), cert. denied, 421 U.S. 1004 (1975). See also Wallace, "Redefining the Foreign Compulsion Defence in U.S. Antitrust Law: The Japanese Auto Restraints and Beyond," *Law and Policy in International Business* 14 (1982), 742; Matsushita and Repeta, "Restricting the Supply of Japanese Automobiles: Sovereign Compulsion or Sovereign Collusion?" *Case Western Reserve Journal of International Law*, 14 (1982), 47.

102. See supra note 14, Title II, section 203. This authority was used in "Specialty Steel," Presidential Proclamation No. 4445, *Federal Register* 41 (1976), 24101; "Nonrubber Footwear," Presidential Proclamation No. 4510, *Federal Register* 42 (1979), 32430; and "Color Television Receivers and Assemblies," Presidential Proclamation No. 4511, *Federal Register* 42 (1977), 32747.

103. Agricultural Act of 1956, Pub. L. No. 540, 70 Stat. 188 (1956).

104. GATT Article XI, BISD, Vol. IV (1969). For a discussion of Article XI, see Jackson, supra note 1, chapter 13; Jackson and Davey, supra note 2, chapter 6.4.

105. American Iron and Steel section 301 complaint, *Federal Register* 41 (1976), 45628; Discontinuance of Investigation, *Federal Register* 43 (1978), 3962.

106. See also the 1982 American Iron and Steel Institute's section 301 complaint. In that case, the USTR decided not to initiate an investigation. See *Federal Register* 48 (1983), 8878. The 1982 case is discussed in Bronckers, supra note 66, 195 et seq.

107. Concerning the economics of voluntary restraint agreements, see "Economic Effects of Export Restraints" USITC Pub. No 1256 (1982); Hamilton, C., 1985, Economic Aspects of Voluntary Export Restraints, in *Current Issues in International Trade*, Brian Greenaway (ed.) London: St. Martin's Press, pp. 99–117; Hindley, supra note 62; Comptroller General of the United States, *Economic and Foreign Policy Effects of Voluntary Restraint Agreements on Textiles and Steel* (Washington, D.C.: GAO B-179342, 1974); W. Max Corden, *Trade Policy and Economic Welfare* (Oxford: Clarendon Press, 1974), 186–187; Tarr and Morkre, supra note 30.

108. The Short-Term Arrangement (1961–2) and the Long-Term Arrangement (1962–1973) were the first attempts to deal with textiles. For an overview of the problem, see Henry R. Zheng, *Legal Structure of International Textile Trade* (Westport, CT: Quorum Books, 1988), chapter 1; William R. Cline, *The Future of World Trade in Textiles and Apparel*, (Washington, D.C.: Institute for International Economics, 1987); Vinod K. Aggarwal, *Liberal Protectionism: The International Politics of Organized Textile Trade* (Berkeley: University of California Press, 1985); David B. Yoffie, *Power and Protectionism* (New York: Columbia University Press, 1983), chapters 2, 3, and 4. See also symposium, "Perspectives on Textiles," *Law and Policy in International Business* 19 (1987), 1–271.

109. *GATT Textiles and Clothing in the World Economy* (Geneva: GATT, 1984). See also *GATT A Study on Cotton Textiles* (Geneva: GATT, 1966).

110. *Arrangement Regarding International Trade in Textiles* (MFA), GATT, BISD, 21 Supp. 3 (1975); 25 UST 1001; TIAS 7840. Regarding the protocols extending the MFA, see *MFA II*, GATT BISD, 24 Supp. 5 (1978); *MFA III*, GATT, BISD 28 Supp. 3 (1982); and *MFA IV*, GATT, BISD 33 Supp. 7 (1987). See also Zheng, supra note 108, 8.

111. The speech was reported in the *New York Times*, September 3, 1960, 1 and 38. After his election, President Kennedy then issued a formal plan for textiles: see *New York Times*, May 3, 1961, 1.

112. However, the GATT report, supra note 109, paragraphs 1.6 to 1.8, notes that this argument only holds good as long as the production of textiles is dependent upon abundant low-skilled labor. The increased levels of automation in the textile industry have possibly moved the comparative advantage back to industrialized, developed countries. This conclusion seems to be partially supported

by Ambassador Yeutter in a article in the *Washington Post*, August 5, 1987, reprinted in *Congressional Record* 134 (1988), S11134.

113. See GATT, *Status of Legal Instruments*, (Geneva: GATT, looseleaf, 1988), chapter 12–7.2.

114. Cline, supra note 108, 158, 167, and 15.

115. See the comments of John H. Jackson, *International Trade Reporter* 2 (1985), 383, 384. Michael K. Levine in *Inside International Trade Policy Formulation* (New York: Praeger, 1986) at page 46 also notes that certain elements of the 1982 U.S.–EC Steel Arrangements seemed to be lifted from the MFA.

116. *Declaration of Ministers*, GATT, BISD 20 Supp. 19, 21 (1973).

117. See *Report of the Director-General of GATT*, supra note 79, 90–95; *Supplementary Report of the Director-General of GATT*, supra note 79, 14–17 and Annex C. See also L. A. Glick, *Multilateral Trade Negotiations: World Trade After the Tokyo Round* (Totowa, NJ: Rowman and Allenheld, 1984), 112–126, 152, 157 and Appendix III; Winham, supra note 79, 123–125, 197–200, 240–247, 278–279.

118. *GATT Ministerial Declaration of 29 November 1982*, GATT, BISD 29 Supp. 12–13 (1982).

119. The Ministerial Declaration called for an understanding to be drawn up by the Council for adoption by the contracting parties not later than their 1983 session. This deadline was not met. Instead, a chairman's report of the 1983 session noted that "in spite of the progress made [a text] has not proved possible at this stage . . ." See *Chairman's Report on Safeguards*, GATT, BISD, 30 Supp. 216, 220 (1983). For further developments, see GATT L/5310 (1982); GATT C/W/437/Rev. 1, 20 (1984); GATT C/W/448/Rev. 1, 35 (1984). See also *Ministerial Declaration*, (GATT, BISD 33 Supp. 19, 24–25 (1987); GATT/1396, 25 September 1986) and *Decision of 28 January 1987* (GATT, BISD 33 Supp. 31, 42 (1987).

120. An analogy can be drawn from the technique of "side-codes," developed in the Tokyo Round negotiations. See Jackson, "The Birth of the GATT-MTN System: A Constitutional Appraisal," *Law and Policy in International Business* 12 (1983), 21; John H. Jackson, Jean-Victor Louis, and Mitsuo Matsushita, *Implementing the Tokyo Round* (Ann Arbor: University of Michigan Press, 1984).

121. See supra note 65.

122. The GATT Secretariat has already assumed some responsibility to report on measures in international trade: see *Developments in the Trading System*, supra note 111. Additionally, each country has assumed the obligation to report trade measures it has taken: see *Understanding Regarding Notification, Consultation, Dispute Settlement and Surveillance*, GATT, BISD 26 Supp. 210 (1979); *Notification and Surveillance*, GATT, BISD 27 Supp. 20 (1980); Notification and Surveillance, GATT C/W/361 (1981); *Improvement of Notification Procedure*, GATT C/W/446 (1984). See also Olivier Long et al. *Public Scrutiny of Protection* (London: Trade Policy Research Centre, 1987).

Chapter 8

1. Article III GATT, BISD, Vol. IV (1969). See, e.g., John H. Jackson, *World Trade and the Law of GATT*, (Indianapolis: Bobbs-Merrill, 1969), chapter 12; John H. Jackson, and William Davey, *Legal Problems Of International Economic Relations* (St. Paul: West, 2d ed., 1986), chapter 8.

2. See Pieter Verloren van Themaat, *The Changing Structure of International Economic Law* The Hague, (Martinus: Nijhoff, 1981), 16 et seq., who notes that nondiscrimination clauses (in the sense of national treatment) were developed as early as the twelfth and thirteenth centuries, especially in the Hansa context. U.S. FCN treaties with a national treatment clause included Reciprocal Trade Agreement with Iceland, Aug. 27, 1943, Art. II, 57 Stat. 1075, E.A.S. No. 342; Treaty of Friendship, Commerce, and Consular Rights with Finland, Feb. 13, 1934, Art. VII, 49 Stat. 2659, T.S. No. 868; Treaty of Friendship, Commerce, and Consular Rights with Germany, Dec. 8, 1923, Art. VIII, 44 Stat. 2132, T.S. 725.

3. The right of establishment is a critical concern with respect to the provision of services (although it may be important with respect to trade in goods). As such, right of establishment is an important issue in the service negotiations in the Uruguay Round. See Jonathan Aronson and Peter Cowhey, *Trade in Services: A Case for Open Markets* (Washington, D.C.: American Enterprise Institute, 1984), 25–26.

4. Our rough calculations indicate that of the 233 disputes formally brought to GATT, 31 concern Article III. See list of some of these disputes in Robert Hudec, *The GATT Legal System and World Trade Diplomacy* (New York: Praeger, 1975); Jackson supra note 1, chapter 12.3–12.4; and Jackson and Davey, supra note 1, 486–496.

5. See Section 9.3.

6. The Treaty of Rome, establishing the European Economic Community, has a parallel provision to GATT Article III:2 — Article 95 and this is one of the more frequently invoked provisions of the treaty in cases before the European Court of Justice. See also supra note 4.

7. See infra chapters 10 and 14.

8. See, in general, Jackson, *World Trade* supra note 1, section 12.3; Jackson and Davey, supra note 1, sections 8.1 and 8.2.

9. *Italian Discrimination Against Imported Agricultural Machinery*, Report by the Panel, GATT, BISD 7 Supp. 60 (1959).

10. Ibid., paragraph 5.

11. *Canada: Administration of the Foreign Investment Review Act*, Report of the Panel, GATT, BISD 30 Supp. 140 (1984).

12. See infra section 10.7.

13. *United States: Imports of Certain Automotive Spring Assemblies*, Report of the Panel, GATT, BISD 30th Supp. 107 (1984). See Jackson and Davey, supra note 1, 519–522.

14. Panel report supra note 13, paragraph 66.

15. See Denton, "The New Commerical Policy Instrument and Akzo v. Du-Pont," *European Law Review* 13 (1988), 3; Litowitz, "European Community Regulation No. 2641/84: A New Challenge to U.S. International Trade Commission's Section 337," *International Business and Trade Law Reporter* (1986), 3.

16. See Schieffelin & Co. v. United States, 424 F. 2d 1396 (CCPA, 1970); Bercut-Vandervoort & Co. v. United States, 46th Court of Customs and Patent Appeals, C.A.D. 691 (1958), cert. den., 359 U.S. 953, 79 S. Ct. 739, 3 L. Ed. 2d 760 (1959). See Jackson and Davey, supra note 1, section 8.2(B).

17. In Schieffelin, the treaties involved were the Ireland–U.S. Treaty of Friendship, Commerce, and Navigation of 1950, and the British–U.S. Treaty of Friendship, Commerce, and Navigation of 1815. The Customs Court had accepted that the British imports were entitled under the MFN clause in the British treaty to whatever tax treatment was required with respect to imports of Irish origin.

18. See generally Jackson and Davey, supra note 1, section 8.2(b), 496.

19. See *Belgian Family Allowances (Allocations Familiales)*, GATT, BISD, 1 Supp. 59 (1953). Belgian law imposed a charge on foreign goods purchased by public bodies when these goods originated in a country whose system of family allowances did not meet certain requirements. The panel noted that this discrimination was inconsistent with the provisions of Article I "and possibly with those of Article III, paragraph 2." See Hudec, supra note 4, chapter 13.

20. See Zenith Radio Corp. v. United States, 437 U.S. 443, 98 S. Ct. 2441, 57 L. Ed. 2d 337 (1978). See also Jackson and Davey, supra note 1, 140–142.

21. See Annex I, Ad Article XVI, *General Agreement on Tariffs and Trade*, GATT, BISD, Vol. IV (1969): "The exemption of an exported product from duties or taxes borne by the like product when destined for domestic consumption, or the remission of such duties or taxes in amounts not in excess of those which have accrued, shall not be deemed to be a subsidy."

22. For example, section 1101(b) (16) of the 1988 Trade Act (Omnibus Trade and Competitiveness Act of 1988, Pub. L. 100–418, 102 Stat. 1125.) states that a principal negotiating objective of the United States in the Uruguay Round regarding border taxes is "to obtain a revision of the GATT with respect to the treatment of border adjustments for internal taxes to redress the disadvantages to countries relying primarily for revenue on direct taxes rather than indirect taxes."
     See also *Tax Adjustments in International Trade: GATT Provisions and EEC Practice*, Executive Branch GATT Study No.1, 93rd Cong., 1st sess., 1973.

23. See, in general, Ballentine, "Uncertainty and the Short-Run Shifting of the Corporate Tax," *Oxford Economic Papers* 19 (1967), 95–110; J. Gregory Ballentine,

Equity, Efficiency and the U.S. Corporation Income Tax (Washington, D.C.: American Enterprise Institute, 1980); Goulder, Shoven and Whalley, 1983, Domestic Tax Policy and the Foreign Sector Formulations to Result from a General Equilibrium Tax Analysis Model, in *Behavioral Simulation Methods in Tax Policy Analysis,* Martin Feldstein (ed). Chicago: University of Chicago Press, pp. 333–364; Oswald Brownlee, *Taxing the Income from U.S. Corporation Investments Abroad* (Washington, D.C.: American Enterprise Institute, 1980); Douglas Kahn and Pamela Gann, *Corporate Taxation and Taxation of Partnerships and Partners* (St. Paul: West, 2d ed., 1985).

24. See John Whalley, *Trade Liberalization Among Major World Trading Partners* (Cambridge, Mass.: MIT Press, 1985); Fullerton, Henderson and Shoven, 1984, A Comparison of Methodologies in Empirical General Equilibrium Models of Taxation," in *Applied General Equilibrium Analysis,* Herbert Scarf and John Shoven (eds.) New York: Cambridge University Press, 367–410.

25. Zenith Electronics Corporation v. U.S., 633 F. Supp. 1385 (CIT 1986).

26. "Television Receivers from Japan; Final Results of an Anti-dumping Duty Administrative Review," *Federal Register* 53 (1988), 4050.

27. The following are some examples:

1. The French requirement that French inspectors inspect the source factory of any pharmaceutical sold in France, combined with the fact that French inspectors do not travel abroad (see *U.S. Export Weekly* 20 [1984], 953)

2. Belgian rules that margarine in Belgium must be sold in cubes, and not in oblong sticks, as in the rest of the Common Market (see, for example, Case 261/81, *Walter Rau Lebensmittelwerke v. De Smedt PvbA* [1982] ECR 3961, [1983] 2 CMLR 496)

3. German requirements that prevent importation of non-fizzy mineral water on the basis that such mineral water, as opposed to fizzy mineral water, does not help kill bacteria (see *The Economist* [June 23, 1984], 29)

4. Pre-1983 Japanese practice of requiring "lot" or "unit" approval for imported products, while allowing "type" approval for Japanese-produced products (see John H. Jackson, Jean-Victor Louis, and Mitsuo Matsushita, *Implementing the Tokyo Round* [Ann Arbor: University of Michigan Press, 1984], 110)

28. See Weil and Glick "Japan—Is the Market Open? A View of the Japanese Market Drawn from U.S. Corporate Experience," *Law and Policy in International Business* 11 (1979), 845. See also Wineburg "The Japanese Patent System: A Non-Tariff Barrier to Foreign Businesses?", *Journal of World Trade,* 22/1 (1988), 11; Edelman, "Japanese Product Standards as Non-Tariff Barriers: When Regulatory Policy Becomes a Trade Issue," *Stanford Journal of International Law* 24 (1988), 389; Jackson, Louis, and Matsushita, supra note 27, 107–115.

29. *Agreement on Technical Barriers to Trade,* GATT, BISD, 26 Supp. 8 (1980), T.I.A.S. 9616, 31 UST 405. See Middleton, "The GATT Standards Code," *Journal of World Trade Law* 14 (1980), 201; Sweeney, "Technical Analysis of the Technical Barriers to Trade Agreement," *Law and Policy in International Business* 12 (1980),

179; Nusbaumer, "The GATT Standards Code in Operation" *Journal of World Trade Law*, 18 (1984) 542.

30. GATT L/6453 (1989). Thirty-six nations are listed as accepting this code.

31. Trade Agreements Act of 1979, Pub. L. 96–39, Title IV, 93 Stat. 242 et seq., 19 USC §2531 et seq. (1980 and Supp. 1988)

32. See Robert Stern, John H. Jackson, and Bernard Hoekman, *An Assessment of the Implementation and Operation of the Tokyo Round Codes* (Brookfield, VT: Gower, 1988). In the case involving metal bats from the U.S., the U.S. claimed that Japanese "lot" inspection of American imports was discriminatory (see supra note 1). A formal bilateral complaint was lodged in August 1982. In March 1983 the Japanese changed the law and permitted U.S. producers to obtain "type" approval. See Edelman, supra note 28, 406–410.

33. See particularly infra section 9.4.

34. Article III, par. 8 GATT, BISD, Vol, IV (1969). For example, paragraph 8(a) used the phrase "products purchased for governmental purposes." The question of what is a "governmental purpose" can be very troublesome indeed. See, for a U.S. example, Bethlehem Steel Corp. v. Board of Commissioners, 276 Cal. App. 2d 221, 80 Cal. Rptr. 800 (1969).

35. See also supra chapter 6. Cf. Edmond McGovern, *International Trade Regulation* (Exeter: Globefield Press, 2d ed., 1986), 213.

36. Kenneth Dam, *The GATT: Law and International Economic Organization* (Chicago: University of Chicago Press, 1970), 199–200.

37. Ibid., 199. See Jackson and Davey, supra note 1, 522–523; for a European view, Bourgeois "Tokyo Round Agreements on Technical Barriers and on Government Procurement in International and EEC Perspective," *Common Market Law Review* 19 (1982), 5. See "International Symposium on Government Procurement Law" in *George Washington Journal of International Law and Economics* 20 (1987), 415–597 and 21 (1987), 1–187.

38. *Agreement on Government Procurement*, Article II, paragraph 1, GATT, BISD, 26th Supp. 33, 35 (1980).

39. For example, the complaint of the U.S. against EC deductions of value-added tax in calculating whether the contract value exceeds the threshold figure. See *Report of the Panel on Value-Added Tax and Threshold*, GATT, BISD, 31st Supp. 247 (1985). A second dispute concerned a French code-covered entity's procurement of a substantial number of microcomputers with allegedly code inconsistent procedures. The U.S. has proposed establishment of a working party to study the problem.

40. See, for example, *International Trade Reporter* 3 (1986), 1427.

41. SDR 150,000 was approximately $149,000 in 1986. This threshold amount has subsequently been lowered to SDR 130,000 (GATT, BISD 33 Supp. 190 [1987])

which for 1988 had a dollar value of $156,000. SDR stands for "special drawing right," a concept developed by the International Monetary Fund.

42. *Agreement on Government Procurement.* Article VIII, See supra note 38.

43. GATT L/6453 (1989).The EC is counted as one country. For the value-of-trade-covered data, see GATT/GPR/W/38 (1983); GPR/W/57 (1984); GPR/24 (1984).

44. In 1981 Fujitsu submitted a bid to supply fiber optic cable to AT&T. When AT&T considered accepting the bid, which AT&T freely admitted was the lowest, Congressman Timothy Wirth wrote to the FCC pointing out the national security implications of such a purchase (*Wall Street Journal,* October 19, 1981, 26; *New York Times,* December 12, 1981, 33 and 34). AT&T later rejected Fujitsu's bid, and decided only to accept tenders from U.S. firms. Eventually, in 1983 AT&T decided in favor of Western Electric, the manufacturing arm of AT&T (*New York Times,* January 18, 1983, D4). However, in 1982, MCI awarded a similar contract to Fujitsu (*Wall Street Journal* June 18, 1982, 12).

45. On state "Buy American" acts, see L. A. Glick, *Multilateral Trade Negotiations: World Trade After the Tokyo Round* (Totowa, NJ: Rowman and Allenheld, 1984), 138.

46. MTN Studies No. 6, Pt. 3, 96th Cong., 1st sess., 1979, 233, 265.

47. McGovern, supra note 35, 213–219.

48. Sections 1 to 3 of Act of March 3, 1933, c. 212 Title III, 47 Stat. 1520, are commonly known as the "Buy American" Act. See 41 USCA §102, (1980 and Supp. 1988); 41 CFR §1–61, 48 *Federal Register* 14899 (1983).

49. The president has set this cost difference at 6 percent, 48 C.F.R. §25.105.

50. Jackson, Louis, and Matsushita, supra note 27, 198–200.

Chapter 9

1. For example, the variable levy of the EEC Common Agricultural Policy has been criticized as skirting the rules of GATT. See John H. Jackson and William Davey, *Legal Problems of International Economic Relations* (St. Paul: West, 2d ed., 1986), 965–968. An "import deposit" is another device. In addition, the extensive use of so-called "voluntary restraint arrangements" also skirts the formal rules of GATT. However, cf. Jackson, "Export Restraints and the Law of GATT," *World Economy* 11 (1988), 485. For a general discussion of NTBs, see supra chapters 5 and 8.

2. See Peter Kenen, *The International Economy* (Englewood Cliffs, NJ: Prentice Hall, 1985), 167 et seq.

3. Article XXI(b), especially iii, GATT, BISD, Vol. IV (1969). See also John H. Jackson, *World Trade and the Law of GATT* (Indianapolis: Bobbs-Merrill, 1969),

748–752; Jackson and Davey, supra note 1, 915–918; Barry Carter, *International Economic Sanctions* (New York: Cambridge University Press, 1988); Knoll, "The Impact of Security Concerns Upon International Economic Law," *Syracuse Journal of International Law and Commerce* 11 (1984), 567.

4. See, for example, Santon, "The National Security Exception to Free Trade," *Federal Business News and Journal* 30 (1983), 293 and Reich, "Beyond Free Trade," *Foreign Affairs* 61 (1983), 773, 787.

5. In 1949, Czechoslovakia brought a complaint against the U.S. practices of export control licenses: see GATT CP.3/33 (1949); CP.3/38; CP.3/SR.22 (1949); CP.3/20 (1949). In 1961, Ghana imposed a ban on all imports from Portugal, invoking Article XXI: see GATT Doc. SR.19/12, at 196 (1961). The 1951 dispute between the United States and Czechoslovakia and the 1955 conflict between Peru and Czechoslovakia may also have involved Article XXI: see Jackson, supra note 3, 749–750. The 1985 dispute between the United States and Nicaragua is discussed infra notes 9 and 10.

6. This contrasts with the provisions of Article XXXV of GATT, which authorize any GATT contracting party to "opt out" of its relationship with any other GATT contracting party or prospective party, at one time only: the time at which one of the two parties enters GATT. There is no provision for such an "opt-out" at some subsequent point in time during GATT membership.

7. GATT, BISD, Vol. II, 36 (1952). See Jackson, supra note 3, 749–750.

8. See cases cited supra note 5 .

9. The embargo was imposed by Presidential Executive Order No. 12,513 of May 1, 1985 (*Federal Register* 50 [1985], 18629). See Whitt, "The Politics of Procedure: An Examination of the GATT Dispute-Settlement Panel and the Article XXI Defense in the Context of the U.S. Embargo of Nicaragua," *Law and Policy in International Business* 19 (1987), 603.

10. A GATT panel report, presented to the council on November 6, 1986, ruled that the U.S. embargo did not constitute a violation of GATT. However, the panel noted that its mandate did not allow it to rule on whether the embargo was consistent with GATT law. The panel also noted that irrespective of Article XXI, the embargo was contrary to the basic objectives of GATT. See *International Trade Reporter* 3 (1986), 1368.

11. Export Administration Act of 1979, Pub. L. 96–72, 93 Stat. 503, as amended, Pub. L. 97–145, 95 Stat. 1727, and Pub. L. 99–64, 99 Stat. 120 (1985), 50 USC § 2402.

12. See 50 USC §§ 2404(a), 2405(a); Jackson and Davey, supra note 1, 899–902, 918–924.

13. Section 232 of the Trade Expansion Act of 1962, Pub. L. No. 87–794, 76 Stat. 872 et seq., 19 USCA § 1862 (1980 and Supp. 1988). See *Threat of Certain Imports to National Security*, S. Hrg. 99–1041, Senate Finance Committee, 99th Cong., 2d sess., 1986. Section 1501 of the Omnibus Trade and Competitiveness Act of 1988 (Pub. L. 100–418, 102 Stat. 1257) amended section 232 to shorten the period in

which the president may respond to a petition. The Secretary of Commerce is also to notify and consult with the Secretary of Defense concerning any petition. See also Vakerics, Wilson, and Weigel, *Antidumping, Countervailing Duty and Other Trade Actions* (New York: Practicing Law Institute, 1987), chapter 8; Jackson and Davey, supra note 1, 924–925. Note also the case of machine tools. Following an investigation which concluded that imports of machine tools could affect U.S. national security, the president sought voluntary export restraints with the countries in question (statement by the president, May 20, 1986, *Public Papers* [1986], 661). The export-restraint agreements were announced in December 1986 (*Weekly Compilation of Presidential Documents* 22 [1986], 1654). See also *Operation of the Trade Agreements Program, 38th Report*, USITC Pub No. 1995 (1987), section 5–20.

14. See section 232, op. cit. supra as amended in 1988. See Vakerics, Wilson, and Weigel, supra note 13, chapter 8.4.

15. Article XX GATT, BISD, Vol. IV (1969). See Jackson, supra note 3, 741–747; Jackson and Davey, supra note 1, 510–522.

16. Article XX, GATT, BISD, Vol. IV (1969). See Jackson, supra note 3, 741–747.

17. *Prohibition of Imports of Tuna Fish and Tuna Products from Canada*, GATT, BISD 29 Supp. 91 (1983).

18. See infra section 10.7.

19. See supra note 13, Omnibus Trade and Competitiveness Act of 1988, section 1301(a), amending section 301(d)(3)(B)(II). The pre-1988 version of section 301 has, however, been used to challenge the intellectual property policies (or lack thereof) of foreign governments. The most notable examples are Docket 301–49, "Brazilian Informatics Policy" (*Federal Register*, 51 (1986) 35993, 52 (1987) 1619, 4207 and 24971), Docket 301–61, "Brazilian Patent Protection of Pharmaceuticals" (*Federal Register* 52 [1987], 28223 and 53 [1988], 28100 and 30894), Docket 301–68, "Argentinian Intellectual Property Protection of Pharmaceuticals" (*Federal Register* 53 [1988], 37668), and Docket 305–32, "South Korean Patent Protection" (*Federal Register* 53 [1988], 22758).

20. See supra note 19, section 1342(a)(1).

21. See the *Ministerial Declaration* (GATT, BISD 33 Supp. 19, 25–26 [1987]; GATT/ 1396, 25 September 1986) and *Decision of 28 January 1987* (GATT, BISD 33 Supp. 31, 45–46 [1987]). The 1988 Act supra note 19, section 1101(b)(10), has the protection of intellectual property as a principal negotiating objective of the Uruguay Round.

22. See supra section 8.3.

23. See Charles Kindleberger, *International Economics* (Homewood, IL: Irwin, 5th ed., 1973), 53–69.

24. See, for example, Kirgis, "Effective Pollution Control in Industrialized Countries: International Economic Disincentives, Policy Responses, and the GATT,"

Michigan Law Review 70 (1972), 859, 889–895; Seymour Rubin and Thomas Graham (eds.), *Environment and Trade: The Relation of International Trade and Environmental Policy* (Totowa, NJ: Allanheld, Osmun, 1980).

25. Kirgis, supra note 24.

26. See, for example, U.S. v. Canada (Trail Smelter case), *United Nations Reports of International Arbitration Awards* vol. III, 1907 et seq. See also Pontavice, 1977. Compensation for Transfrontier Pollution Damage. In *Legal Aspects of Transfrontier Pollution Damage*, Paris: OECD, p. 409.

27. For example, the 1977 Berne Convention on the Protection of the Rhine Against Chemical Pollution; the 1975 Paris Convention for the Prevention of Marine Pollution from Land-Based Sources; the 1976 Barcelona Convention on the Protection of the Mediterranean Sea Against Pollution.

28. See infra chapter 11.

29. The United Nations Environment Program, established in 1972 as a coordinating agency, might play a role in international regulation or harmonization of pollution controls. Cf. Pieter Verloren van Themaat, *The Changing Structure of International Economic Law* (The Hague: Martinus Nijhoff, 1981), 101–102.

30. See, for example, Wolfgang Friedmann, *The Changing Structure of International Law* (New York: Columbia University Press, 1964), 40–45, 232–253.

31. See Jackson, supra note 1, 8, 187, 402. See, on FCN Treaties, Youngquist, "United States Commercial Treaties: Their Role in Foreign Economic Policy," *Studies in Law and Economic Development*, Vol. 2, Study No. 1, Washington, D.C.: George Washington University International Law Society 1967).

32. During the 1960s, the British Steel Corporation offered a rebate to its customers if they certified that they had not used imported steel in their products. This was challenged by the U.S. in the GATT and eventually the measure was withdrawn. More generally, see Yamamura, 1986. *Caveat Emptor*: The Industrial Policy of Japan. In *Strategic Trade Policy and the New International Economics*, Paul Krugman (ed.) Cambridge, Mass.: MIT Press, pp. 167–210, 180–181. The issue of loyalty rebates in order to prevent import penetration was raised in the massive Zenith v. Matsushita litigation. However, such rebates arguably assisted in the alleged predation of the U.S. market, secret rebates being a way of circumventing U.S. antidumping regulation. A criminal case was brought against Sears Roebuck for false declaration on customs documents since the price declared was overstated to the extent of the secret rebate received. See also Dealers Wholesale Supply Inv. v. Pacific Steel and Supply Co., and Mitsui, 1984–2 Trade Cas. P66,109.

33. See "GM Switch: Will Now Buy Foreign Steel," *Dunn's Business Month* 125 (1985), 30.

34. At the conclusion of the Havana Conference, the Final Act and Related Documents of the United Nations Conference on Trade and Employment, which included the text of the Havana Charter for an International Trade Organization,

was published by the United Nations, the United States, and the United Kingdom governments. The following refers, respectively, to the UN and U.S. documents: *Final Act and Related Documents*, UN Conference on Trade and Employment, held at Havana, Cuba, from November 21, 1947, to March 24, 1948; Interim Commission for the International Trade Organization, Lake Success, New York, April 1948; UN Doc. E/Conf.2/78, (chapter V of this charter, E/Conf.2/C.4/1–25, dealt with restrictive business practices); Havana Charter for an International Trade Organization, U.S. Department of State Commercial Policy Series, *114 Pub. No. 3117, 1948*.

35. *Proposal of Denmark, Norway, Sweden*, GATT L/283 (1954). *Proposal of West Germany*, GATT L/261/Add.1, 41 (1954). See also *Restrictive Business Practices* (Geneva: GATT, 1959). See also Jackson, supra note 3, 522–527.

36. *OECD Guidelines for Multinational Enterprises* (OECD: International Investment and Multilateral Enterprises, rev. ed., 1979) as amended, *OECD International Investment and Multilateral Enterprises: The 1984 Review of the 1976 Declaration and Decisions* 9 (1984). See Coolidge, Spina, Wallace (eds.), *The OECD Guidlines for Multinational Enterprises* (Paris: OECD, 1980); Wallace, "International Codes and Guidelines for Multinational Enterprises: Update and Selected Issues," *International Law* 17 (1983), 435; Grosse, "Codes of Conduct for Multinational Enterprises," *Journal of World Trade Law* 16 (1982), 414. See also "UN Draft Code of Conduct for Transnational Corporations," *International Legal Materials* 24 (1984), 624.

37. *The Set of Multilaterally Agreed Equitable Principles and Rules for the Control of Restrictive Business Practices*, U.N. Doc. TD/RBP/10 (1980). See Brusick, "UN Control of Restrictive Business Practices," *Journal of World Trade Law* 17 (1983), 337; Miller and Davidson, "Antitrust at the UN: A Tale of Two Codes," *Stanford Journal of International Law* 18 (1982), 347; "Recent Developments: *The Set of Multilaterally Agreed Equitable Principles and Rules for the Control of Restrictive Business Practices*," *Law and Policy in International Business* 13 (1981), 313.

38. See supra note 19, section 1301(a), amending section 301(d)(3)(B)(III).

39. On the IMF, see, in general, Jackson and Davey, supra note 1, 284–293, 826–883; Kenneth Dam, *The Rules of the Game: Reform and Revolution in the International Monetary System* (Chicago: University of Chicago Press, 1982); Joseph Gold, *Legal and Institutional Aspects of the International Monetary System: Selected Essays* (Washington, D.C.: IMF, 1984); Gold, "Developments in the International Monetary System, The International Monetary Fund, and International Monetary Law Since 1971," *Receuil des Cours* 174 (1982), 107. See also John K. Horsefield (ed.), *The International Monetary Fund, 1945–1965*, 3 vols. Washington, D.C.: IMF, 1969); Margaret Garritsen de Vries, *The International Monetary Fund, 1966–1971: The System Under Stress* (Washington, D.C.: IMF, 1976); Richard W. Edwards, *International Monetary Collaboration* (Dobbs Ferry, NY: Transnational Publishers, 1985).

40. See Jackson, supra note 3, 711–716; Jackson and Davey, supra note 1, 875–876. A list of tariff surcharges coming within the cognizance of GATT can be

found in GATT COM.TD/F/W.3 (1965). Of course, there have been a number of subsequent tariff surcharges that are not included.

41. See Jackson, supra note 3, 711–716. A list of documents for each surcharge case can be found in GATT COM.TD/F/W.3, 4–3 (1965). The following is a list of the action taken in each case: GATT, BISD, 3 Supp. 26 (1955), France; GATT, BISD, 7 Supp. 37 (1959), Peru; GATT, BISD, 8 Supp. 29 (1960), Chile; GATT, BISD, 8 Supp. 52 (1960), Nicaragua; GATT, BISD, 10 Supp. 35 (1962), Ceylon; GATT, BISD, 10 Supp. 51 (1962), Uruguay; GATT, BISD, 11 Supp. 57 (1963), Canada; GATT L/2477 (1965), India, (Statement of removal without action taken); GATT Doc. C/50 (1964) and L/2651 (1965), United Kingdom; GATT L/3573 and L/3647 (1971) United States.

42. See Kindleberger, supra note 23, chapter 7, Kenen, supra note 2, 172–177; Jackson and Davey, supra note 1, 17–18. See also GATT COM.TD/F/W.3 (1965) (policy reasons).

43. See "Address to the Nation Outlining a New Economic Policy: 'The Challenge of Peace,'" *Public Papers of the President, Richard Nixon* (1971), 886–890.

44. Ibid. The decision was implemented by Executive Order No. 11615, *Federal Register* 36 (1971), 15727. See also infra note 47.

45. See GATT, BISD 23 Supp. 98 (1977). See Jackson, "The Jurisprudence of International Trade: The DISC Case in GATT," *American Journal of International Law* 72 (1978), 747. See also Hudec "Reforming GATT Adjudication Procedures," *Minnesota Law Review* 72 (1988), 1443. See Jackson and Davey, supra note 1, 744–746.

46. See Jackson and Davey, supra note 1, 107–108. Nevertheless, the congressional delegation was upheld by the court in Amalgamated Meat Cutters & Butcher Workmen of North America, AFL-CIO v. Connally, 337 F. Supp. 737 (D.D.C. 1971).

47. See supra note 47. The tariff surcharge was upheld in United States v. Yoshida International, Inc., 526 F. 2d 560 (CCPA. 1975), reversing 378 F.Supp. 1155; and in Alcan Sales, Div. of Alcan Aluminum Corp. v. United States, 534 F.2d 920 (CCPA), cert. denied, 429 U.S. 986, 97 S. Ct. 506, 50 L. Ed. 598 (1976).

48. See, in general, Roessler, "Selective Balance-of-Payment Adjustment Measures Affecting Trade: The Roles of the GATT and the IMF," *Journal of World Trade Law* 9 (1975), 622.

49. Cf. C. Fred Bergsten and William Cline, *Trade Policy in the 1980s* (Washington, D.C.: Institute for International Economics, Policy Analyses in International Economics No. 3, 1982), 54–55, who recognize the link but recommend "a much greater degree of equilibrium among the major currencies. . . ."

50. *Declaration on Trade Measures Taken for Balance-of-Payment Purposes*, GATT, BISD, 26th Supp. 205 (1980).

51. Ibid.

52. See cases cited supra note 48.

53. Section 122 of the Trade Act of 1974, Pub. L. 93–618, 88 Stat. 1978, 19 USC § 2132. See also S. Rep. No. 93–1298, Senate Finance Committee, 93d Cong., 2d sess., 1974, 87–89.

54. Ibid., section 122(d)(4).

55. Cf. Bergsten and Cline, supra note 50, 78.

56. Private discussions with government officials: see *GATT Focus* 52 (1988), 3, where it is stated that a number of views had been expressed supporting the continued existence of Article XVIII:B.

Chapter 10

1. See Jacob Viner, *Dumping: A Problem in International Trade* (New York: Kelley, 1966); Edwin A. Vermulst, *Antidumping Law and Practice in the United States and European Communities* (New York: North Holland, 1987); Richard Dale, *Antidumping Law in a Liberal Trade Order* (New York: St. Martin's Press, 1980); John H. Jackson and William Davey, *Legal Problems of International Economic Relations* (St Paul: West, 2d ed., 1986), chapter 10. See also Barcelo, "The Antidumping Law: Revise It or Repeal It," *Michigan Yearbook of International Legal Studies* 1 (1979), 53; Ehrenhaft, "What the Antidumping and Countervailing Duty Provisions (Can) (Will) (Should) Mean for U.S. Trade Policy," *Law and Policy in International Business* 11 (1979), 1361.

2. See, for example, *The Unfair Foreign Competition Act 1985: Hearings on S. 1655*, S. Hrg. 99–643, Senate Judiciary Committee, 99th Cong., 1st sess., 1985 and *Remedies Against Dumping of Imports: Hearings on S. 1655*, S. Hrg. 99–897, Senate Finance Committee, 99th Cong., 2d Sess., 1986.

3. See, for example, a section 301 action brought by the specialty steel industry which resulted in a request from the president that the ITC open a section 201 action (*Federal Register* 47 [1982], 51717). A section 201 action was initiated (*Federal Register* 47 [1982], 56218) and the positive determination of injury by the ITC (*Federal Register* 48 [1983]), 22373) led to a presidential proclamation placing quantitative restrictions on some kinds of steel (*Federal Register* 48 [1983], 33233). See also Lowenfeld, "Fair or Unfair Trade: Does It Matter?", *Cornell International Law Journal* 13 (1980), 205; Nicolaides, "How Fair is Fair Trade?", *Journal of World Trade Law* 21 (1987), 147.

4. See Ambassador Yeutter's comments on the conclusion of the Punta del Este declaration (*International Trade Reporter* 3 [1986], 1150) where he stated that: "the Punta del Este meeting means that GATT can remain relevant to the needs of our economy. We have a chance to eliminate their unfair foreign trade practices that are hurting American farmers and establish new rules to expand trade in services, America's fastest-growing sector, and provide new protection for U.S. intellectual property, including patents, copyrights and trademarks, establish international rules on foreign investment and improve our ability to settle disputes

arising over interpretations of international trading rules. All these actions would help to level the playing field for American exporters." See also Senator John Dingell (*International Trade Reporter* 3 [1986], 1198): "all the companies and workers of this country ask is a level playing field. Yet with few exceptions, this Administration continues to turn the other cheek when country after country targets industry after industry. . . .First the intellectual property of our industry is stolen, then our foreign markets are flooded with counterfeit, profits are used to dump in the U.S. market. Finally our firms are driven out of business, or close to it—and all the while, their markets are insulated from meaningful competition.

5. The infra text is adapted from Jackson and Davey, supra note 1, pages 650–2, and appears by permission of the authors. The concept first appeared in Jackson. J. H., 1978. United States Policy Regarding Disruptive Imports from State Trading Countries or Government-Owned Enterprises. In *Interface One: Conference Proceedings on the Application of U.S. Antidumping and Countervailing Duty Law to Imports from State-Controlled Economies or State-Owned Enterprises*, Don Wallace, George Spina,Richard Rawson and Brian McGill (eds.) Washington, D.C: Institute for International and Foreign Trade Law, Georgetown University Law Center, pp. 1–20.

6. See infra chapter 12.

7. See supra note 1. The author also acknowledges the special assistance of Professor Alan Deardorff of the Department of Economics, University of Michigan, in the preparation of this section. Apart from the extensive discussions we have had on subjects covered here, the author is indebted to a tentative manuscript, prepared by Professor Deardorff for a symposium volume on comparative antidumping law, to be published by the University of Michigan Press under the editorship of John H. Jackson and Edwin A. Vermulst.

8. One should note, however, that certain economists believe that dumping *may* have beneficial effects in certain circumstances—for example, where the ability to dump allows a certain scale of production and consequent cost reduction which, without the ability to dump, could not have been achieved. See, for example, Joan Robinson, *Economics of Imperfect Competition* (London: Macmillan, 2d ed., 1969), chapter 16, 204–205. See also the speech of Milton Friedman, "In Defense of Dumping," reported in *International Trade Reporter* 4 (1987), 935.

9. See *General Agreement of Tariffs and Trade*, Article VI. See also *Agreement on the Implementation of Article VI of the General Agreement on Tariffs and Trade* (the "1979 Code"), GATT, BISD 26 Supp. 171 (1980); 31 UST 4919; TIAS No. 9650.

10. 19 USC §1677b (1980 and Supp. 1987). See also 19 CFR. §353.19 (1987).

11. See William Wares, *The Theory of Dumping and American Commercial Policy* (Lexington, Mass.: Lexington Books, 1977), 68; Fisher, "The Antidumping Law of the United States: A Legal and Economic Analysis," *Law and Policy in International Business* 5 (1973), 85.

12. "An act to amend section 2 of the act entitled 'An Act to supplement existing law against unlawful restraints and monopolies, and for other purposes' approved

October 1914 as amended" (the "Robinson–Patman Act"), ch. 592, 49 Stat. 1526 (1936) amending §2 of the Clayton Act (current version at 15 USC §13[a] [1976 and Supp. 1982]). See U.S. Department of Justice, *Report on the Robinson-Patman Act*, (Washington, D.C.: USGPO, 1977); Philip Areeda, *Antitrust Analysis: Problems Texts, Cases* (Boston: Little, Brown, 3d ed., 1981, supp. 1986), chapter 7. See also "The Robinson-Patman Act: A Symposium on Its Fiftieth Anniversary," *Antitrust Bulletin,* XXXI (1986), 571; "The Robinson–Patman Act Revisited in Its 50th Year," *Antitrust Law Journal* 55 (1986), 133; "Living with the Robinson–Patman Act," *Antitrust Law Journal* 53 (1985), 845, in particular Calvani, "Government Enforcement of the Robinson–Patman Act," 921.

13. See Richard Posner, *The Robinson–Patman Act: Federal Regulation of Price Differences* (Washington, D.C.: American Enterprise Institute, 1976); Levi, "The Robinson–Patman Act—Is it in the Public Interest?", *ABA Antitrust Section* 1 (1952); Ross, "Winners and Losers under the Robinson–Patman Act," *Journal of Law and Economics* 27 (1984), 243.

14. See F. W. Taussig, *Principles of Economics* (New York: Macmillan, 3d ed., 1928, revised 1935), volume 1, 153.

15. See, for example, Matsushita Electric Industrial Co. v. Zenith Radio Corp., 475 U.S. 574. In the domestic context, see, for example, Cargill v. Monfort of Colorado, 93 L. Ed. 2d. 427.

16. Sherman Act, ch. 647 §2, 26 Stat. 209 (1890) (current version at 15 USC §2 [1973]). See Areeda, supra note 12, 214–215.

17. See Viner, supra note 1, 120: "In the absence of world-wide monopoly, the dumping concern will have to share with rival concerns in its own country or in other foreign countries the benefit accruing from the destruction of the native industry in the country dumped on." However, he continues: "There are, however, sufficient instances of trusts and combinations, many of them international in their membership or affiliations, that are within reach of a world-wide quasi-monopolistic control of their industry, to make the danger of predatory competition a real one even if this reasoning is unqualifiedly accepted."
   In Matsushita v. Zenith (supra note 15, 588–593), the Supreme Court noted that *conspiracies* to predate were even more unlikely than single predatory actions. However, a growing body of literature, while accepting that price predation is unlikely, emphasizes the possibility of *non-price* predation. For a summary of these ideas, see Ordover and Wall, "Proving Predation After Monfort and Matsushita: What the 'New Learning' Has to Offer," *Antitrust* 1 (1987), 5.

18. See Fisher, supra note 11 and the comments of Senator Dingell, supra note 4.

19. See Barcelo, supra note 1.

20. See supra note 7.

21. See supra chapter 7.

22. Alexander Hamilton, *Report on Manufactures* (1791), quoted in Viner, supra note 1, 37.

23. See Viner, supra note 1, 38–39.

24. Viner states that the Tariff Act of 1816 was "the first distinctly protectionist tariff of the United States, and it has been claimed that the threat to American industries from English dumping, and especially Brougham's frank utterances with respect thereto, was an important influence contributing to this, as well as to subsequent, protectionist legislation." (See Viner, supra note 1, 40–44.) However, cf. F. W. Taussig, *The Tariff History of the United States* (New York: G. P. Putnam's 8th. ed., 1931, Johnson reprint, 1966), 68.

25. See Viner supra note 1, 51.

26. The Revenue Act of 1916, ch. 463, sections 800–801, 39 Stat. 798 (commonly referred to as the "Antidumping Act of 1916," 15 USC §72 [1976]); "An Act imposing temporary duties upon certain agricultural products to meet certain emergencies, and to provide revenue; to regulate commerce with foreign countries; to prevent dumping of foreign merchandise on the markets of the United States; to regulate the value of foreign money, and for other purposes . . ." (The Emergency Tariff Act of 1921, ch. 14, Title II, 42 Stat. 9 [current version, Tariff Act of 1930, Title VII §731, as added July 26, 1979, Pub. L. 96–39, Title I, §101, 93 Stat. 162, 19 USCA §1673 (1980 and Supp. 1988)]).

27. See, for example, Article IX:2 of *1938 Reciprocal Trade Agreement between the United States and United Kingdom* (54 Stat. 1897), where a provision allowed the U.K. to take measures which it deemed necessary to act as an effective deterrent to the practice. No mention was made of an equivalent U.S. right. Cf. *1938 Reciprocal Trade Agreement between the U.S. and Canada* (54 Stat. 2348), where no such antidumping provision is to be found.

28. *General Agreement of Tariffs and Trade*, Article VI. October 30, 1947, 61 Stat. (5), (6), TIAS No. 1700, 55 UNTS 194 (1948) as amended and Vol. IV BISD. However, N.B. *Protocol of Provisional Application to the GATT*, October 30, 1947, 61 Stat. (5), (6), TIAS No. 1700, 55 UNTS 308.

Article VI, entitled "Antidumping and Countervailing Duties," at paragraph 1 reads as follows:

1. The contracting parties recognize that dumping, by which the products of one country are introduced into the commerce of another country at less than the normal value of the products, is to be condemned if it causes or threatens material injury to an established industry in the territory of a Contracting Party or materially retards the establishment of a domestic industry. For the purposes of this Article, a product is to be considered as being introduced into the commerce of an exporting country at less than its normal value, if the price of the product exported from one country to another

   a. is less than the comparable price, in the ordinary course of trade, for the like product when destined for consumption in the exporting country, or,

   b. in the absence of such a domestic price, is less than either

i. the highest comparable price for the like product for export to any third country in the ordinary course of trade, or

ii. the cost of production of the product in the country of origin plus a reasonable addition for selling cost and profit

Due allowance shall be made in each case for differences in conditions and terms of sale, for differences in taxation, and for other differences affecting price comparability.

29. *Agreement on the Implementation of Article VI (the "1967 Code")*, 651 UNTS 320, GATT, BISD 15 Supp. 24 (1968). See Jackson and Davey, supra note 1, 670–674. See also John W. Evans, *The Kennedy Round in American Trade Policy: The Twilight of the GATT?* (Cambridge, Mass.: Harvard University Press, 1971), 106–110.

30. Section 201 of 1968 Renegotiations Amendment Act, Pub. L. No. 90–634, 82 Stat. 1345. See Jackson and Davey, supra note 1; John H. Jackson, Jean-Victor Louis, and Mitsuo Matsushita, *Implementing the Tokyo Round* (Ann Arbor: University of Michigan Press, 1984), 146; Thomas Curtis and John Vastine, *The Kennedy Round and the Future of American Trade* (New York: Praeger, 1971), chapter 14. See also Pintos and Murphy, "Congress Dumps the International Code," *Catholic University Law Review* 18 (1968), 180.

31. See Jackson, Louis, and Matsushita, supra note 30, 164–165; Vermulst, supra note 1, 544–545; J. F. Beseler and A. N. Williams, *Anti-Dumping and Anti-Subsidy Law: The European Communities*, (London: ICC/Sweet and Maxwell, 1986), 11–13.

32. *The Tokyo Round of Multilateral Trade Negotiations: Report by the Director-General of GATT* (Geneva: GATT, 1979), 181 and *The Tokyo Round of Multilateral Trade Negotiations: Supplementary Report by the Director-General of GATT* (Geneva: GATT, 1980), chapter 3(b).

33. The 1979 Code, supra note 9, had a number of significant alterations. First, the injury test was arguably weakened, since the causation standard was reduced. Article 3 of the 1967 Code talked of the dumped imports being "demonstrably the principal cause of material injury," whereas the 1979 Code did not have such a provision, merely stating in Article 3(4) that the dumped imports through the effects of dumping are causing the injury. Second, the criteria for assessing what amounted to injurious effects on a domestic industry were made more explicit. Third, the rules on price undertakings were expanded. Fourth, a provision on dispute settlement was added (Article 15). Fifth, signatories were obligated under Article 16(6)(b) to notify the Committee on Antidumping Practices of any changes in its laws or regulation. Finally, there was a new article (Article 13) inserted, concerning developing countries.

34. In general, see Article 59 of *Vienna Convention on the Law of Treaties* (UN Doc. A/CONF.39/27, [1969]). In addition, see Article 16(5) supra note 9 of the 1979 Antidumping Code: "Acceptance of this Agreement shall carry denunciation of the Agreement on the Implementation of Article VI of the General Agreement on Tariffs and Trade, done at Geneva on 30 June 1967, which entered into force on 1 July 1968, for Parties to the 1967 Agreement. Such denunciation shall take

effect for each Party to this Agreement on the date of entry into force of this Agreement for each such Party."

35. The countries who have accepted the Code are Australia, Austria, Brazil, Canada, Czechoslovakia, Egypt, Finland, Hong Kong, Hungary, India, Japan, Republic of Korea, Mexico, New Zealand, Norway, Pakistan, Poland, Romania, Singapore, Spain, Sweden, Switzerland, the United Kingdom (the territories for which it has international responsibility, except for Antigua, Bermuda, Brunei, Cayman Islands, Monserrat, St. Kitts-Nevis, Sovereign Base Areas Cyprus and the Virgin Islands), the United States of America, Yugoslavia, and the European Community. For detailed information on the signatories, see GATT L/6453 (1989).

36. The European Community is a signatory of the 1979 Code. It has exclusive legislative competence with respect to antidumping legislation in the community. This means that after the end of the transitional period applicable to Spain and Portugal, Portugal, as part of the European Community, will be subject to the provisions of the Code. See Jackson, Louis, and Matsushita, supra note 30, 47–48. The twenty-five signatories of the AD code counts the EC as one.

37. See the 1979 Code, supra note 9, Article 2. See Ehrenhaft, supra note 1; Lorenzen, "Technical Analysis of the Antidumping Agreement and Trade Agreements Act," *Law and Policy in International Business* 11 (1979), 1405.

38. Indeed, a GATT panel (GATT, BISD 30 Supp. 140, 164 [1984] has stated: "In particular, the General Agreement does not impose on contracting parties the obligation to prevent enterprises from dumping."

39. Malcolm Baldrige, "There Won't Be a Trade War," *Washington Post* (April 10, 1987), A27: "Dumping is . . . anti-free trade and is illegal under U.S. laws as well as under the General Agreement on Tariffs and Trade. In short, sanctions against illegal dumping and for opening markets are pro-, not anti-free trade." See also Clyde Prestowitz, Jr., in his recent book *Trading Places* (New York: Basic Books, 1988), where at page 38 he states: "The only problem was that dumping is illegal under both U.S. trade law and under the international rules of GATT." See statement of Senator Heflin, in *The Unfair Foreign Competition Act of 1985: Hearings on S.1655 Senate Judiciary Committee*, supra note 2, 72 where he says, "'Dumping' is clearly unlawful." Cf. John H. Jackson, *World Trade and the Law of GATT* (Indianapolis: Bobbs-Merrill, 1969), 412, nn.9, 10, and accompanying text.

40. The Committee on Antidumping Practices publishes the relevant figues as an appendix to its report, which can be found in the the BISD volume for that year. Its first report can be found in GATT, BISD 16 Supp 43 (1970). This committee produced eleven reports before being reconstituted following the signing of the 1979 Code. The first report of the "new" Committee on Antidumping Practices can be found in GATT, BISD 27 Supp. 44 (1981).

41. On December 24, 1986, the Japanese government issued new guidelines to strengthen the implementation of the 1979 Antidumping Code. See Hagiwara, Noguchi, and Masui, "Anti-Dumping Laws in Japan," *Journal of World Trade* 22/4 (1988), 35. See also Jackson, Louis, and Matsushita, supra note 30, 102–107; Matsushita, comment in Jackson and Vermulst, supra note 7.

42. See supra note 26.

43. In re *Japanese Electronic Products Antitrust Litigation*, 723 F. 2d 238 (CA3 1983); 513 F. Supp. 1100 (ED Pa. 1981). See also Zenith Radio Corp. v. Matsushita Electric Industrial Co., 494 F. Supp. 1190 (ED Pa. 1980); In re *Japanese Electronics Products Antitrust Litigation*, 723 F. 2d 319 (CA3 1983); Matsushita Electric Industrial Co. v. Zenith Radio Corp, 475 U.S. 574.

44. See, for example, S. 1655, 99th Cong., 1st sess., 1985, and hearings, supra note 2. The House version of the 1987 trade bill (HR 3, 100th Cong., 1st sess., 1987 §166) provided for a repeal of the criminal sanction in the 1916 Antidumping Act, and the introduction of a private right to obtain single damages. There was also a provision which would have allowed domestic industries injured by dumped imports to apply to have some or all of the antidumping duties paid to them as some form of compensation (see HR 3, 100th Cong., 1st sess., 1987 §167. Neither provision was included in the bill which eventually formed part of the Omnibus Trade and Competitiveness Act of 1988 (Pub. L. 100–418, 102 Stat. 1107 et seq.).

45. "An Act imposing temporary duties upon certain agricultural products to meet certain emergencies, and to provide revenue; to regulate commerce with foreign countries; to prevent dumping of foreign merchandise on the markets of the United States; to regulate the value of foreign money, and for other purposes . . ." (The Emergency Tariff Act of 1921), ch. 14, Title II, 42 Stat. 9 [current version, Tariff Act of 1930, Title VII §731, as added July 26, 1979, Pub. L. 96–39, Title I, §101, 93 Stat. 162, (19 USC §1673 [1980 and Supp. 1987])]).

46. See infra section 10.5.

47. This inventory of U.S. trade actions has been prepared by my assistants, based on U.S. government documents available as of September 1988.

48. Trade Act of 1974, Pub. L. 93–618, §321(f)(3), 88 Stat. 1978 amending 28 USC §§2632.

49. Trade Agreements Act of 1979, Pub L. 96–39, Title I, section 101, 93 Stat. 144, amending the Tariff Act of 1930, 19 USCA 1671 et seq. (1980 and Supp. 1988).

50. See 19 USC §§1330–1338 (International Trade Commission). See also Vermulst, supra note 1, 37–40; Jackson and Davey, supra note 1, 547–9. However, one should note that in the case of third-country dumping, under section 1317 of the 1988 Trade Act (supra note 44) the USTR is required, upon determination that products are being dumped and that injury results to a U.S. industry, to request that the third nation undertake an investigation.

51. A single- or multiple-firm action is in theory possible under the 1979 Code, but most jurisdictions do not use either for fear of the action being manipulated to suit the domestic industry—for example, when a U.S. firm imports Korean cars and then brings a single-firm action against a Korean producer (while excluding its own imports from the scope of the investigation). The U.S. Department of Commerce discourages petitioners from attempting such a case. The EC has, however, opened a single-firm action against two named Japanese firms (OJ [1987] C.256/15). However, cf. Beseler and Williams, supra note 31, 186. The

recent EC "parts amendment" (Regulation [EEC] 1761/87, OJ [1987] L.167/9 adding to Article 13 of Regulation [EEC] 2176/84, OJ [1984] L.201/1) to the anti-dumping regime also raises issues analogous to single-firm actions. In theory, an EC petitioner may request that the commission impose duties upon a foreign firm, already found to be dumping, who assembles in the EC, and not have similar duties imposed on itself, even though it uses exactly the same parts in the same amounts as the foreign assembler.

52. See the 1979 Antidumping Code, supra note 9, Article 6, paragraph 8, and *Recommendations Concerning Best Information Available in Terms of Article 6:8*, GATT BISD 31st. Supp 283 (1985). In the U.S., see 19 CFR §207.8 (1988); 19 CFR §353.51 (1988). See also Vermulst, supra note 1, 61–64, 207–208.

53. See generally Vermulst, supra note 1; Peter Feller, *U.S. Customs and International Trade Guide* (New York: Matthew Bender, 1979), chapter 18.

54. The figures for each jurisdiction for each year appear as an appendix to the *Antidumping Committee Report* found in the annual GATT *Supplement to Basic Instruments and Selected Documents*.

55. See supra note 41.

56. See *The Commerce Department Speaks on Import and Export Administration 1984* (New York: Practicing Law Institute, 1984), vols. 1 and 2; Vermulst, supra note 1; Feller, supra note 53, chapter 18.

57. 19 USCA §1673 (1980 and Supp. 1988) states:

If

1. the administering authority determines that a class or kind of foreign merchandise is being, or is likely to be sold in the United States at less than fair value, and

2. the Commission determines that

   a. an industry in the United States

      i. is materially injured, or

      ii. is threatened with material injury, or

   b. the establishment of an industry in the United States is materially retarded, by reason of imports of that merchandise,

then there shall be imposed upon such merchandise an antidumping duty, in addition to any other duty imposed, in an amount equal to the amount by which the foreign market value exceeds the United States price for the merchandise. For the purposes of this section and section 1673d(b)(1) of this title, a reference to the sale of foreign merchandise includes the entering into of any leasing arrangement regarding the merchandise that is equivalent to the sale of the merchandise.

58. See "Fresh Winter Vegetables, Mexico," *Federal Register* 45 (1980), 20512. The case was appealed: South West Florida Vegetable Growers Association v. United States, 583 F. Supp. 10 (CIT). See also note, "Applying Antidumping Law to Perishable Agricultural Goods," *Michigan Law Review* 80 (1982), 524.

59. The CIT has held that the Department of Commerce must state why the margin was held to be *de minimis* in each case: see Carlisle Tire and Rubber Co. v. United States, USCIT slip op. 86–45 (April 29, 1986). Following the remand of the CIT, Commerce adopted a rule regarding *de minimis* (0.5 percent) dumping and subsidization (*Federal Register* 52 (1987), 30660; 19 CFR §353.24 [1988]). See also Feller, supra note 53, §18.04 (18–16.3). See also Thomas Schoenbaum, *Antidumping and Countervailing Duties and the GATT: An Evaluation and a Proposal for an Unified Remedy for Unfair International Trade* (Athens, GA: Dean Rusk Center for International and Comparative Law, University of Georgia Law School, 1987), 14.

60. See Vermulst, supra note 1, 495. See also Feller, supra note 53, §18.02[1]. Cf. *Report of Group of Experts on Anti-Dumping and Countervailing Duties* (Geneva: GATT, 1961), 7.

61. See Vermulst, supra note 1, 384–386; Schoenbaum, supra note 59, 10–15.

62. See Ehrenhaft and Meriwether, "The Trade Agreements Act of 1979: Small Aid for Trade," *Tulane Law Review* 58 (1984), 1107, 1131. Cf. statement of Gary Horlick, *Options to Improve the Trade Remedy Laws: Comm. Ser. 98–15*, House Ways and Means Committee, 98th Cong., 1st sess., 1983, 565. Horlick points out that, at least as far as the complainant is concerned, a dumping action need cost them no money or effort since the actual investigation is carried out by the Department of Commerce and the International Trade Commission. Most of the time and money expended by the complainants is used to check on the governmental agencies' results.

63. The so-called ESP offset (19 CFR §353.15c) problem has become one of the most notorious elements of antidumping law in the United States See *SCM Group v. United States*, 713 F. 2d 1568 (Fed. Cir. 1983) cert. den., 104 S. Ct 1274. See Crawford and Hunter, "The ESP Offset" in *The Commerce Department Speaks*, supra note 56, vol. 2, 57. Senator Hollings proposed an amendment to the 1987 Trade Bill bringing the ESP offset into line with the more rigorous version used in the EC. This was adopted by voice vote on June 30, 1987 (*International Trade Reporter* 4 [1987], 864) and became §339 of HR3 as passed by the Senate. The amendment was seen as very significant (see statement of Senator Bentsen, *International Trade Reporter* 4 [1987], 810). In October 1987, a report was released quantifying the effects of the Hollings amendment on imports to the United States. The report was very critical of the amendment, saying that up to 800,000 U.S. jobs could disappear and that a decline in living standards of close to $39 billion may occur (*International Trade Reporter* 4 [1987], 1290). The Hollings Amendment was not included in the 1988 Omnibus Trade and Competitiveness Act (supra note 44).

64. 19 USC §1677b (1980 and Supp. 1987), 19 CFR §353.5 (1987).

65. 19 USCA §1677b(e) (1980 and Supp. 1988), 19 CFR §353.6 (1987).

66. See supra note 48, Title III, chapter 2, §321(d), amending 28 USC §164 (current version 19 USCA §1677b[b] [1980 and Supp. 1987], 19 CFR §353.7 [1988]).

67. See Crawford and Koteen, "Constructed Value" in *The Commerce Department Speaks*, supra note 56, vol. 2, 43.

68. 19 USC §1677b(e)(1)(B) (1980 and Supp. 1987), 19 CFR §353.6(2) (1987). Cf. the practice of the EC: see Beseler and Williams, supra note 31, 60–61.

69. See the 1979 Code, supra note 9, Article 2, paragraph 4.

70. See GATT, Article VI, see also the code, supra note 9.

71. See supra chapter 7.

72. See S. Rep. 93–1298, Senate Finance Committee, 93d Cong., 2nd sess., 1974, reprinted in *U.S. Code Congressional and Administrative News*, 7187, 7317: "In short the Committee does not view injury caused by unfair competition, such as dumping, to require as strong a causation link to imports, as would be required for determining the existence of injury under fair trade conditions."

73. See Jackson, Louis, and Matsushita, supra note 30, 164–5; Vermulst, supra note 1, 544–545; Beseler and Williams, supra note 31, 11–13.

74. See supra note 48, Title III, chapter 3, §331, amending 28 USC §1303 (current version 19 USCA §1303 and §1671b and d [1980 and Supp. 1988].

75. See infra chapter 11.

76. See statement of Richard O. Cunningham, *Comparison of Recommendations Received from Public Witnesses on Multilateral Trade Negotiations Implementing Legislation, WMCP 96–20*, Subcommittee on Trade, House Ways and Means Committee, 99th Cong. 1st sess., 1979 46, 50. See also Jackson and Davey, supra note 1, 698–699; Jackson, Louis, and Matsushita, supra note 30, 164.

77. See, for example, *Cast Iron Soil Pipe, Poland*, USTC Pub. 214 (1967), 6. This interpretation of the commission lasted until 1975. See Vermulst, supra note 1, 546–547.

78. HR Rep.96–317, House Ways and Means Committee, 96th Cong., 1st sess., 1979, 46.

79. S. Rep. 96–249, Senate Finance Committee, 96th Cong., 1st sess., 1979, 87. See also supra note 78.

80. Private discussions with the author.

81. The injury test found in Article 6 of the Subsidies Code (*Agreement on the Interpretation and Application of Articles VI, XVI and XXIII of the General Agreement on Tariffs and Trade, 31 UST 513, TIAS No. 9619, 26 BISD 56 [1980]*) differs in some respects from the test found the Antidumping Code (Article 3). It includes most of the definition of industry found in a separate article (Article 4) in the Antidumping Code. Also, the Subsidies Code does not have the explicit reference to threat of material injury or material retardation found in footnote 3 of the Antidumping Code. It is unclear whether this is significant, since Article VI:6(a) of the GATT seems to extend the application of countervailing duties to these other situations.

82. 19 USC §1677(7) (1980 and Supp. 1987). See supra notes 78 and 79. See also section 1329(b) of the *1988 Trade Act*, supra note 44.

83. See, for example, *Certain Carbon Steel Products, Certain European Countries*, USITC Pub. No. 1064, 14–15 (views of Vice Chairman Alberger) and 64–67 (views of Commissioner Stern); *Certain Carbon Steel Products, Certain European Countries*, USITC Pub. No. 1221, 16–17 (views of Commissioners Alberger, Stern, and Eckes). See also Vermulst, supra note 1, 575–583; Mock, "Cumulation of Import Statistics in Injury Investigations Before the International Trade Commission," *Northwestern Journal of International Law and Business* 7 (1986), 433.

84. Trade and Tariff Act of 1984, Pub. L. 98–573, §612, 98 Stat. 2948 amending 19 USC §1677 (current version 19 USCA §1677[7][C][iv] [1980 and Supp. 1988]).

85. The 1988 Trade Act, supra note 44, contains a provision (section 1330[b]) on negligible imports. Under it the ITC is not required to cumulate imports as required under section 1330(a) if they have "no discernable impact on the domestic industry."

86. See also section 1330(a) of the 1988 Trade Act, supra note 44. Under this provision the ITC *may* cross-cumulate among various actions in the assessment of *threat* of material injury.

87. See *ITC General Counsel Memoranda*, GC-E-065 (March 17, 1981), Memo from General Counsel to Commissioner Stern, and GC-F-345 (October 8, 1982) Memo from General Counsel to the Commission. See also Vermulst, supra note 1, 563–575; Easton, "Administration of the Import Trade Statutes: Possibilities for Harmonizing the Investigative Techniques and Standards of the ITC," *Georgia Journal of International and Comparative Law* 10 (1980), 78; Easton and Perry, "The Causation of Material Injury: Changes in the Antidumping and Countervailing Duty Investigations of the International Trade Commission," *UCLA Pacific Basin Law Journal* 2 (1983), 43.

88. In Hyundai Pipe Co. v. International Trade Commission (Slip Op. 78–18), the CIT held that the Commission is not required to examine margins, but that it is not barred from examining them if it so wishes. See also Easton, and Easton and Perry, supra note 87.

89. See Vermulst, supra note 1, 570–571. Cf. Easton, supra note 87.

90. The 1979 Subsidies Code, supra note 81, Article 6, paragraph 4.

91. The 1979 Antidumping Code, supra note 9, Article 3, paragraph 6.

92. The American Law Institute, *Restatement of the Law (Third): Foreign Relations Law of the United States*, 1987, 329–330.

93. See in general Alan Rugman and Andrew Anderson, *Administered Protection in America*, (London: Croom-Helm, 1987) in particular 6–8. See also Vermulst, supra note 1, 703.

94. Article 13 (3) of Council Regulation (EEC) 2176/84 of July 23, 1984, *Protection against Dumped or Subsidized Imports from Countries not Members of the European*

Economic Community (OJ [1984] L.201); Article 13(3) Commission Decision 2177/84/ECSC of July 27 1984, *Protection against Dumped or Subsidized Imports from Countries not Members of the European Coal and Steel Community* (OJ [1984] L.201). See also the decision of the European Court of Justice in case 53/83, Allied Corporation v. Council of the European Communities ("Allied II') (1985) ECR 1621, (1986) 3 CMLR 605, where the court held that the council must ascertain whether the amount of duty imposed "is necessary in order to remove the injury."

95. See the 1979 Code, supra note 9, Article 8, paragraph 1.

96. 19 USC §1673 (1980 and Supp. 1988).

97. The United States share of Canadian merchandise exports was 70.2 percent in 1983, 75.6 percent in 1984 and 78 percent in 1985 (compared with 65 percent in 1975). By way of contrast, U.S. merchandise exports destined for Canada in 1984 were 21.4 percent of the total; in 1985, they were 22.2 percent; and they fell to 20.9 percent in 1986. In the United States in 1986, exports of goods and services accounted for 8.8 percent of GNP; in Canada in 1986, exports of goods and services accounted for 27.3 percent of GDP. In 1986, Canadian exports were worth $110.4 billion; U.S. exports were worth $373 billion. Imports into Canada in 1986 were $104 billion; and imports into the United States were $477.3 billion (Figures complied from the Economic Intelligence Unit, *Economic Indicators* (London: Economic Intelligence Unit]).

98. A number of attempts have been made to introduce an effective private right of action for dumping in the United States. Concern has been expressed as to whether *any* remedy other than duties would be compatible with GATT. There is also a question of to what extent the United States can alter the 1916 act without losing the grandfather rights. At the moment, section 801 of the Revenue Act of 1916 (ch. 463, 39 Stat. 798, current version 15 USC §72 [1976]) contains a criminal prohibition on predatory dumping. The requirement of intent has never been legally satisfied.

99. See HR3, 100th Cong., 1st sess., 1987, §167. This provision was not accepted into the trade bill which eventually became the Trade Act of 1988 (see supra note 44).

100. Article III of GATT provides for national treatment, under which imported goods should be treated no worse than their domestic equivalents. It has been suggested that since the United States does not enforce a prohibition on price discrimination within the United States, it may not treat imports any more stringently [see letter from Professor John H. Jackson to the Honorable Dan Rostenkowski, March 13, 1987 [unpublished]; see also *Hearings on S.1655*, supra note 2 (statements of Alan Holmer, 20, and Gary Horlick, 132]). It has also been suggested that the clear implication of Article VI:2 of GATT is that the only legitimate response to dumping is the imposition of duties, this narrow remedy being an exception to Article III: see *Hearings on S.1655*, supra note 2 (statements of Alan Holmer, 28, Gilbert Kaplan, 37, and Gary Horlick, 130). Cf. *The Unfair Foreign Competition Act of 1985: Hearings on S.1655*, Senate Judiciary Committee, supra note 2 (statements of Peter Ehrenhaft, 55 and Richard O. Cunningham, 43), 1985.

101. See *Decision of 28 January 1987*, GATT, BISD 33 Supp. 28, 43 (1987).

102. See Jackson and Davey, supra note 1, section 10.4.

103. The unfair-trade practice of export targeting was included in the 1988 Trade Act (supra note 44, section 1301). For an analysis of targeting practices, see *Foreign Industrial Targeting and Its Effects on U.S. Industries, Phase I: Japan*, USITC Pub. No. 1437 (1983); *Foreign Industrial Targeting and Its Effects on U.S. Industries, Phase II: The European Community and Member States*, USITC Pub. No. 1517 (1984); *Foreign Industrial Targeting Practices*, S. Hrg. 98–522, Joint Economic Committee, 98th Cong., 1st sess., 1983. There is also great debate as to the effectiveness of targeting from an economic standpoint: see Krugman, "The U.S. Response to Foreign Industrial Targeting," *Brooking Papers on Economic Activity* (1984/1), 77. Cf. *The Effect of Government Targeting on World Semiconductor Competition* (Cupertino, CA: Semiconductor Industry Association, 1983). See also Jackson and, Davey, supra note 1, section 22.2.

104. Industrial policy is extremely difficult to define. See, for example, William Diebold, *Industrial Policy as an International Issue* (Washington, D.C.: Council on Foreign Relations, 1980); John Pinder (ed.), *National Industrial Strategies and the World Economy* (London: Croom-Helm, 1982); Hindley, "Empty Economics in the Case for Industrial Policy," *World Economy* 7 (1984), 277; "Industrial Policy: An Unfair Trade Practice?", *Congressional Quarterly Weekly Reports* 41 (1983), 211.

105. See supra sections 1.2 and 1.3.

106. See, for example, *Product Liability Reform Proposals*, S. Hrg. 99–1004, Senate Commerce, Science and Transportation Committee, 99th Cong., 2d sess., 1986 (testimony of Secretary Baldridge) ; *Problems Confronting Small Manufacturers in Automating Their Plants*, S. Hrg. 100–455, Senate Committee on Small Businesses, 100th Cong., 1st sess., 1987. See also Liebman, "The European Community's Products Liability Directive: Is the U.S. Experience Applicable?", *Law and Policy in International Business* 18 (1986), 795; Maddox, "Products Liability in Europe," *Journal of World Trade Law* 19 (1985), 508; *U.S. Export Weekly* 18 (1983), 684, 686.

107. Tariff Act 1922, c. 356 Title III, § 316, 42 Stat. 943, superseded by § 337 of Tariff Act 1930 as amended in 1974 and 1979 (19 USC §§1337 and 1337[a] [1980 and Supp. 1988]). See Thomas Vakerics, David Wilson, and Kenneth Weigel, *Antidumping, Countervailing and Other Trade Actions* (New York: PLI, 1987), chapter 7; Jackson and Davey, supra note 1, chapter 10.4; see also Brandt and Zeitler, "Unfair Import Trade Practice Jursidiction: The Applicability of Section 337 and the Countervailing Duty and Antidumping Laws," *Law and Policy in International Business* 12 (1980), 95; Zeitler, "A Preventative Approach to Import-Related Disputes: Antidumping, Countervailing, and Section 337 Investigations," *Harvard International Law Journal* 28 (1987), 69.

108. 19 USCA §1337(a) (1980 and Supp. 1988).

109. See the 1988 Trade Act, supra note 44, section 1342. See also *Congressional Record* 134 (1988), H2043.

110. See Jackson and Davey, supra note 1, 799; Vakerics, Wilson, and Weigel, supra note 107, 503–506.

111. 19 USCA §1337(e) (1980 and Supp. 1988). The ITC has refused to provide relief on these grounds in at least two cases: *Automatic Crankpin Grinders*, USITC Pub No. 1022 (1979); and *Inclined Field Acceleration Tubes*, USITC Pub. No. 1119 (1980).

112. See supra chapter 8.2. See also GATT, BISD 30 Supp. 107 (1984).

Chapter 11

1. See supra section 10.1.

2. See, generally, G. C. Hufbauer and J. Shelton Erb, *Subsidies in International Trade* (Washington, D.C.: Institute for International Economics, 1984); Barcelo, "Subsidies and Countervailing Duties — Analysis and a Proposal," *Law and Policy in International Business* 9 (1977), 779; *The Commerce Department Speaks on Import and Export Administration 1984* (New York: Practising Law Institute, 1984), volume 1; Wallace, Loftus and Krikorian, eds., *Interface III: Legal Treatment of Domestic Subsidies* (Washington, D.C.: International Law Institute, 1984); John H. Jackson, *World Trade and the Law of GATT* (Indianapolis: Bobbs-Merrill, 1969), 365–438; Harald B. Malmgren, *International Order for Public Subsidies* (London: Trade Policy Research Centre, 1977); Rivers and Greenwald, "The Negotiation of a Code on Subsidies and Countervailing Measures: Bridging Fundamental Policy Differences," *Law and Policy in International Business* 11 (1979), 1477.

3. See supra section 10.5.

4. See *The Tokyo Round of Multilateral Trade Negotiations: Report by the Director-General* (Geneva: GATT, 1979), 181; *The Tokyo Round of Multilateral Trade Negotiations: Supplementary Report by the Director-General* (Geneva: GATT, 1980), 10. See also Tarullo, 1984. The MTN Subsidies Code: Agreement Without Concensus. In *Emerging Standards of International Trade and Investment*. Seymour Rubin and Gary Hufbauer (eds.) Totowa, NJ: Rowman and Allenheld, pp. 63–99.

5. See, for example, Barcelo, "Subsidies, Countervailing Duties, and Antidumping after the Tokyo Round," *Cornell International Law Journal* 13 (1980), 257, 282–285; Barcelo, supra note 2, 794–835.

6. See, for example, Geoffrey Denton and Seamus O'Cleirearain, *Subsidy Issues in International Commerce* (London: Trade Policy Research Centre, 1972), 33–45, 52–59. If the government of an importing country has accepted a tariff binding, and the government of the exporting country could, at the time of the negotiation of the tariff binding, not reasonably have expected the subsequent introduction of a subsidy, then it is possible that such a subsidy constitutes a *prima facie* case of nullification or impairment in the sense of GATT Article XXIII.

7. See, for example, for the EC: Council Regulation (EEC) 2176/84, OJ (1984) L. 201 and Decision 2177/84/ECSC, OJ (1984) L.201; for Canada: Special Import Measures Act 1984, 32–33 Eliz. II, c. 25.

8. Inventory of U.S. trade actions has been prepared by my assistants, based on U.S. government documents available as of September 1988.

9. See, for example, Deardorff and Stern, 1987, Current Issues in Trade Policy: An Overview, and Dixit, 1987, How Should the United States Respond to Other Countries' Trade Policies? both in *U.S. Trade Policies in a Changing World Economy*, Robert M. Stern (ed.) Cambridge, Mass.: MIT Press, pp. 15–68 and pp.245–282; Sykes, "Countervailing Duty Law: An Economic Perspective," *Columbia Law Review* 89 (1989), 199. Brander, 1986, Rationales for Strategic Trade and Industrial Policy, in *Strategic Trade Policy and the New International Economics*, Paul R. Krugman (ed.) Cambridge, Mass.: MIT Press, pp.23–46; W. M. Corden, *Trade Policy and Economic Welfare* (Oxford: Clarendon Press, 1974), chapter 2; Steven J. Warnecke, ed., *International Trade and Industrial Policies* (New York: Holmes and Meier, 1978).

10. See Dixit, supra note 9.

11. Ibid., 252; see also Deardorff and Stern, supra note 9.

12. Deardorff and Stern, supra note 9, 55.

13. On subsidies and predation, see for example Ordover, Sykes, and Willig, "Unfair International Trade Policies," *New York University Journal of International Law and Politics* 15 (1983), 323, 332; Epstein, 1985, Foreign Predation against U.S. Firms: Reconciling International and Domestic Policies, in *1984 Fordham Corporate Law Institute*, Barry Hawk (ed.) New York: Matthew Bender, pp.41–61.

14. See supra section 10.2.

15. Arguably, the subsidy on the imports is irrelevant in this context. This may, again, show that the difference between measures against fair and unfair trade is often very vague. See supra section 10.1. On trade actions and national security, see generally Jackson, supra note 1, 748–752.

16. See, for example, Wonnacott, *The United States and Canada: The Quest for Free Trade: An Examination of Selected Issues* (Washington, D.C: Institute for International Economics, Policy Analyses in International Economics No. 16, 1987), 7.

17. A clear, but controversial, example of this is the U.S. "commitments" policy. See, for example, "Brass Sheet and Strip from Brazil," *Federal Register* 51 (1986), 40837, 40840. On the "commitments" policy, see infra section 11.2, text accompanying notes 40–42.

18. See generally Walker, *International Limits to Government Intervention in the Marketplace: Focus on Subsidies to the Private Sector* (London: Trade Policy Research Centre, Lectures in Commercial Diplomacy No. 1, 1976), 2–3.

19. Alexander Hamilton, for example, stated in his 1791 Report on Manufacturers:

[T]he greatest obstacle of all to the succesfull prosecution of a new branch of industry in a country, in which it was before unknown, consists, as far as the instances apply, in the bounties premiums and other aids which are granted, in a variety of cases, by the nations, in which the establishments to be imitated, are previously introduced. It is well known ... that certain nations grant bounties on the exportation of particular commodities, to enable their own workmen to under sell and supplant all competitors, in the country to which the commodities are sent. Hence the undertakers of a new manufacture have to contend not only with the natural disadvantages of a new undertaking, but with the gratuities and renumerations which other governments bestow. To be enabled to contend with success, it is evident, that interference and aid of their own governments are indispensable.

(See Alexander Hamilton's Famous *Report on Manufactures*: [Washington, D.C.: U.S. Department of Treasury, 1892] See, also Adam Smith, *Wealth of Nations (1776)*, book IV, chapter 5.

20. Tariff Act of 1897, ch. 11; 30 Stat. 151, 205.

21. In 1923 Viner found twenty-nine treaties containing a pledge against subsidies, of which seven were signed after 1900: see Jacob Viner, *Dumping: A Problem in International Trade* (New York: Kelley, 1966), 166–168. Countervailing duties were also discussed in the framework of the League of Nations. For a discussion on countervailing duties and the most-favored-nation principle, see League of Nations, Committee of Experts for the Progressive Codification of International law, *Report of the Subcommittee* (V. Legal, 1927, v. 10), reprinted in *American Journal of International Law* 22 (Supp., special no., 1928), 134.

22. A majority of the bilateral treaties concluded by the United States had only implicit references to the use of countervailing duties as a way of offsetting subsidies. See, for example, Article VI:2 of the 1942 Reciprocal Trade Agreement between the United States and Mexico (57 Stat. 833, 839). However, at least one *(1938 Reciprocal Trade Agreement between the United States and United Kingdom*, Article XI:2 [54 Stat. 1897]) had explicit provisions dealing with the use of countervailing duties. But this provision related to U.K. action against *U.S.* subsidies.

23. See Jackson, supra note 1, chapters 15 and 16.

24. Ibid., section 15.3

25. Several GATT dispute resolution panels have dealt with this issue: *French Assistance to Exports of Wheat and Wheat Flour*, GATT, BISD 7 Supp. 46 (1959); *European Economic Community: Subsidies on Exports of Wheat Flour* (1985); *European Economic Community: Subsidies on Exports of Pasta* (1985), all (partially) reprinted in John H. Jackson and William Davey, *Legal Problems of International Economic Relations* (St. Paul: West, 2d ed., 1986), 732–743. See also *European Communities: Refunds on Exports Complaint by Australia*, GATT, BISD 26 Supp. 290 (1980); and *European Communities: Refunds on Exports—Complaint by Brazil*, GATT, BISD 27 Supp. 69 (1981).

26. See, for example, the DISC case, GATT BISD 23 Supp. 98 (1977), partially reprinted in Jackson and Davey, supra note 25, 744.

27. GATT L/1864 (1962); 445 U.N.T.S. 294 (1962); See Jackson, supra note 2, 373.

28. See Jackson, supra note 2, 666.

29. See Tariff Act of 1897, supra note 20, 30 Stat. 151, 205; The language of this act evolved out of two earlier countervailing duty provisions that had been applicable only to sugar exports. These first U.S. countervailing duty provisions were section 237 of the Tariff Act of 1890 (26 Stat. 567, 584) and paragraph 182½ of the Tariff Act of 1894 (28 Stat. 521). See also supra sections 2.2 and 2.3.

30. See, for trade reform, House Ways and Means Committee, 99th Cong., 1st sess., 1973, 4088–4097 part 12, (testimony of Dan Gerhardstein, Director, American Institute for Imported Steel); see also John H. Jackson, Jean-Victor Louis, and Misuo Matsushita, *Implementing the Tokyo Round* (Ann Arbor: University of Michigan Press, 1984) 156.

31. Reorganisation Plan No. 3 of 1979, § 2(a); Executive Order No. 12188, 3 CFR §131, (1981), *Federal Register* 44 (1979), 69273, 69274; 19 U.S.CA § 2171 (1980 and Supp. 1988).

32. Trade Act of 1974, Pub. L. No. 93–618, Title I, chapters 1 and 2, 88 Stat. 1978.

33. Section 331 of the Trade Act of 1974, supra note 32 amending section 303 of the *Tariff Act of 1930*, 19 USCA §1303 (1980 and Supp. 1988). See also H. Rep. 93–571, House Ways and Means Committee, 93d Cong., 1st sess., 1973, 76; S. Rep. 93–1231, Senate Finance Committee, 93d Cong., 1st sess., 1973, 185.

34. *Agreement on Interpretation and Application of Articles VI, XVI and XXIII of the General Agreement on Tariffs and Trade*, GATT, BISD 26 Supp. 56 (1980); 31 UST 513; T.I.A.S. No. 9619 (hereinafter cited as Subsidies Code). See *The Tokyo Round of Multilateral Trade Negotiations, Report by the Director-General*, supra note 4, 53–61; Rivers and Greenwald, supra note 2; Tarullo, supra note 4.

35. See Subsidies Code, supra note 34, Article XI.

36. *Report Adopted on November 19, 1960*, GATT, BISD 9 Supp. 185, 186 (1961).

37. See, for example, "Railcars from Canada," *Federal Register* 48 (1983), 6569, 6579, in which the U.S. Commerce Department in a countervailing duty case declined to follow the "cost to the government" approach of paragraph (k) of the Illustrative List of Export Subsidies, and, instead, calculated the amount of the subsidy on the basis of the benefit conferred upon the recipient. For a discussion of this position, see Simon, "Can GATT Export Subsidy Standards Be Ignored by the United States in Imposing Countervailing Duties?" *Northwestern Journal of International Law and Business* 5 (1983), 183.

38. Trade Agreements Act of 1979, Pub. L. No. 96–39, 93 Stat. 144 (1979).

39. See supra section 3.3.

40. "Countries under the Agreement" for the purposes of section 701(b)(1), (2), and (3) of the 1930 Tariff Act are those who have (1) signed the Subsidies Code (infra note 41); (2) concluded an agreement with the United States that includes obligations substantially equivalent to those under the Subsidies Code; or (3)

through other means have the right to be treated in a manner similar to the above two categories.

41. See GATT L/6453 (1989). The signatories of the code as of January 1989 are Australia, Austria, Brazil, Canada, Chile, Egypt, the EEC, Finland, Hong Kong, India, Indonesia, Israel, Japan, Korea, New Zealand, Norway, Pakistan, the Philippines, Spain, Sweden, Switzerland, Turkey, the United States, and Uruguay. EEC member states are obligated by the EEC status, and thus the total industrial countries could be listed as 35.

42. The countries who have assumed obligations which are substantially similar to those of the agreement (section 701(b)(2) of the 1930 Tariff Act, as amended) are Taiwan and Mexico. The countries who are entitled to the injury test by virtue of section 701(b)(3) of the 1930 Tariff Act, as amended, are Venezuela, Honduras, Nepal, North Yemen, El Salvador, Paraguay, and Liberia. LDC code signatories (see 41 supra note) are Brazil, Chile, Egypt, Hong Kong, India, Indonesia, Israel, Korea, Pakistan, Philippines, Turkey, and Uruguay. From most of these, the United States has received some sort of "commitment." Special problems also exist vis-à-vis New Zealand. The extact status of all these countries is not clear on the public record, and inquiry to the office of the U.S. trade representative is necessary. Under section 1336(b) of the Omnibus Trade and Competitiveness Act of 1988 (Pub. L. 100–418, 102 Stat. 1210), USTR is to review "all subsidy commitments" undertaken by foreign governments, with a view to assessing compliance with the obligations undertaken.

43. Rivers and Greenwald, supra note 2, 1482.

44. See *Panel on United States Countervailing Duties*, GATT, BISD 28 Supp. 113 (1982); "Determination Regarding the Application of Certain International Agreements," *Federal Register* 46 (1981), 48391. See, generally, Jackson and Davey, supra note 25, 479–480; a.c. Hufbauer, Shelton Erb, and Starr, "The GATT Codes and the Unconditional Most-Favored-Nation Principle," *Law and Policy in International Business* 12 (1980), 59; Tarullo, supra note 4, 92.

45. For example, the U.S. Economic Joint Committee in 1965 offered the following definition: "An act by a governmental unit involving either (1) a payment, (2) a remission of charges, or (3) supplying commodities or services at less than cost or market price, with an intent of achieving a particular economic objective, most usually the supplying to a general market a product or service which would be supplied in as great a quantity only at higher prices in absence of the payment or remission of charges." (*Subsidies and Subsidy-Effect Programs of the U.S. Government*, Joint Economic Committee Print, 89th Cong., 1st sess., 1965.)

46. See generally Hunter, W.D., and Kuhbach, S. A., 1987. Subsidies and Countervailing Duties: Highlights Since 1984. In *The Commerce Department Speaks, 1987*, New York: Practicing Law Institute, pp. 491–625, 543–550.

47. See the Subsidies Code, supra note 34, annex.

48. See, for example, *Oversight Hearings on U.S. Trade Policy*, S. Hrg. 99–624, Senate Finance Committee, 99th Cong., 1st sess., 1985, 289 (testimony of John H. Jackson). Reprinted in *International Business Law* 14 (1986), 123.

49. See *The Tokyo Round of Multilateral Trade Negotiations: Report by the Director-General*, supra note 4, 57; Hufbauer and Erb, supra note 2, 22.

50. See infra section 11.4.

51. Other examples are environmental and employment aid and aid for industrial restructuring. See Subsidies Code, supra note 34, Article 11(1).

52. For a detailed overview of the methodologies used by the U.S. Commerce Department for the calculation of a subsidy, see the Subsidies Appendix, "Cold-Rolled Carbon Steel Products from Argentina," *Federal Register* 49 (1984), 18006, 18018, reprinted in Jackson and Davey, supra note 25, 764; See also Holmer, Haggerty, and Hunter, 1984. Indentifying and Measuring Subsidies under the Countervailing Duty Law: An Attempt at Synthesis. In *The Commerce Department Speaks on Import and Export Administration 1984*, New York: Practicing Law Institute, vol. 1, pp. 301–562.

53. See, for example, Paul Samuelson, *Economics* (New York: McGraw-Hill, 10th ed., 1976), 470–462; Schwartz and Harper, "The Regulation of Subsidies Affecting Trade," *Michigan Law Review* 70 (1973), 831, 843.

54. See Tarullo, supra note 4. Also Horlick, 1983. Current Issues in Countervailing Duty Law. In *The Trade Agreements Act of 1979 — Four Years Later* (New York: Practicing Law Institute, 1983), 11, 35. See also Tarullo, "Logic, Myth and the International Order," *Harvard International Law Journal* 26 (1985), 533; Tarullo, "Beyond Normalcy in the Regulation of International Trade," *Harvard Law Review* 100 (1987), 546.

55. See, for example, Peter Kenen, *The International Economy* (Englewood Cliffs, NJ: Prentice Hall, 1985), 203–205; Denton and O'Cleirearain, supra note 6, 52–59.

56. An exception to this should be made with regard to the responsibility of the industrialized countries for the development of the less-developed countries.

57. Tariff Act of 1930, §771(6), 19 USC §1677(6) (1980 and Supp. 1988). The legislative history of the Trade Agreements Act of 1979 makes it clear that "increased costs as a result of locating in an underdeveloped area, are not … permitted as offsets." (S. Rep. 96–249, 96th Cong., 1st sess., 1976, 86, reprinted in *U.S. Code Congressional & Administrative News* [1979], 381, 472). See also H. Rep. 96–317, 96th Cong., 1st sess., 1979, 74. This approach is not always consistent with the suggested purpose of countervailing duty law — i.e., to offset only the benefits of a subsidy that affects international trade.

58. The specificity test in U.S. law was first applied in "Certain Steel Products from Belgium," *Federal Register* 47 (1982), appendix 4, 39304, based on explicit statutory language. The European Commission also later accepted the principle of specificity: see Decision 85/223/EEC, OJ (1985) L. 106/19, Recital 7.3.

59. Tariff Act of 1930 as amended, section 771(5), 19 USCA §1677(5) (1980 and Supp. 1988).

60. See especially supra note 2 and infra note 64.

61. See Bello and Holmer, "Subsidies and Natural Resources: Congress Rejects a Lateral Attack on the Specificity Test," *George Washington Journal of International Law and Economics* 18 (1984), 297.

62. "Certain Softwood Lumber Products from Canada," *Federal Register* 48 (1983), 24159; "Certain Softwood Lumber Products from Canada," *Federal Register* 51 (1986), 37453, see supra note 60; Holmer and Bello, "The U.S.–Canada Lumber Agreement: Past as Prologue," *International Lawyer* 21 (1987), 1185.

63. "Anhydrous and Aqua Ammonia from Mexico," *Federal Register* 48 (1983), 28522; "Carbon Black from Mexico," *Federal Register* 48 (1983), 28564; "Lime from Mexico," *Federal Register* 48 (1983), 35672; "Portland Hydraulic Cement and Cement Clinker from Mexico," *Federal Register* 48 (1983), 43063.

64. U.S. Department of Commerce practice, several court cases, and section 1312 of the 1988 Omnibus Trade and Competitiveness Act (supra note 42) all stress the need for *"de facto"* or actual nonspecificity rather than mere "nominal" availability of benefits programs. See Horlick, Bello and Levine, 1985. The Countervailability of Subsidies: Specificity. In *United States Import Relief Laws: Current Developments in Law and Policy* New York: Practicing Law Institute, p. 47; Cabot Corp. v. U.S., 620 F. Supp. (CIT, 1985), appeal dismissed, 788 F. 2d 1539 (Fed. Cir., 1986); PPG v. U.S., 661 F. Supp. 285 (CIT, 1987); *Al Tech v.* U.S. 661 F. Supp. 1206 (CIT, 1987); Can-Am v. U.S. 8 ITRD 2510 (CIT, 1987). The legislative history of the 1988 Act states: "The amendment codifies the holding by the U.S. Court of International Trade in *Cabot Corporation v. United States,* 620 F. Supp. 722 (CIT, 1985) that, in the order to determine whether a domestic subsidy is countervailable, the Commerce Department must examine on a case-by-case basis whether the benefits provided by a program are bestowed upon a specific enterprise or industry, or group of enterprises or industries." (Omnibus Trade Act of 1987, S. Hrg. 100–71, Senate Finance Committee, 100th Cong., 1st sess., 1987, 122.)

65. Carlisle Tire and Rubber Co. v. United States supra note 60.

66. "Fresh Asparagus from Mexico," *Federal Register* 48 (1983), 21618. For a list of cases reflecting the Commerce Department's approach, see Holmer, Haggerty, and Hunter, supra note 52, 378.

67. See generally Jackson, "Perspectives on the Jurisprudence of International Trade: Costs and Benefits of Legal Procedures in the United States," *Michigan Law Review* 82 (1984), 1570.

68. For an overview of different issues, see Bello and Holmer, "The Tariff and Trade Act of 1984: The Road to Enactment," *International Lawyer* 19 (1985), 287 and "The Tariff and Trade Act of 1984: Principal Antidumping and Countervailing Duty Provisions," *International Lawyer* 19 (1985), 639. See also S. 490 §326, 100th Cong., 1st sess., 1987.

69. See *Ministerial Declaration*, GATT, BISD 33 Supp. 19, 25 (1987); *Decision of January 28, 1987*, GATT, BISD 33 Supp. 31, 43–44.

70. See *Oversight Hearings on U.S. Trade Policy*, supra note 48, 289.

71. See supra section 11.2.

72. See supra note 37.

73. Following the remand by the CIT in the case of Carlisle Tire and Rubber Co. v. United States (Slip. Op. 86–45, 29 April 1986), the Commerce Department adopted a rule regarding *de minimis* dumping and subsidization (*Federal Register* 52 [1987], 30660) now found in 19 CFR §353.24 (1988).

74. A similar analysis is sometimes used for the determination under section 771A of the Tariff Act of 1930 (19 USCA §1677[1] [1980 and Supp. 1988] ["upstream subsidies"]) whether a subsidy to a producer of an input – the "upstream" producer – that is passed through to a "downstream" producer has a significant effect on the cost of manufacturing the product under investigation. See, for example, "Agricultural Tillage Tools from Brazil," *Federal Register* 50 (1985), 34525, 34530.

75. Jackson, supra note 67. For a discussion on the actual costs of countervailing duty proceedings, see *Options to Improve the Trade Remedy Laws*, Comm. Ser. 98–15, House Ways and Means Committee, 98th Cong., 1st sess., 1983, 535–587.

76. See supra section 10.5.

77. In November 1986 the Canadian authorities preliminarily determined that the Canadian grain corn producers were materially injured by U.S. subsidies on grain corn. Although the amount of imports into Canada was small, the overproduction and high inventories created by the subsidy in the United States were found to have caused – through potential imports – a significant decline in the Canadian market price. See *International Trade Reporter* 3 (1986), 1358; 4 (1987), 334 and 608.

78. Some see the dispute-settlement provisions of chapter 19 (*International Legal Materials* XXVIII [1988], 281) of the Canada–U.S. Trade Agreement as a model for future GATT negotiations. See, for example, *Congressional Record* 134 (1988), H6626 (testimony of Mr. Crane) and H6640 (testimony of Mr. Bereuter). The provisions of chapter 19 were implemented into U.S. law by Title IV of the United States-Canada Free Trade Implementation Act of 1988, Pub. L. 100–449; 102 Stat. 1878 et seq.

Chapter 12

1. See generally John H. Jackson, *World Trade and the Law of GATT* (Indianapolis: Bobbs-Merrill, 1969), chapter 25; John H. Jackson and William Davey, *Legal Problems of International Economic Relations* (St. Paul: West, 2d ed., 1986), chapter 20. For more specific works, see Robert E. Hudec, *GATT and the Developing Countries*, (Brookfield, VT: Gower/Trade Policy Research Centre, 1988); Jagdish Bhagwati, *The Economics of Underdeveloped Countries* (New York: McGraw-Hill,

1966); Jagdish Bhagwati, *The International Crisis and the Developing Countries* (Bombay: Economic Research and Training Foundation, 1975); Anne O. Krueger et al., eds., *Trade and Employment in Developing Countries*, 3 vols. (Chicago: University of Chicago Press, 1981); Pomfret, "The Effects of Trade Preferences for Developing Countries," *Southern Economic Journal* 53 (1986), 18; Djojohadikusumo, "Common Interests of Industrial and Developing Countries," *World Economy* 8 (1985), 325; Takase, "The Role of Concessions in the GATT Trading System and Their Implications for Developing Countries," *Journal of World Trade Law* 21 (1987), 67.

2. Srinivasan, "Why Developing Countries Should Participate in the GATT," *World Economy* 5 (1982), 85. See also Jackson and Davey, supra note 1, 1153–4.

3. GATT, *Trends in International Trade* (Sales No. GATT/1958–3) (also known as the Haberler Report). See Jackson, supra note 1, section 25.4.

4. See supra chapter 2 and section 11.2 (the U.S. "commitments" policy). The four Tokyo Round codes having special provisions are the *Agreement on Technical Barriers to Trade* (Article XII), the *Agreement on Government Procurement* (Article III), the *Subsidies Code* (part III, Article 14) and the *Antidumping Code* (Article 14). The text of all the MTN codes can be found in GATT, BISD, 26 Supp. (1980).

5. *Differential and More Favourable Treatment Reciprocity and Fuller Participation of Developing Countries*, GATT, BISD 26 Supp. 203 (1980). See also infra section 12.2.

6. See supra section 6.3. The Third Lome Convention was signed in Lome on December 8, 1985 and was implemented on the community side by the Decision of the Council and Commission, OJ (1986) L. 86/1. Currently sixty-six African Caribbean and Pacific (ACP) states have signed the convention.

7. See supra chapter 6, notes 26 and 70.

8. See Jackson, supra note 1, section 25.7.

9. See, for example, GATT Article XVI:3. See Jackson, supra note 1, sections 15.7 and 15.8.

10. See supra sections 4.3 and 4.4

11. See *Declaration on Trade Measures Taken for Balance of Payment Purposes*, GATT, BISD 26 Supp. 205 (1980), and *Statement of the Chairman of the Committee on Balance of Payments Restrictions*, GATT, BISD, 31 Supp. 56 (1985).

12. Such tariff escalation was a major concern of developing countries during the Tokyo Round, since the linear tariff method used in the Kennedy Round tended not to address this question, see GATT, *The Tokyo Round of Multilateral Trade Negotiations, Report by the Director-General* (Geneva: GATT, 1979), 164–5. However, it should be noted that the developing countries wanted the reduction in tariff levels on industrial goods to be on a preferential basis so as to preserve an advantage over developed exporters: see Cline, Kawanabe, and Kronsjo, eds., *Trade Negotiations in the Tokyo Round* (Washington, D.C.: Brookings, 1978), 220–24.

13. See supra section 6.3.

14. See supra sections 4.3 and 4.4

15. Mexico and the People's Republic of China have expressed such concerns. The accession of India to the Subsidies Code was also based upon such considerations. See supra section 6.5 and chapter 11.

16. See Hudec, *Developing Countries in the GATT Legal System*, supra note 1, 210 et seq.; Jagdish Bhagwati, *Anatomy and Consequences of Exchange Control Regimes* (New York: NBER, 1978); Ewing, "The Assault on Development Economics," *Journal of World Trade Law* 18 (1984), 189. See also Cline, W. R., 1983. Introduction and Summary. In *Trade Policy in the 1980s* Washington D.C.: Institute of International Economics, pp. 1–54, 23–26. Cf. Yusuf, "Differential and More Favorable Treatment: The GATT Enabling Clause," *Journal of World Trade Law* 14 (1980), 488.

17. Graduation refers *inter alia* to the removal of a country from GSP eligibility in general with respect to specific individual products based on the degree of competitiveness the developing country has achieved with the products. The policy is partly a result of the fact that certain countries, like Brazil and Mexico, have become major exporters of certain industrial products. The developing nations reject graduation as arbitrary and damaging. See Yusuf, supra note 16, 504 and "Address of Alister McIntyre, Acting Head of UNCTAD," reported in *International Trade Reporter* 2 (1985), 932. The U.S. Congress has been instrumental in encouraging the U.S. administration to undertake a graduation program: see Trade Agreements Act of 1979, Senate Report 96–249, 96th Cong., 1st Sess., 1979, 273.

18. The graduation rules are found at 19 USCA § 2464(a) (1980 and Supp. 1988). As noted in note 17, a country can be completely graduated or graduated with respect to particular articles. For a recent example of the operation of the rules with respect to individual products, see *Federal Register* 53 (1988), 1302, list 1. From this list it appears that the following countries have been partially "graduated": Argentina, Bahamas, Brazil, Chile, Colombia, Hong Kong, Israel, Mexico, Peru, Singapore, South Korea, Taiwan, Turkey, Yugoslavia, Zambia. See also Jackson and Davey, supra note 1, capter 20.3(c).

19. See the "Address of Acting Head of UNCTAD," supra note 17; Bohn, "Governmental Response to Third World Debt: The Role of the Export-Import Bank," *Stanford Journal of International Law* 21 (1985), 461. See also Jackson and Davey, supra note 1, section 20.5.

20. See supra chapter 6.

21. See Jackson and Davey, supra note 1, section 20.3.

22. GATT, BISD 18 Supp. 24 (1972). See Espiell, "GATT: Accomodating Generalized Preferences," *Journal of World Trade Law* 8 (1974), 341.

23. The U.S. GSP system was authorized by Title V of the 1974 Trade Act, Pub. L. 93–618, 88 Stat. 2067; 19 USCA §2461 et seq (1980 and Supp. 1988): see Senate

Rep. No. 93–1298 (1973), reprinted in *U.S. Code Congressional and Adminstrative News* 4 (1974), 7186. However, the system did not come into effect until January 1976. See infra section 12.3.

24. See, for example, supra note 1 and the annual *General Report on the Implementation of the Generalized System of Preferences*, prepared by the UNCTAD secretariat. Cf. "Study of the Effects of the Generalized System of Preferences on U.S. Trade in the Program's First Year of Operation," *ITC Staff Research Study No. 12* (Washington, D.C.: ITC, 1978); "An Evaluation of U.S. Imports Under the Generalized System of Preferences," USITC Pub. No. 1379 (1983). See also Brown, "General Equilibrium Effects of the U.S. Generalized System of Preferences," *Institute of Public Policy Studies Discussion Paper No. 237* (1985).

25. GATT, BISD 26 Supp. 203 (1980). See also Jackson and Davey, supra note 1, 1149.

26. Cf. Yusuf, supra note 16, 504–505.

27. See Krishnamurti, "Trade Preferences in Favour of the Developing Countries," *Journal of World Trade Law* 1 (1967), 643, 656–7. See also Jackson and Davey, supra note 1, 1160 et seq.

28. See supra note 23, section 502(b), 88 Stat. 2067; 19 USCA §2462(b) (1980 and Supp 1988). See also Senate Rep. No. 93–1298 (1973), reprinted in *U.S. Code Congressional and Adminstrative News* 4 (1974), 7186, 7351–2. However, the system did not come into effect until January 1976: see infra section 12.3.

29. See supra note 23, section 502(b)(2); 19 USCA §2462(b)(2) (1980 and Supp. 1988).

30. See supra note 23, section 503(c); 19 USCA §2463(c)(1) (1980 and Supp. 1988). The articles are textiles under trade agreements, watches, certain electronic articles, certain steel articles, certain footwear, certain semimanufactured and manufactured glass products, and other items designated by the president as import-sensitive.

31. See supra note 23, section 504; 19 USCA §2464 (1980 and Supp. 1988). See also Senate Rep. No. 93–1298 (1973), reprinted in *U.S. Code Congressional and Adminstrative News*, 4 (1974), 7186, 7355–7357.

32. Ibid. See also S. Rep. 96–249, supra note 17.

33. In 1982, the trade covered was $8.3 billion, in 1983 $10.8 billion, in 1984 $billion, in 1985 $13.3 billion and in 1986 $13.9 billion. Figures *Operation of the Trade Agreements Program* (34th through 38th reports), USITC Publication Nos. 1414 (1983), 1535 (1984), 1725 (1985), 1871 (1986), and 1995 (1987).

34. In 1982 the GSP coverage as a percentage of total U.S. imports was 3 percent, in 1983, 4.2 percent, in 1985, 3.9 percent and in 1986, 3.8 percent.

35. Trade and Tariff Act of 1984, Pub. L. 98–573, Title V, 98 Stat. 3018, 19 USCA §2461 et seq. (1988 and Supp. 1988). For an overview of the GSP renewal program, see *Operation of the Trade Agreements Program, 35th Report*, USITC Publication No. 1535 (1984), chapter 1.

36. The amount of "graduation" with respect to products has been gradually increasing. In 1982, the president removed $651 million from the list of eligible items. In 1983, the figure was $900 million, in 1984, the figure was $1.2 billion, in 1985, $1.8 billion and in 1986, $2.4 billion.

37. See Proclamation 5758 of December 24, 1987, *Federal Register* 52 (1987), 49129.

Chapter 13

1. See generally John H. Jackson, *World Trade and the Law of GATT* (Indianapolis: Bobbs-Merrill, 1969), chapter 2; John H. Jackson and William Davey, *Legal Problems of International Economic Relations* (St. Paul: West, 2d ed., 1986), 293–298.

2. In general, see Thomas Hoya, *East West Trade: COMECON Law: American/ Soviet Trade* (New York: Oceana, 1984); M. M. Kostecki, *East-West Trade and the GATT System*, (New York: St. Martin's Press, 1979); Wallace et al., eds., *Interface Two: Conference Proceedings on the Legal Framework of East-West Trade* (Washington, D.C.: International Law Institute, Georgetown University Law Center, 1982); Nyilas, ed., *Integration in the World Economy: East-West and Inter-State Relations* (Leyden: A. W. Sijthoff, 1978). See also Jackson and Davey, supra note 1, chapter 21.

3. See Jackson, supra note 1, section 14.7.

4. See panel report (GATT, BISD 30 Supp. 140) on the Canadian FIRA legislation, where the panel said: "The Panel saw great force in Canada's argument that only the most-favored nation and not the national treatment obligations fall within the scope of the general principles of non-discriminatory treatment referred to in Article XVII:1(a). However the Panel did not consider it necessary to decide in this particular case whether the general reference to the principles of non-discriminatory treatment referred to in Article XVII:1 also comprises the national treatment obligation since it had already found the purchase undertakings to be inconsistent with Article III:4 which implements the national treatment principle specifically in respect of purchase requirements."

5. See the report of a 1988 U.S. position paper on state trading under the GATT sytem: *International Trade Reporter* 5 (1988), 795.

6. See supra section 2.4(e).

7. Zarin, "Countertrade and the Law," *George Washington Journal of International Law and Economics* 18 (1984), 235; Walsh, "The Effects on Third Countries of Mandated Countertrade," *Journal of World Trade Law* 19 (1985), 592; Kostecki, "Should One Countertrade?" *Journal of World Trade Law* 21 (1987), 5. See also "Interface IV: East-West Countertrade," *Journal of Comparative Business and Capital Markets* 5 (1983), 327 et seq., Nugent, "U.S. Countertrade Policy: Is it Economically Sound?" *George Washington Journal of International Law and Economics* 19 (1985), 829.

8. See Roessler, "Countertrade and the GATT Legal System," *Journal of World Trade Law* 19 (1985), 604; Gadbaw, "The Implications of Countertrade under the

General Agreement on Tariffs and Trade," *Journal of Comparative Business and Capital Markets* 5 (1983), 355; Verdun, "Are Governmentally Imposed Countertrade Requirements Violations of the GATT?" *Yale Journal of International Law*, 11 (1985), 191; Liebman, "GATT and Countertrade Requirements," *Journal of World Trade Law*, 18 (1984), 252.

9. With respect to the NMEs that have joined GATT since its inception, see for *Yugoslavia: Report of the Working Party on the Accession of Yugoslavia*, GATT, BISD 14 Supp 49 (1967) and *Protocol for the Accession of Yugoslavia*, GATT, BISD 15 Supp. 53 (1968); for Poland: *Protocol for the Accession of Poland*, GATT, BISD 15 Supp 46 (1968) and *Report of the Working Party on the Accession of Poland*, GATT, BISD 15 Supp 109 (1968); for Romania: *Protocol for the Accession of Romania*, GATT, BISD 18 Supp. 5 (1972) and *Report of the Working Party on the Accession of Romania*, GATT, BISD 18 Supp. 94 (1972); Hungary: *Protocol for the Accession of Hungary*, GATT, BISD 20 Supp. 3 (1974) and *Report of the Working Party on the Accession of Hungary*, GATT, BISD 20 Supp. 34 (1974).

10. See Patterson, "Improving GATT Rules for Non-Market Economies," *Journal of World Trade Law* 20 (1986), 185. See also Ianni, "The International Treatment of State Trading," *Journal of World Trade Law* 18 (1982), 480; Grzybowski, "Socialist Countries in GATT," *American Journal of Comparative Law* 28 (1980), 539.

11. Kennedy, "The Accession of the Soviet Union to the GATT," *Journal of World Trade Law* 21 (1987), 23; Dirksen, "What if the Soviet Union Applies to Join the GATT?" *World Economy*, 10 (1987), 228.

12. See, for example, M. M. Kostecki, *East-West Trade and the GATT System* (New York, St. Martin's Press, 1979), 43–52.

13. See, for example, *Agreement of July 28 Between the European Economic Community and the Socialist Republic of Romania on Trade in Industrial Products* (OJ [1980] L. 352/5) and *Trade and Economic Co-Operation Agreement Between the European Economic Community and the People's Republic of China* (OJ [1986] L.257/54).

14. See supra chapter 7. See also Trade Act of 1974, Pub. L. 93–618, §406, 88 Stat. 2062., 19 USCA §2436 (1980 and Supp. 1988).

15. See supra note 9.

16. Ibid.

17. Ibid.

18. Ibid.

19. See Li, "Resumption of China's GATT Membership," *Journal of World Trade Law* 21 (1987), 25; Herzstein, "China and the GATT: Legal and Policy Issues Raised by China's Participation in GATT," *Law and Policy in International Business* 18 (1986), 371. See also Sheridan, "The Accession to GATT of the People's Republic of China: New Challenges for the World Trade Regime," *Willamette Law Review* 23 (1987), 737.

20. The People's Republic of China was recognized as the representative of China in the IMF on April 17, 1980. See IMF, *Summary Proceedings* 35 (1980), 99–103. See also documents regarding the recognition of the People's Republic of China as the representative of China in the World Bank, in *International Legal Materials* 20 (1980), 777–781.

21. See GATT L/6017 and *International Trade Reporter* 3 (1986), 135, 846, 915 and 4 (1987), 349. See also *Journal Of Commerce*, July 16, 1986, 5A.

22. Cf. Li, supra note 19, 44–47.

23. See, for example, *International Trade Reporter* 5 (1988), 253, concerning the GATT working group's work on the accession/resumption of China.

24. See supra note 11.

25. See Richard Cooper. 1986. Trade Policy as Foreign Policy. In *U.S. Trade Policies in a Changing World Economy*. R Stern (ed.) Cambridge, Mass: MIT Press, pp. 291–322. See also Jackson, supra note 1, chapter 1, especially 9–12.

26. See supra chapter 1.

27. See supra section 10.1.

28. An Act to extend the authority of the President to enter into trade agreements under section 350 of the Tariff Act of 1930, as amended, and for other purposes, Pub. L. No. 49, ch 139, §5, 65 Stat. 73 (1951).

29. GATT, 2 BISD 36 (1952).

30. See Jackson and Davey, supra note 1, 1188.

31. Ibid.

32. Trade Act of 1974, Pub. L. 93–618, Title IV, §409, 88 Stat. 2064, 19 USC §2439(b).

33. Ibid. See also Paula Stern, *The Water's Edge: Domestic Politics and the Making of American Foreign Policy* (Westport, CT: Greenwood Press, 1979); Lansing and Rose, "The Granting and Suspension of Most-Favored-Nation Status for Non-Market Economy States: Policy and Consequences," *Harvard International Law Journal* 25 (1984), 329.

34. See *Department of State Bulletin* 72 (1975), 139–40.

35. The risk of annual review in the U.S. Congress is not particularily desirable.

36. Trade Act of 1974, §406, 88 Stat. 2062, 19 USC §2436. See Thomas Vakerics, David Wilson, and Kenneth Weigel, *Antidumping, Countervailing Duty, and Other Trade Actions* (New York: Practicing Law Institute, 1987), chapter 5. See also Erlick, "Relief from Imports from Communist Countries: The Trials and Tribulations of Section 406," *Law and Policy in International Business* 13 (1981), 617. See also Jackson and Davey, supra note 1, 586–589.

37. July 1988.

38. *International Legal Materials* and the *Federal Register*. See also the annual *Operation of the Trade Agreements Program* reports issued by the ITC.

39. In 1988, Romania renounced its renewal of MFN status under the Jackson-Vanik clause (*International Trade Reporter* 5 [1988], 286). The U.S. State Department announced suspension of the MFN provisions of the agreement on April 4, 1988 (*International Trade Reporter* 5 [1988], 499). See agreement signed in Bucharest, April 2, 1975, in force August 3, 1975: TIAS 8159; *International Legal Materials* 14 (1975), 671. See also *Waiver of Trade Restrictions Against Romania, Message from the President*, H. Doc. 94–113, 94th Cong., 1st sess., 1975; *Trade Agreement Between the U.S. and Romania, Communication from the President*, H. Doc. 94–114, 94th Cong., 1st sess., 1975; *U.S.–Romanian Trade Agreement*, House Ways and Means Committee, 94th Cong., 1st sess., 1975; *Extension of Non-Discriminatory Treatment to Products of Romania*, H. Rpt. 94–359 (recommends passage of H. Con. Res. 252), 94th Cong., 1st. sess., 1975; *Romanian Trade Agreement: Senate Finance Committee*, 94th Cong., 1st sess., 1975; *Bilateral Commercial Agreements Between the U.S. and the Socialist Republic of Romania*, S. Rpt. 94–281 (recommends passage of S. Con. Res. 25), 94th Cong., 1st sess., 1975. Regarding renewals, see "Presidential Determination No. 81–9 of June 2, 1981," *Federal Register* 46 (1981), 29921; "Presidential Determination No. 84–10 of May 31, 1984," *Federal Register* 49 (1984), 23025; "Presidential Determination No. 87–16 of June 24, 1987," *Federal Register* 52 (1987), 23931.

40. Budapest, 17 March 1978, in force 7 July 1978: TIAS 8967; 17 *International Legal Materials* 17 (1978), 1475. See also *U.S.–Hungary Trade Agreement, Communication from the President*, H. Doc. 95–318, 95th Cong., 2d sess., 1978; *Extension of Trade Agreement with Romania and Hungary, Message from the President*, H. Doc. 95–345, 95th Cong., 2d Sess., 1978; *MFN Treatment with Respect to the Products of Hungary*, House Ways and Means Committee, 95th Cong., 2d sess., 1978; *Extension of Non-Discriminatory Treatment to Products from Hungary*, H. Rpt. 95–1106 (recommends passage of H. Con. Res. 555), 95th Cong., 2d sess, 1978; *MFN Treatment for Hungary*, Senate Finance Committee, 95th Cong., 2d sess., 1978; *Extension of Nondiscriminatory Treatment to Products of Hungary*, S. Rpt. 95–949 (recommends passage of H. Con. Res. 555), 95th Cong., 2d Sess., 1978. For renewals, see "Presidential Determination No. 81–9 of June 2, 1981," *Federal Register* 46 (1981), 29921; "Presidential Determination No. 84–10 of May 31, 1984," *Federal Register* 49 (1984), 23025; "Presidential Determination No. 87–15 of June 23, 1987," *Federal Register* 52 (1987), 23785.

41. Beijing, 7 July 1979, in force 1 February 1980: TIAS 9360; *International Legal Materials* 18 (1979), 1041. See also *Agreement on Trade Relations Between the U.S. and People's Republic of China, Communication from the President*, H. Doc 96–209, 96th Cong., 1st sess., 1979; *U.S.–China Trade Agreement*, Comm. Ser. No. 96–63, House Ways and Means Committee, 96th Cong., 1st sess., 1979; *Approving the Extension of Non-Discriminatory Treatment to Products of The People's Republic of China*, H. Rpt. 96–733 (recommends passage of H. Con. Res. 204), 96th Cong., 2d sess., 1980; *Agreement on Trade Relations Between the U.S. and People's Republic of China*, Comm. Ser. No. 96–57, Senate Finance Committee, 96th Cong., 1st sess., 1979; *Extension of Non-Discriminatory Treatment to Products of The People's Republic of China*, S. Rep. 96–549 (recommends passage of S. Con. Res. 47). See also *Federal Register* 47 (1982), 57653.

42. Section 1106 of the Omnibus Trade and Competitiveness Act of 1988 (Pub. L. 100–418, 102 Stat. 1133).

43. The nonmarket economy rules with respect to antidumping actions are found in Trade Agreements Act 1979, Pub. L. 96–39, Title I, §101, 93 Stat. 182, amending the Tariff Act of 1930, currently at 19 USCA §1677b(c) (1980 and Supp. 1988). See also 19 CFR 353.8 (1987). See Horlick and Shuman, "Non-Market Economy Trade and U.S. Antidumping/Countervailing Duty Laws," International Lawyer 18 (1984), 807; Soltysinski, "U.S. Antidumping Laws and State-Controlled Economies," *Journal of World Trade Law* 15 (1981), 251. See also Jackson and Davey, supra note 1, 695–698.

44. See supra chapter 10.

45. See Horlick and Shuman, supra note 43; Meuser, "Dumping from 'Controlled Economy' Countries: The Polish Golf Car Case," *Law and Policy in International Business* 11 (1979), 777.

46. See, for example, Alford, "When is China Paraguay? An Examination of the Application of Antidumping and Countervailing Duty Laws of the U.S. to China and Other 'Nonmarket Economy Nations,'" *Southern California Law Review* 61 (1987), 79.

47. In an investigation concerning Finnish carbon steel plate (*Federal Register* 49 [1984], 8973), the Commerce Department stated: "The allegation of sales at less than fair value of this merchandise from Finland is supported by comparisons of the estimated Finnish home market prices (derived from data used by the Department of Commerce in its section 751 review of the suspension agreement in the antidumping proceeding on carbon steel plate from Romania) with the weighted average f.a.s. Finnish port value of the product imported into the U.S. . . . In the Romanian case the value of the Finnish carbon steel plate was used as a surrogate for the foreign market value of Romanian carbon steel plate." For example, Cotton Shop Towels from the People's Republic of China, *Federal Register* 48 (1983), 37055.

48. See "Initiation of Countervailing Duty Investigations, Textiles, Apparel and Related Products from the People's Republic of China," *Federal Register* 48 (1983), 46600. The Commerce Department stated that the action contained "novel issues," including whether a bounty or grant may be found in a nonmarket economy.

49. "Textiles, Apparel and Related Products from the People's Republic of China, Termination of Countervailing Duty Investigations," *Federal Register* 48 (1983), 55492. The termination was without prejudice to the issues involved: see, for example, "Carbon Steel Wire Rod From Poland, Initiation of Countervailing Duty Investigation," *Federal Register* 48 (1983), 56419.

50. "Carbon Steel Wire from Czechoslovakia, Final Negative Countervailing Duty Determination," *Federal Register* 49, (1984), 19370. During the course of the examination of the steel wire case, two new cases were brought, and all three were decided in a similar manner and proceeded through the appeals together:

see "Potassium Chloride from the Soviet Union, Recission of Initiation of Countervailing Duty Investigation and Dismissal of Petition," *Federal Register* 49 (1984), 23428. "Potassium Chloride from the German Democratic Republic. Recission of Initiation of Countervailing Duty Investigation and Dismissal of Petition," *Federal Register* 49 (1984), 23428.

51. Continental Steel Corp. v. United States, 614 F. Supp 548 (1985, CIT); Georgetown Steel Corp. v. United States, 801 F.2d 1308 (CAFC, 1986).

52. Section 325 of the Senate version of HR3, 100th Cong., 1st sess., 1987, would have used a trade-weighted average price of comparable merchandise, as sold at arm's-length in the United States, to determine the foreign market value of the nonmarket economy products. The provision was not included in the 1988 Trade Act (the Omnibus Trade and Competitiveness Act of 1988 [Pub. L. 100–418, 102 Stat. 1107 et seq.]).

53. For the reasoning of the Department of Commerce, see the decisions supra note 50.

54. See supra note 43.

55. This approach is typified by the so-called Heinz Bill. It was first proposed as S. 1966 in 1979 (96th Cong., 1st sess.) and has been resubmitted subsequently under other numbers. However, see also, for example, the "Hecht" proposal, *International Trade Reporter* 4 (1987), 1064.

56. The Heinz Bill in its 1983 form (S. 1531, 98th Cong., 1st sess.) was adopted by the Senate but later dropped in conference at the end of the 1984 congressional session.

Chapter 14

1. See W. Max Corden, *Trade Policy and Economic Welfare* (Oxford: Clarendon Press, 1974). See also W. Max Corden, *The Theory of Protection* (Oxford: Clarendon Press, 1971).

2. See International Chamber of Commerce, *The Organization for Trade Cooperation and the New GATT* (New York: United States Council of the International Chamber of Commerce, 1955); *Organization for Trade Cooperation*, Hearing before the House Ways and Means Committee, 84th Cong., 2d sess., 1956. See also Jackson, J.H., 1989. Strengthening the International Legal Framework of the GATT–MTN System: Reform Proposals for the New GATT Round. In *The New GATT Round of Multilateral Trade Negotiations: Legal and Economic Aspects*, Mcinhard Hilf and Ernst-UlrichPetersmann (eds.) Deventer: Kluwer [forthcoming]).

3. See supra chapter 4.

4. See, for example, Borrus and Goldstein, "United States Protectionism: Institutions, Norms and Practices," *Northwestern Journal of International Law and Business* 8 (1987), 328.

5. See Jackson, supra note 2. See John H. Jackson and William Davey, *Legal Problems of International Economic Relations* (St. Paul: West, 2d ed., 1986), section 23.3.

6. See Gary Hufbauer, Jeffrey Schott, and Kimberley Elliott, *Economic Sanctions Reconsidered* (Washington, D.C.: Institute for International Economics, 1985) and Carter, "Improving International Economic Sanctions: Improving the Haphazard U.S. Legal Regime," *California Law Review* 75 (1987), 1159.

7. See, for example, Jackson, "Perspectives on the Jurisprudence of International Trade: Costs and Benefits of Legal Procedures in the United States," *Michigan Law Review,* 82 (1984), 1570.

8. See *Ministerial Declaration,* GATT, BISD 33 Supp. 19, 26 (1987); GATT/1396, September 25, 1986; see also *Decision of 28 January 1987,* GATT, BISD 33 Supp. 31, 47 (1987); GATT/1405, February 5, 1987.

Index